T0295682

Modeling Economic Growth in Contemporary India

ENTREPRENEURSHIP AND GLOBAL ECONOMIC GROWTH

Series editor: Bruno S. Sergi, Harvard University, USA & University of Messina, Italy

Entrepreneurship and Global Economic Growth is Emerald's cutting-edge Global Economic Growth book series, presenting modern examinations of economic growth at national, regional, and global levels. Each book in this series discusses different dimensions of the changing economic and industrial contexts and examines in detail their impact on the nature of growth and development. For academics and senior practitioners, this series puts forward significant new research in the global economic growth field, opening discussions regarding new topics and updating existing literature.

Published Titles in This Series

Modeling Economic Growth in Contemporary Russia, edited by Bruno S. Sergi

Modeling Economic Growth in Contemporary Belarus, edited by Bruno S. Sergi

Modeling Economic Growth in Contemporary Malaysia, edited by Bruno S. Sergi and Abdul Rahman Jaaffar

Modeling Economic Growth in Contemporary Greece, edited by Vasileiois Vlachos, Aristidis Bitzenis and Bruno S. Sergi

Modeling Economic Growth in Contemporary Indonesia, edited by Bruno S. Sergi and Dedhy Sulistiawan

Modeling Economic Growth in Contemporary Hong Kong, edited by Michael K. Fung and Bruno S. Sergi

Modeling Economic Growth in Contemporary Poland, edited by Elżbieta Bukalska, Tomasz Kijek and Bruno S. Sergi

Modeling Economic Growth in Contemporary Czechia, edited by Daniel Stavárek and Michal Tvrdoň

Forthcoming Titles in This Series

Modeling Economic Growth in Contemporary Slovakia, edited by Michael Augustín, Peter Jančovič and Bruno S. Sergi

Modeling Economic Growth in Contemporary India

EDITED BY

BRUNO S. SERGI
University of Messina, Italy; Harvard University, USA

AVIRAL KUMAR TIWARI
*Indian Institute of Management Bodh Gaya (IIM Bodh Gaya)
Uruvela, India*

AND

SAMIA NASREEN
Lahore College for Women University, Pakistan

United Kingdom – North America – Japan – India – Malaysia – China

Emerald Publishing Limited
Emerald Publishing, Floor 5, Northspring, 21-23 Wellington Street, Leeds LS1 4DL

First edition 2024

British Library Cataloguing in Publication Data
A catalogue record for this book is available from the British Library

ISBN: 978-1-80382-752-0 (Print)
ISBN: 978-1-80382-751-3 (Online)
ISBN: 978-1-80382-753-7 (Epub)

INVESTOR IN PEOPLE

Contents

List of Figures and Tables

Figures

Tables

About the Editors

Bruno S. Sergi is an Instructor at Harvard University, where he teaches courses on development economics and the economics of emerging markets. At Harvard, he is also a Faculty Affiliate at the Harvard Center for International Development and an Associate at the Asia Centre. He is codirector of the Lab for Entrepreneurship and Development (LEAD), a research lab based in Cambridge, USA. LEAD aims to generate and share knowledge about entrepreneurship, development, and sustainability.

Dr Aviral Kumar Tiwari is an Associate Professor of Economics at the Indian Institute of Management Bodh Gaya (IIMBG) in the Department of Economics and Business Environment. Prof Tiwari is a C-EENRG Fellow at the Department of Land Economy, University of Cambridge and Research Fellows, University of Economics Ho Chi Minh City, Vietnam. Before joining IIMBG, he worked as an Associate Professor at Rajagiri Business School (RBS), India, and Montpellier Business School (MBS), Montpellier, France, from where he received his post-doc. After graduating with a degree in Economics from Lucknow University, Lucknow, India, he received his MPhil (in Labour Economics) and PhD (in Energy and Environment) from ICFAI University Tripura. He is basically an Applied Economist with broad empirical interests focusing on, but not limited to, emerging economies, particularly Asia. His research interests focus on various issues concerning energy, environment, tourism, macroeconomy and growth and development, etc. He has published widely in peer-reviewed international journals and contributed more than 100 ABDC-A &A* research papers so far. He is the only economist from India in the career ranking of the world's top 2% scientists list of 2021, 2022, 2023 and 2024 published by Stanford University Study. He is ranked in first position in India as a researcher by IDEAS. He is one of the Highly Cited Researchers 2020, 2022 and 2023 by Clarivate™ of Web of Science™. He is one of the recipients of M J Manohar Rao Award (for young econometrician) for 2014 from The Indian Econometric Society, 2015. He is a life member of the Indian Economic Association, India, and a member of several other international associations such as the International Association for Energy Economics (IAEE), USA, Association for Comparative Economic Studies, USA, Western Economic Association International, USA, etc. He holds different editorial positions at more than 10 journals of international repute (ABDC, Scopus and ABS-indexed journals).

Samia Nasreen is an Associate Professor in the Department of Economics at Lahore College for Women University, Lahore, Pakistan. Her primary research interests are in development economics, energy economics, environmental economics, and financial economics.

About the Contributors

Bhavya Advani is a Research Scholar pursuing her PhD in the department of Humanities and Social Sciences at Maulana Azad National Institute of Technology, Bhopal, India. Her current areas of research are environmental economics and economics of happiness. She has delivered research paper presentations in conferences at Gokhale Institute, Maharashtra and at Rajagiri Business School, Kerala. She has qualified 2021 UGC NET JRF and has completed her Master's in Economics from the Institute for Excellence in Higher Education in the year 2021. She has a corporate working experience of 2 years.

Shilpa Ahuja is a PhD Research Scholar at the Department of Economics, Indian Institute of Technology, Bombay. Prior to this, she was working as an Assistant Professor in the Department of Business Economics, Sri Guru Gobind Singh College of Commerce, University of Delhi. She has taught subjects like International Economics, International Finance and Investment Analysis and Portfolio Management to undergraduate students. She has a keen interest in the area of international capital flow movements, monetary policy, and financial markets. She has completed her postgraduation from Delhi School of Economics, University of Delhi.

Namrata Barik, a PhD Scholar at IIT Bombay, specializes in Energy Economics. Her research focuses on the economic aspects of renewable energy adoption.

Anusuya Biswas is an Associate Professor at Alliance University, Bangalore. She holds a PhD degree in Economics from Amity University Uttar Pradesh. She has qualified UGC-NET exam in Economics. Dr Anusuya has an experience of over 11 years as an academician, researcher, and administrator. Her research interest entails Applied Econometrics, International Trade, Timeseries Forecasting, Prescriptive and Predictive Analysis, Macroeconomic Analysis, and Environmental Sustainability. As a researcher, she has presented her papers in more than 30 conferences and published above 10 research papers in various peer-reviewed international and national journals including SCOPUS, Web of Science, and one paper accepted in ABDC. She also published six book chapters in reputed journals.

Sukhmani Bhatia Chugh is an Assistant Manager at Canara Bank, Chandigarh. She has done her MBA in Finance from Punjab Agriculture University, Ludhiana. She also has done various certifications from IIBF including JAIIB and

CAIIB. She has about 12 years of corporate experience in banking, project finance, and sales and marketing in various organizations. Her areas of interest in research include Mergers and Acquisitions, Economic policy, strategy etc. She has attended international and national conferences and presented her work there. She is pursuing her PHD in Management from Chitkara Business School, Chitkara University.

Varsha Singh Dadia is currently a Senior Research Scholar at the Department of Humanities and Social Sciences, Indian Institute of Technology Roorkee, Roorkee, India. She completed her Bachelor in Economics (Honors) from the University of Delhi. She received her Master of Economics from the Central University of Haryana, Haryana, India. She qualified National Eligibility Test (NET-JRF) for Lectureship and Junior Research Fellowship conducted by the University Grant Commission-UGC, New Delhi, India. Her research interests include efficiency and productivity analysis and the thermal power sector. She has also presented several papers at National and International conferences.

Ruchika Dawar, with a strong academic background, PhD from HNB Garhwal University (A Central University) and MBA from IMS, Dehradun. Having experience of more than 24 years with 7 years in the corporate sector that is in sales and marketing and 17 years in teaching. Currently associated with the National Institute of Fashion Technology (NIFT), Jodhpur since 2012. Published and presented many papers, posters, and case studies at reputed national and international platforms. With vast experience in industry and academics also involved in various projects at NIFT and giving a sincere effort to bring the Department of Fashion Management Studies (FMS) at its best expertise includes entrepreneurship management, consumer buying behavior, organizational behavior, marketing management, professional practices, etc.

Shilpa Deo is currently working as an Assistant Professor in the School of Humanities and Social Sciences at DES Pune University, India. Dr Deo has completed her doctoral degree (PhD) from the premier and India's top-ranked institutes in economics – Gokhale Institute of Politics and Economics, Pune, India. Her teaching and research interests have been in development economics, micro and macroeconomics, research methods, and international business. She has won the "Best Research Paper Award" for a paper presentation at two international conferences. She has been a reviewer and editorial board member for reputed journals. Currently, she serves as a Research Fellow at the Center for International Trade and Business in Asia, James Cook University, Australia.

Narayanage Jayantha Dewasiri is a Professor attached to the Department of Accountancy and Finance, Sabaragamuwa University of Sri Lanka. Further, he currently serves as the Brand Ambassador at Emerald Publishing, UK, and the Vice President of the Sri Lanka Institute of Marketing. He is a pioneer in applying triangulation research approaches in the management discipline. He is currently serving as the Co-Editors-in-Chief of the *South Asian Journal of Marketing* published by Emerald Publishing, Managing Editor of the *Asian Journal of*

Finance, and *South Asian Journal of Tourism and Hospitality*, published by the Faculty of Management Studies, Sabaragamuwa University of Sri Lanka.

Ekta Duggal, MCom, MPhil, PhD, is working as a Professor, Department of Commerce, Motilal Nehru College, University of Delhi. She has done her doctorate in marketing from FMS, University of Delhi. Her areas of teaching and research include business organization and management, e-commerce, services marketing, and retail quality. She has taught courses in master's programmes at Department of Commerce, Delhi School of Economics, and Guru Gobind Singh College of Commerce, University of Delhi. She has also participated in numerous conventions and seminars. She has published 28 research papers in various journals of repute including *International Journal of Business Ethics in Developing Economies, Journal of Marketing and Business Communication*, and *South Asian Journal of Global Business Research*. She participated in the third Academy of Indian Marketing–American Marketing Association Sheth Foundation Doctoral Consortium as the Consortium Fellow at Dubai.

Thilini Chathurika Gamage is a Professor attached to the Department of Marketing Management, Sabaragamuwa University of Sri Lanka. Her research interests center on Digital Marketing, Technology Management, Tourism and Hospitality Marketing, and Entrepreneurship. Her research works were published in top-tier management and marketing journals, including the *Journal of Strategic Marketing*, the *Journal of Product and Brand Management, Tourism Management*, and the *International Journal of Hospitality Management*. Further, she is an Editor of the South Asian Journal of Marketing, published by the Sri Lanka Institute of Marketing in collaboration with Emerald Publishing.

Athula Gnanapala is a well-respected expert in Tourism Management and currently serves as a Professor at the Sabaragamuwa University of Sri Lanka. He is also the Dean of the Faculty of Management Studies at SUSL. Prof Gnanapala is the Co-editor-in-chief of the *South Asian Journal of Tourism and Hospitality* and has an impressive research record with over 50 articles published in indexed and refereed journals, 25 books, and book chapters and has presented at more than 70 international conferences. He serves as a consultant, reviewer, editorial member, and scientific committee member for nationally and internationally recognized academic journals.

Archana Goel is an Assistant Professor at Chitkara Business School. She has done MCom, BEd, and PhD and has 12 years of corporate and academic experience. Her PhD is in corporate governance. Her research areas include corporate governance, mergers and acquisitions, financial reporting, ESG, etc. She specializes in teaching accounts, statistics, research methodology, and finance courses. She has around 25 papers published in national and international journals of repute and has attended many national and international conferences. Several patents have been granted to her. Currently, she is guiding two PhD scholars as well.

Bhumika Goswami, a dedicated student currently pursuing a Master's in Economics at Riga Technical University. With a strong foundation in the field, Bhumika completed her BSc Hons in Economics from MIT WPU. Alongside her academic pursuits, Bhumika has developed a keen interest in the fascinating realms of neuroeconomics, behavioral science, and neuromarketing. This unique blend of disciplines allows her to explore the intricate connections between economics and the human mind, unraveling the complexities of decision-making and consumer behavior. Bhumika's passion for understanding the interplay between economics and psychology highlights her drive to uncover new insights and bridge the gap between theory and practice. With her enthusiasm and dedication, Bhumika is poised to make meaningful contributions to the field.

Rachita Gulati is an Associate Professor of Economics at the Department of Humanities and Social Sciences, Indian Institute of Technology (IIT), Roorkee, Uttarakhand. She received the Subir Chowdhury Visiting Fellowship 2017–2018 from the India Observatory, London School of Economics and Political Sciences, London, UK. Her teaching and research interests relate to applied econometrics, banking efficiency, financial stability, corporate governance, and efficiency and productivity analysis. She has published over two dozen articles in top-ranked journals, including Omega, Quarterly Review of Finance and Economics, Economic Modelling, and The North American Journal of Finance and Accounting, among others. She has worked on project studies awarded/sponsored by the Reserve Bank of India, the State Finance Commission of Haryana, the Ministry of Tribal Affairs, and ICSSR (IMPRESS Scheme). She is also a member of several national and international associations, including the International Society of Efficiency and Productivity Analysis, the Indian Econometric Society, the International Corporate Governance Society, the International Econometric Society, etc.

Kokila K is a research scholar in Finance at VIT Business School, Chennai. Prior to this, she completed her MBA in finance and marketing. She has work experience in the stock market and commodities market trading. Her area of interest is financial market, stock market anomalies, investor sentiments, and macroeconomic variables.

Anuja Kure, currently a Financial Analyst at Wipro, possesses a deep-seated passion for both economics and finance. With an academic background that includes graduating with honors in Economics from Dr Vishwanath Karad MIT-WPU, Pune, India, she skillfully applies her analytical prowess to navigate the financial landscape. Apart from her academic and professional role, she is deeply committed to giving back to the society. This commitment is evident in her involvement with S.H.E, a social enterprise dedicated to empowering women artists in rural Kerala. Through this initiative, she has not only explored the mental health needs of rural women but has also demonstrated her leadership and persuasive communication skills by securing seed funding for the cause through a compelling presentation at Dunin Deshpande Queen's Innovation Center (DDQIC).

Bhajan Lal holds the position of Assistant Professor within the domain of Human Resource Management at the Institute of Management, Nirma University, located in Ahmedabad, Gujarat, India. He has successfully attained his doctoral credentials from the esteemed Indian Institute of Technology, Roorkee, focusing on Human Capital Creation. Accumulating over a span of 9 years, Dr Lal has garnered a wealth of expertise in the realms of pedagogy, scholarly inquiry, and professional advisement. His scholarly pursuits primarily revolve around the spheres of HR analytics, performance assessment, measurement methodologies, and the intricate realm of human capital generation.

J. Divya Merry Malar is an Assistant Professor in the Department of Commerce at Holy Cross College (Autonomous) in Nagercoil, Tamilnadu, India. Affiliated with Manonmaniam Sundaranar University, Tirunelveli. With a wealth of knowledge and experience in the field of Commerce, Dr Malar is dedicated to imparting valuable insights to her students and contributing to the academic community. Dr Malar holds a PhD in Commerce and has a profound interest in accounting and commerce.

Priya Mandleshwar is a Doctoral Scholar in the area of Finance and Accounting at the Indian Institute of Management Indore. Her research interests cover Corporate Social Responsibility (CSR), corporate finance, mergers and acquisitions, and corporate governance. Along with that, she is working on papers in the area of institutional investors. Prior to her doctoral studies, she completed MCom with a finance specialization at Banaras Hindu University. Her academic prowess earned her a gold medal during her undergraduate studies at Guru Ghasidas Central University. Passionate about unraveling the link between responsible business practices, Priya aspires to contribute significant insights into the realm of ethical corporate frameworks.

Srishti Nagarajan is an MPhil Scholar, Department of Commerce, Delhi School of Economics, University of Delhi. She has done her Master's (MCom) from Ramjas College, University of Delhi, India. She has presented papers in International Conferences. She has won the best paper award for presentation of a paper in the 10th International Conference on Business and Management organized by the Department of Commerce, Shaheed Bhagat Singh College, University of Delhi. She has published a chapter in an edited book titled *Paradigm Shift in Marketing and Finance* by Bharti Publications. Her research interest includes areas such as international business and financial management.

Prof Puja Padhi is a distinguished academic professional renowned for her expertise in Economics. She holds a PhD from the Central University of Hyderabad. She has significantly contributed to the field, particularly in financial economics, applied econometrics, and macroeconomics. Since 2008, she has been an integral faculty member at the Department of Economics, IIT Bomby, where her impactful research and multidisciplinary approach have influenced the academic discourse.

Anuradha S Pai is currently working as an Assistant Professor at the Department of Economics, PES University, Bangalore. She is pursuing PhD in the area of Organ Donation. Her areas of interest include Law and Economics and Development Economics. She has one book chapter and two articles to her credit. She has won Best Paper Award at an International Conference. She has completed a certificate program from Gokhale Institute for Politics and Economics on Computer Applications in Economics. She teaches papers like law and economics and tries to deliver through innovative teaching learning pedagogies.

Pratham Parekh has completed a PhD from the Center for Studies in Society and Development, School of Social Sciences, Central University of Gujarat. He has to his credit 15 research papers to his credit and nine book chapters from reputed publishers. He has authored two scholarly acclaimed books titled *Epistemes of Death* and *Infrastructure Growth & Human Development in Gujarat*. He has 7 years of experience working on the policy interventions with the Government of Gujarat. He has prepared and contributed to 16 policy intervention documents. He is appraised by the Government of Gujarat for his contribution in developing Outcome Budget, Gender Budget, Development Program, SDG monitoring system, and CM Dashboard. His interdisciplinary research interests' range across sociological aspects related to public policy, governance, information technology, data analytics & visualization, human resources management, labor laws, social policy, gender & women studies, mythology, medical sociology, and development studies.

Ashis Kumar Pradhan is currently positioned as an Assistant Professor in the department of Humanities and Social Sciences at Maulana Azad National Institute of Technology, Bhopal, India. He has completed his PhD in Financial Economics from Indian Institute of Technology Kharagpur, India. His current area of research includes International Finance, Corporate Finance, Macroeconomics, and Energy Economics. His teaching interests are Corporate Finance and Macroeconomics.

Mananage Shanika Hansini Rathnasiri is a Lecturer attached to the Department of Marketing Management, Faculty of Management Studies, Sabaragamuwa University of Sri Lanka. She serves as an Associate Editor cum Editorial Assistant of the *South Asian Journal of Marketing*, published by Emerald Publishing. She also serves as the Associate Editor of the Sri Lankan Marketer Magazine, published by the Sri Lanka Institute of Marketing. Furthermore, she contributes as the Editor-in-chief of FMS Today published by the Faculty of Management Studies, Sabaragamuwa University of Sri Lanka.

E. Joseph Rubert, Professor and Head, Department of Management Studies, Arunachala College of Engineering for Women, Manavilai, Kanyakumari District, Tamilnadu, He has successfully completed his PhD in Management Studies from Noorul Islam University, Kumarkovil. He is the Guest Editor of UGC CARE Listed and Scopus Journals. He has published 35 research articles in various reputed journals including UGC Care, Scopus, Peer Refereed and Conference Proceedings. He is the Editor of 25 ISBN Edited books and has presented more than 16 papers in various national and international conferences including International Conference conducted by IIT, Chennai. He guided 4 PhD Research Scholars in Manonmaniam Sundaranar University, Tirunelveli. He has organized 7 National, International Conference, 50 Seminars, Workshops and Business Conclaves. He is a Doctorate Committee member of the Department of Management Studies, Manonmaniam Sundaranar University and Nesamoney Memorial Christian College. He is a member of Board of Studies in St. Xavier's College (Autonomous) Tirunelveli. He was the convenor of different academic programs and coordinators of various academic committees.

Anshita Sachan is a Research Scholar pursuing her PhD in the department of Humanities and Social Sciences at Maulana Azad National Institute of Technology, Bhopal, India. Her academic achievements include successfully clearing the UGC NET 2019; MPSET 2019 examinations. She specializes in the fields of macroeconomics, environmental economics, and energy economics, showcasing a keen interest in addressing critical issues at the intersection of economics and sustainability. She has authored and published papers in esteemed international SCIE and SSCI journals. She has also presented her research papers at prestigious institutes such as IIT Bombay, India; IIM Bodhgaya, India; and Rajagiri Business School, India.

Udit Kumar Sahu is a Research Scholar pursuing his PhD in the department of Humanities and Social Sciences at Maulana Azad National Institute of Technology, Bhopal, India. He qualified UGC NET in the year 2019. His research areas of interests are energy economics, environment, macroeconomics, and financial economics. He has coauthored two research papers published in SCI and SSCI journals. He has also presented research papers in the conferences held at IIT Bombay, IIT Roorkee, and other reputed institutes of India. He has also worked in S&P Global Market Intelligence, Hyderabad, India for one year and seven months.

Shaik Saleem, currently working as an Assistant Professor in Finance at VIT Business School, Chennai. He holds a PhD in management and his area of specialization is finance. He has eight years of teaching experience, and his area of interest includes Corporate Finance, Business Valuation, Financial Modeling, capital markets, and mergers and acquisitions. He has participated and presented papers at several national and international conferences. Also, he has published research papers in various journals and conference proceedings.

Ananya Sarkar is a recent BSc (Hons) Economics graduate at Dr Vishwanath Karad MIT-WPU University, with a keen interest in macroeconomics, development economics, international economics, and quantitative research. Ms Sarkar has actively pursued academic excellence. She has presented her research findings at two international conferences, showcasing her dedication to advancing knowledge in the field. Ms Sarkar's commitment to rigorous economic analysis developed through various academic and professional research reflects her potential to make meaningful contributions in the field of economics.

Sapna Sehrawat is a student in the National Institute of Fashion Technology, Jodhpur, India in the Department of Fashion Management Studies.

Atreyee Sengupta is a BSc (Hons) Economics graduate from Dr Vishwanath Karad MIT World Peace University, Pune, India. Her research interests have been in the areas of international economics and trade, labor economics, and developmental economics. She possesses a strong academic foundation and has consistently directed her endeavors toward economic research and analysis. Ms Sengupta participated in several academic research projects in the fields of micro and macroeconomics during her university days and employed various statistical and econometric methods and models. She is a former member of her university's research club and presented some of her research findings at an international conference. In the forthcoming years, Ms Sengupta aspires to delve deeper into her areas of interest through advanced studies while maintaining a commitment to making substantial contributions to the progressive development of knowledge in the field of economics and business.

J. Sahaya Shabu is a dedicated Research Scholar currently pursuing her PhD studies at Holy Cross College (Autonomous) in Nagercoil, Tamilnadu, India. Affiliated with Manonmaniam Sundaranar University, Tirunelveli. His research interests span asset pricing, market dynamics, investor sentiment, etc. Mr. Shabu brings a wealth of academic expertise to his research, holding an MBA in finance and marketing. With a passion for advancing knowledge in finance and accounting, he is committed to contributing valuable insights to the academic community. In addition to his current role as a Research Scholar, J. Sahaya Shabu is working as an Assistant Professor in Xavier Institute of Business Administration, Palayamkottai, Tirunelveli.

Bharti Singh is a Professor at the Institute of Management Technology Center for Distance Learning, Ghaziabad, Uttar Pradesh, India. She holds a PhD in Economics from the University of Lucknow. She has about three decades of teaching and research experience. Her areas of academic interests include international trade, development economics, environmental economics, and consumer behavior. Prof Singh has supervised PhD candidates, authored books, published research papers in journals, and created academic resources for distance education. She has been associated with corporate trainings at prestigious public and private sector organizations like NTPC, THDC, Genpact, Ericsson, Hero Motocorp Ltd., American Express, RBS, Hindalco, Sopra Steria, Unichem Laboratories Ltd. and Sunlife.

Dr Anju Singla is working as a Head and Professor in the Centre of Management and Humanities (CMH), Punjab Engineering College (PEC), Deemed to be University, Chandigarh. Apart from this, she has also served as a Head of the Entrepreneurship and Incubation Cell, President of Institute Innovation Council, PEC under MHRD Innovation Cell (MIC), Govt. of India and Coordinator of National Innovation and Startup Policy (NISP) under AICTE. She has twenty-two years of teaching and research experience in Management and Finance. Her research areas include Micro Financing, MSMEs, Entrepreneurship, Financial Inclusion, Financial Literacy and Financial Technology (Fintech). She has published more than 80 research papers in reputed International/National Journals and Conference Proceedings and presented papers in numerous International/National Conferences and Seminars. She has also completed a course on "Entrepreneurship in Emerging Economies" from Harvard Business School, Harvard University.

Sonika Siwach is an Assistant Professor with the Department of Fashion Management Studies in National Institute of Fashion Technology, Jodhpur. She is a NIFT graduate in Fashion Technology and MBA in Operations. She has worked in the Fashion e-commerce industry for a decade as Category Manager, Buyer and Merchandising Manager. She specializes in Online Retailing, Fashion Merchandising, and Digital Marketing. Her research interests are based on fashion business landscape and e-commerce development.

Prihana Vasishta is a Senior Research Fellow at the Center of Management and Humanities (CMH), Punjab Engineering College (Deemed to be University), Chandigarh, India. Her research interests include FinTech Adoption, Financial Literacy, Financial Inclusion, and Artificial Intelligence. She has participated in various international conferences and also been a reviewer for some reputed journals indexed in Scopus. She has delivered expert presentations/ invited talks on various topics such as Startups, Academic Research Writing, Cyber security and Financial Literacy.

Chapter 1

Forecasting Major Macroeconomic Variables of the Indian Economy

Bhavya Advani, Anshita Sachan, Udit Kumar Sahu and Ashis Kumar Pradhan

Maulana Azad National Institute of Technology, India

Abstract

A major concern for policymakers and researchers is to ascertain the movement of price levels and employment rates. Predicting the trends of these variables will assist the government in making policies to stabilize the economy. The objective of this chapter is to forecast the unemployment rate and Consumer Price Index (CPI) for the period 2022 to 2031 for the Indian economy. For this purpose, the authors analyse the prediction capability of the univariate auto-regressive integrated moving average (ARIMA) model and the vector autoregressive (VAR) model. The dataset for India's annual CPI and unemployment rate pertains to a 30-year time period from 1991 to 2021. The result shows that the inflation forecasts derived from the ARIMA model are more precise than that of the VAR model. Whereas, unemployment rate forecasts obtained from the VAR model are more reliable than that of the ARIMA model. It is also observed that predicted unemployment rates hover around 5.7% in the forthcoming years, while the forecasted inflation rate witnesses an increasing trend.

Keywords: Forecasting; inflation; consumer price index; unemployment rate; ARIMA; VAR

1. Introduction

The Reserve Bank of India (RBI) underlines that the Indian economy is confronting the strong headwinds of global recessionary risks with sound macroeconomic fundamentals (RBI Press release, 2022). The fifth largest economy of the world has been able to stand firm amid the COVID-19 pandemic and the

Modeling Economic Growth in Contemporary India, 1–24
doi:10.1108/978-1-80382-751-320241001

Russia–Ukraine war. India occupies a significant place in the world economy as it contributes 7% to the global GDP (in purchasing power parity) which is the third highest after the United States and China (World Bank blog, 2019). Additionally, in terms of GDP growth, India is the second largest emerging economy after China and shares 16% of the global GDP growth (World Economic Forum, 2024). The country is also a prominent member of major international trade blocks such as G-20 and BRICS.

The economic march of India, however, has been quite challenging over the years. Every decade since 1990, India is undergoing an economic crisis. First in the year 1991, India faced the balance of payment emergency and currency crisis that prompted the country to liberalize its economy and integrate with the world economy. Further, in the year 2008, the country experienced twin deficit problem which was ensue of the global financial crisis. Later in the year 2015–2016, the Indian economy started experiencing a slowdown as several indicators, viz. GDP growth, private investment, consumption demand and a number of new projects encountered a declining trend (Upadhyay, 2019). The monetary and financial sector also got affected and the country's fiscal deficit shot up to 4.6%, higher than the anticipated figure of 3.5% in the year 2019–2020 (Dev & Sengupta, 2020). Further, in the year 2020, the COVID-19 pandemic afflicted the country and aggravated the state of affairs of already falling Indian economy. The GDP of the country contracted by 23.9% in the first quarter and subsequently by 7.5% in the second quarter of the year 2020 (Economic Survey, 2020–21). The two major contributors of Indian economy – manufacturing and service sector, were badly hit due to the nationwide lockdown imposed by the Government. Nevertheless, agriculture was the only sector that witnessed a positive growth during the first wave of COVID-19.

The COVID-19 emerged as a health crisis and gradually transformed into an economic crisis across the globe. It impacted the world's major economies resulting in 3.4% decline in their collective GDP (Statista, 2023). For a highly populated Indian economy with high population density, greater population of elderly people and with 69% of total population living in rural area, it was unlikely to escape from such crisis (Economic Survey, 2020–21). Despite these impuissance and vulnerabilities, the economy of India was able to recover faster than its counterfeits during the pandemic. The faster recovery can be attributed to the introduction of supply side measures, structural reforms and demand reforms. Moreover, India is witnessing a V-shaped economic recovery and the performance of Indian economy post pandemic has been phenomenal. According to the projections made by the Asian Development Bank (ADB), the International Monetary Fund (IMF) and the World Bank, Indian economy will be the fastest growing economy in the world during the year 2021–2024. It is also expected to grow up to five trillion dollar economy by the year 2025 (Sawhney, 2021). Looking at the growing prominence of the Indian economy, we take a keen interest to look into the trends of certain macro-economic variables of the country and predict their future prospects. In the context of economic development, inflation and unemployment are a couple of factors that hold a direct impact on the general mass of the country as explained theoretically by the Phillips curve. At the same time such factors get majorly affected in case of a crisis. For instance, CPI was among the most affected variable during the COVID-19 pandemic. CPI measures prices at the retail level and determines the general purchasing power of the consumers. At the time when the zoonotic virus started spreading at the global level, people were very uncertain about the longevity of the virus among humans. As a result, people started hoarding necessary goods in their houses which resulted in an increase in overall prices. Citing another instance, during the fall-out of Russia–Ukraine war, the CPI peaked to 7.8% in April 2022. Howsoever, the figure moderated to 5.7% in December with the prompt and adequate efforts made by the RBI and the Government of India (Ministry of finance, Press Release, 2023). Therefore, frequent investigations into the trends of general prices in the second largest emerging market become crucial as the variable also holds a close link with the standard of living of the people.

Similarly, unemployment is another significant element which is frequently discussed at every level of the economy and society. Unemployment constrains the income level of the population which can further limit the per capita income of the country. Notably, as per Lai et al. (2021) the COVID-19 pandemic created a challenging scenario of employment in India. Given this, the study attempts to forecast the CPI inflation and unemployment in India by using Box–Jenkins' ARIMA model along with VAR model. The two noble models also enable us to make a comparative analysis of the results obtained from the same. The study is based on a time series dataset ranging from the period 1991 to 2021 and provides a forecast of the two variables up to 2031.

The current study enhances the extant literature in several aspects. First, the study's data period encompasses a series of crisis including East Asian financial crisis, the global financial crisis and the pandemic period. Second, we employed ARIMA and VAR forecasting models in our study which are considered better than the other estimation techniques namely exponential smoothing. Moreover, our findings provide a comparative analysis about the trend prediction of the CPI and unemployment. Third, the study is based on India, the second largest emerging economy worldwide. Examining the trend and accurately forecasting the variables CPI and unemployment in such an economy is itself a challenging chore. Finally, the study will also suggest appropriate policies and direct the regulatory bodies to be vigilant about the future phase of any crisis.

2. Theoretical Framework

Inflation is the persistent increase in the general price level of services and goods within an economy (Omar et al., 2022). It declines the purchasing power of the currency. It is a monetary phenomenon which is affecting most economies of the world, both developed and developing (Abdulrahman et al., 2018). Different theories of inflation are given by various economists. For instance, classical economists believed in full employment and operation of Say's law in an economy, which is supply creates its own demand. According to Quantity theory of Money (QTM) given by Classical economist, Irving Fisher, there is a direct and proportional association between quantity of money and price level. This relationship is described by an equation of exchange, $MV = PT$, where M denotes money supply, V stands for circulation or velocity of money, P refers to the general price level index and T is the volume of trade. The velocity of money (V) in any economy is determined by institutional factors that are constant in the short run. The volume of trade or transactions (T) is also assumed fixed under the scenario of full employment level. Therefore, any variation in money supply will have a proportionate change in the level of prices. A change in money supply (M) impacts aggregate demand, and with aggregate supply being fixed at full employment level, it will cause inflation (Fisher, 1911). However, Keynes and his followers believed that the non-monetary impulses are responsible for changes in price level (Gordon, 1976).

According to Keynes, when the economy reaches beyond full employment level, increase in aggregate demand is responsible for rise in the price level. Beyond full employment level, aggregate supply of goods and services cannot be altered. So, any change in aggregate demand in the form of consumption expenditure, investment expenditure or government expenditure, will have a direct influence on the price level. Therefore, at full employment level, when aggregate demand exceeds aggregate supply, an inflationary gap is created in an economy. This inflationary gap will lead to price rise in an economy which is termed as demand pull inflation.

The Monetarist school of thought also contributed towards theory of inflation. According to them, a rise in aggregate demand, due to change in money supply, is responsible for increase in the price level. Milton Friedman is the main proponent of the monetarist school. There is similarity between Keynesian and Monetarist schools, as both these schools have considered aggregate demand responsible for rise in price level. However, in Keynesian school, increase in aggregate demand is due to change in components of aggregate demand (autonomous investment, government expenditure or consumption expenditure or net exports), which is independent of money supply. Whereas, monetarists considered fluctuations in money supply responsible for any changes in aggregate demand (Totonchi, 2011).

In any economy, prices of goods are determined by their cost of production. Therefore, alteration in cost of production, due to any reason, will have a direct impact on price. The alteration in cost can be due to supply shocks, raise in wage rate or higher profit motives among many reasons. This resultant increase in price due to rise in cost of production is known as cost push inflation. Here, increase in cost takes place without any change in aggregate demand. Hence, a price increase, without any change in wage rate, will lead to price wage spiral in an economy. Due to rising prices, wage earners will seek greater nominal wages, in order to keep their real wages to the same level as before. This rise in wage rate will further lead to rise in prices and this process continues. This type of inflation is also called price–push inflation (Gordon, 1976; Totonchi, 2011).

Besides inflation, unemployment is another unsettling issue which affects both developing and developed economies (Dev & Venkatanarayana, 2011). Unemployment is a situation when there is scarcity of jobs for the employable and willing labour force of a country. There can be multiple scenarios that lead to unemployment in an economy. As per Singh and Verma (2016), unemployment usually arises when there is a mismatch between the demand and supply of labour in the labour market. That is, the demand of labour is less than the supply of labour.

The unemployment rate is measured by total unemployed labour force as a percentage of labour force (PIB, 2022a). Labour force refers to the people in the population who are either seeking work or already working (PIB, 2022a). The unemployment rate in India is measured based on usual status, current weekly status and current daily status (Dev & Venkatanarayana, 2011). The Ministry of Statistics and Programme Implementation (MoSPI) and the National Statistical Office (NSO) are responsible to gather data on unemployment and employment for Indian economy and for conducting periodic labour force survey (PIB, 2022b).

Inflation and unemployment are among the crucial indicators of the health of an economy. Notably, the two indicators are also associated with each other as exhibited by A.W. Phillips. In the 1960s, A.W. Phillips introduced the concept of the Phillips curve, depicting an inverse association between the wage rate (inflation) and unemployment level. The Phillips curve shows that a rise in the wage rate will lead to a fall in unemployment, and a decline in the wage rate will result in an increase in unemployment. Therefore, in any economy, inflation can be managed by altering the level of unemployment (Totonchi, 2011).

The further stage of the Phillips curve is given by Phelps and Milton Friedman and is called natural rate of unemployment hypothesis. This stage distinguishes between a short-run and long-run Phillips curve. In the short term, there is a negative association between inflation and unemployment, but over a period of time, unemployment becomes stable and does not alter with any change in the inflation rate. This stable unemployment rate is known as the natural rate of unemployment, and the Phillips curve is a vertical, straight line at this level. This stage of Phillips Curve is based on an assumption that people make expectations about inflation on the basis of adaptive or past expectations (Frisch, 1983).

The latter stage of the Phillips curve is given by new classical or rational expectation economists. In this approach, there is no distinction between the short-run and the long-run, and the Phillips curve is a vertical straight line at the natural rate of unemployment level. It is based on the assumption that economic agents act rationally and take decisions on the basis of all the past and current available information (Totonchi, 2011).

3. Literature Review

Forecasting is the mechanism of predicting future trends on the basis of prior data. There has been a quest in the extant literature regarding the appropriate selection of models for forecasting.

One side of literature views linear models are better in forecasting than non-linear models (Awel, 2018; Liu et al., 2012), while the other side offers an opposing view (Marcellino, 2008). However, economic indicators for different countries can be forecasted by using either or both the methods. In time series forecasting, the statistical and primitive methods of forecasting are considered linear, whereas Artificial Neural Networks (ANN) emerged as a non-linear tool (Stock & Watson, 1998). For instance, in the study by Awel (2018) the economic growth for Ethiopia is predicted for the period 2015 to 2017 by considering the sample from the period 1980 to 2014, by employing the Box–Jenkins Approach. The study discusses the importance of the univariate time series model in a data limited environment and also compares the prediction precision of the univariate model with other forecasters. It is found that the ARIMA (1,1,1) model performs better than the IMF World Economic: Forecasting GDP Growth Outlook (1990–2014) and World Bank Global Economic Prospects (2007–2014) forecasters based on Root Mean Square Error (RMSE) and Mean Absolute Errors (MAE). In addition, the study proposes to look into the VAR model to improve the forecasting. In a similar study, Rahman et al. (2019) uses Exponential Smoothing and ARIMA model to project the ten years growth rates of Bangladesh by taking the data for the period 1982 to 2018. In another study by Liu et al. (2012) the real economic growth for ten Latin American countries namely Brazil, Ecuador, Argentina, Venezuela, Dominican Republic, Chile, Peru, Mexico, Colombia and Uruguay is estimated by using five models: bridge equations, autoregressive model, Bayesian VAR (BVAR) model, dynamic factor model (DFM) and bi-variate VAR model. Moreover, the author evaluates the quarterly nowcast and estimates the quarterly value. The author observes that the auto-regressive model provides reliable and more accurate results using monthly data than quarterly data. Secondly, the nowcast and forecast results of the DFM model are more precise than other used models. And lastly, external indicators improve forecast values for most Latin American economies. Marcellino (2008) also conducted the study using the real-time data for the USA from the period 1980 to 2004 and analysed whether complicated time series models perform better than linear models in forecasting economic growth and inflation by employing fifty-five alternative sequences. The comparison results obtained are evaluated using a bootstrap algorithm. The author concludes that linear models outperform the non-linear models, and their relative performance is better assessed using out of sample evaluation.

However, Higgins et al. (2016) predict the economic growth and CPI inflation of China for the time period 2011 to 2015 by employing BVAR methodology and other competing models. These models are Benchmark model, the BVAR model with Sims–Zha (SZ) US prior, No Prior VAR model, Blue Chip Economic Indicators (BCEI) forecasts, the BVAR model with PLR prior, the gold standard random walk model, the BVAR model with Minnesota prior, the BVAR model with GLP prior, auto-regressive (AR) model without trend, that is AR(1), AR(6) and AR(12) and AR with trend at AR(1), AR(6) and AR(12). On the basis of comparative results, it is proven that the benchmark model yields much more reliable outcomes. Similarly, Chuku et al. (2019) depict the benefits of using ANN and non-parametric models for developing economies and observe that ANN have superior accuracy in predicting economic growth than ARIMA and structural econometric models in developing economies that are exposed to chaotic factors and external shocks. The economic growth is estimated for South Africa, Kenya and Nigeria using primary commodity prices, inflation, trade intensity and interest rates by using the data from 1970 to 2016.

The study by De Gooijer and Hyndman (2006) throws light on the overall time series forecasting literature. The authors consider the period from 1982 to 2005 and cover nine hundred and forty papers that are summarized and classified either by models or by problems they addressed or on several issues. It is observed that the proportion of papers concerned with time series forecasting is constant over time. However, the quality of papers has changed over time in terms of statistical models, forecast calculation approaches and evaluation tools.

With regards to the variables, inflation is an important macroeconomic variable which is widely considered by researchers globally for predicting in advance. To forecast the inflation rate of different countries, the ARIMA method is highly used by several researchers. ARIMA method is generally used because of its ability to handle all types of data – stationary, non-stationary or seasonal (Chuku et al., 2019). The study made by Youness and Driss (2022), estimates the dynamics of inflation rate for Morocco by considering the data from 1971 to 2019 using the ARIMA model. The inflation rate is estimated for five years from 2020 to 2024 and findings reveal that ARIMA is the appropriate method for forecasting and ARIMA (0,1,1) provides the best result. Similarly, Omar et al. (2022) use the inflation data of Egypt from the year 2018 to 2022 in order to predict five months' inflation rate from August to December 2022 and found that ARIMA (1,1,1) is an appropriate model to foresee inflation rates. Likewise, Vafin (2020) forecasts the major macro-economic indicators, namely real exports, real investment, real consumption and real GDP, in the context of seven major economies, viz. China, France, India, Japan, Russia, the US and the UK using the ARIMA forecasting technique for the period 2020–2024. Varying results are obtained for different economies. For India, the author finds that the inflation rate will rise from a projected 6.19% in 2020 to reach 7.842% in 2021 and will be stable in subsequent years, from 2021 to 2024. The author also predicts the unemployment rate to rise in the same period. In a similar fashion, Abdulrahman et al. (2018) conducted a study on the Sudan economy. The authors employ the ARIMA methodology to estimate the inflation rates for the period 2017–2026 by taking annual data from the period 1970 to 2016 and find that the ARIMA (1,2,1) is an appropriate model for prediction and that inflation will increase in the coming years for Sudan.

On the similar grounds, Adubisi et al. (2018) predict inflation rate of Nigeria for a six-year period from 2015 to 2020 by using the data from 2006 to 2017. The findings of the research suggest that the ARIMA (1,2,1) produces best forecasted values with minimal forecast errors. Ahmar et al. (2018) conducted a study on the Indonesian economy by taking the data from January 2005 to December 2015 and confirm that the model ARIMA (1,0,0) produces best results. Similarly, Habibah et al. (2017) forecast inflation for the period 2017–2021 in the context of SAARC region by considering the economies of Pakistan, Sri Lanka, Bangladesh and India. By considering yearly data for the period 1981–2016, the authors find that the inflation rates will be higher in future for the SAARC region but still is lower than the average inflation rate of the prior year.

Several models other than Box–Jenkins ARIMA are also used to forecast inflation values. Gjika et al. (2018) use the multiple regression model and seasonal autoregressive integrated moving average (SARIMA) model to predict CPI of Albania for the years 2017 and 2018. The authors opine that for a short-term graphical projection, the results of SARIMA model are more satisfactory than that of multiple regression models. Similarly, Thakur et al. (2016) analyse the monthly data for inflation in India for the period January 2000 to December 2012 and predict the inflation for the year 2013 using feed forward back propagation neural networks. As per the authors, satisfactory results are obtained by using neural networks model. The authors also identify a set of variables namely, GDP, exchange rate, imports and exports, foreign reserves and oil and gold prices as significant factors impacting inflation in India. With the quest to find out the best model to forecast, Hussain et al. (2022) employ both ARIMA and ANN to forecast inflation rates, GDP and exchange rate for Pakistan economy. It is found that ANN-based forecasts are more precise to estimate inflation as compared to the ARIMA model. However, ARIMA-based forecasts are comparatively better to predict GDP and exchange rate than that of the ANN model.

The study by Jose et al. (2021) tests the suitability of a Phillips curve relationship for forecasting CPI inflation using ARIMA and SVAR models in the context of India. The out of sample forecast are obtained for the period 2017–2018: Q4 to 2019–2020: Q4 by using the data from the period 1996–1997: Q1 to 2017–2018: Q3. The findings confirm the existence of Phillips curve relationship. Secondly, it is found that while Phillips curve-based models perform better for four-quarters ahead forecast horizon, the univariate models (SARIMA) outperform in forecasting one-quarter ahead inflation in the case of core inflation. Thirdly, SVAR model proved useful for assessing the impact of different shocks on inflation.

The inflation rate of any economy is affected by several factors. Totonchi (2011) reviews and analyses the theories of inflation and reveals that the origins of inflation can be attributed to any of these mentioned factors, mainly supply side shock, demand side shock, monetary shocks, political factors (or the role of institutions) and structural factors. Also, it is observed that inflation is a consequence of dynamic interactions of these independent variables. The author also observes that it is not easy to attribute observed inflation into any one of its components. The author asserts that inflation is always an institutional and macro-economic phenomenon and inflation itself has a tendency to cause further inflation. Likewise, Osorio and Unsal (2013) discussed the inflation dynamics in Asia using Global Vector Autoregression (GVAR) model and Structural Vector Autoregression (SVAR) model. The authors analyse the impact of demand shock and supply shock in price rise and the extent to which these shocks are derived from foreign and domestic sources. In analysis, demand sources comprise output gaps and monetary shocks (interest rates, money supply and exchange rates) while supply factors comprise producer prices and commodity prices. The author uses the GVAR model for thirty-three countries over the period from 1986 to 2010. It is observed that supply pressures and monetary pressures are major forces for driving Inflation in Asia while demand shocks have played a relatively smaller role. Also, the relative role of these factors is changing over time. The output gaps play a significant role in driving inflation in recent years, while the role of supply shocks has reduced slightly. Secondly, the impact of monetary shock has diminished in some economies of Asia. Thirdly, ASEAN economies and India are exposed to inflationary developments happening in China and these spillovers from China region are both significant and large. Spillovers cause inflationary pressure directly through increased imported commodity prices and indirectly through higher good prices.

On similar grounds, Mohanty and John (2015) identified the factors of inflation in India by considering the data from the period 1996–1997 to the period 2013–2014. The identified determinants of inflation are fiscal policy, output gap, crude oil prices and monetary policy. The relation of these determinants with inflation is studied using the SVAR model. It is observed that the inflation in India was moderate before the global financial crisis. However, inflation rose to around 10% during 2010–2011 and 2011–2012, which however declined again in 2012–2013. It is found that from the supply-side, exchange rates and crude oil prices played a dominant role in defining prices and from the demand side, output gap has an asymmetric effect on the prices. It is also found that the fiscal deficit played a significant role in inflation during the post crisis period. Similarly, Gjika et al. (2018) looked into the inflation data of Albania from 1990 to 2017. It is observed that during the period 1996–1997, inflation rose rapidly in Albania and is almost three times higher than the previous year. This rise in figures was attributed to pyramid schemes and the premise for further growth.

The level of unemployment is also an important determination of inflation. Unemployment rate is an authentic indicator for the prevalent conditions of the labour market (Chakraborty et al., 2021). Various studies are carried on forecasting unemployment rates using alternative methods. Forecasting unemployment is defined as the expected value for the number of unemployed persons as a percentage of the total labour force. Chakraborty et al. (2021) conducted the study on the unemployment rate of seven countries namely, Japan, Canada, Switzerland, New Zealand, Germany, Sweden and Netherlands, by using the proposed hybrid model of ARIMA and Auto Regressive Neural Networks (ARNN). ARIMA method is applied in the first phase of the model to catch linear trends and ARNN is applied in the second phase to catch non-linear trends present in the dataset. It is found that the proposed hybrid ARIMA–ARNN model predicts better results and better forecast accuracy as compared to traditional hybrid and single models. The proposed method is also found useful for both long-term and short-term forecasts.

In a different study, Katris (2021) studied the impact of COVID-19 pandemic on the unemployment rates in Greece economy in comparison to the European Union comprising of twenty-seven countries (EU27), on general population, on females and on youth population using VAR Model, ARIMA and ANN. It is found that the effect of COVID-19 is lower on unemployment rates in Greece as compared to EU27 countries. In terms of forecasting ability, other approaches are preferred in comparison to the VAR Model. Alternatively, Dritsakis and Klazoglou (2018) aim to identify appropriate forecasting model for predicting

US unemployment rate by using combinations of either one or two models from the SARIMA, autoregressive conditional heteroscedasticity and the generalized autoregressive conditional heteroscedasticity (GARCH) model. It is found that the SARIMA (1,1,2) (1,1,1)12 – GARCH (1,1) model is the better predictor to project US unemployment rates by considering the monthly data from January 1995 to July 2017. Likewise, Sermpinis et al. (2014) observe that hybrid genetic algorithm–support vector regression (GA-SVR) model outperforms random walk model, genetic programming algorithm, multi-layer perceptron, moving average convergence/divergence model, neural networks and auto-regressive moving average (ARMA) model while predicting US inflation and unemployment rates for a period 1974 to 2012. GA-SVR provides the lowest statistics for MAE, RMSE, mean absolute percentage error (MAPE), and Theil's U. The lower the statistics, the better is the prediction accuracy of the model. The second-best model is genetic programming algorithm as it outperformed recurrent neural network and multi-layer perceptron. Kurita (2010) uses fractionally integrated autoregressive and moving average (ARFIMA) models to predict unemployment rate by considering the monthly sample data for Japan from January 1995 to August 2008. It is found that the ARFIMA model depicts a fair representation of data and, hence, provides accurate results.

There are certain challenges that need to be overcome while forecasting. Liebermann (2012) discusses the problem faced during estimation due to delay in publications and delay in official release of data. The author focuses on Irish economies and predicts nowcast GDP growth by factor model approaches and bridge equations. So, in order to solve the problem of publication lag, an early estimate of GDP is predicted before its official release using high frequency information and many indicators to effectively assess and monitor the economy. Likewise, Chuku et al. (2019) highlight the problem of estimation faced by developing economies due to presence of several complexities in these economies.

By examining the existing literature, it is found that there are limited studies that forecast both CPI inflation and unemployment in the context of India until 2031. Hence, the current study tries to fill this gap by forecasting the two variables for next ten years with the help of ARIMA and VAR models.

4. Materials and Methods

4.1 Data Collection

The dataset utilised for empirical analysis includes yearly rates of CPI (indicator of inflation) and UNE (unemployment rate) for the Indian economy over the years 1991–2021. The data are fetched from the World Bank open database. The purpose of the study is to analyse and anticipate the values of CPI and UNE from 2022 to 2031. The study applies the ARIMA model and the VAR model to predict and estimate the CPI and UNE. The ARIMA model is executed using R studio, while STATA software is employed for the VAR model.

4.2 Model Description

4.2.1 The ARIMA Model

The ARIMA model constitutes of autoregressive process (AR), integrated process (I), the moving average process (MA) and the differencing process (*d*) (Adubisi et al., 2018). For the implementation of the ARIMA model by the Box–Jenkins approach, we must consider following parameters: identifying, estimating and forecasting (Mossad & Alazba, 2015; Tang et al., 2020). The initial step starts with identification, wherein we check the stationarity property of the time series data. If the variable is non-stationary at level form, we use the differentiating technique. This step decides the value of *d*. The second step includes estimating the appropriate model from all the available models of *p,d,q*. The final step involves the calculation of future values of the variables.

The autoregressive model (AR) denoted by AR (*p*) is represented as follows:

$$Y_t = \alpha_0 + \alpha_1 Y_{t-1} + \alpha_2 Y_{t-2} + \ldots\ldots\ldots\ldots + \alpha_p Y_{t-p} + \mu_t \tag{1.1}$$

where u_t shows a white noise error term. We will forecast the future observations using the first component, i.e. AR time series model.

The Moving Average (MA) model is the second component, which assist in predicting the future observations of the dependent variable. Unlike AR model, MA model utilizes prior forecast errors in a regression and not the past values. The following is the mathematical expression of the MA order. MA of the current and the past white noise error component denoted by MA (*q*) will also stimulate Y_t.

$$Y_t = C_0 + C_1 \mu_t + C_2 \mu_{t-1} + \ldots\ldots\ldots\ldots + C_p \mu_{t-p} \tag{1.2}$$

The integration of stationary AR and MA components constitutes the ARMA (*p,q*) model. The third component is integration which is employed when we convert the input data into stationary form by applying the differencing technique. Following is the mathematical expression given by Rohrbach and Kiriwaggulu (2001) and Nau (2017).

$$\Delta y_t = y_t - y_{t-1} \tag{1.3}$$

where Δy_t represents change in the variable of interest, y_t is the original series and y_{t-1} exhibits 1-year lagged term. The combinations of all the three components assist in better estimation and forecasting.

4.2.2 VAR Model

According to Sims (1980), the multivariate VAR model considers all variables as endogenous and each equation considers the same set of regressors. We represent the bivariate VAR model as follows:

$$CPI_t = \alpha + \beta_1 CPI_{t-1} + \ldots\ldots\ldots + \beta_j CPI_{t-j} + \beta_1 UNE_{t-1} \ldots\ldots\ldots\ldots + \beta_i UNE_{t-i} + \mu_{1t} \tag{1.4}$$

$$\text{UNE}_t = \alpha' + \beta_1 \, \text{UNE}_{t-1} + \ldots\ldots + \beta_i \, \text{UNE}_{t-i} + \beta_1 \, \text{CPI}_{t-1} \ldots\ldots\ldots + \beta_j \, \text{CPI}_{t-j}$$
$$+ \mu_{2t} \quad (1.5)$$

where u is the stochastic error term and is also called as innovations or shocks.

5. Application of Models

5.1 Application of Box–Jenkins Methodology

The process of ARIMA modelling involves three major steps.

Step 1: Identification
In the identification step, the values of p, d and q are determined. The partial autocorrelation function (PACF) and autocorrelation function (ACF) are the primary tools used to find these values. PACF determines correlation within time series observations, that is, between present observation and 'm' period prior observation, after controlling for observations at intermediate lags (i.e. all lags $<$ m). In other words, the correlation between Y_t and Y_{t-m}, after eliminating the impact of in-between lags, i.e. $Y_{t-m+1}, Y_{t-m+2,...}, Y_{t-1}$. ACF is a complete auto-correlation function which provides with the values of auto-correlation of any series along with its lagged values. It describes the extent by which the present value of the series is related to its past values.

The first step is to check the stationarity of our time series dataset. We have shown the results of Augmented Dickey–Fuller test and Phillips–Perron test of stationarity. The null hypothesis for both the stationarity test is that there is existence of unit root in the time series. Both the results and graphs (Figs. 1.1 and 1.2) show that the variables are stationary in level form, i.e. I(0) (Table 1.1). The value of parameter d is determined on the basis of stationarity. As both these variables are stationary at level form, the parameter d is equal to zero.

The values of PACF and ACF determine the appropriate order of the parameters, p and q of ARIMA model respectively. The correlogram in Fig. 1.3 helps us to choose a lag length to execute the suitable model. The blue line represents 95% confidence interval and lags beyond that level are considered for finding the values of p and q. We can now formulate models for CPI and UNE. The proposed sets of p,d,q that we identify for CPI is ARIMA (1,0,1) and ARIMA (5,0,2) and for UNE is ARIMA (0,0,1).

Step 2: Estimation
The next procedure is to estimate the parameters of the model specified in step 1 and further, select the best model. In Table 1.2, we evaluate the right fit model using Akaike's information criterion (AIC), log likelihood and Sigma SQ. We select the model with the minimum values of these parameters. After comparing the values of both the model, Sigma SQ and AIC criterion confirm ARIMA (5,0,2) for CPI is appropriate for our study.

Table 1.3 reports the AR and MA characteristics. As all the estimates of the AR and MA characteristics are less than 1, hence, the predicted AR and MA are stationary and stable.

Table 1.4 depicts the Sigma SQ, log likelihood and AIC characteristics of ARIMA (0,0,1) for UNE. Since ACF and PACF suggested only one set of values for p,d,q, we proceed with ARIMA(0,0,1) for UNE.

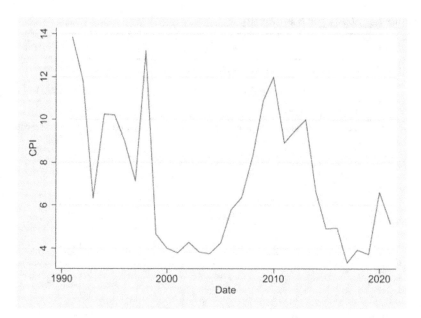

Fig. 1.1.   CPI Inflation Over the Years 1991–2021. *Source:* Author's
Computation.

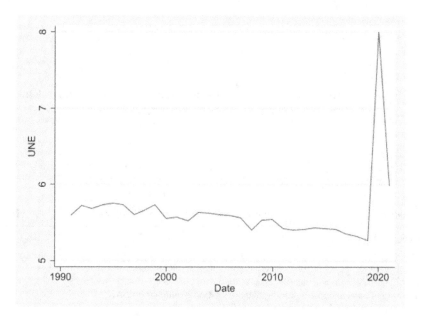

Fig. 1.2.   Unemployment Rate Over the Years 1991–2021. *Source:*
Author's Computation.

Table 1.1. Tests for Stationarity.

Variables	ADF (Levels)	Phillips–Perron Test
CPI	−3.129***	−3.131***
UNE	−4.822***	−4.805***

Source: Author's computation.

Note: ***denotes 1% level of significance. The authors have reported the results of *t*-statistics.

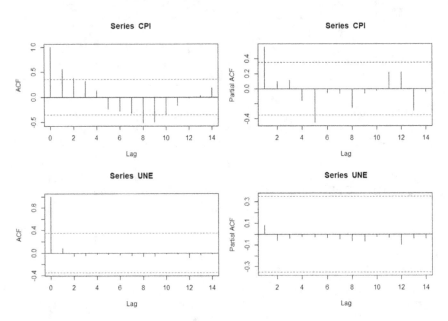

Fig. 1.3.   ACF and PACF for CPI Inflation and Unemployment Rate.
Source: Author's Computation.

Table 1.2. Comparison of Tentative ARIMA (*p*,0,*q*) Models for CPI.

Models	Selection Criteria		
	Sigma SQ	Log Likelihood	AIC
ARIMA (1,0,1)	6.014	−72.09*	152.18
ARIMA (5,0,2)	3.154*	−65.56	149.12*

Source: Author's computation.

Note: *indicates the lowest among Sigma SQ, Log likelihood and AIC.

Table 1.3. Parameter for ARIMA (5,0,2) Model for CPI.

Model Fit Statistics		
Sigma SQ	**Log Likelihood**	**AIC**
3.154	−65.56	149.12
Coefficients	*Estimates*	*Std. Error*
AR(1)	0.574	0.1870
AR(2)	−0.4270	0.2042
AR(3)	0.5110	0.1917
AR(4)	0.0906	0.2205
AR(5)	−0.3648	0.1834
MA(1)	−0.1103	0.1331
MA(2)	1.000	0.1727
Cons	7.3287	0.9725

Source: Author's computation.

Table 1.4. ARIMA $(p,0,q)$ Model for UNE.

	Selection Criteria		
Models	**Sigma SQ**	**Log Likelihood**	**AIC**
ARIMA (0,0,1)	0.2053	−19.45	44.89

Source: Author's computation.

Table 1.5 depicts the MA characteristics for unemployment rate. The MA characteristic is found to be stationary and stable because the estimates of MA are less than 1.

Table 1.5. Parameter for ARIMA (0,0,1) Model for UNE.

Model Fit Statistics		
Sigma SQ	**Log Likelihood**	**AIC**
0.2053	−19.45	44,89
Coefficients	*Estimates*	*Std. Error*
MA(1)	0.0866	0.1830
Cons	5.6449	0.0882

Source: Author's computation.

Before proceeding further, performing some diagnostic checks is ideal for effective prediction. Table 1.6 shows autocorrelation and normality test results for both the variables. We use Ljung–Box test to find the presence of autocorrelation in our time-series model. This test is applied to the residuals of a time series after fitting an ARIMA (p,d,q) model on the dataset. The results of Ljung–Box depict that the model does not show lack of fit and there is absence of autocorrelation in our model for both the variables. The Shapiro–Wilk test is a test of normality and it examines how close the sample data fit to a normal distribution. The high p-value of the Shapiro–Wilk test for the variable CPI denotes that we fail to reject the null hypothesis and our sample is normally distributed. However, the result from Shapiro–Wilk test for the variable UNE shows that the variable is non-normally distributed.

Step 3: Forecasting an ARIMA model
The final step of the model includes prediction of the variables for the next 10 years. From the above discussion, we have identified the ARIMA (5,0,2) parameter for the variable CPI. Hence, the ARIMA model for CPI Inflation will predict the future values based on the 5-year lags (or AR) of the previous values of CPI and 2-year lags of the error terms (or MA). Similarly, based on ARIMA (0,0,1) parameter, the variable UNE will predict based on its 1-year MA value. The final results of the predicted values are provided in Table 1.9.

5.2 Application of VAR Model

Step 1: We first find the stationarity of both the variables. As mentioned in Table 1.1, all the variables are stationary at level form.

Step 2: The second step is to determine the appropriate lag length (LL). We employ the AIC, Schwarz criterion (SC) and Hannan–Quinn information criterion (HQIC), Final prediction error (FPE) and Likelihood ratio (LR) characteristics to determine the suitable lag length. The results of LR, FPE, HQIC and SBIC criterion confirm lag 1 (Table 1.7) as appropriate lag length.

5.3 Testing Granger Causality

As we employ multivariate VAR model, it is ideal to check the Granger causality between the variables CPI and UNE. Granger causality test is conducted to find out

Table 1.6. Model Residuals Adequacy Analysis (Diagnostic Tests).

CPI				UNE		
Test	Test Statistics	Degree of Freedom	P-Value	Test Statistics	Degree of Freedom	P-Value
Ljung–Box	0.0267	1	0.87	1.8624e-05	1	0.996
Shapiro–Wilk	0.97946	–	0.7974	0.42618	–	6.523e-10

Source: Author's computation.

cause and effect relationship among the variables of interest. The null hypothesis of Granger causality test states no granger causality between the variables. The insignificant p-values presented in Table 1.8 confirm the absence of any granger causality between the variables.

Step 3: Forecasting the model
The final step is to predict the future values of the selected variables. Based on the lag order selection, obtained from lowest values of FPE, AIC, HQIC and SBIC (Table 1.7), the VAR model will provide the predicted values by taking 1-year lag of the previous values. The final results are shown in Table 1.9.

Table 1.7. VAR Lag Order Selection Criteria.

Lag	LL	LR	Df	P	FPE	AIC	HQIC	SBIC
0	−85.414				2.224	6.475	6.503	6.571
1	−77.72	15.38*	4	0.004	1.695*	6.201	6.287*	6.489*
2	−76.591	2.266	4	0.687	2.110	6.414	6.556	6.894
3	−75.769	1.644	4	0.801	2.712	6.649	6.849	7.321
4	−73.901	3.736	4	0.443	3.269	6.807	7.064	7.671

Source: Author's computation.
Note: *indicates lag order selected by choosing the highest LR and lowest AIC, HQIC and SBIC.

Table 1.8. Results of Granger Causality Wald Testing.

Direction Causality	*P*-Value
CPI → UNE	0.470
UNE → CPI	0.563

Source: Author's computation.

6. Findings and Discussions

We present the predicted values of CPI and UNE in Table 1.9. The table contains the results of both ARIMA and VAR models. As per the ARIMA model, the CPI inflation upsurges and goes beyond 7% from the year 2024 onwards. The CPI is even predicted to go beyond 7.5% in the year 2027, 2028 and 2031 as per the model. While considering the results of VAR model, the CPI inflation remains below 6.5% up to 2031. In the context of unemployment, the ARIMA model predicts a constant value of 5.644% from 2023 to 2031. Similarly, the VAR model also predicts the unemployment rate to hover around 5.7% from 2023 to 2031. The results are also depicted graphically in Fig. 1.6.

While plotting the results on a graph, we assert that the CPI inflation maintains an upsurge trend as per ARIMA (Fig. 1.4a) and remains almost horizontal as per

Table 1.9. Forecasted Results of ARIMA Model and VAR Model.

Year	ARIMA Results		VAR Results	
	CPI	UNE	CPI	UNE
2022	6.075	5.655	5.501093	5.709373
2023	6.411	5.644	5.890947	5.679444
2024	7.463	5.644	6.133889	5.670762
2025	7.215	5.644	6.27872	5.666245
2026	7.425	5.644	6.364627	5.663611
2027	7.875	5.644	6.415554	5.662052
2028	7.890	5.644	6.445741	5.661129
2029	7.407	5.644	6.463636	5.660581
2030	7.463	5.644	6.474243	5.660257
2031	7.673	5.644	6.48053	5.660064

Source: Author's computation.

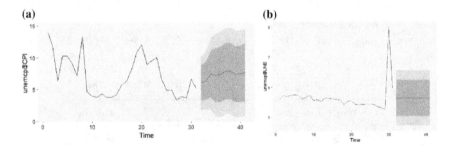

(a)   **(b)**

Fig. 1.4.   Forecasts From ARIMA for CPI Inflation and Unemployment. (a) Forecasts From ARIMA (5,0,2) With Non-Zero Mean. (b) Forecasts From ARIMA (0,0,1) With Non-Zero Mean. *Source:* Author's computation.

VAR (Fig. 1.5a). Moreover, in case of unemployment, the predicted graphical trend stays almost parallel to the horizontal axis as per both the models (Fig. 1.4b and Fig. 1.5b). The shaded areas show the tentative volatility with regards to the predicted values.

While we employ both ARIMA and VAR models for our analysis, we incisively comprehend an in-sample forecasting exercise to discover the best model between the two models to predict variables – CPI and UNE.[1] Based on the results of the in-sample forecasting, we assert that the ARIMA model better predicts CPI whereas

---

[1]The authors present the results of in-sample forecasting in the appendix.

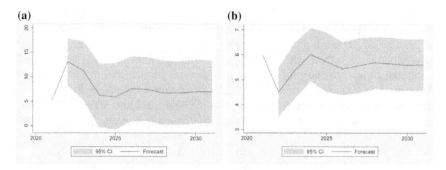

Fig. 1.5. Forecasts From VAR. (a) Forecast for CPI. (b) Forecast for UNE. *Source:* Author's computation.

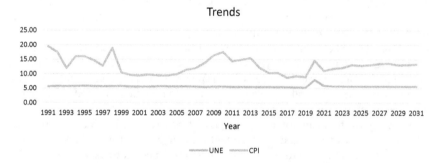

Fig. 1.6. Trends for CPI Inflation and Unemployment Rate. *Source:* Author's Computation.

the VAR model is more suitable for UNE. Therefore, for our ultimate forecasting, we refer to the results of ARIMA for CPI and the results of VAR for UNE. Even though we aim at predicting the future values of the two important variables representing economic stability of a country, the prediction of these crucial variables not necessarily provides accurate forecasts. Many forecasting techniques have failed because of several reasons. For instance, Barbate et al. (2021) projected that unemployment rate and inflation for the year 2024–2025 will hover between 12.13% to 18.13% and 8%–14% respectively due to COVID-19 and these projections depends upon the rate of COVID-19 recovery. The failure of these predictions is primarily because of more vivid speculations and implementation of certain theoretical assumptions. Some of the models predicted long-term outcomes whereas others which focus on short-term forecasting have also produced confusing results with highly uncertain figures. Contrary to our findings, Sharma and Soni (2021) asserted that the ARIMA model results outperformed the findings of other exponential smoothing techniques while forecasting the youth unemployment rate for India from 2019 to 2023.

The forecasted results of ARIMA model for CPI falls in line with the findings of Vafin (2020) as the author predicts more than 7% inflation rates in India from 2021 to 2024. The inflation rate surging beyond 7% is however, an unwelcome phenomenon for a developing country like India. Nevertheless, it is the aftermath of globalization that any international shock such as the fall-out of the Russia–Ukraine war can elevate the price levels in the country. Reportedly, the global growth has been estimated to slowdown in the year 2023 and afterwards whereas the global commodity prices stay elevated (Economic survey, 2022–23). Under such a scenario, it brings up the risks of increasing price levels in India in the coming years if the economy remains susceptible to the world economy.

The economic survey (2022–23) also underlines the probability of rupee depreciation under the likelihood of further increment in the policy rates by the US Fed. It can eventually decrement the purchasing power of rupee and push up the price levels, majorly impacting imports and imported items. Under such circumstances, the CPI inflation of more than 7% can continue for successive years. Howsoever, the appropriate and timely actions taken by the RBI and the government of India can carve down the high inflation risks in the long run. It is evident that India has performed well to restrain the rising inflation in the year 2022 from 7.8% in April to 5.7% in December amid the global recessionary headwinds. Hence, it can be assumed that inflation in India in the coming years will remain within the forecasted values of CPI estimated through our model. As a domestic policy measure, India should also strive to enhance the agricultural productions in order to maintain the food prices which will strengthen the root of the economy.

With regards to unemployment, Vafin (2020) has exhibited an incline in the rate, whereas we project a static unemployment rate for India through the VAR model that circles around 5.7%. However, India's unemployment rate has been predicted to upsurge in some other studies as well viz., Sharma and Soni (2021) and Lai et al. (2021). Nevertheless, our projection of a static unemployment rate is based on the conception that with the growing skilled labour market in India, several global companies prefer India for outsourcing and professional jobs. At domestic level, propagation of Make in India and the re-emergence of start-ups and MSMEs, especially after the COVID-19 pandemic, have been setting new platforms for employment creation in the country. As per the Economic survey 2022–23, the government schemes such as the Mahatma Gandhi National Rural Employment Guarantee Scheme (MGNREGS) have been implemental in meliorating the rural employment. Thus, the continuity of such factors unanimously can help in constraining the unemployment rate over the long run. Notwithstanding to the fact that India is the second highest populated country of the world, creating employment for the entire labour force is certainly a baffling chore. Hence, our models forecast an approximate stable unemployment rate in India till 2031.

7. Conclusion

It is crucial and challenging at the same time to predict the variables such as CPI inflation and unemployment for a rapid advancing country like India. In this study we have attempted to predict the future trends of the two well-discussed variables by employing the ARIMA and the VAR models. As per our findings, we exhibit an increasing trend for CPI and an approximate stability for unemployment rates for next 10 years predicted from 2022 to 2031. The possible rise in CPI inflation can be attributed to the international events and increasing global commodity prices. Besides, the development of skilled labour market and India's preference for labour outsourcing are responsible for constant unemployment rate in the India economy. The rising inflation levels can be detrimental for the economy which can be carved down through incessant efforts from the RBI as well as the government.

The accurate prediction of the discussed variables – CPI inflation and unemployment is however, a knotty chore and requires more elaboration of the entire economic scenario. Besides, the ARIMA and VAR models applied in the study have forecasted the variables based on their own lagged terms and their error components. Hence, the study limits itself with regards to the accuracy of the prediction. Moreover, the emergence of unforeseen events, viz. the COVID-19 pandemic, can even worsen the predictions made on any ground.

References

Abdulrahman, B. M. A., Ahmed, A. Y. A., & Abdellah, A. E. Y. (2018). Forecasting of Sudan inflation rates using ARIMA model. *International Journal of Economics and Financial Issues, 8*(3), 17.

Adubisi, O. D., David, I. J., James, F. E., Awa, U. E., & Terna, A. J. (2018). A predictive autoregressive integrated moving average (ARIMA) model for forecasting inflation rates. *Research Journal of Business and Economic Management, 1*(1), 1–8.

Ahmar, A. S., Gs, A. D., Listyorini, T., Sugianto, C. A., Yuniningsih, Y., Rahim, R., & Kurniasih, N. (2018, June). Implementation of the ARIMA (p, d, q) method to forecasting CPI Data using forecast package in R Software. In *Journal of physics: Conference series* (Vol. 1028, No. 1, p. 012189). IOP Publishing.

Awel, Y. M. (2018). Forecasting GDP growth: Application of autoregressive integrated moving average model. *Empirical Economic Review, 1*(2), 1–16.

Barbate, V., Gade, R. N., & Raibagkar, S. S. (2021). COVID-19 and its impact on the Indian economy. *Vision, 25*(1), 23–35.

Chakraborty, T., Chakraborty, A. K., Biswas, M., Banerjee, S., & Bhattacharya, S. (2021). Unemployment rate forecasting: A hybrid approach. *Computational Economics, 57*(1), 183–201.

Chuku, C., Simpasa, A., & Oduor, J. (2019). Intelligent forecasting of economic growth for developing economies. *International Economics, 159*, 74–93.

De Gooijer, J. G., & Hyndman, R. J. (2006). 25 years of time series forecasting. *International Journal of Forecasting, 22*(3), 443–473.

Dev, S. M., & Sengupta, R. (2020, April). *Covid-19: Impact on the Indian economy.* Indira Gandhi Institute of Development Research.

Dev, S. M., & Venkatanarayana, M. (2011). *Youth employment and unemployment in India.* Indira Gandhi Institute of Development Research.

Dritsakis, N., & Klazoglou, P. (2018). Forecasting unemployment rates in USA using Box-Jenkins methodology. *International Journal of Economics and Financial Issues*, *8*(1), 9.

Economic Survey. (2020-21). https://www.indiabudget.gov.in/budget2021-22/economicsurvey/index.php

Economic Survey. (2022-23). State of the Economy 2022-23: Recovery complete. https://www.indiabudget.gov.in/economicsurvey/doc/eschapter/echap01.pdf

Fisher, I. (1911). "The equation of exchange," 1896–1910. *The American Economic Review*, *1*(2), 296–305.

Frisch, H. (1983). *Theories of inflation*. Cambridge University Press.

Gjika, E., Puka, L., & Zaçaj, O. (2018, May). Forecasting consumer price index (CPI) using time series models and multi regression models (Albania case study). In 10th International Scientific Conference "Business and Management 2018". https://doi.org/10.3846/bm.2018.51

Gordon, R. J. (1976). Recent developments in the theory of inflation and unemployment. *Journal of Monetary Economics*, *2*(2), 185–219.

Habibah, U., Bhutto, N. A., & Ghumro, N. H. (2017). Inflation forecasting in SAARC region using ARIMA models. *Sukkur IBA Journal of Economics and Finance*, *1*(1), 38–58.

Higgins, P., Zha, T., & Zhong, W. (2016). Forecasting China's economic growth and inflation. *China Economic Review*, *41*, 46–61.

Hussain, L., Ghufran, B., & Ditta, A. (2022). Forecasting inflation, exchange rate, and GDP using ANN and ARIMA models: Evidence from Pakistan. *Sustainable Business and Society in Emerging Economies*, *4*(1), 25–32.

Jose, J., Shekhar, H., Kundu, S., Kishore, V., & Bhoi, B. B. (2021). Alternative inflation forecasting models for India – What performs better in practice? *Reserve Bank of India Occasional Papers*, *42*(1).

Katris, C. (2021). Unemployment and COVID-19 impact in Greece: A vector autoregression (VAR) data analysis. *Engineering Proceedings*, *5*(1), 41.

Kurita, T. (2010). A forecasting model for Japan's unemployment rate. *Eurasian Journal of Business and Economics*, *3*(5), 127–134.

Lai, H., Khan, Y. A., Thaljaoui, A., Chammam, W., & Abbas, S. Z. (2021). COVID-19 pandemic and unemployment rate: A hybrid unemployment rate prediction approach for developed and developing countries of Asia. *Soft Computing*, 1–16.

Liebermann, J. (2012). Short-term forecasting of quarterly gross domestic product growth. *Quarterly Bulletin Articles, Central Bank of Ireland*, *1*, 74–84.

Liu, P., Matheson, T., & Romeu, R. (2012). Real-time forecasts of economic activity for Latin American economies. *Economic Modelling*, *29*(4), 1090–1098.

Marcellino, M. (2008). A linear benchmark for forecasting GDP growth and inflation? *Journal of Forecasting*, *27*(4), 305–340.

Ministry of finance, Press Release, 2023. https://pib.gov.in/PressReleasePage.aspx?PRID=1894925

Mohanty, D., & John, J. (2015). Determinants of inflation in India. *Journal of Asian Economics*, *36*, 86–96.

Mossad, A., & Alazba, A. A. (2015). Drought forecasting using stochastic models in a hyper-arid climate. *Atmosphere*, *6*(4), 410–430.

Nau, R. (2017). ARIMA models for time series forecasting. Statistical Forecasting: Notes on Regression and Time Series Analysis. Duke University, Durham.

Omar, M. A., Shahin, S. E., & Roshdy, M. (2022). Forecasting inflation in Egypt (2019–2022) by using autoregressive integrated moving average (ARIMA) models. *Journal of Advanced Veterinary Research*, *12*(6), 670–676.

Osorio, C., & Unsal, D. F. (2013). Inflation dynamics in Asia: Causes, changes, and spillovers from China. *Journal of Asian Economics, 24*, 26–40.

PIB. (2022a). Periodic labour force survey (PLFS) – Quarterly Bulletin [April – June 2022]. https://pib.gov.in/PressReleasePage.aspx?PRID=1855783

PIB. (2022b). Steps taken to reduce unemployment. https://pib.gov.in/PressReleasePage.aspx?PRID=1809229

Rahman, M., Voumik, L. C., Rahman, M., & Hossain, S. (2019). Forecasting GDP growth rates of Bangladesh: An empirical study. *Indian Journal of Economics and Development, 7*(7), 1–11.

RBI Press release December 2022. https://www.rbi.org.in/Scripts/BS_PressReleaseDisplay.aspx?prid=54955

Rohrbach, D. D., & Kiriwaggulu, J. A. B. (2001). Commercialization prospects for sorghum and pearl millet in Tanzania. Working Paper Series no. 7. *Journal of SAT Agricultural Research, 3*(1), 1–28.

Sawhney, A. (2021). Striving towards a circular economy: Climate policy and renewable energy in India. *Clean Technologies and Environmental Policy, 23*, 491–499.

Sermpinis, G., Stasinakis, C., Theofilatos, K., & Karathanasopoulos, A. (2014). Inflation and unemployment forecasting with genetic support vector regression. *Journal of Forecasting, 33*(6), 471–487.

Sharma, S., & Soni, H. K. (2021). An unemployment prediction rate for Indian youth through time series forecasting. In *Machine intelligence and smart systems: Proceedings of MISS 2020* (pp. 315–335). Springer.

Sims, C. A. (1980). Macroeconomics and reality. *Econometrica: Journal of the Econometric Society*, 1–48.

Singh, D., & Verma, N. (2016). Tradeoff between inflation and unemployment in the short run: A case of the Indian economy. *International Finance and Banking, 3*(1), 77.

Statista. (2023). *Impact of the coronavirus pandemic on the global economy*. https://www.statista.com/topics/6139/covid-19-impact-on-the-global-economy/

Stock, J. H., & Watson, M. W. (1998). *A comparison of linear and nonlinear univariate models for forecasting macroeconomic time series*. https://www.nber.org/papers/w6607

Tang, R., Zeng, F., Chen, Z., Wang, J. S., Huang, C. M., & Wu, Z. (2020). The comparison of predicting storm-time ionospheric TEC by three methods: ARIMA, LSTM, and Seq2Seq. *Atmosphere, 11*(4), 316.

Thakur, G. S. M., Bhattacharyya, R., & Mondal, S. S. (2016). Artificial neural network based model for forecasting of inflation in India. *Fuzzy Information and Engineering, 8*(1), 87–100.

Totonchi, J. (2011, July). Macroeconomic theories of inflation. In *International conference on economics and finance research* (Vol. 4, No. 1, pp. 459–462). IACSIT Press.

Upadhyay, R. K. (2019). *Slowdown creeps in Indian economy*. https://doi.org/10.2139/ssrn.3442600

Vafin, A. (2020). Forecasting macroeconomic indicators for seven major economies using the ARIMA model. *Sage Science Economic Reviews, 3*(1), 1–16.

World Bank. (2019). Tracking GDP in PPP terms shows rapid rise of China and India. https://blogs.worldbank.org/opendata/tracking-gdp-ppp-terms-shows-rapid-rise-china-and-india%20(worldbank.org)

World Economic Forum. (2024, January 15). India could become the world's 3rd largest economy in the next 5 years. Here's how. https://www.weforum.org/agenda/2024/01/how-india-can-seize-its-moment-to-become-the-world-s-third-largest-economy/

Youness, J., & Driss, M. (2022, May). An ARIMA model for modeling and forecasting the dynamic of univariate time series: The case of Moroccan inflation rate. In 2022 International Conference on Intelligent Systems and Computer Vision (ISCV) (pp. 1–5). IEEE.

Appendix

Before proceeding towards predicting the future values of both the variables of interest, it is ideal to check the applicability of both the models on our variables and compare the forecasted values with the actual values for a specific time period. To do so, we have taken the actual and predicted values of CPI and UNE for a comparative analysis from 2016 to 2021 in order to perform in-sample forecasting which is reported in Table A1.1 and A1.2.

Table A1.1. In-Sample Forecasting.

| Year | ARIMA | | | VAR | | |
	CPI Actual	UNE Actual	CPI Predicted	UNE Predicted	CPI Predicted	UNE Predicted
2016	4.948216	5.42	5.849	5.62	4.906973	5.43
2017	3.328173	5.36	4.849	5.62	6.588745	5.444503
2018	3.938826	5.33	5.551	5.62	7.405035	5.464191
2019	3.729506	5.27	5.849	5.62	7.751936	5.483541
2020	6.623437	8.00	5.909	5.62	7.856546	5.500269
2021	5.131407	5.98	5.849	5.62	7.845631	5.513747

Source: Author's Computation.

Table A1.2. Mean Absolute Percentage Error (MAPE).

| Year | Mean Absolute Percentage Error (MAPE) | | | |
| | ARIMA | | VAR | |
	CPI	UNE	CPI	UNE
2017	45.696	4.851	97.969	1.577
2018	40.930	5.441	88.001	2.518
2019	56.830	6.641	107.854	4.052
2020	−10.786	−29.750	18.617	−31.247
2021	13.984	−6.020	52.894	−7.797

Source: Author's Computation.

Chapter 2

ICT Sector Development and Its Contribution to Innovation and Economic Growth in South Asia: A Critique

Thilini Chathurika Gamage, Narayanage Jayantha Dewasiri, Athula Gnanapala and Mananage Shanika Hansini Rathnasiri

Sabaragamuwa University of Sri Lanka, Sri Lanka

Abstract

South Asian countries have recently shown tremendous advancement in Information and Communication Technology (ICT) deployment and have been identified as one of the fastest-growing regions in the world. This chapter reviews 43 state-of-the-art scholarly articles on the role of ICT in accelerating economic growth by fostering innovations in South Asian countries. A seven-step approach to the literature review is used for synthesizing relevant data. The findings indicate that although many South Asian countries understood ICT innovations as an approach that provides a competitive edge to business firms and the country's economic growth, their full potential remains untapped due to many barriers. Some significant barriers include the digital divide, ICT infrastructure, existing ICT policies, and data governance and social trust. The results of this chapter would help policymakers understand the vital role of ICT in fostering innovation and uplifting economic growth in the South Asian region.

Keywords: Development; economic growth; information and communication technology; innovation; South Asia

1. Introduction

Intuitively, most scholars (e.g., Appiah-Otoo & Song, 2021; Niebel, 2018) acknowledge that Information and Communication Technologies (ICT) lead to a

Modeling Economic Growth in Contemporary India, 25–33
doi:10.1108/978-1-80382-751-320241002

country's economic growth and innovation potential, as the notion of state development is the consequence of the interplay between its socio-technical components (Salakhova et al., 2021). It is believed that ICT undeniably has tremendous potential to increase the productivity of almost all economic sectors in a country, fostering innovations (Appiah-Otoo & Song, 2021; Usman et al., 2021). The outstanding examples of recently industrialized countries such as Singapore and South Korea, which have placed ICT and innovation at the core of their economic growth policies, are often quoted to confirm this widely held purview. Consequently, the notion of ICT for development (ICT4D) was introduced in the late 1980s (Schelenz & Pawelec, 2022). It is a multiplex notion that integrates the broader perspectives of three disciplines: computer science, information systems and development studies (Jimenez et al., 2022).

From the technological viewpoint, ICT progresses through radio, television, the Internet and mobile technologies. However, not all ICT applications are innovations. If ICT applications are to be considered an innovation, they must be designed to operate in complex social, political, economic, human, financial, and cultural contexts (Hussain et al., 2021; Jimenez et al., 2022). As a result, ICT innovations are considered necessary to achieve the sustainable development goals introduced by the United Nations to alleviate poverty, improve healthcare, provide better education and create global partnerships for development in developing countries (Schelenz & Pawelec, 2022). Consequently, ICT innovations have become an essential part of the development agenda of many developing countries, including countries in South Asia (Hussain et al., 2021).

Although many ICT applications and systems are available in the market, it is still challenging to find solid evidence of scholarly research on how ICT innovations have induced economic development by fostering innovations in South Asian countries (Hussain et al., 2021; Kaplinsky & Kraemer-Mbula, 2022). More specifically, prior literature indicates that numerous projects focusing on ICT innovations in the South Asian region have failed to achieve the anticipated benefits at their full potential (Usman et al., 2021). This suggests that there is still a need to undertake a holistic research approach to understand how ICT innovations could contribute to economic development in South Asia. Consequently, this chapter aims to fill this void in prior literature by investigating the role of ICT in accelerating economic growth by fostering innovations in South Asian countries.

Several reasons inspire the choice of the South Asian region for this chapter. In Asia, where many countries are underdeveloped, rapid growth in the ICT sector has been recently observed (Kaplinsky & Kraemer-Mbula, 2022). Hussain et al. (2021) further revealed that most South Asian countries are paying sincere attention to their competitiveness by focusing on ICT innovations over the last few years and thus experiencing economically positive momentum globally. They also claimed that the South Asia region is becoming the fastest-growing region of the world in innovation, technology and business competitiveness. However, despite the rapid growth of ICT in the South Asian region, there is a severe lack of research that provides insights into how implementing ICT innovations contributes to the economic growth and development of the region (Appiah-Otoo & Song, 2021).

It is essential to acknowledge that the vital role of ICT innovations in a country's economic development process can vary within the different development paradigms we consider. For instance, a transition can take place from a more technologically oriented viewpoint toward a more socially-oriented view, as the term "development" is also linked to a change in the quality of life, empowerment, enhancing human capabilities, equality and poverty reduction. However, how ICT innovations enable economic growth in South Asian countries has yet to be studied from a socially-oriented viewpoint (Kaplinsky & Kraemer-Mbula, 2022). From this perspective, we investigate the role of ICT in accelerating economic growth by fostering innovations in South Asian countries in this chapter.

The rest of the chapter is organized as follows. The next section illustrates the literature review approach adopted. Then, the key findings stemming from the literature review are presented, followed by a discussion on the research gaps identified. Finally, we suggest future research directions before we conclude.

2. Approach to Literature Review

A comprehensive and a critical literature review can create a solid foundation for advancing knowledge by identifying the current status of the research, existing research gaps and where future research is needed (Webster & Watson, 2002). This chapter used the seven-step model postulated by Williams (2018), commonly used in conducting comprehensive literature reviews (see Fig. 2.1). The model guided the relevant literature search from the Web of Science and Scopus databases using keywords such as "ICT innovations," "ICT development," "economic growth," "economic development" and "South Asia" to identify papers about the impact of ICT in accelerating economic growth by fostering innovations in South Asian countries. The search was limited to peer-reviewed articles published in English, and this method generated a complete list of 119 peer-reviewed articles. Then, three authors independently read and shortlisted the titles and abstracts of the 119 papers to identify a set of highly relevant articles. By doing so, we excluded the papers oriented toward software development, technological development in general and any not explicitly focused on South Asian countries. By doing so, we selected 43 state-of-the-art scholarly articles that are highly relevant to the topic of investigation. Later, these selected articles were thoroughly reviewed against the aim of the chapter and then categorized into various groups based on the theme of each article.

3. Findings

Based on the comprehensive review of the 43 selected peer-reviewed articles, it was apparent that in most South Asian countries, ICT innovations are understood as an approach that provides a competitive edge to business firms by creating novel market opportunities and diversification potentials. Consequently, in the recent past, extensive theoretical and empirical research on the use of ICT in fostering innovations and enhancing economic growth has been conducted,

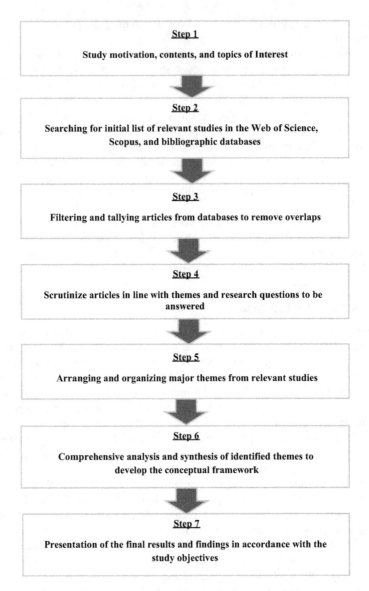

Fig. 2.1.   Literature Review Process Adapted (Williams, 2018).

covering various industries and organizational settings in different South Asian countries. As revealed in the review, although some business firms and industries in South Asian countries benefit from access to novel product and service portfolios, employment creation opportunities and reduced transaction costs by fostering ICT innovations, its full potential remains still untapped due to many reasons (Hussain et al., 2021; Usman et al., 2021). Some significant barriers identified to ICT innovations in the South Asian region are delineated as follows.

3.1 Digital Divide

As Khanra and Joseph (2019) emphasized, the notion "digital divide" is not surprising to the South Asian region. Instead, it manifests other divides and disparities that already exist within the region. The digital divide refers to unequal access to digital technology, including smartphones, tablets, laptops and the Internet. Many factors, such as lack of electricity and other infrastructures, language barriers, costly access to computers, lack of ICT policies, and poor education, have added more complexity to this phenomenon. Prior literature indicates a strong correlation between ICT and poverty (Dutta, 2007; Goswami et al., 2009; Latif et al., 2017). However, this does not mean that poverty in the South Asian region has resulted due to a lack of ICT infrastructure and innovations. Instead, it sets the background for poor governance of these countries for which ICT penetration is low and subsequently represents the low level of knowledge and use of these tools to eradicate poverty (Latif et al., 2017). However, surprisingly, most of the decision-makers in South Asian countries still think of a sequential mode of development where many other elements come first on development agendas other than ICT applications and innovations (Hussain et al., 2021; Nipo & Bujang, 2014). Further, it was revealed that most South Asian countries might be unaware or have not yet used the full potentiality and applicability of ICT tools and innovations in development processes.

3.2 ICT Infrastructure

A large stream of studies (e.g., Latif et al., 2017; Swar & Khan, 2014) has shown how the development of ICT infrastructure has contributed to the economic growth of South Asian countries, especially after the late 1980s. For instance, Khan and Majeed (2020) observed that within the South Asian region, ICT infrastructure facilities have been relatively well developed over the last two decades. Hussain et al. (2021) emphasized that, as in many other countries, even in South Asian countries, the number of mobile SIMs has surpassed the population due to multiple SIM usage. However, although most South Asian countries have expanded 4G mobile networks over the previous 5 years (Blumenfeld et al., 2019), broadband Internet and smartphones remain unaffordable for the region's poorest people. For instance, 61% of South Asians live within the range of telecommunication networks but still do not use the Internet, contributing to the most significant usage gap in the world (Hussain et al., 2021). Moreover, international bandwidth is costly in landlocked countries such as Nepal.

3.3 Existing ICT Policies

ICT is undoubtedly strategically crucial for the economic growth of all developing countries and is particularly true for South Asian countries. However, existing ICT policies in the South Asian region tend to emphasize the export-led growth potential of ICT innovations (Aziz, 2020). The region's emerging prominence of India as an ICT superpower is an ideal example. For instance, most ICT innovations from India address the needs of the importing countries, and they gain significantly from using ICT innovations produced at low cost in India. It is essential to recognize that while ICT export-led growth is an attractive goal as it may enable foreign exchange earnings, it cannot deliver sustainable economic growth to any country (Biryukova & Matiukhina, 2019). In contrast, recently, some scholars (e.g., Aziz, 2020; Bhujabal & Sethi, 2020) pointed out that a policy that stresses the use of ICT innovations within the country serves as an engine of economic growth by directly contributing to job creation and per capita GDP growth.

3.4 Data Governance and Social Trust

Although South Asia is now catching up on ICT innovations, Liu (2022) noted that data governance and ensuring social trust are essential for protecting vulnerable populations. Data is at the heart of any ICT innovation and is especially important in its application to human capital development. Yet, it is essential to acknowledge that data can be misused for exclusion and discrimination. At the same time, "data invisible" groups, such as women and marginalized poor communities, will not be benefited, leading to potential bias in automated decision-making or the development of personalized solutions within the region. For example, less than 40% of women own a mobile phone in India and Pakistan, compared with 80% of men in India and 70% in Pakistan (Hussain et al., 2021).

3.5 ICT and Economic Growth and Development

Literature indicates that ICT innovations have strongly influenced economic growth in developed countries and emerging economies such as South Korea and Singapore in recent years (Appiah-Otoo & Song, 2021; Niebel, 2018). Admittedly, however, South Asian countries seem to have neither invested in ICT innovations nor benefited from such investments to the same extent as developed countries (Aziz, 2020; Bhujabal & Sethi, 2020). On the other hand, it is essential to focus on the fact that information is becoming a decision criterion, like income and wealth, by which countries are classified as rich and poor. To prevent this from happening, South Asian countries need to formulate national ICT strategies to promote the use of emerging technologies. It is important to note that today investment in ICT innovations, even for South Asian countries, is not an option; instead, it is an absolute necessity to ensure economic growth and development.

4. Gaps in Existing Research and Future Research Directions

Based on our comprehensive analysis, we identified four research gaps, and accordingly, four future research directions are formulated as follows. First, more research is still needed to explore the link between ICT innovations and their contribution to economic development. Even though several scholars have emphasized the need to understand this connection (Appiah-Otoo & Song, 2021; Kaplinsky & Kraemer-Mbula, 2022), little has been done to address this aspect from a socially-oriented perspective. One of the main reasons why this has not yet been comprehensively addressed is due to the difficulty in identifying and isolating the factors that explain how ICT innovations contribute to economic development since there is an ongoing interplay between ICT innovations and their subsequent consequences, such as the social, cultural, political, and economic-related changes (Jimenez et al., 2022). Therefore, various research approaches and methods should be used to identify the complex interplay between ICT innovations and economic development. By combining various theoretical perspectives, such as human capital, and social capital theories, with the actor-network theory or social exchange theory, we may increase our understanding of social changes associated with ICT innovations and their contribution to a country's economic development.

Second, there is a need to clarify and explore the concept of development concerning the ICT innovations research domain. More research is needed to identify how various views on development (e.g., economic perspective, socio-cultural perspective) influence the growth of ICT innovations within the South Asian region. Future research should also investigate stakeholders' views on how ICT innovations contribute to economic development. For instance, future research could investigate the views of different stakeholders, such as government authorities, business practitioners, customers and the general public, as this might increase our understanding of how various views on development influence and foster ICT innovations within the region.

Third, unique social-cultural issues endemic to the South Asian region, such as politicization, corruption, bureaucracy, and context-dependent power structures, are currently less investigated in the ICT innovations research domain (Kaplinsky & Kraemer-Mbula, 2022). However, these sociocultural issues will influence the complex interplay between ICT innovations and their subsequent economic consequences, which need to be studied in detail.

Fourth, the ICT innovation literature is thus far dominated by either qualitative or quantitative-based research studies (Park & Choi, 2019; Vu et al., 2020). Such studies are needed to explore and explain the complexity involved in ICT innovations. However, this discussion on the research gaps and the areas identified for further research does call for the use of mixed methods research design in exploring the link between ICT innovations and economic growth. For instance, a qualitative research approach is required to comprehensively understand barriers that hamper ICT innovations within the region, such as the digital divide, data governance, social trust, and various views on development. Likewise, a quantitative research approach is needed to ascribe a causal relationship between ICT innovations and economic growth and to generalize and compare the results. However, in the context of ICT innovations research, in particular, the role of researchers should not be confined to understanding the problem. Instead, it should also involve introducing changes associated with implementing ICT innovations. Therefore, ICT innovations can be further studied by applying different research methods and paradigms, such as an action research design.

5. Conclusion and Study Implications

Until the 1990s, scholars were inclined to focus explicitly on the economic growth of nations, ignoring or isolating the role of ICT innovations from it. However, it is apparent in the contemporary business landscape that there is a strong interplay between ICT innovations and the economic growth of countries globally. Therefore, in this literature review, we aimed to address this void by identifying the role of ICT in the economic development of countries, focusing on countries in South Asian, which have received scant attention in scholarly literature. Based on a comprehensive review of 43 peer-reviewed articles published in leading scholarly journals, we found that linking ICT to economic growth and development has become a common topic of ongoing discussion among business firms and academia in the South Asian region. However, current uses of ICT applications and innovations are not necessarily focused on the development of South Asian countries from a socially-oriented perspective. As the findings imply, to effectively use ICT innovations in socio-economic development in the region, there should be a paradigm shift in thinking about ICT applications and innovations. This includes rethinking and reformulating ICT policies, integrating ICT policies with socio-economic development goals and combining ICT innovations with other development projects to encourage active participation from the general public.

References

Appiah-Otoo, I., & Song, N. (2021). The impact of ICT on economic growth – Comparing rich and poor countries. *Telecommunications Policy*, *45*(2), 102082.

Aziz, A. (2020). Digital inclusion challenges in Bangladesh: The case of the National ICT Policy. *Contemporary South Asia*, *28*(3), 304–319.

Bhujabal, P., & Sethi, N. (2020). Foreign direct investment, information and communication technology, trade, and economic growth in the South Asian association for regional cooperation countries: An empirical insight. *Journal of Public Affairs*, *20*(1), e2010.

Biryukova, O. G. V., & Matiukhina, A. I. (2019). ICT services trade in the BRICS countries: Special and common features. *Journal of the Knowledge Economy*, *10*(3), 1080–1097.

Blumenfeld, M., Wemakor, W., Azzouz, L., & Roberts, C. (2019). Developing a new technical strategy for rail infrastructure in low-income countries in Sub-Saharan Africa and South Asia. *Sustainability*, *11*(16), 4319.

Dutta, D. (2007). Role of ICT in development process: A review of issues and prospects in South Asia. In *Information and communication technologies for economic and regional developments* (pp. 240–258). https://doi.org/10.4018/978-1-59904-186-5.ch012

Goswami, R., De, S. K., & Datta, B. (2009). Linguistic diversity and information poverty in South Asia and Sub-Saharan Africa. *Universal Access in the Information Society*, *8*(3), 219–238.

Hussain, A., Batool, I., Akbar, M., & Nazir, M. (2021). Is ICT an enduring driver of economic growth? Evidence from South Asian economies. *Telecommunications Policy*, *45*(8), 102202.

Jimenez, A., Abbott, P., & Dasuki, S. (2022). In-betweenness in ICT4D research: Critically examining the role of the researcher. *European Journal of Information Systems*, *31*(1), 25–39.

Kaplinsky, R., & Kraemer-Mbula, E. (2022). Innovation and uneven development: The challenge for low-and middle-income economies. *Research Policy*, *51*(2), 104394.

Khan, F. N., & Majeed, M. T. (2020). ICT and e-Government as the sources of economic growth in information age: Empirical evidence from South Asian economies. *South Asian Studies*, *34*(1).

Khanra, S., & Joseph, R. P. (2019). Adoption of e-Governance: The mediating role of language proficiency and digital divide in an emerging market context. *Transforming Government: People, Process and Policy*. https://doi.org/10.1108/TG-12-2018-0076

Latif, Z., Xin, W., Khan, D., Iqbal, K., Pathan, Z. H., Salam, S., & Jan, N. (2017). ICT and sustainable development in South Asian countries. *Human Systems Management*, *36*(4), 353–362.

Liu, J. (2022). Social data governance: Towards a definition and model. *Big Data & Society*, *9*(2). https://doi.org/10.1177/20539517221111352

Niebel, T. (2018). ICT and economic growth – Comparing developing, emerging and developed countries. *World Development*, *104*, 197–211.

Nipo, D. T., & Bujang, I. (2014). Global digital divide: Determinants of cross-country ICT development with special reference to Southeast Asia. *International Journal of Business and Economic Development (IJBED)*, *2*(3).

Park, H., & Choi, S. O. (2019). Digital innovation adoption and its economic impact focused on path analysis at national level. *Journal of open innovation: Technology, market, and complexity*, *5*(3), 56.

Salakhova, V. B., Erofeeva, M. A., Pronina, E. V., Belyakova, N. V., Zaitseva, N. A., & Ishmuradova, I. I. (2021). State regulation and development of digital educational platforms. *World Journal on Educational Technology: Current Issues*, *13*(4), 956–966.

Schelenz, L., & Pawelec, M. (2022). Information and communication technologies for development (ICT4D) critique. *Information Technology for Development*, *28*(1), 165–188.

Swar, B., & Khan, G. F. (2014). Mapping ICT knowledge infrastructure in South Asia. *Scientometrics*, *99*(1), 117–137.

Usman, A., Ozturk, I., Hassan, A., Zafar, S. M., & Ullah, S. (2021). The effect of ICT on energy consumption and economic growth in South Asian economies: An empirical analysis. *Telematics and Informatics*, *58*, 101537.

Vu, K., Hanafizadeh, P., & Bohlin, E. (2020). ICT as a driver of economic growth: A survey of the literature and directions for future research. *Telecommunications Policy*, *44*(2), 101922.

Webster, J., & Watson, R. T. (2002). Analyzing the past to prepare for the future: Writing a literature review. *MIS Quarterly*, *26*(2), xiii–xxiii.

Williams, J. K. (2018). A comprehensive review of seven steps to a comprehensive literature review. *Qualitative Report*, *23*(2), 345–350.

Chapter 3

Crisis Chronicles: Unraveling the Russo-Ukrainian Impact on the Indian Stock Market – An Event Study

J. Sahaya Shabu[a], *E. Joseph Rubert*[b] *and J. Divya Merry Malar*[a]

[a]Holy Cross College, India
[b]Arunachala College of Engineering for Women, India

Abstract

Event studies have gained lots of popularity and momentum since 1960. It is an effective method to understand the event impact on the variables being tested. This paper aims to examine the reaction of Indian stock market to Russo–Ukrainian Crisis 2022, it is to understand the efficiency of Indian stock market for international events and how information content flow into the market is reflected in the stock prices and how the whole market reacts to the new information. The Event Study methodology is employed in this paper to investigate the effect of an event (Russo–Ukrainian Crisis) on a specific dependent variable (Stock Prices). The Small, Mid and Large cap indices of the Indian Stock exchange were taken for the Event Study. However, the abnormal return, standard deviation and t-statistics were calculated to examine the event effect on stock prices. It is found that there is a significant negative effect of the event on the stock prices.

Keywords: Russo; Ukrainian war; Event Study; stock prices; abnormal return; economic disruption

1. Introduction

During the past decades, many researchers have studied the factors affecting stock returns and volatility in the market and they have identified numerous factors that can affect stock return and volatility in the market such as fundamental factors, economic factors, political factors, international factors and so on. Geopolitical factor is also an

Modeling Economic Growth in Contemporary India, 35–48
doi:10.1108/978-1-80382-751-320241003

important factor that can affect stock return and volatility whether it is trade tension or border tension the market tend to react based on its impact on the whole market. During such geopolitical crisis market witnesses a minor to major corrections. Therefore the purpose of the study is to examine the Indian stock market reaction to Russia–Ukrainian crisis.

Since 2014 the relation between Russia and Ukraine has been unfriendly. On February 24, 2022 Russia announced the full-scale invasion of Ukraine mainland, the Russia's announcement creates tension globally, since then there was a huge disruption in trade and supply chain across the world. Russia and Ukraine are the major producers and exporters of key food produces, minerals and energy, therefore the geopolitical developments in Europe, the sanctions on Russia and trade and supply disruptions have caused surge in prices of those products, the price uncertainty due to the war has had adverse effect on the economic growth of the countries globally. India is one of the major trading country with Russia and Ukraine, the war has stoked uncertainty and marginal impact on the trades between the countries, the war also had triggered chaos in the financial markets of the country and had increase the fear of uncertainty among the investors.

In the modern finance theory, efficient market hypothesis (EMH) developed by Paul A. Samuelson (1965) and Eugene F. Fama (1965) is a milestone and it has become the spotlight for investment in which investors have perfect information and they can act rationally according to such information. The theory states that asset prices reflect all available information in the market. The two main points associated with the theory is firstly, the price changes in the financial market is random in nature and secondly, the prices of the securities reflect economic fundamentals. If the market is informational efficient then the price changes are random and unforeseeable.

2. Literature Reviews on Event Study Methodology

Event Study methodology is a widely used econometric model for examining the impact of an event on a variable during a particular period. The key assumption underlying the Event Study is that markets are efficient and that any new information is quickly impounded into stock prices (Fig. 3.1). This makes it possible to identify the abnormal return of stocks, which is a key measure of the event effect. There is a vast literature on Event Study methodology, including its applications and limitations.

Campbell et al. (1997) were the pioneers of the Event Study methodology. They aimed to determine whether an event affected a company's value by examining whether an anomaly impacted the expected "normal return." This methodology's roots can be traced back to Fama's Theory of Efficient Markets, which posits that markets assimilate available public information and reflect it in stock prices.

Agrawal and Kamakura (1995) utilized the Event Study methodology to study the impact of celebrity endorsement contracts on a firm's expected profitability. They assumed that the celebrity endorsement announcement, published in

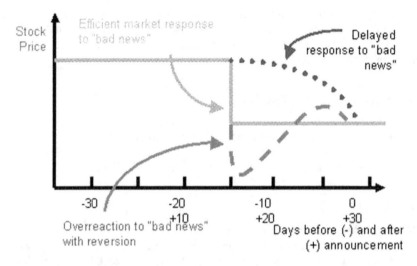

Fig. 3.1.   Reaction of Stock Price to New Information in Efficient
and Inefficient Markets.

newspapers, was widely used by market analysts to evaluate expected returns. The
results showed that such announcements had a positive effect on stock returns.

Cowan (1992) conducted a study on non-parametric Event Study and examined the power and the specification of the generalized sign test. The study found
that under ideal conditions, the rank test is more powerful. However, the
generalized sign test is a viable alternative when there is an increase in the length
of the event window, an increase in return variance or thin trading.

Kolari and Pynnönen (2010) examined cross-sectional correlation issues in
Event Studies. They have found that when there is event date clustering then there
is relatively serious low cross-correlation among abnormal returns. To solve this
issue, they have proposed a new test statistic that modifies the 0-statistic of
Boehme.

In a study conducted by Campbell et al. (2010), they presented simulation
findings regarding the effectiveness of the Event Study test in multi-country non-
US samples. Their research indicated that non-parametric rank and generalized
sign tests are more effective than two frequently used parametric tests, particularly
in multi-day windows. Additionally, they observed that the parametric stan-
dardized cross-sectional test can serve as a reliable check, but it is not as potent as
the non-parametric tests and can result in frequent rejections in single-market
samples and when firm-specific events impact the market index.

Lyon et al. (1999) conducted a study to examine tests for long-run abnormal
returns and identified two distinct approaches: the conventional Event Study
framework and buy-and-hold abnormal returns that are calculated using reference portfolios. The inference is based on either a skewness-adjusted t-statistic or
the distribution of long-run abnormal returns that is generated empirically.

He et al. (2020) employed the Event Study methodology to investigate the impact of COVID-19 on stock prices in various sectors. Through the utilization of three models, they determined that the pandemic had a significant impact on stock prices in different sectors.

3. Objectives of the Study

• To examine the evidences of abnormal return and volatility of the stocks during the event period.
• To understand Indian stock market reaction to geopolitical crisis.

4. Research Method

Modern Finance theories states that capital market reflects all available information of a firm stocks in the stock prices of the firm. This basic knowledge motivates to study the effects of an event on the prices of stocks by quantifying the effects of an event on the stock prices. Event Study is a methodology to perform the analysis of event effect on stock market. Event Study examines the abnormal return of stock prices immediately after the occurrence of an event, returns study quantify the economic effect of an event on the abnormal return of stocks. The event Russia–Ukrainian Crisis 2020 has been examined in this study. The event Russia invasion of Ukrainian was publicly announced on February 24, 2022. Hence the time line of the widow for analysis is given below:

• *Estimation Window:* This window stabilizes the normal return expected from the securities, i.e. from March 12, 2021 to February 9, 2022. Here we will have a standard to compare the event, since these data have not been "contaminated" by the news of the event.
• *Event Window:* It is the time the news about Russia and Ukrainian Crisis get in. The zero moment (0) will be the exact date that the event came public (i.e.) February 24, 2022, we also stabilize a safety window to get the information leak before, from February 10, 2022 to February 23, 2022.
• *Post Event Window:* It is Moment after the event and market position (i.e.) February 25, 2022 to March 11, 2022.

In this chapter, we have used Constant Mean Return Model, Market Adjusted Model and Capital Assets Pricing Model to examine the evidence of abnormal return. Three broad Market Indices such as BSE Mid Cap, Small Cap, All Cap and the Benchmark Index Sensex of Bombay Stock Exchange were taken under study.

5. Hypothesis

Null Hypothesis: There is no abnormal return and no effect of the event on the stock prices.

Alternative Hypothesis: There is abnormal return and event has an effect on the stock prices.

6. Data Analysis

By using the normal return models such as constant return model, market model and economic model, the selected indices representing the stocks were analyzed and the results are given in Tables 3.1–3.4 and Figs. 3.2–3.5:

Table 3.1. Log Return.

	Log Return			
Event Window	S&P BSE Sensex	S&P BSE Mid Cap	S&P BSE Small Cap	S&P BSE All Cap
−10	0.01	0.00	0.00	0.01
−9	−0.01	−0.02	−0.02	−0.01
−8	−0.03	−0.04	−0.04	−0.03
−7	0.03	0.03	0.02	0.03
−6	0.00	0.00	0.00	0.00
−5	0.00	0.00	−0.01	0.00
−4	0.00	−0.01	−0.01	0.00
−3	0.00	−0.01	−0.02	−0.01
−2	−0.01	−0.01	−0.02	−0.01
−1	0.00	0.01	0.01	0.00
0	−0.05	−0.06	−0.06	−0.05
1	0.02	0.04	0.04	0.03
2	0.01	0.01	0.01	0.01
3	−0.01	0.00	0.00	−0.01
4	−0.01	−0.01	0.00	0.00
5	−0.01	−0.02	−0.02	−0.02
6	−0.03	−0.02	−0.02	−0.02
7	0.01	0.01	0.01	0.01
8	0.02	0.02	0.02	0.02
9	0.01	0.01	0.01	0.01
10	0.00	0.00	0.01	0.00

Source: Authors Calculation.

Table 3.2. Constant Return Model.

| Event Window | Constant Return Model | | | |
	S&P BSE Sensex	S&P BSE Mid Cap	S&P BSE Small Cap	S&P BSE All Cap
−10	0.72%	0.21%	0.15%	0.51%
−9	−1.38%	−1.92%	−1.98%	−1.53%
−8	−3.07%	−3.60%	−3.66%	−3.41%
−7	3.01%	2.59%	2.53%	2.68%
−6	−0.32%	−0.12%	−0.18%	−0.14%
−5	−0.25%	−0.30%	−0.37%	−0.24%
−4	−0.17%	−0.89%	−0.95%	−0.49%
−3	−0.32%	−0.88%	−0.95%	−0.94%
−2	−0.73%	−0.79%	−0.85%	−0.87%
−1	−0.19%	0.52%	0.46%	0.10%
0	−4.79%	−5.61%	−5.67%	−5.21%
1	2.37%	3.98%	3.92%	2.96%
2	0.63%	0.75%	0.69%	0.76%
3	−1.45%	−0.25%	−0.32%	−0.83%
4	−0.73%	−0.73%	−0.79%	−0.50%
5	−1.46%	−2.45%	−2.51%	−1.75%
6	−2.81%	−2.34%	−2.40%	−2.50%
7	1.03%	1.37%	1.31%	0.99%
8	2.22%	2.28%	2.22%	1.95%
9	1.43%	0.98%	0.92%	1.37%
10	0.09%	0.36%	0.30%	0.28%

Source: Authors Calculation.

Table 3.3. Market Adjusted Return Model.

| Event Window | Market Adjusted Return Model | | |
	S&P BSE Mid Cap	S&P BSE Small Cap	S&P BSE All Cap
−10	0.23%	−0.02%	0.53%
−9	−1.90%	−1.96%	−1.51%
−8	−3.58%	−4.22%	−3.39%
−7	2.61%	1.91%	2.70%
−6	−0.10%	0.35%	−0.12%

Table 3.3. *(Continued)*

Event Window	Market Adjusted Return Model		
	S&P BSE Mid Cap	S&P BSE Small Cap	S&P BSE All Cap
−5	−0.28%	−0.74%	−0.23%
−4	−0.87%	−0.87%	−0.47%
−3	−0.86%	−2.27%	−0.92%
−2	−0.77%	−1.69%	−0.85%
−1	0.54%	0.87%	0.12%
0	−5.59%	−5.84%	−5.19%
1	4.00%	4.11%	2.98%
2	0.77%	0.73%	0.78%
3	−0.23%	−0.18%	−0.81%
4	−0.71%	0.28%	−0.48%
5	−2.43%	−1.70%	−1.73%
6	−2.32%	−2.37%	−2.48%
7	1.39%	1.26%	1.01%
8	2.30%	2.09%	1.97%
9	1.00%	1.12%	1.39%
10	0.38%	0.84%	0.30%

Source: Authors Calculation.

Table 3.4. CAPM.

Event Window	CAPM		
	S&P BSE Mid Cap	S&P BSE Small Cap	S&P BSE All Cap
−10	0.00%	−0.02%	0.02%
−9	−0.16%	−0.17%	−0.13%
−8	−0.29%	−0.34%	−0.27%
−7	0.18%	0.12%	0.18%
−6	−0.03%	0.01%	−0.03%
−5	−0.04%	−0.07%	−0.04%
−4	−0.08%	−0.08%	−0.05%

(Continued)

Table 3.4. *(Continued)*

| | CAPM | | |
Event Window	S&P BSE Mid Cap	S&P BSE Small Cap	S&P BSE All Cap
−3	−0.08%	−0.19%	−0.09%
−2	−0.08%	−0.15%	−0.08%
−1	0.02%	0.05%	−0.01%
0	−0.44%	−0.46%	−0.41%
1	0.28%	0.29%	0.20%
2	0.04%	0.04%	0.04%
3	−0.04%	−0.03%	−0.08%
4	−0.07%	0.00%	−0.06%
5	−0.20%	−0.15%	−0.15%
6	−0.19%	−0.20%	−0.21%
7	0.09%	0.08%	0.06%
8	0.15%	0.14%	0.13%
9	0.06%	0.06%	0.08%
10	0.01%	0.04%	0.00%

Source: Authors Calculation.

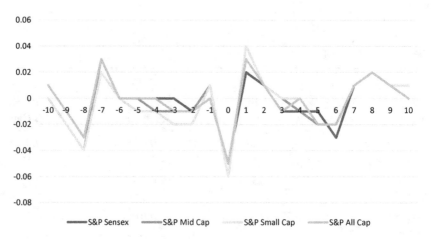

Fig. 3.2.   Log Return.

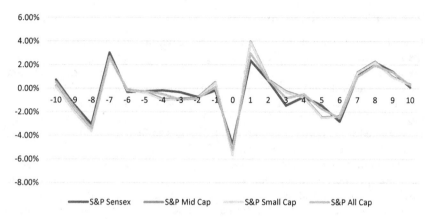

Fig. 3.3.   Abnormal Return Constant Mean Return Model.

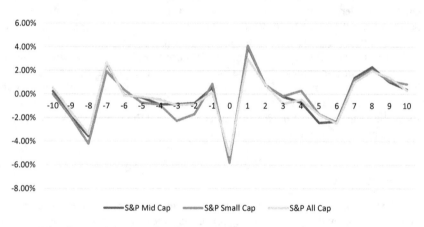

Fig. 3.4.   Abnormal Return Market Adjusted Return Model.

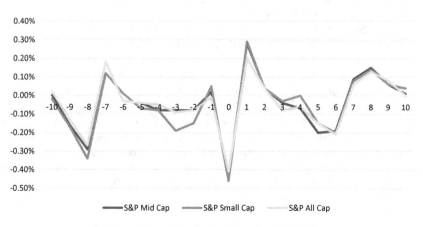

Fig. 3.5.   Abnormal Return CAPM.

7. Results and Discussion

Using the various return estimation models, the selected indices were analyzed for the evidences of abnormal return during the time period of the event. It was observed that the event has negatively influenced on the return of the stocks and increased the volatility of the stocks during the event time (Tables 3.5–3.7). Further it is understood that the news about global geopolitical tension has strong negative effect on Indian stock market and the effect was for short period of time, the obtained results are consistent with the results of Suleman (2012), Sarkar and Bhanja (2016), and Garg and Agarwal (2017).

The result of the models used in the study suggests that systematic risk had an influence on stock price behavior in the market; this result is consistent with the results of Limmack and Ward (1990) and Mehdian et al. (2008).

It is understood that the information about the event has been quickly observed by the market and it has been immediately reacted in the stock prices and the reaction was negative and short period. The Indian stock market as a whole has over reacted to bad news with reversion. Therefore the moods and beliefs of the investors have been changed negatively and as a result the stocks have abnormal negative return during the period of the event.

In the above table using Cumulative Abnormal Return and Buy-and-hold abnormal return approach, the three indices were tested during the event windows for testing the hypothesis. The result shows that for all the three models, null hypothesis is rejected and the alternative hypothesis is accepted. Therefore it shows that the event has an effect on stock prices and the Indian stock market has negatively over reacted to the event.

8. Conclusion

Event Study approach has been used in this study to empirically explore and to understand the evidences of event effect on the stock prices and the Indian stock markets on the whole. The various benchmark indices were analyzed using different models and we found that the event negatively impacted the stock prices and the Indian stock markets.

Indian Stock markets are the developing market, the investor's beliefs and sentiments are the driving force of the market. Global tensions like Russia–Ukrainian geopolitical crisis may quickly influence the investor's beliefs and sentiments on the markets like India. The trade shocks and supply chain crisis due to Russia–Ukrainian war and the sanction on Russia by world organizations have greatly affected the trade across the world, especially India. EU is the biggest market for India's export as well as import, any disruptions in the supply chain may greatly affect the economic growth of the country. As stock markets are the economic barometer for the growth of economy, it has been signaling the negative effect that the event has made on the economic growth, already investors have lost huge amount of money in the stock market, this war will further increase market volatility.

Table 3.5. Constant Return Model.

Return	Window	Return			t-Statistics			p Value		
		MC	SC	AC	MC	SC	AC	MC	SC	AC
CAR	Event	-5.61%	-5.67%	-5.21%	-5.12	-5.17	-5.79	0.00**	0.00**	0.00**
	Anticipation	-5.18%	-5.80%	-4.33%	-3.22	-3.61	-2.80	0.00**	0.00**	0.01**
	Adjustment	3.95%	3.33%	2.74%	1.84	1.55	1.42	0.07	0.12	0.16
	Total	-6.84%	-8.15%	-6.80%	-3.19	-3.80	-3.52	0.00**	0.00**	0.00**
BHAR	Event	-5.61%	-5.67%	-5.21%	-5.12	-5.17	-5.79	0.00**	0.00**	0.00**
	Anticipation	-5.17%	-5.77%	-4.35%	-3.21	-3.58	-2.82	0.00**	0.00**	0.01**
	Adjustment	3.8%	3.2%	2.6%	1.79	1.49	1.37	0.07	0.14	0.17
	Total	-6.94%	-8.24%	-6.92%	-3.24	-3.84	-3.58	0.00**	0.00**	0.00**

Notes: The *p*-values marked with ** (double asterisks) indicate that the corresponding results are statistically significant at the conventional significance level of 0.05 or smaller.
The absence of asterisks would typically indicate that the results are not statistically significant at the chosen level.

Table 3.6. Market Adjusted Return Model.

Window	Return			t-Statistics			p Value		
	MC	SC	AC	MC	SC	AC	MC	SC	AC
Return (CAR)									
Event	−5.59%	−5.84%	−5.19%	−5.10	−5.37	−5.77	0.00**	0.00**	0.00**
Anticipation	−4.99%	−8.63%	−4.15%	−3.10	−4.90	−2.68	0.00**	0.00**	0.01**
Adjustment	4.15%	6.18%	2.93%	1.93	2.76	1.52	0.05	0.01	0.13
Total	−6.43%	−8.30%	−6.41%	−3.00	−3.71	−3.32	0.00**	0.00**	0.00**
Return (BHAR)									
Event	−5.59%	−5.84%	−5.19%	−5.10	−5.37	−5.77	0.00**	0.00**	0.00**
Anticipation	−4.99%	−8.44%	−4.17%	−3.10	−4.79	−2.70	0.00**	0.00**	0.01**
Adjustment	4.0%	6.2%	2.8%	1.89	2.77	1.47	0.06	0.01**	0.14
Total	−6.54%	−8.08%	−6.53%	−3.05	−3.61	−3.38	0.00**	0.00**	0.00**

Notes: The *p*-values marked with ** (double asterisks) indicate that the corresponding results are statistically significant at the conventional significance level of 0.05 or smaller.

The absence of asterisks would typically indicate that the results are not statistically significant at the chosen level.

Table 3.7. CAPM.

Window		Return			t-Statistics			p-Value		
		MC	SC	AC	MC	SC	AC	MC	SC	AC
Return (CAR)	Event	−0.44%	−0.46%	−0.41%	−5.33	−5.61	−6.05	0.00**	0.00**	0.00**
	Anticipation	−0.57%	−0.84%	−0.50%	−4.70	−6.36	−4.35	0.00**	0.00**	0.00**
	Adjustment	0.12%	0.27%	0.03%	0.73	1.61	0.18	0.46	0.11	0.85
	Total	−0.89%	−1.03%	−0.89%	−5.52	−6.12	−6.12	0.00**	0.00**	0.00**
Return (BHAR)	Event	−0.44%	−0.46%	−0.41%	−5.33	−5.61	−6.05	0.00**	0.00**	0.00**
	Anticipation	−0.57%	−0.84%	−0.50%	−4.69	−6.34	−4.34	0.00**	0.00**	0.00**
	Adjustment	0.1%	0.3%	0.0%	0.73	1.61	0.18	0.47	0.11	0.86
	Total	−0.89%	−1.03%	−0.89%	−5.52	−6.11	−6.12	0.00**	0.00**	0.00**

Notes: The *p*-values marked with ** (double asterisks) indicate that the corresponding results are statistically significant at the conventional significance level of 0.05 or smaller.

The absence of asterisks would typically indicate that the results are not statistically significant at the chosen level.

References

Agrawal, J., & Kamakura, W. A. (1995). The economic worth of celebrity endorsers: An event study analysis. *Journal of Marketing, 59*(3), 56–62.

Campbell, C. J., Cowan, A. R., & Salotti, V. (2010). Event-study test robustness in a multi-country world. *Journal of Financial and Quantitative Analysis, 45*(1), 99–118.

Campbell, J. Y., Lo, A. W., & MacKinlay, A. C. (1997). *The econometrics of financial markets.* Princeton University Press.

Cowan, A. R. (1992). Non-parametric event study testing. *Journal of Financial Economics, 31*(2), 255–279.

Fama, E. F. (1965). The behavior of stock-market prices. *The Journal of Business, 38*(1), 34–105. https://doi.org/10.1086/294743

Garg, R., & Agarwal, N. (2017). Impact of geopolitical risks on stock markets: Evidence from India. *IUP Journal of Applied Finance, 23*(3), 7–23.

He, P., Sun, Y., Zhang, Y., & Li, T. (2020). Impact of Covid 19 on stock prices across different sectors: An event study analysis. *Journal of Risk and Financial Management, 13*(7), 146.

Kolari, J. W., & Pynnönen, S. (2010). Cross-sectional correlation in event studies. *Journal of Financial Economics, 96*(1), 1–19.

Limmack, R. J., & Ward, C. W. R. (1990). The October 1987 stock market crash: An exploratory analysis of share price models. *Journal of Banking & Finance, 14*(2–3), 273–289.

Lyon, J. D., Barber, B. M., & Tsai, C. L. (1999). Improved methods for tests of long-run abnormal stock returns. *The Journal of Finance, 54*(1), 165–201.

Mehdian, S., Nas, T., & Perry, M. J. (2008). An examination of investor reaction to unexpected political and economic events in Turkey. *Global Finance Journal, 18*(3), 337–350.

Samuelson, P. A. (1965). Proof that properly anticipated prices fluctuate randomly. *Industrial Management Review, 6*(2), 41–49.

Sarkar, S., & Bhanja, N. (2016). Impact of global political crisis on stock market: Evidence from Ukraine-Russia conflict. *Journal of Applied Accounting Research, 17*(3), 296–308.

Suleman, M. T. (2012). Stock market reaction to good and bad political news. *Asian Journal of Finance & Accounting, 4*(1), 299–312.

Chapter 4

Calendar Effects in the Indian Stock Market Sustainability Index

Kokila. K and Shaik Saleem

Vellore Institute of Technology, India

Abstract

The world of investing has changed drastically. Investors are willing to invest the companies that give high priority to environmental, social and governance issues (ESG). This study delves into the performance of the BSE CARBONEX index in comparison to the BSE 100, BSE Sensex, BSE Energy and BSE Oil & Gas. It seeks to examine the impact of calendar anomalies, particularly focusing on the day-of-the-week effect, on these indices. To accomplish this, daily closing prices of the BSE CARBONEX, BSE 100, BSE Sensex, BSE Energy and BSE Oil & Gas were gathered from the BSE official website. The study period was divided into three segments: the full period, period I (2017–2020) and period II (2020–2022). The study's findings reveal that throughout the full period, period I and period II, BSE Energy exhibited the highest mean daily return compared to the other selected indices. There appears to be a discernible Tuesday effect on the daily average mean returns of BSE CARBONEX, BSE 100, BSE Sensex, BSE Energy and BSE Oil & Gas in both the full sample period and period II. Results from ordinary least squares (OLS) analysis by day indicate a notably high positive and statistically significant daily return on Tuesdays, particularly during the full sample period and period II. Furthermore, the GARCH (1,1) model suggests a significant Tuesday effect on the BSE Energy and BSE Oil & Gas indices.

Keywords: Calendar anomalies; BSE CARBONEX; BSE 100; BSE sensex; BSE energy; BSE oil & gas; GARCH (1,1) model

Modeling Economic Growth in Contemporary India, 49–64
Copyright © 2024 Kokila. K and Shaik Saleem
Published under exclusive licence by Emerald Publishing Limited
doi:10.1108/978-1-80382-751-320241004

1. Introduction

The world is witnessing the adverse effects of climate change and global warming. It has a serious impact on health (Rushton & Kett, 2015), food production (Wheeler & von Braun, 2013), water supply (Miller, 2008), energy consumption (King & Gulledge, 2013), etc. Historically, the industrialized world was primarily responsible for rising greenhouse gas emissions. But the growing share of emissions is from developing nations (Kanitkarameer et al., 2009) also. Countries are taking steps to tackle climate change. According to a recent survey, the nations that are best prepared for a low-carbon future are Iceland, Denmark and the Netherlands. The United Kingdom, Norway, Finland, France, Germany, Sweden and South Korea are the other nations in the top 10 of the Green Future Index 2022 (Source: MIT Technology Review Insights, 2022). Socially accountable investments (Ameer & Othman, 2012) have attracted more importance among market participants globally. Investors are more concerned about the environmental aspect of doing business. In both developed and developing economies, investors are keen on investments in stocks that not only create value for shareholders (Tripathi & Bhandari, 2015) but are also able to manage risk associated with climate change over the long term. Now investors are interested in the stock that utilize eco-friendly business practices (Patel & Kumari, 2020) to reduce their carbon emissions.

The term 'sustainable investment' refers to an investing strategy that takes into account ESG factors while choosing and monitoring a portfolio. There are some concepts relating to sustainability investment, such as green investment, socially responsible investment (SRI), ESG investment and ethical investment. All of these concept themes aim to encourage environment-friendly investment.

Investment strategies that take into account ESG factors are not new; date back many centuries (Schueth, 2003). The idea of ethical investment was the first widely adopted in 1970 in value-based institutions like charities and NGOs. After 1990 the focus switched to SRI which is a combination of social, environmental and financial goals (Eccles & Viviers, 2011). The first worldwide benchmark for sustainability index, the Dow Jones Sustainability Indexes (DJSI), was introduced in 1999. It covers a number of factors, including stakeholder well-being, energy usage, climate change and corporate governance, across all global capital markets. India has also joined the rest of the world by launching its own benchmark index S&P BSE GREENEX in February 2012. It is the 25th index of the Bombay stock exchange and measures the company's performance in terms of carbon emission. BSE CARBONEX, a carbon-based thematic index was also introduced. It is based on the organization's stance on climate change.

Sustainable investment has steadily increased over the past few years (Global Sustainability Investment Review, 2020). Banks (Avrampou et al., 2019; Jeucken & Bouma, 2017; Nizam et al., 2019), companies (Knoepfel, 2001; Rueda et al., 2017), stock exchanges (Cunha et al., 2020; De Souza Cunha & Samanez, 2013), mutual funds (Ielasi et al., 2018; Soler-Domínguez et al., 2021), regulators

(Conley & Williams, 2011) and other agents interested in sustainable investment participation and promoting initiatives to speed the growth of these investments. New products have been created by stock exchanges to encourage sustainable investing.

In the stock market, there is evidence of calendar impacts (Urquhart & McGroarty, 2014) that will produce larger (Engelberg et al., 2018) or lower returns than their intrinsic value. Due to the fact that it cannot be explained by pre-existing theories. This is said to as an anomaly. One of the most well-known phenomena of abnormal returns is the calendar effect. Many researchers analysed the sustainable indices performance. This chapter contributes to the literature studies by studying the day of the week effect on BSE CARBONEX, BSE 100, BS Sensex, BSE Energy and BSE Oil & Gas. Furthermore, the day of the week effect is analysed by dividing the sample period into two equal halves to know about the return and volatility pattern.

The article is structured in the following way. Section 2 gives information about sustainable investments and day of the week effect. Section 3 represents the methods and data. Section 4 deals with empirical results and discussion. Section 5 includes the conclusion and scope for future research.

2. Review of Literature

Sustainable investing is a way of investing that considers society and the natural environment in a responsible way (Ang, 2015). Investments in clean technologies, participation in ecologically sustainable businesses and a reduction in toxic-producing companies are all part of socially responsible investing. De Souza Cunha and Samanez (2013) examined the performance of sustainability indices in Brazilian Mercantile, Futures and Stock Exchange's (BM&FBOVESPA) Corporate Sustainability Index (ISE) from December 2005 to December 2010. To achieve this purpose, they compared its performance with the market portfolio (IBOVESPA) and other BM&FBOVESPA sectoral indexes. They concluded that restrictions placed on this type of investment may be damaging their return and risk.

There are various studies that focus on Socially Responsible Investment (SRI) and stock return. Brzeszczynski et al. (2016) found the that annual average return of the SRI was higher than other benchmark indices. Another study Xiao et al. (2017) expressed that in the US equity market there is no Asset pricing impact because of SRI. A study by Vasal (2009) examined the performance of socially responsible stocks in the Indian capital market. He used ESG index, CNX 500 index and Nifty for the period 2005 to 2008 to know about their stock performance. He concluded that there is a positive excess return during the study period. In contrast, Makni et al. (2009) argued that environmental stocks are not considered sound investment avenues in the short run in the Canadian stock market.

Benson et al. (2010) state that sustainable stocks provide steady returns for a long period of time. Ahmed et al. (2017) analysed the Corporate Social Performance (CSP) of the 30 banking and 23 finance sectors listed on the Dhaka Stock

Exchange (DSE). Their findings revealed that investors are keener on CSP and it has a positive impact on stock return. Some of this research (Belghitar et al., 2014; Hawn et al., 2018; Lean & Nguyen, 2014) evaluated a variety of sustainability indices in advanced economies, while others concentrated on developing nations (Ang, 2015; Ortas et al., 2012; Ur Rehman et al., 2016; Wai Kong Cheung, 2011).

Delsen and Lehr (2019) examined sustainable investments in pension funds. They analysed 2,486 pension funds in the Netherland using socio-demographic test factors. They concluded that there is a demand for sustainability investment across developed economies. Chan and Walter (2014) used samples from 748 green companies listed on US stock exchanges to learn how socially responsible investing (SRI) affects stock investment returns, as well as Initial Public Issues and Equity Offers. The empirical analyses show positive and statistically significant excess returns for environmentally friendly enterprises and their IPOs and Equity Offers. Another researcher Lesser et al. (2014) revealed that there is solid evidence in terms of financial performance and risk, green investments differ significantly from SRI investments. But Silva and Cortez (2016) study result indicates that green indices underperformed when compared to market indices. As per their study results in times of crisis, US green funds outperform other socially conscious funds but European green fund underperforms during the non-crisis period. Another author Chang et al. (2012) reveals that lower returns have been produced by green mutual funds, compared to conventional mutual funds in their respective categories. On a risk-adjusted basis, green mutual funds underperformed.

In financial markets, the existence of calendar anomalies has been extensively studied over a long period of time. The Day of the Week Effect is the most prevalent one. There are several studies relating to the existence of the day of the week effect on emerging markets to name a few (Chiah & Zhong, 2021; Hui & Chan, 2015; Islam & Sultana, 2015; Zhang et al., 2017). Bolek et al. (2022) examined the effect of the day of the week effect anomaly during the pandemic period in OMX exchange. They concluded that there is a pandemic impact on market efficiency.

3. Methods and Data

India is a big developing nation, approximately two-thirds of the population directly depends on climate-sensitive industries like agriculture, fisheries and forests. Food production, water resources, biodiversity and lifestyle are expected to be impacted by climate change. The primary source of climate change is human activity, when fossil fuels like coal and oil are burnt carbon dioxide levels in our atmosphere increase. This will automatically affect the climatic conditions globally. This study is about how the CARBONEX index is performing in comparison with BSE 100, BSE SENSEX, BSE Energy and BSE Oil & Gas indices. For that, the study applied descriptive statistics, and calendar anomaly such as the day-of-week effect to check the return of the BSE CARBONEX, BSE 100, BSE

SENSEX, BSE Energy and BSE Oil & Gas indices. It also aims to check the volatility of these indices during the study period.

The daily closing price of the indices was collected from BSE India for the span of 1 August 2016, to 31 July 2022. The data were downloaded from the BSE portal. The selected period covers 1,239 observations. Daily returns are calculated as follows.

$$R_t = \ln(P_t/P_{t-1})*100$$

Here P_t is the present day return and P_{t-1} is the previous day return.

To test the stationarity of the return of indices, the present study applied the ADF test and PP test 1988. ADF test is one of the most frequently used statistical methods to test the stationarity of given time series data. There are three basic regression models in the ADF test. They are

(1) If there is no constant and no trend:

$$\Delta y_t = Y y_{t-1} + v_t$$

(2) If there is a constant and no trend:

$$\Delta y_t = \alpha + Y y_{t-1} + v_t$$

(3) If there is a constant and trend:

$$\Delta y_t = \alpha + Y y_{t-1} + \lambda_t + v_t$$

This test adds lagged differences to these models. PP test is like the ADF test. But it ignores serial correlation.

The distribution of stock returns is not the same for all days. Because of the existence of some calendar anomalies in the Indian stock market. A calendar anomaly is a pattern of stock returns that is unpredictable and dependent on a calendar date or year. The study aims to know about the presence of the day of the week effect of these indices. The following Ordinary Least Square (OLS) model is used for empirical analysis.

$$R_t = \beta_1 + \beta_2 D_1 + \beta_3 D_2 + \beta_4 D_3 + \beta_5 D_4 + \varepsilon_t$$

R_t is the daily return of the indices, D_1 to D_4 dummy variables and ε_t is the random error term.

To test the volatility of the indices during the study period GARCH(1,1) model is used. The basic GARCH model (1,1) equation is:

$$\sigma_t^2 = \alpha_0 + \alpha_1 U_{t-1}^2 + \beta_1 \sigma_{t-1}^2$$

The variance of the ARCH and GARCH model is the same. But in GARCH model the error term (σ_{t-1}^2) is used to predict the previous time period error term.

4. Results and Discussions

To get a clear outcome of this study, the analysis is carried out in three ways. First, the summary of statistics discussing the day-wise daily return of the BSE CARBONEX, BSE 100, BSE SENSEX, BSE Energy and BSE Oil & Gas indices. Then OLS is applied to check the day of the week effect on the indices. Further GARCH (1,1) model is used to check the volatility of these indices.

The summary statistics for the whole study period, period I, period II of BSE CARBONEX, BSE 100, BSE SENSEX, BSE Energy and BSE Oil & Gas indices are presented in Table 4.1. The study result indicates during the whole period, period I and period II, BSE Energy has the highest mean daily return (0.064), (0.055) and (0.073) compared to all other selected indices. BSE 100 has the lowest standard deviation (1.212) followed by BSE CARBONEX (1.216) and BSE Sensex (1.236). As per the study result, BSE energy and BSE oil & gas have a higher standard deviation, are negatively skewed and have high Kurtosis values during the full period and period II.

Table 4.1. Summary of Statistics.

Indices	Mean	SD	Minimum	Maximum	Kurtosis	Skewness
Full Period						
Sensex	0.046	1.236	−14.102	8.595	21.402	−1.536
BSE 100	0.042	1.212	−13.881	8.143	20.877	−1.627
CARBONEX	0.042	1.216	−13.961	8.312	21.210	−1.626
BSE energy	0.064	1.678	−13.722	9.699	9.483	−0.459
BSE oil & gas	0.024	1.549	−13.561	8.665	12.619	−1.125
P – I						
Sensex	0.040	0.793	−2.367	5.186	3.561	0.445
BSE 100	0.027	0.812	−2.628	5.380	3.641	0.410
CARBONEX	0.026	0.810	−2.588	5.377	3.594	0.412
BSE energy	0.055	1.303	−8.907	5.993	5.724	−0.457
BSE oil & gas	0.006	1.329	−13.561	5.743	19.196	−1.844
P – II						
Sensex	0.052	1.537	−14.102	8.595	16.342	−1.606
BSE 100	0.056	1.490	−13.881	8.143	16.761	−1.771
CARBONEX	0.057	1.497	−13.961	8.312	16.945	−1.763
BSE energy	0.073	1.963	−13.722	9.699	8.327	−0.437
BSE oil & gas	0.039	1.728	−13.179	8.665	9.311	−0.798

Source: Authors calculation.

Figures 4.1−4.5 indicated the daily return of the indices. It is clear from the figures that there is a presence of volatility in all five indices.

The unit root test result of the indices was presented in Table 4.2. The study applied the ADF test and PP test 1988 to test the stationarity of the time series data. The null hypothesis for this test is there is a presence of unit root in the time series data. The study result shows that the series is stationarity at level. So, the alternative hypothesis is accepted.

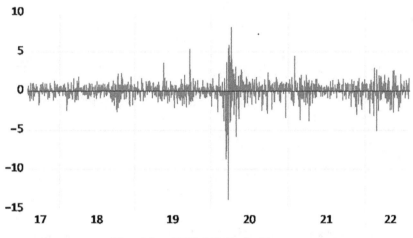

Fig. 4.1.   BSE 100 Daily Return.

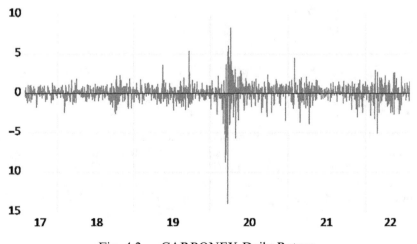

Fig. 4.2.   CARBONEX Daily Return.

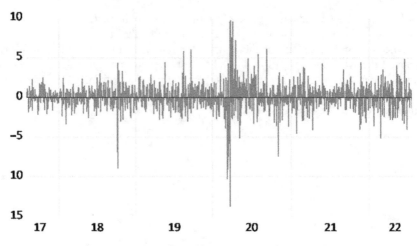

Fig. 4.3.   BSE Energy Daily Return.

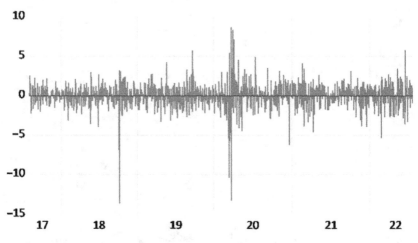

Fig. 4.4.   BSE Oil & Gas Daily Return.

The day-wise summary of statistics of the indices has been presented in Table 4.3. The overall study results show that the highest mean average daily return was observed on Tuesday, i.e. (BSE Sensex (0.225), BSE 100 (0.222), BSE CARBONEX (0.219), BSE Energy (0.327), BSE Oil & gas (0.271)) and the lowest was on Monday (BSE Sensex (−0.149), BSE 100 (−0.222), BSE CAR-BONEX (−0.161), BSE Energy (−0.269), BSE Oil & gas (−0.271)) in full

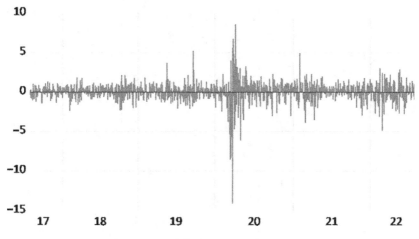

Fig. 4.5.   BSE Sensex Daily Return.

sample period. The result of period I indicates that the highest average mean return was found on Friday (Berument & Kiymaz, 2001; Zhang et al., 2017) (except for BSE Sensex and BSE Energy). The possible reason for this might be there are weekend expectations of the investors.

Traders in the stock market have had a belief that certain days' returns are better than others. It is clear from Table 4.4 that the Tuesday effect is present and statistically significant in the full sample period study. A possible reason might be Tuesday is the second day of the week obviously having a few more trading days before and after any transaction. So investors have more time to respond to the information on Tuesday because they have information sets for the previous day as well as forecasts for the next three days. Further analysis of sub-periods denotes that there is a statistically significant Tuesday effect present in period II.

GARCH(1,1) model is used to check the volatility (Table 4.5) of the BSE CARBONEX, BSE 100, BSE Sensex, BSE Energy and BSE Oil & Gas indices during the day of the week. The overall result of the mean equation shows that a significant mean return was observed on Tuesday for BSE Energy and BSE Oil & Gas. This result is consistent with Islam and Sultana (2015). The sum of the coefficient of the GARCH model (except the error term) is 0.982 which is less than 1 and there is the existence of volatility in BSE CARBONEX, BSE 100, BSE Energy and BSE Oil & Gas indices.

RESID $(-1)^2$ (ARCH variable) is positive and statistically significant at a 5% level in all models for all indices. It is clear that the previous day's return has an effect on the present-day return.

Table 4.2. Unit Root Test Results of the Indices.

ADF Test	Sensex		BSE 100		CARBONEX		BSE Energy		BSE Oil & Gas	
	Crit.	Abs.	Crit.	Abs.	Crit.	Abs.	Crit.	Abs.	Crit.	Abs.
Intercept	−2.863	−12.091	−2.863	−11.923	−2.863	−11.835	−2.863	−36.625	−2.863	−35.845
Trend & intercept	−3.413	−12.088	−3.413	−11.927	−3.413	−11.838	−3.413	−36.612	−3.413	−35.842
None	−1.941	−12.024	−1.941	−11.870	−1.941	−11.783	−1.941	−36.585	−1.941	−35.851
PPT Test										
Intercept	−2.863	−36.680	−2.863	−36.406	−2.863	−36.365	−2.863	−36.624	−2.863	−35.840
Trend & intercept	−3.413	−36.669	−3.413	−36.401	−3.413	−36.360	−3.413	−36.610	−3.413	−35.836
None	−1.941	−36.632	−1.941	−36.377	−1.941	−36.338	−1.941	−36.585	−1.941	−35.846

Source: Authors calculation.

Note: Abbreviations used Critical (Crit.), Absolute (Abs.).

Table 4.3. Day-Wise Summary of Statistics.

Indices/Days	Monday		Tuesday		Wednesday		Thursday		Friday	
Full Period	Mean	SD	Mean	SD	Mean	SD	Mean	SD	Mean	SD
Sensex	−0.149	1.647	0.225	1.048	0.071	1.050	0.024	1.190	0.066	1.121
BSE 100	−0.161	1.612	0.222	1.025	0.063	0.995	0.028	1.176	0.064	1.124
CARBONEX	−0.161	1.616	0.219	1.030	0.063	1.000	0.029	1.183	0.066	1.123
BSE energy	−0.269	1.983	0.327	1.583	0.115	1.421	0.034	1.606	0.119	1.711
BSE oil & gas	−0.222	1.800	0.271	1.400	−0.041	1.143	0.025	1.546	0.090	1.737
P – I										
Sensex	0.095	0.897	−0.005	0.682	0.027	0.674	−0.010	0.750	0.090	0.932
BSE 100	0.067	0.919	−0.006	0.699	−0.009	0.697	−0.016	0.742	0.096	0.972
CARBONEX	0.067	0.916	−0.005	0.695	−0.016	0.693	−0.013	0.744	0.092	0.972
BSE energy	0.034	1.376	0.212	1.282	0.013	1.009	−0.020	1.316	0.033	1.498
BSE oil & gas	−0.034	1.296	0.155	1.038	−0.094	1.165	−0.073	1.259	0.074	1.777
P – II										
Sensex	−0.372	2.092	0.437	1.264	0.111	1.303	0.055	1.485	0.043	1.280
BSE 100	−0.369	2.033	0.432	1.218	0.128	1.202	0.069	1.467	0.034	1.257
CARBONEX	−0.370	2.040	0.426	1.229	0.135	1.211	0.068	1.478	0.040	1.256
BSE energy	−0.546	2.379	0.433	1.816	0.208	1.710	0.085	1.836	0.203	1.898
BSE oil & gas	−0.393	2.152	0.377	1.664	0.007	1.126	0.113	1.769	0.105	1.704

Source: Authors calculation.

Table 4.4. Day-Wise Returns – OLS.

Indices/Days	Monday	Tuesday	Wednesday	Thursday	Friday	R^2	D.W - Stat.
Full Period							
Sensex	-0.153	0.378*	0.224*	0.177	0.219	0.009	2.080
BSE 100	-0.165*	0.387*	0.228*	0.194	0.230*	0.010	2.065
CARBONEX	-0.165*	0.384*	0.228*	0.195	0.231*	0.010	2.062
Energy	-0.271*	0.598*	0.387*	0.306*	0.391*	0.013	2.074
Oil & gas	-0.222*	0.492*	0.181	0.246	0.311*	0.010	2.030
P – I							
Sensex	0.097	-0.102	-0.070	-0.107	-0.008	0.003	1.875
BSE 100	0.069	-0.075	-0.078	-0.086	0.025	0.003	1.846
CARBONEX	0.071	-0.076	-0.087	-0.083	0.021	0.003	1.850
Energy	0.035	0.176	-0.022	-0.055	-0.002	0.003	1.818
Oil & gas	-0.030	0.186	-0.063	-0.041	0.104	0.005	1.823
P – II							
Sensex	-0.382*	0.819*	0.493*	0.437*	0.424*	0.029	2.125
BSE 100	-0.379*	0.811*	0.507*	0.449*	0.414*	0.030	2.121
CARBONEX	-0.381*	0.806*	0.515*	0.448*	0.421*	0.030	2.117
Energy	-0.551*	0.984*	0.759*	0.635*	0.754*	0.029	2.172
Oil & gas	-0.396*	0.773*	0.403*	0.509*	0.500*	0.021	2.143

Source: Authors calculation.

Note: *Statistically significant at 5% level.

Table 4.5. Indices Volatility.

Variables	Sensex	BSE 100	CARBONEX	BSE Energy	BSE Oil & Gas
Mean Equation					
Intercept	0.042	0.020	0.022	−0.086	−0.090
Indices	0.067*	0.077*	0.076*	0.069*	0.078*
Tuesday	0.128	0.142	0.134	0.367*	0.331*
Wednesday	−0.016	−0.024	−0.025	0.154	−0.031
Thursday	0.059	0.083	0.079	0.168	0.148
Friday	0.026	0.045	0.043	0.146	0.160
Var. Equation					
Intercept	0.026*	0.031*	0.030*	0.150*	0.174*
RESID(−1)^2	0.125	0.125*	0.121*	0.106*	0.136*
GARCH(−1)	0.857	0.852*	0.857*	0.832*	0.782*
R^2	−0.007	−0.007	−0.007	0.000	0.000
D–W test	2.216	2.221	2.217	2.219	2.189

*Significant at 5% level.

Source: Authors calculation.

Note: Indices indicate respective lag values of the selected indices.

5. Conclusion

This research paper analyses the presence of the day of the week effect in the selected indices for the period of 1 August 2016, to 31 July 2022. The study first applied descriptive statistics to know about their mean return during the full study period, period I and period II. It is clear from the descriptive statistics that during the whole period, period I and period II, BSE Energy has the highest mean daily return compared to all other selected indices. There is a Tuesday effect on the daily average mean returns of BSE CARBONEX, BSE 100, BSE Sensex, BSE Energy and BSE Oil & Gas in the full sample period and period II. The day-wise OLS results indicate a high positive and statistically significant daily return for Tuesday particularly during the full sample period and period II. GARCH(1,1) model indicates there is a significant Tuesday effect on BSE Energy and BSE Oil & Gas indices.

As per the study result, CARBONEX index performance is still in a growing stage. During the study period, the BSE Energy index's performance is high compared to other indices. The result obtained in this chapter is useful to investors to frame their investment strategy, and for academicians to know the performance of these indices for different periods. The scope of the study is it can be extended to other countries' indices also.

References

Ahmed, S. U., Abdullah, M., & Ahmed, S. P. (2017). Linkage between corporate social performance and stock return: An evidence from financial sector of Bangladesh. *The Journal of Developing Areas, 51*(2), 287–299.

Ameer, R., & Othman, R. (2012). Sustainability practices and corporate financial performance: A study based on the top global corporations. *Journal of Business Ethics, 108*(1), 61–79.

Ang, W. R. (2015). Sustainable investment in Korea does not catch a cold when the United States sneezes. *Journal of Sustainable Finance & Investment, 5*(1–2), 16–26.

Avrampou, A., Skouloudis, A., Iliopoulos, G., & Khan, N. (2019). Advancing the sustainable development goals: Evidence from leading European banks. *Sustainable Development, 27*(4), 743–757.

Belghitar, Y., Clark, E., & Deshmukh, N. (2014). Does it pay to be ethical? Evidence from the FTSE4Good. *Journal of Banking & Finance, 47*, 54–62.

Benson, C. C., Gupta, N., & Mateti, R. (2010). Does risk reduction mitigate the costs of going green? – An empirical study of sustainable investing. *An Empirical Study of Sustainable Investing*, 7–25.

Berument, H., & Kiymaz, H. (2001). The day of the week effect on stock market volatility. *Journal of Economics and Finance, 25*(2), 181–193.

Bolek, M., Gniadkowska-Szymańska, A., & Lyroudi, K. (2022). Covid-19 pandemic and day-of-the-week anomaly in Omx markets. *Central European Economic Journal, 9*(56), 158–177. https://doi.org/10.2478/ceej-2022-0010

Brzeszczynski, J., Ghimire, B., Jamasb, T., & McIntosh, G. (2016). *Socially responsible investment and market performance: The case of energy and resource firms.* Energy Policy Research Group, University of Cambridge. http://www.jstor.org/stable/resrep30376

Chan, P. T., & Walter, T. (2014). Investment performance of "environmentally-friendly" firms and their initial public offers and seasoned equity offers. *Journal of Banking & Finance, 44*, 177–188.

Chang, C. E., Nelson, W. A., & Witte, H. D. (2012). Do green mutual funds perform well? *Management Research Review, 35*(8), 693–708.

Chiah, M., & Zhong, A. (2021). Tuesday blues and the day-of-the-week effect in stock returns. *Journal of Banking & Finance, 133*, 106243.

Conley, J. M., & Williams, C. A. (2011). Global banks as global sustainability regulators?: The equator principles. *Law & Policy, 33*(4), 542–575.

Cunha, F. A. F. D. S., de Oliveira, E. M., Orsato, R. J., Klotzle, M. C., Cyrino Oliveira, F. L., & Caiado, R. G. G. (2020). Can sustainable investments outperform traditional benchmarks? Evidence from global stock markets. *Business Strategy and the Environment, 29*(2), 682–697.

De Souza Cunha, F. A. F., & Samanez, C. P. (2013). Performance analysis of sustainable investments in the Brazilian stock market: A study about the corporate sustainability index (ISE). *Journal of Business Ethics, 117*(1), 19–36. http://www.jstor.org/stable/42001964

Delsen, L., & Lehr, A. (2019). Value matters or values matter? An analysis of heterogeneity in preferences for sustainable investments. *Journal of Sustainable Finance & Investment, 9*(3), 240–261.

Eccles, N. S., & Viviers, S. (2011). The origins and meanings of names describing investment practices that integrate a consideration of ESG issues in the academic literature. *Journal of Business Ethics, 104*(3), 389–402.

Engelberg, J., McLean, R. D., & Pontiff, J. (2018). Anomalies and news. *The Journal of Finance, 73*(5), 1971–2001.

Hawn, O., Chatterji, A. K., & Mitchell, W. (2018). Do investors actually value sustainability? New evidence from investor reactions to the Dow Jones Sustainability Index (DJSI). *Strategic Management Journal, 39*(4), 949–976.

Hui, E. C., & Chan, K. K. K. (2015). Testing calendar effects on global securitized real estate markets by Shiryaev-Zhou index. *Habitat International, 48*, 38–45.

Ielasi, F., Rossolini, M., & Limberti, S. (2018). Sustainability-themed mutual funds: An empirical examination of risk and performance. *The Journal of Risk Finance.* https://doi.org/10.1108/JRF-12-2016-0159

Islam, R., & Sultana, N. (2015). Day of the week effect on stock return and volatility: Evidence from Chittagong stock exchange. *European Journal of Business and Management, 7*(3), 165–172.

Jeucken, M., & Bouma, J. J. (2017). The changing environment of banks. In *Sustainable banking* (pp. 24–38). Routledge.

Kanitkarameer, T., Jayaraman, T., D'Souza, M., Purkayastha, P., Ragunandan, D., & Talwar, R. (2009). How much "carbon space" do we have? Physical constraints on India's climate policy and its implications. *Economic and Political Weekly, 44*(41/42), 35–46. http://www.jstor.org/stable/25663678

King, M. D., & Gulledge, J. (2013). The climate change and energy security nexus. *Fletcher Forum of World Affairs, 37*(2), 25–44. http://www.jstor.org/stable/45289586

Knoepfel, I. (2001). Dow Jones sustainability group index: A global benchmark for corporate sustainability. *Corporate Environmental Strategy, 8*(1), 6–15.

Lean, H. H., & Nguyen, D. K. (2014). Policy uncertainty and performance characteristics of sustainable investments across regions around the global financial crisis. *Applied Financial Economics, 24*(21), 1367–1373.

Lesser, K., Lobe, S., & Walkshäusl, C. (2014). Green and socially responsible investing in international markets. *Journal of Asset Management, 15*(5), 317–331.

Makni, R., Francoeur, C., & Bellavance, F. (2009). Causality between corporate social performance and financial performance: Evidence from Canadian firms. *Journal of Business Ethics, 89*(3), 409–422. http://www.jstor.org/stable/40295064

Miller, K. A. (2008). Climate change and water resources: The challenges ahead. *Journal of International Affairs, 61*(2), 35–50. http://www.jstor.org/stable/24358110

Nizam, E., Ng, A., Dewandaru, G., Nagayev, R., & Nkoba, M. A. (2019). The impact of social and environmental sustainability on financial performance: A global analysis of the banking sector. *Journal of Multinational Financial Management, 49*, 35–53.

Ortas, E., Moneva, J. M., & Salvador, M. (2012). Does socially responsible investment equity indexes in emerging markets pay off? Evidence from Brazil. *Emerging Markets Review, 13*(4), 581–597.

Patel, S. K., & Kumari, P. (2020). Indian stock market movements and responsiveness of sustainability indices: A risk-adjusted analysis. *International Management Review, 16*(1), 55–64.

Rueda, X., Garrett, R. D., & Lambin, E. F. (2017). Corporate investments in supply chain sustainability: Selecting instruments in the agri-food industry. *Journal of Cleaner Production, 142*, 2480–2492.

Rushton, S., & Kett, M. (2015). Climate change and health: Rising to the challenge? *Medicine, Conflict and Survival, 31*(3/4), 141–143. https://www.jstor.org/stable/27017906

Schueth, S. (2003). Socially responsible investing in the United States. *Journal of Business Ethics, 43*(3), 189–194.

Silva, F., & Cortez, M. C. (2016). The performance of US and European green funds in different market conditions. *Journal of Cleaner Production, 135*, 558–566.

Soler-Domínguez, A., Matallín-Sáez, J. C., de Mingo-López, D. V., & Tortosa-Ausina, E. (2021). Looking for sustainable development: Socially responsible mutual funds and the low-carbon economy. *Business Strategy and the Environment, 30*(4), 1751–1766.

Tripathi, V., & Bhandari, V. (2015). Socially responsible stocks: A boon for investors in India. *Journal of Advances in Management Research*. https://doi.org/10.1108/JAMR-03-2014-0021

Ur Rehman, R., Zhang, J., Uppal, J., Cullinan, C., & Akram Naseem, M. (2016). Are environmental social governance equity indices a better choice for investors? An Asian perspective. *Business Ethics: A European Review, 25*(4), 440–459.

Urquhart, A., & McGroarty, F. (2014). Calendar effects, market conditions and the adaptive market hypothesis: Evidence from long-run US data. *International Review of Financial Analysis, 35*, 154–166. https://doi.org/10.1016/j.irfa.2014.08.003

Vasal, V. K. (2009). Corporate social responsibility & shareholder returns – Evidence from the Indian capital market. *Indian Journal of Industrial Relations, 44*(3), 376–385. http://www.jstor.org/stable/27768210

Wai Kong Cheung, A. (2011). Do stock investors value corporate sustainability? Evidence from an event study. *Journal of Business Ethics, 99*(2), 145–165.

Wheeler, T., & von Braun, J. (2013). Climate change impacts on global food security. *Science, 341*(6145), 508–513. http://www.jstor.org/stable/23491201

Xiao, Y., Faff, R., Gharghori, P., & Min, B.-K. (2017). The financial performance of socially responsible investments: Insights from the intertemporal CAPM. *Journal of Business Ethics, 146*(2), 353–364. http://www.jstor.org/stable/45022323

Zhang, J., Lai, Y., & Lin, J. (2017). The day-of-the-week effects of stock markets in different countries. *Finance Research Letters, 20*, 47–62.

Chapter 5

Social Predictors of Money Management Behaviour Among Emerging Adults

Prihana Vasishta and Anju Singla

Punjab Engineering College, India

Abstract

An individual's capacity to manage finances has become critical in today's environment. The availability of various sophisticated financial instruments, combined with the economy's complexity and rising uncertainty, has prompted a significant push to analyse from where the youth learn about managing their money. This study intends to investigate the differences in the selected social predictors (Parents, Friends, School, Books, Job Experiences, Life experiences and Media) that influence the money management behaviour of emerging adults. The data was collected through a structured questionnaire from 230 undergraduates in the age group of 18–22 years. To test the normality of data, Kolmogorov–Smirnov (KS) test was applied and further Kruskal–Wallis test was found to be the appropriate method based on the identification of statistically significant deviations. The results show that parents have been considered as the most influential predictor ($X =$ 3.565) of money management behaviour among emerging adults. followed by Life Experiences ($X =$ 3.526). Whereas School and Job Experience were the least influential social predictors with mean value of 2.278 and 2.130 respectively. The study provides insights to the regulators, academicians and policymakers to initiate innovative strategies and processes for helping emerging adults for effective money management to increase their academic performance in a stress-free environment. Further, this paper contributes towards effective money management advice by recommending implementation of tools, apps and programs relating to Financial Literacy for better Financial Behaviour. Lastly, the paper provides implications that focus on enhancing the financial literacy of the parents as they act as role models for their children by teaching them skills to manage money.

Modeling Economic Growth in Contemporary India, 65–79

Copyright © 2024 Prihana Vasishta and Anju Singla

Published under exclusive licence by Emerald Publishing Limited

doi:10.1108/978-1-80382-751-320241005

Keywords: Money management behaviour; money management; social predictors; emerging adults; financial literacy

1. Introduction

Money management is the ability to deal with money efficiently to avoid financial troubles. Poor money management has been a serious concern for many young adults, prompting various researchers to investigate it throughout the years (Bamforth et al., 2018; Bapat, 2020; Sachitra et al., 2019; Sundarasen & Rahman, 2017). College students are not just future managers and money earners for their organizations but also for the nation. In addition, the financial habits established by these students are likely to be carried forward into their careers (Xiao et al., 2007). Further, the advent of the gig economy has transferred society's financial responsibilities from the government to the individual. At the same time, due to the pandemic, consumer spending trends in India have shown a huge rise with youngsters trying new shopping behaviours (Ho et al., 2020). Emerging adults can be greatly impacted by irresponsible spending, which further affect their academic performance, physical and emotional well-being, and social relationships (Xiao et al., 2007). The struggles of young people to manage their finances, such as growing credit card debt, school loan debt, lack of savings, inconsistent income and limited financial knowledge (ANZ, 2008), make it challenging for them to achieve financial success. To help address this, multiple stakeholders, including organizations, parents, educational and financial institutions, and the government, need to have a better understanding of the financial habits of emerging adults (Solis & Durband, 2015).

Various studies in the past have focused on studying the money management behaviour of emerging adults based on the linkages between credit usage, financial literacy, academic accomplishment, debt management and well-being (Chun et al., 2021; Xiao et al., 2008; Zhang & Kemp, 2009). However, a person's ability to effectively manage their financial resources depends on various factors other than the level of financial literacy such as psychological, economic and social (ANZ, 2008; Roy Morgan Research, 2003; Simon, 1986; Singh et al., 2005). A thorough review of the literature reveals that various developed economies such as the United Kingdom, Australia and the United States have focused on researching the social, economic and psychological aspects that predict the behaviour of emerging adults towards money management (Capuano & Ramsay, 2011; Gudmonson & Danes, 2011; Hodson & Dwyer, 2014). However, the evidence from developing countries in this context is limited (Sachitra & Wijesinghe, 2018; Zulfaris et al., 2020). Most previous studies have focused on financial knowledge (Bapat, 2020), peer influence (Bursztyn et al., 2012) and parental influence (Zhao & Zhang, 2020; Zulfaris et al., 2020) as predictors of students' money management behaviour. However, limited research has been conducted to investigate the social predictors of money management, such as Media, Teachers and Life Experiences (Fig. 5.1).

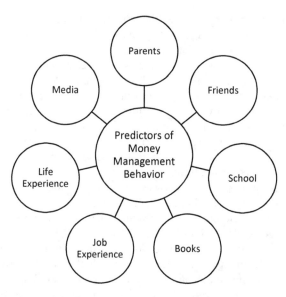

Fig. 5.1.   Social Predictors of Money Management Behaviour.
Source: Author's Own Compilation.

Therefore, it is necessary to conduct a more in-depth investigation into the predictors that influence the behaviour of emerging adults on money management and financial decision-making in India. The present study aims to accomplish the following objectives:

- To investigate the social predictors (Parents, Friends, School, Books, Job Experience, Life experience and Media) of money management behaviour among emerging adults.
- To explore the differences in the selected predictors that influence the behaviour of emerging adults towards money management and to provide recommendations for future policies in terms of regulation and educational programs at the school and university level.

2. Review of Literature

The previous studies have examined the relationship between money and individuals through development of behavioural scales with regard to money (Tang, 1995; Tang et al., 2006; Yamauchi & Templer, 1982). Ridhayani and Johan (2020) asserted that money is a potent driver of human behaviour. Further, Van Raaij (2016) in his book discussed money management as a subfield of financial behaviour. Teachers, parents, classmates and the media are social agents who can impact a person's financial behaviour (Campenhout, 2015) or how individuals use the money to meet their final demands. As one of the major components of financial management behaviour, few researchers have studied the money management behaviour of students (Bamforth et al., 2018; Sachitra et al., 2019; Sachitra & Wijesinghe, 2018; Zulfaris et al., 2020) and discovered that the factors other than financial literacy, debt management and financial well-being such as attitudes towards money, financial goals and peer influence have a favourable and statistically significant impact on the behaviour of university students towards money management.

A study by Nidar and Bestari (2012) at Padjadjaran University in Indonesia aimed to determine the factors affecting the personal financial literacy of 400 students. The results showed that education level, faculty, personal income, insurance ownership, parental knowledge and parental income significantly impacted personal financial literacy. Moreover, financial skills and attitudes, parental occupation, and parental involvement were found to positively influence young adults' financial decisions, particularly regarding the use of student credit cards (Bamforth et al., 2017; Gudmonson & Danes, 2011; Limbu et al., 2012; Norvilitis & MacLean, 2010). In addition, Lusardi et al. (2010) revealed that less than one-third of young adults had a fundamental understanding of inflation, risk diversification and interest rates. However, there was a considerable correlation between financial literacy, socioeconomic factors and family financial sophisti-cation. Jorgensen (2007) assessed the personal financial literacy of college students based on gender, class rank and socioeconomic background. Further, the research analysed the parental and peer influence on the level of financial literacy among college students. It was revealed in the study that students had low financial knowledge, attitudes and behaviours, but their scores increased dramatically from undergraduate to master's level. Additionally, the study found that students had higher scores for financial knowledge, attitude and behaviour when their financial habits were influenced by their parents. It was also noted that students with a higher level of financial knowledge displayed higher scores for financial attitude and behaviour. Chen and Volpe (1998) studied the level of financial literacy among 924 college students from 14 institutions to understand why some students are more financially knowledgeable than others. The study found that students with business majors had higher financial literacy compared to those with other majors. The researchers also observed that students with greater financial knowledge were more likely to retain financial information and make the correct decision in hypothetical financial scenarios. In general, one can obtain basic financial information from parents, but numerous studies have revealed that parents frequently lack the necessary financial expertise to teach their children (Moschis, 1985). Researchers uncovered a similar pattern between adolescents and their parents. People who participated in or heard little or no discussion about finances during childhood were more likely to remain ignorant about various financial goods and become irrational consumers (Lyons & Hunt, 2003). From the literature review, it can be inferred that personal financial literacy among college students is influenced by various factors such as education level, faculty, personal income, insurance ownership, parental knowledge and income, financial skills and attitudes, parental occupation and involvement. The studies also reveal that students with business majors and higher financial knowledge tend to display better financial literacy and decision-making abilities. Parental influence, as well as socioeconomic factors, family financial sophistication and peer influence also play a role in students' financial literacy. However, many parents lack the necessary financial expertise to effectively teach their children, leading to a lack of financial knowledge and irrational financial behaviour in some individuals.

As the dynamics have changed over time, according to Sachitra et al. (2019), undergraduates in Sri Lanka utilize both careful and risky strategies when managing their finances. Young adults are aware that budgeting skills are necessary for them to manage their limited funds. In addition, effective money management practices, including saving, spending, budgeting and investing, have been demonstrated to prevent overspending and reduce the risk of personal debt (Godwin & Koonce, 1992). The capacity to manage one's finances is crucial to achieving success in life. Further, adopting efficient financial management tactics is a requisite for adults, adolescents and college students. A person's effective management practices improve his quality of life through improving social interactions and mental health (Sachitra & Bandara, 2017). As a result of their high monthly expenses, they must practise prudent financial management (Aung & Mon, 2020).

Past research has examined the money management practices of young adults based on the interrelationships between credit utilization, financial literacy, academic achievement, debt management and well-being (Xiao et al., 2008; Zhang & Kemp, 2009). Nevertheless, a person's capacity to efficiently manage their financial resources depends not just on their level of financial literacy but also on a variety of psychological, economic and social aspects (ANZ, 2008; Roy Morgan Research, 2003; Simon, 1986; Singh et al., 2005). Studies in the past have delved into the money management behaviours of emerging adults and the connections between credit usage, financial literacy, academic success, debt management and overall well-being. However, managing finances effectively is not just dependent on financial literacy but also on psychological, economic and social factors. Although developed economies have explored the social, economic and psychological factors that predict money management behaviours, evidence from developing countries is limited. Previous studies have mainly focused on the effects of financial knowledge, peer influence and parental influence on money management, but limited research has been done on the effects of social predictors such as media, teachers and life experiences. This research gap highlights the need for further examination into the social predictors of money management behaviours in developing countries, as these findings can provide valuable insights and inform policies and initiatives aimed at improving financial literacy and stability among emerging adults.

3. Material and Methods

This paper aims to assess differences in the selected social predictors (Parents, Friends, School, Books, Job Experience, Life experience and Media) of money management behaviour across emerging adults. Emerging adults include individuals who fall in the age group of 18–24 years (Bosch et al., 2016). The following research question was developed in response to the objectives mentioned above:

RQ. Is there a difference in selected social predictors that influence money management behaviour among emerging adults?

The study considered the data collected from undergraduate students of various colleges of the Tricity (Chandigarh, Panchkula and Mohali, India) through a well-structured questionnaire using Google Form. The questionnaire was sent to 300 emerging adults through various social media platforms such as Whatsapp, Facebook, Instagram and LinkedIn. A total of 230 duly filled questionnaires were received. The results of socio-demographic profile of the respondents are shown in Table 5.1.

The data shows that the sample of 230 respondents consisted of 128 males (55.7 %) and 102 females (44.3 %) in the age group of 18–22 years. 36.9% of the respondents had a family income of less than 2.5 lakh per annum. More than half of the respondents (51.7%) belonged to urban areas.

Table 5.1. Socio-Demographic Profile of the Respondents.

Profile Variables		No. of Participants	Percentage
Gender			
a.	Male	128	55.7
b.	Female	102	44.3
Area			
a.	Rural	60	26.1
b.	Semi-urban	51	22.17
c.	Urban	119	51.7
Family Income Per Annum			
a.	<2.5 lakh	85	36.9
b.	≥2.5 lakh to <5 lakh	52	22.6
c.	≥5 to <7.5 lakh	25	10.8
d.	≥7.5 to <10 lakh	32	13.9
e.	>10 lakh	36	15.9

Source: Primary Data.

Further, the selection and application of relevant methodology were dependent on the fulfilment of the assumption of normality, Kolmogorov–Smirnov (KS) test was conducted to check the normality of the data. Further, the Kruskal–Wallis test was selected as an appropriate approach for assessing the differences based on the results of normality tests. This test can discover differences across independent observations. However, it cannot establish the category in which difference occurred or which category obtained a higher rank (Bačík et al., 2020). Hence, descriptive analysis, including mean and standard deviation, was conducted to overcome this drawback.

4. Analysis and Results

According to Table 5.2, the results of the KS normality test reveal that the social predictors included in this study have p-value below 0.05, indicating statistically significant deviations from the normal distribution.

As a result, the Kruskal–Wallis test was selected as a non-parametric alternative to the ANOVA test based on the identification of statistically significant deviations. The following statistical hypothesis was developed.

H1. Differences among social predictors (Parents, Friends, School, Books, Job Experience, Life experience and Media) are statistically significant.

Table 5.3 reveals the results of the Kruskal–Wallis test.

Evidently, the asymptotic significance is less than 0.05. Therefore, the alternative hypothesis (*H1*) is accepted. It infers that there is an observable difference between selected predictors influencing the money management behaviour among emerging adults. The results further indicate a positive response to the research question posted in the methodology section of this study.

Table 5.2. Results of Kolmogorov–Smirnov Normality Tests.

Predictors of Money Management Behaviour	Kolmogorov–Smirnov		
	Statistic	Df	Sig.
Parents	0.249	230	0.000
Friends	0.223	230	0.000
School	0.182	230	0.000
Books	0.233	230	0.000
Job experience	0.248	230	0.000
Life experiences	0.254	230	0.000
Media	0.259	230	0.000

Source: Primary Data.

Table 5.3. Results of Kruskal–Wallis Test.

Test Statistic	Value
Chi-Square	282.548
df	7
Asymp. Sig.	0.000

Source: Primary Data.

Table 5.4. Descriptive Statistics of the Sample.

Predictors of Money Management Behaviour	Mean	Standard Deviation
Parents	3.565	1.244
Friends	2.469	1.009
School	2.278	1.057
Books	2.756	1.201
Job experience	2.130	1.267
Life experiences	3.526	1.252
Media	3.021	1.258

Source: Primary Data.

The descriptive statistics of the predictors that influence the money management behaviour of young people are shown in Table 5.4. With a focus on the mean, the results show the values and their relative deviations from the normal distribution.

The results of descriptive analysis depict that Parents have the highest mean value ($X = 3.565$), followed by Life Experiences ($X = 3.526$) as the most influential predictors of Money Management Behaviour among emerging adults. Whereas School and Job Experience with a mean value of 2.278 and 2.130 were the least influential social predictors.

5. Discussion

The results from descriptive statistics highlight that parents are viewed as the most influential factor in determining money management behaviour among emerging adults. This finding aligns with previous research done by Novitasari et al. (2021) and Norvilitis and MacLean (2010). Studies have shown that parents play a crucial role in imparting financial education to their children (Clarke et al., 2005; Ivan & Dickson, 2008; Shim et al., 2009; Shim et al., 2010; Xiao et al., 2007). According to Shim et al. (2009), adults who have strong financial literacy skills often received substantial parental guidance and formal financial education in their childhood. Similar to previous studies, this research also demonstrates a beneficial and significant influence of parents on behaviour of their children's money management. Undergraduates who live with their parents are more likely to receive financial assistance for necessities such as food and transportation, as indicated by Sachitra et al. (2019). Hence, they are disciplined by their parents not to overspend and practice money control behaviour. It is recommended for the policymakers to focus on enhancing the financial literacy of the parents as they act as role models for their children by teaching them skills to manage money more effectively.

The findings of this study found Life Experiences to be one of the most influential social predictors of money management behaviour among emerging adults. Further, Sachitra et al. (2019) confirmed the findings of the study wherein the respondents stated that they learnt from their mistakes when they realized they were spending too much without an income. Life experiences play a significant role in shaping the money management behaviour of emerging adults and have a strong influence on their spending habits. The result of the study depicts that media has been ranked third impacting the money management behaviour. The result is consistent with the findings of Lyons et al. (2006) and Loibl and Hira (2005). They emphasized that the use of media has a significant impact on the financial decisions of less self-confident adolescents. For emerging adults, media is a significant socialization tool. Loibl and Hira (2005) discovered that people who used media as a data source for financial engagements had better monetary behaviours and financial fulfilment. Media sources serve as an important foundation for self-education for enhancing money management behaviour. Through various forms of media, such as television, print and online sources, people can access information and resources to improve their financial literacy and make informed decisions about managing their finances. However, educating emerging adults about the selection and use of authenticated media sources is recommended for effective money management strategies.

On the other hand, the influence of peers on the financial behaviour of undergraduates was found to be relatively lower and ranked fifth ($X = 2.469$) among the seven predictors considered in the study. However, these findings are in contrast to previous research studies that have emphasized the critical role that peers play in shaping an individual's financial behaviour (Kretschmer & Pike, 2010; Masche, 2010; Moore & Bowman, 2006). Despite these differing results, it is widely recognized that peers are an integral part of the factors that determine an individual's monetary behaviour (Delfabbro & Thrupp, 2003; Kretschmer & Pike, 2010; Masche, 2010; Moore & Bowman, 2006). In addition, according to Sachitra and Bandara (2017), peers appear to exert distinct effects on learning and decision-making processes of the undergraduates.

This study also found that job experience ($X = 2.130$) was the least influential factor on money management behaviour among emerging adults. However, previous research by Mortimer et al. (2003) suggested that young people who work gain valuable financial lessons, such as a sense of responsibility and improved money management skills. The study's results showed that Books ($X = 2.756$) and School ($X = 2.278$) had a lower impact on money management behaviour, ranked fourth and sixth respectively out of the seven predictors analysed. Sachitra et al. (2019) confirmed the findings of this study. The influence of teacher over the money management behaviour of undergraduates was not evident in their study, reinforcing the conclusion drawn from this study. However, Shim et al. (2015) indicated that teachers could play a significant role as financial intermediaries. Hence, teachers are required to constantly motivate students since a lack of motivation can result in poor financial capability (Mandell & Klein, 2009; McCormick, 2009). Most educational institutions in India lack initiatives to promote financial literacy, such as incorporating financial education into their curricula. As a result, teachers and schools have no effect on the money management practices of students. Hence it is recommended to introduce the basic concepts of financial literacy at the school level which will increase the financial capability, thereby leading to the financial well-being of emerging adults.

6. Implications

The study was conducted to identify the existing contextual factors that affect money management behaviour among emerging Indian adults. The findings of this study confirm that various contextual factors such as parents, peers, life experiences, school, books and social media significantly impact the money management behaviour of emerging adults. The study found that, as a developing country, India differs structurally from wealthy nations, where most previous research has been conducted. India is well-known for its wide cultural and socioeconomic diversity. Furthermore, there is concern that young adults are not financially prepared to deal with today's complex financial reality, owing to the current economic crisis and an increase in the number of bankruptcies reported in India. The complexity of financial services and products has increased the demand for financial literacy in today's environment. These occurrences, in turn, have impacted the environmental factors influencing monetary behaviour. The results of this article have academic and managerial implications for academicians, policymakers and the government.

6.1 Implications for Academicians

This study found that young adults in India are not influenced much by schools and books, stating the loopholes in the Indian education system. Due to this, the undergraduates are still dependent on their parent's income. Further, the students having a slight interest in finance gets abandoned due to the unavailability of knowledge at the school level. Thus, including a module that deals with enhancing financial literacy at the school level would be a great step towards generating interest of the students in money management. The government should also conduct quizzes and webinars at national level for the students at school and undergraduate level. Moreover, schools can also play a vital role by conducting similar type of fun quizzes and sessions which helps in exploring the financial interests of the students. Various financial organizations can partner with educational institutions to support the delivery of financial education through school savings initiatives, offering students practical experience by teaching them the concept of saving money in an insured financial institution while simultaneously fostering development of financial skills and confidence. The Central Bank of Papua New Guinea in collaboration with the Centre for Excellence in Financial Inclusion (CEFI), launched the "Savings campaign for young minds," a national initiative that catered to children and young adults between the ages of 6 and 25. In order to reach out to emerging adults and assist them in opening student accounts, financial institutions should be encouraged to collaborate with educational institutions at all levels (primary, secondary and senior-secondary).

6.2 Implications for Government and Policymakers

Governments and regulators could play a significant role in developing customized products for emerging adults by developing mechanisms to incentivize Fin-Tech firms. In some countries, such as the United States, under the Community Reinvestment Act, banks are given preferential treatment when they are responsive to community needs, especially when implementing programmes related to financial literacy for low- and moderate-income youth. Through this study, various conclusions and policy options may be drawn for advancing emerging adults' financial inclusion. Various rules and regulations governing Digital Financial Inclusion for emerging adults by studying their money management behaviour must be considered as policy options. Further, financial awareness campaigns are an integral way to engage individuals (particularly emerging adults) in discussions about money management and financial issues. World Savings Day, Global Money Week, and Dutch Money Week are successful examples of global initiatives that involve a diverse range of stakeholders for financial awareness. The initiatives can also reach their target audiences through various campaigns and initiatives on emerging platforms such as social media, interactive films, interactive games and mass communication methods that are quite common among emerging adults.

7. Conclusion

This study observed that parents, life experiences and media significantly influence the money management behaviour among emerging adults in India. However, the influence of books, school and friends is considered low. There is a fundamental need for a better level of financial education in the school curriculum and appropriate inputs at the college level, based on the student's level of financial literacy, to avoid emerging adults from being vulnerable to several malpractices and frauds. In addition to inputs relating to knowledge, the curriculum should also cover the attitudinal and behavioural aspects of financial literacy. This will have a positive impact on students' economic as well as social circumstances and will serve as both a preventative and curative measure for them. Securities Board Exchange of India (SEBI) has been reaching out to the masses through trainers/resource persons (RPs) to spread financial literacy/education across the country.

Further, National Centre for Financial Education (NCFE) is delivering unbiased financial education in schools to improve financial literacy, a vital life skill for each student's holistic development. However, the impact analysis of these initiatives is recommended at the national level. Due to the continuous transformation of the financial landscape, it is necessary to examine the extent and interplay of economic, social, psychological and technological predictors on the money management behaviour of emerging adults. In addition, empirical studies are needed to investigate the role of various FinTech apps in better money management techniques (Spending, Saving, Investing and Budgeting) for emerging adults. The study provides specific insights to the regulators, academicians and policymakers to initiate innovative strategies and processes for helping emerging adults for effective money management to increase their academic performance in a stress-free environment. In the end, future research should inspect the financial behaviour among Indian youths so that they can become financially independent and supportive of their family. Further, this paper contributes towards practical money management advice by recommending the implementation of tools, apps and programs relating to Financial Literacy for better Financial Behaviour.

References

ANZ. (2008). *ANZ survey of adult financial literacy in Australia*. The Social Research Centre. www.anz.com/Documents/AU/Aboutanz/AN_5654_Adult_Fin_Lit_Report_08_Web_Report_full.pdf. Accessed on July 27, 2022.

Aung, N. N., & Mon, H. H. (2020). Budgeting habit behavior of undergraduate students in Yangon University of economics. *Journal of the Myanmar Academy of Arts and Science*, *2*(1).

Bačík, R., Fedorko, R., Gavurova, B., Ivankova, V., & Rigelský, M. (2020). Differences in financial performance between various categories of hotels in the Visegrad group countries. *Journal of International Studies*, *13*(2).

Bamforth, J., Jebarajakirthy, C., & Geursen, G. (2017). Undergraduates' responses to factors affecting their money management behaviour: Some new insights from a qualitative study. *Young Consumers*, *18*(5).

Bamforth, J., Jebarajakirthy, C., & Geursen, G. (2018). Understanding undergraduates' money management behaviour: A study beyond financial literacy. *International Journal of Bank Marketing*, *36*(7).

Bapat, D. (2020). Antecedents to responsible financial management behavior among young adults: Moderating role of financial risk tolerance. *International Journal of Bank Marketing*, *38*(5), 1177–1194.

Bosch, L. A., Serido, J., Card, N. A., Shim, S., & Barber, B. (2016). Predictors of financial identity development in emerging adulthood. *Emerging Adulthood*, *4*(6), 417–426.

Bursztyn, L., Ederer, F., Ferman, B., & Yuchtman, N. (2012). *Understanding peer effects in financial decisions: Evidence from a field experiment (No. w18241)*. National Bureau of Economic Research.

Campenhout, G. (2015). Revaluing the role of parents as financial socialization agents in youth financial literacy programs. *Journal of Consumer Affairs, 49*(1), 186–222.

Capuano, A., & Ramsay, I. (2011). *What causes cause a sub optimal financial behaviour? An exploration of financial literacy, social influences and behavioural economics.* Research paper No. 540, University of Melbourne Legal Studies.

Chen, H., & Volpe, R. P. (1998). An analysis of personal financial literacy among college students. *Financial Services Review, 7*(2), 107–128.

Chun, Y. K., Fenn, C. J., & Al-Khaled, A. A. S. (2021). The relationship between socio-demographics and financial literacy with financial planning among young adults in Klang Valley, Malaysia. *Jurnal Pengurusan, 63*, 1–14.

Clarke, M. C., Heaton, M. B., Israelsen, C. L., & Eggett, D. L. (2005). The acquisition of family financial roles and responsibilities. *Family and Consumer Sciences Research Journal, 33*(4), 321–340.

Delfabbro, P., & Thrupp, L. (2003). The social determinants of youth gambling in South Australian adolescents. *Journal of Adolescence, 26*(3), 313–330.

Godwin, D. D., & Koonce, J. C. (1992). Cash flow management of low-income newlyweds. *Financial Counseling and Planning, 3*(1), 17–42.

Gudmonson, C. G., & Danes, S. M. (2011). Family financial socialization: Theory and critical review. *Journal of Family and Economic Issues, 32*, 644–667.

Ho, J., Kim, A., & Yamakawa, N. (2020). *Survey: Asian consumer sentiment during the COVID-19 crisis.* McKinsey & Company report. https://www.mckinsey.com/featured-insights/asia-pacific/survey-asian-consumersentiment-during-the-covid-19-crisis. Accessed on August 22, 2022.

Hodson, R., & Dwyer, R. E. (2014). *Financial behavior, debt and early life transitions: Insights from the national longitudinal survey of youth.* 1997 Cohort. OH State University.

Ivan, B., & Dickson, L. (2008). Consumer economic socialization. In *Handbook of consumer finance research* (pp. 83–102). Springer.

Jorgensen, B. L. (2007). *Financial literacy of college students: Parental and peer influences.* Doctoral dissertation, Virginia Tech.

Kretschmer, T., & Pike, A. (2010). Links between non-shared friendship experiences and adolescent siblings' differences in aspirations. *Journal of Adolescence, 33*(1), 101–110.

Limbu, Y. B., Huhmann, B. A., & Xu, B. (2012). Are college students at greater risk of credit card abuse? Age, gender, materialism and parental influence on consumer response to credit cards. *Journal of Financial Services Marketing, 17*(2), 148–162.

Loibl, C., & Hira, T. K. (2005). Self-directed financial learning and financial satisfaction. *Journal of Financial Counseling and Planning, 16*(1), 11.

Lusardi, A., Mitchell, O. S., & Curto, V. (2010). Financial literacy among the young. *Journal of Consumer Affairs, 44*(2), 358–380.

Lyons, A., & Hunt, J. (2003). The credit practices and financial education needs of community college students. *Journal of Financial Counseling and Planning, 14*(2).

Lyons, A. C., Scherpf, E., & Roberts, H. (2006). Financial education and communication between parents and children. *The Journal of Consumer Education, 23*(2006), 64–76.

Mandell, L., & Klein, L. S. (2009). The impact of financial literacy education on subsequent financial behavior. *Journal of Financial Counseling and Planning, 20*(1).

Masche, J. G. (2010). Explanation of normative declines in parents' knowledge about their adolescent children. *Journal of Adolescence, 33*(2), 271–284.

McCormick, M. H. (2009). The effectiveness of youth financial education: A review of the literature. *Journal of Financial Counseling and Planning, 20*(1).

Moore, E. S., & Bowman, G. D. (2006). Of friends and family: How do peers affect the development of intergenerational influences? *Advances in Consumer Research, 33*, 536–542.

Mortimer, J. T., Staff, J., & Oesterle, S. (2003). Adolescent work and the early socioeconomic career. In *Handbook of the life course* (pp. 437–459). Springer.

Moschis, G. P. (1985). The role of family communication in consumer socialization of children and adolescents. *Journal of Consumer Research, 11*(4), 898–913.

Nidar, S. R., & Bestari, S. (2012). Personal financial literacy among university students (case study at Padjadjaran University students, Bandung, Indonesia). *World Journal of Sport Sciences, 2*(4), 162–171.

Norvilitis, J. M., & MacLean, M. G. (2010). The role of parents in college students' financial behaviors and attitudes. *Journal of Economic Psychology, 31*(1), 55–63.

Novitasari, D., Juliana, J., Asbari, M., & Purwanto, A. (2021). The effect of financial literacy, parents' social economic and student lifestyle on students personal financial management. *Economic Education Analysis Journal, 10*(3), 522–531.

Ridhayani, F., & Johan, I. R. (2020). The influence of financial literacy and reference group toward consumptive behavior across senior high school students. *Journal of Consumer Sciences, 5*(1), 29–45.

Roy Morgan Research. (2003). *ANZ survey of adult financial literacy in Australia.* www.financialliteracy.gov.au/media/465156/anz-survey-of-adult-financial-literacy-2003.pdf. Accessed on May 16, 2008.

Sachitra, K. M. V., & Bandara, U. (2017). Measuring the academic self-efficacy of undergraduates: The role of gender and academic year experience. *World Academy of Science, Engineering and Technology, 11*(11), 2320–2325.

Sachitra, K. M. V., & Wijesinghe, D. (2018). What determine money management behaviour of undergraduates an examination in an emerging economy. *Journal of Education, Society and Behavioural Science, 26*(4), 1–14.

Sachitra, V., Wijesinghe, D., & Gunasena, W. (2019). *Exploring undergraduates' money-management life: Insight from an emerging economy.* Young Consumers.

Shim, S., Barber, B. L., Card, N. A., Xiao, J. J., & Serido, J. (2010). Financial socialization of first-year college students: The roles of parents, work, and education. *Journal of Youth and Adolescence, 39*(12), 1457–1470.

Shim, S., Serido, J., Tang, C., & Card, N. (2015). Socialization processes and pathways to healthy financial development for emerging young adults. *Journal of Applied Developmental Psychology, 38*, 29–38.

Shim, S., Xiao, J. J., Barber, B. L., & Lyons, A. C. (2009). Pathways to life success: A conceptual model of financial well-being for young adults. *Journal of Applied Developmental Psychology, 30*(6), 708–723.

Simon, H. A. (1986). Rationality in psychology and economics. *Journal of Business, 59*(4), 209–224.

Singh, S., McKeown, W., Myers, P., & Shelly, M. (2005). *Literature review on personal credit and debt: Families at risk deciding on personal debt.* RMIT University. http://mams.rmit.edu.au/fjefpb2zv2q7.pdf. Accessed on September 8, 2016.

Solis, O., & Durband, D. B. (2015). Financial support and its impact on undergraduate student financial satisfaction. *College Student Journal, 49*(1), 93–105.

Sundarasen, S. D. D., & Rahman, M. S. (2017). Attitude towards money: Mediation to money management. *Academy of Accounting and Financial Studies Journal, 21*(1), 80–96.

Tang, T. L. P. (1995). The development of a short money ethic scale: Attitudes toward money and pay satisfaction revisited. *Personality and Individual Differences, 19*(6), 809–816.

Tang, T. L. P., Sutarso, T., Akande, A., Allen, M. W., Alzubaidi, A. S., Ansari, M. A., … Vlerick, P. (2006). The love of money and pay level satisfaction: Measurement and functional equivalence in 29 geopolitical entities around the world. *Management and Organization Review, 2*(3), 423–452.

Van Raaij, W. F. (2016). *Understanding consumer financial behavior: Money management in an age of financial illiteracy.* Springer.

Xiao, J. J., Shim, S., Barber, B., & Lyons, A. (2007). *Academic success and well-being of college students: Financial behaviours matter, take charge America institute for consumer financial education and research.* The University of Arizona. www.cefe.illinois.edu/research/reports/Academic%20Success%20and%20WellBeing%20of%20College%20Students_112007.pdf. Accessed on May 17, 2022.

Xiao, J. J., Tang, C., & Shim, S. (2008). Acting for happiness: Financial behaviour and life satisfaction of college students. *Social Indicators Research, 92*(1), 53–68.

Yamauchi, K. T., & Templer, D. J. (1982). The development of a money attitude scale. *Journal of Personality Assessment, 46*(5), 522–528.

Zhang, J., & Kemp, S. (2009). The relationships between student debt and motivation, happiness, and academic achievement. *New Zealand Journal of Psychology, 38*(2), 24–29.

Zhao, H., & Zhang, L. (2020). Talking money at home: The value of family financial socialization. *International Journal of Bank Marketing, 38*(7).

Zulfaris, M. D., Mustafa, H., Mahussin, N., Alam, M. K., & Daud, Z. M. (2020). Students and money management behavior of a Malaysian public university. *The Journal of Asian Finance, Economics and Business, 7*(3), 245–251.

Chapter 6

Life Insurance Industry in India: The Inside Story

Srishti Nagarajan and Ekta Duggal

University of Delhi, India

Abstract

The present study aims to provide an overview of the life insurance industry in India and scrutinise various dimensions impacting life insurance uptake in accordance with the views of the management representatives. An exploratory study was assumed by conducting in-depth face-to-face/telephonic interviews with six employees and one agent affiliated to the most prominent life insurance companies operating in India. The interviews focused on operation of life insurance companies in general, their work culture, approach towards individuals/customers, steps taken to attract and retain their human capital (agents), the overall impact of reforms on the life insurance industry and their tactics which make them unique in the market. The study observed that life insurance uptake in India is discernibly affected by an individual's financial knowledge, needs and the level of trust they have on the company apart from brand of the life insurance company and grievance redressal system. It was also found that reforms (Foreign Direct Investment (FDI) Policy, entry of private players) did bring about a difference in work culture, improved employment opportunities and increased the reach of the insurance industry in the country. The study highlights dimensions that life insurance companies constantly work/need to work upon to remain at the zenith of success, broadens the horizons of the life insurance industry in an emerging nation like India as it is one of the few studies to have probed the management's outlook of the Indian life insurance industry and holds scope for future theoretical investigation and development of a comprehensive model as well.

Keywords: Life insurance; management; trust; brand; financial literacy; need; insurance uptake

Modeling Economic Growth in Contemporary India, 81–108
Copyright © 2024 Srishti Nagarajan and Ekta Duggal
Published under exclusive licence by Emerald Publishing Limited
doi:10.1108/978-1-80382-751-320241006

1. Introduction

Plato once said –

"Nothing in the affairs of men is worthy of great anxiety".

However, one cannot be completely oblivious to the uncertainty that surrounds the everyday life. The unpredictable happenings like death, fire, natural calamities, accidents, etc. nevertheless make an individual anxious and sometimes scared as well. These situations necessitate some form of risk cover/corpus fund to rely upon which is what is provided by modern day insurance. The central idea of insurance is to combine resources and share the risk/losses suffered by a few due to some unfortunate events among all those subjected to such events (Insurance Institute of India, 2016). The lack of such facility is most likely to put a lot of pressure on individuals to deal with serious health ailments, accidents and deaths which can exhaust them both emotionally and financially. Insurance helps individuals plan their lives better by making provision for various risks that may arise in the future. Thinking and providing for risk related to property/goods is much easier than doing the same for living beings. The mere thought of losing a loved one makes people cringe and thus life insurance may not be one of the most sought-after products. Nevertheless, variety of life insurance products are available with a few being able to catch the imagination of people.

In 2022, the global insurance demand is forecasted to grow at 3.9%; India ranked 11th in the top 20 global insurance markets (ranked by premium volume) as on 2020 and its global market share stood at 1.7% (Swiss Re Institute, 2021). Insurance penetration in India was 4.2% in 2020 with 3.2% for life insurance and 1% for non-life insurance (Swiss Re Institute, 2021). In India, the total insurance density was US $78 with US $59 for life insurance and US $19 for non-life insurance business (Swiss Re Institute, 2021). The increase in penetration levels is an encouraging sign as it shows the improvement in risk awareness levels and knowledge about insurance protection among people.

The insurance industry deals very closely with individuals/customers and hence provides a fertile ground for investigation into its various aspects. Insurance business to a great extent relies on agents who sell policies of various insurers to the individuals/customers. The role of the agents thus becomes extremely crucial for insurers to further their clientele. Agents are required to keep talking to individuals/customers in order to identify their needs and establish a unique link with the individuals/customers to be able to provide them with the right type of policy that best matches their needs/requirements (Chee & Sin, 2020). However, there are some individuals who also purchase policies due to a sense of responsibility towards their immediate family and dependants. Post the pandemic, people in general have become more self-conscious which is why it is no surprise that many are keen to take term plans especially the well-educated who have high sense of responsibility. This is in sync with findings of Deb et al. (2021) wherein a few respondents who were young preferred term plans rather than traditional plans and ULIPs as they considered life insurance as a tool purely for protection.

Although agents are inarguably the most significant element of the insurance industry, its distribution channel is also strengthened by the banks which provide the necessary infrastructure and clientele base for the sale of insurer's policies. The ability of banks to push policies to individuals is thus humongous. This is precisely the reason why banks have emerged as a feasible distribution channel for various insurance companies to sell their policies to the clients of the banks. The sheer reach of the banks makes them a viable distribution channel. Selling of insurance products through banks is essentially termed as 'Bancassurance'; the banks and insurance companies tie up wherein the banks agree to sell the attached insurance company's various products to their huge clientele (The Economics Times, 2022). Many private life insurers operating in India have used Bancassurance as their route for distribution of insurance products, which has accelerated their penetration in the market (Sinha, 2005). The close link between insurance and banking cannot be denied especially because of the reach of a bank's branches to the nook and corner of the country, making it a desirable mechanism for distribution of insurance.

A robust, well-structured and functioning insurance industry is important as it helps individuals and businesses minimise their risk by providing appropriate financial cover and aids in the growth and development of the economy. Thus, a competitive insurance industry with the participation of private and public sector would aid in providing cost-effective policies to the ultimate consumer (Skipper, 1997). It is often seen how the government is burdened with various welfare objectives, thus reiterating the significance of privately provided insurance (Washid & Kazmi, 2000). The private life insurance companies broadened the horizons of the life insurance market, thanks to the reforms; and also brought in the much-needed competition and efficiency (Krishnamurthy et al., 2005) which are essential for growth and development of the industry.

The insurance industry in India has long been protected due to the government rules and regulations. The inability of private insurance companies to make strong inroads can largely be attributed to the protected nature of the industry and the stringent FDI rules which restricted foreign participation in the industry, curbing it at 26% initially. In the life insurance industry, it was particularly difficult for the private players to fight the life insurance giant – LIC (Life Insurance Corporation of India). However, when LIC was the sole life insurance provider prior to the reforms, the industry suffered from lack of competition and/ or low penetration levels (Rajendran & Natarajan, 2009; Sinha, 2005), while the private players post reforms, brought in the much-required variety in their product offerings (Rastogi & Sarkar, 2007) which yielded better results in terms of insurance penetration.

The insurance industry's growth trajectory can be visualised on a continuum as it has moved from being a highly regulated industry to a less regulated one, thanks to the reforms which set the industry onto the path of growth. The extant literature has effectively documented this journey of insurance industry. Literature has abundance of studies on individuals/consumers of insurance services, however there are little studies on the management's perspective on insurance services. Further, Sinha and Jain (2014) point out that the role of top management in Indian life insurance industry has received little thought in the literature. This makes it even more necessary to bring their perspective to the forefront. Through our study, we aim to shed some light on the management's perspective on India's life insurance industry as it would prove to be very beneficial for policymakers and the marketers alike.

The present study is divided into six sections. Section 2 discusses the Background followed by Section 3 which provides the Methodology adopted in the study. Section 4 contains the Analysis and Discussion while Section 5 puts forth the Implications of the study. Section 6 details the Concluding remarks.

2. Background

In India, insurance has deep origins as writings of Manu (Manusmrithi), Yagnavalkya (Dharmasastra) and Kautilya (Arthasastra) talk about insurance as a means of putting together resources which can be used when calamities like fire, floods, epidemics, famine, etc. strike (IRDAI, 2020). The first insurance company to be set up in India was the Oriental Life Insurance Company Limited (an English Company) in Calcutta in 1818 (which however failed in 1834) and was trailed by Bombay Assurance Company in 1823 and the Madras Equitable Life Insurance Society in 1829 (IRDAI, 2020; Sinha, 2005). It was only in the early 1900s, when the focus was shifted to the Indian insurance companies with the enactment of Indian Life Assurance Companies Act and Provident Fund Act in 1912 to regulate the life insurance business while in 1928 the enactment of Indian Insurance Companies Act took place which empowered the government to collect statistical data about life and non-life insurance business along with provident insurance societies (Insurance Institute of India, 2016; IRDAI, 2020).

Though the insurance sector continued its growth, the need for reforms was felt, owing to improvements needed in service provided to customers, optimal insurance coverage and allocation of resources, innovation in the products offered to cater to the everchanging needs of customers and to portray insurance as a financial instrument to cover risks and not just as a mere instrument for claiming tax exemption (Rastogi & Sarkar, 2007). The reforms carried out in 2000, opened the gates for private sector in the industry. Almost all domestic private companies operating in India have a joint venture with a foreign partner onboard. With regulations in place for private players to enter the insurance markets, these insurance companies had to first address questions relating to timing of entry in the markets, the joint venture partners desired, services they inclined to offer, market segments to focus on, etc. (Krishnamurthy et al., 2005). The Indian partners majorly benefitted from the financial and technical expertise that was provided by their foreign partners. Through the joint collaboration, the foreign players too benefitted through access to new and unexplored market which aided their expansion activities. The stringent regulation however also discouraged many global reinsurers from entering the Indian market directly (Sinha, 2005).

The arrival of new players was a game changer for the insurance industry which had previously suffered from little penetration and inefficient operations.

The overall evolution of the Indian Insurance industry can be summarised in the three phases of Pre-Nationalisation, Nationalisation and Privatisation as shown in Fig. 6.1.

Out of the 24 life insurers operating in the Indian insurance market presently, LIC is the only public sector company along with Exide Life Insurance Co. Ltd., Kotak Mahindra Life Insurance Co. Ltd. and Sahara India Life Insurance Co. Ltd. from the private sector which are 100% domestic companies (IRDAI, 2021). All the rest 20 private life insurers have foreign investment as they are mostly joint ventures with a foreign company. The private players along with their foreign counterparts have helped the industry grow from strength to strength. While the new companies battled their initial hiccups, LIC too started rallying for the imminent competition. Ever since, the life insurance industry has witnessed better growth, increased market reach and has made considerable progress with respect

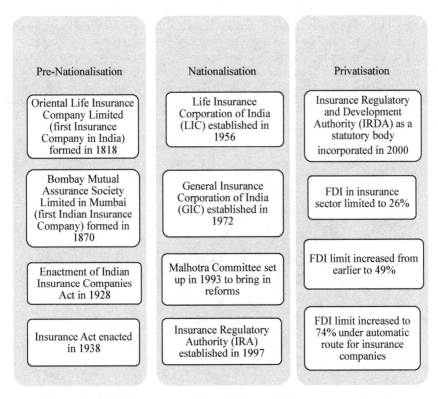

Fig. 6.1.   The Evolution of Insurance Industry in India. *Source:*
Author Compilation from DPIIT (2020, 2021); IRDAI (2020); Insurance
Institute of India (2016); Krishnamurthy et al. (2005)

to insurance penetration and density which are very crucial especially for emerging nations like India.

The trust of people on LIC (public sector life insurer in India) is still strong going by the number of new individual policies issued by the life insurers in 2020–2021 as represented in Chart 6.1.

The market share of LIC has definitely reduced with the entry of private players. However, the trust on LIC has not completely faltered. It still has a huge grip in the life insurance business in India as reiterated in the study by Chakraborty (2017). The ability of LIC to evolve with the changing times has hugely benefitted the company as it still enjoys a significant market share despite the tough competition from private life insurers.

The private players after initial teething problems seem to have created a space for themselves. The benefit of this highly competitive market inarguably accrues to the individual/customer as they now have an array of products and services to choose from (Skipper, 1997). The life insurance industry is considered unique from the other financial services as the customers are associated with the company for the long haul usually spanning over their lifetime (Krishnamurthy et al., 2005). Hence, providing quality service, ensuring cost-effective policies become extremely important for insurance companies to retain their customer base.

The life insurance companies are required to constantly evolve with the dynamic environment and aim for long-term relationship with their customers to stay profitable in their business. With economies around the world slowly bouncing back to business, the insurance industry is likely to witness an upward

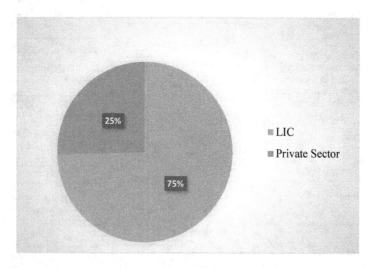

Chart 6.1.   Percentage of New Individual Policies Issued by Life Insurers in 2020–2021. *Source:* Adapted from IRDAI (2021). *Note:* Figures are rounded off (74.57% and 25.43% respectively).

growth, in particular the life insurance industry is bound to benefit from the increased risk awareness among individuals owing to a lot of factors including the pandemic. The life insurance companies hence need to focus on different means by which they can retain and proliferate their market share.

3. Methodology

The primary motive behind the study was to gain insights into the working of the life insurance companies. The idea was to comprehend the life insurance industry from 'the other side of the table' i.e. from the management's perspective as they deal with the individuals/customers on a day-to-day basis. The outlook of management representatives about the life insurance industry, products sold, agent training, customer's apprehensions, etc. are likely to illustrate a thorough and novel understanding of the life insurance industry. To achieve this objective, an exploratory study (Ghauri & Grønhaug, 2005; Zikmund, 2000) was assumed by undertaking in-depth qualitative telephonic/face-to-face interviews of seven employees/agents representing the management in order to have better understanding of the life insurance industry in India.

Prior permission was obtained from the interviewees along with the suitable time for the interview. The background of the researcher as well as the study was explained to interviewees, post which the interviews were conducted.

Table 6.1 provides the credentials of the interviewees and the life insurance companies included in the present study. There were five private and domestic life insurance companies with foreign capital and one public and domestic life insurance company along with an agent belonging to the sole public life insurance company. While the public life insurer is decades old, the private life insurers also go a long way as few Indian partners have decades old history but are in the life insurance business under joint-venture with foreign partners. The interviewees of the present study varied in their designation from Business Associate to Regional Manager providing the perfect mix of knowledge and experience. The life insurance companies included in the study together account for 82.93% market share based on first year premium for the period ended 28th February, 2022 (IRDAI, 2022).

The management's view of the life insurance industry, its working, business environment, etc. are of great use to analyse opportunities and threats surrounding this sector. Some specific open-ended questions were utilised to obtain the information relevant for the study. The questions that were asked covered a vast range of topics such as rules and regulations governing the insurance industry, the competition levels due to opening up of the industry, impact of foreign participants, tactics of insurance companies, individual/customer preferences of products, their apprehensions, financial literacy, the company's grievance redressal system and the role of IRDAI. The data was analysed by using Grounded Theory approach (Glaser, 1978; Glaser & Strauss, 1967; Strauss & Corbin, 1998) which included the iterative process of reading the interviews repeatedly in order to extract the major dimensions and themes. The data was

Table 6.1. Credentials of the Interviewees.

S. No. of Interviewee	1	2	3	4	5	6	7
Company/ Agent	A	B	C	D	E	F	Agent
Type of company	Public life insurance company	Private life insurance company	Private life insurance company	Private life insurance company	Private life insurance company	Private life insurance company	Public life insurance company
Ownership of company	Domestic life insurance company	Domestic life insurance company with foreign capital	Domestic life insurance company with foreign capital	Domestic life insurance company with foreign capital	Domestic life insurance company with foreign capital	Domestic life insurance company with foreign capital	Domestic life insurance company
Company's history	More than 65 years	More than 20 years	More than 20 years	More than 20 years	More than 20 years	More than 20 years	More than 65 years
Designation of the interviewee	Assistant Branch Manager	Business Associate	Regional Manager	Ex Area Manager	Area Manager	Regional Head	Agent
Gender of the interviewee	Male	Female	Male	Male	Male	Male	Female

further probed to identify linkages of the identified dimensions with life insurance uptake among individuals/consumers.

4. Analysis and Discussion

The life insurance industry in India has become highly competitive over the decades. The opening up of the insurance sector in 2000 with the formation of Insurance Regulatory Development Authority (IRDA) aided the private companies enter the insurance market. Insurance being a financial service plays a great role in the development of the economy and the reforms and changes in policies aided the process of increasing the reach, effectiveness and competitiveness in the industry (Krishnamurthy et al., 2005). In particular, the life insurance industry has been on an interesting journey as it has moved past the times of Life Insurance Corporation of India (LIC) being the public and only player in the market to the times of 23 other private life insurance companies emerging as new challengers.

The journey of the life insurance industry has been very long. However, the effective progress of private life insurers and increased insurance penetration is testimony of the fact that with reforms at the appropriate time, any industry can prosper and simultaneously ensure growth of the economy as well. The rules and regulations governing the insurance industry initially added to the entry barriers making it difficult for new companies to enter the market. While rules and regulations governing the insurance industry in India have seen reforms and a lot of amendments from time-to-time, the history of insurance in India at a glance is given in Table 6.2.

Key findings from the interviews

The interviewees while providing an overview of the life insurance industry talked about the difficulty of entry for private insurers and emphasised on the shortcomings of the industry prior to the reforms. Of the *management representatives* interviewed, a few pointed towards the fact that despite being the only player in life business for decades together, LIC couldn't increase insurance penetration levels and suggested it to be one of LIC's failure as they opined that insurance penetration in India increased significantly post the entry of private players in the market. They firmly believe that people are now more open to the idea of procuring life insurance from private insurers though a few challenges do remain. A few excerpts from the interview are as follows:

The *management representative of Company B* said:

> ...... initially people in the local areas wanted LIC, so we had to convince them by saying how you prefer private schools for your children, similarly we are private life insurers who are also governed by the same IRDAI that governs LIC as well. As customer service in private is better, why do you want to go to public only? For 8–10 years now people don't want LIC.

Table 6.2. Timeline: Evolution and Development of Insurance Industry in India.

Phase	Year	Event
I	1818	The formation of Oriental Life Insurance Company limited (first insurance company in India)
	1829	Madras Equitable Life Insurance Society transacting life insurance business in Madras Presidency
	1870	Passing of British Insurance Act; The setting up of Bombay Mutual Assurance Society Limited in Mumbai (first Indian insurance company)
	1897	The setting up of Empire of India insurance company in the Bombay Residency
	1912	Enactment of Indian Life Assurance Companies Act and Provident Fund Act (to regulate the life insurance business)
	1928	Enactment of Indian Insurance Companies Act (enabled the government to collect statistical data about life and non-life insurance business along with provident insurance societies)
	1938	Insurance Act enacted (to regulate the insurance companies)
II	1956	Nationalisation of life insurance sector and establishment of Life Insurance Corporation of India (LIC)
	1972	Enactment of General Insurance Business Nationalisation Act and establishment of General Insurance Corporation of India (GIC)
	1993	Setting up of Malhotra Committee (to make the insurance sector competitive and bring in reforms)
	1994	Report submitted by the committee under the chairmanship of R. N. Malhotra
	1997	Insurance Regulatory Authority (IRA) established
III	1999	The passing of Insurance Regulatory and Development Act and formation of Insurance Regulatory and Development Authority (IRDA) (as an autonomous body to regulate the insurance industry)
	2000	Incorporation of Insurance Regulatory and Development Authority (IRDA) as a statutory body (for regulating the insurance industry- life, non-life, health)
	2000	Foreign companies allowed ownership of up to 26% (FDI in insurance sector limited to 26%)
	2000	Restructuring of subsidiaries of General Insurance Corporation of India (GIC) as independent companies and conversion of GIC as the only national re-insurer of the country

Table 6.2. *(Continued)*

Phase	Year	Event
IV	2014	Renaming of Insurance Regulatory and Development Authority (IRDA) as Insurance Regulatory and Development Authority of India (IRDAI)
	2015	Amendment of Insurance Act (addition of provisions regarding definition and formation of insurance companies in India)
	2015	Foreign companies allowed ownership of up to 49% (FDI limit increased from earlier 26%)
	2021	Increase in the FDI limit under automatic route for insurance companies to 74% (from 49%) and 100% for insurance intermediaries under automatic route

Source: Author Compilation from DPIIT (2020, 2021); IRDAI (2020); Insurance Institute of India (2016); Krishnamurthy et al. (2005).

Another *management representative belonging to Company C* said:

> ...... challenges are still there as LIC is like TATA Salt, for LIC all will say that first; it was difficult to bring in private life insurance due to the earlier government rules and regulations.

The interviewees provided a lot of insight into the life insurance industry. With the entry of private players, the market structure did see some changes and the various dimensions which emerged after repeated analysis of the interviews are presented for discussion below.

4.1 Agents: The Core/Base of Life Insurance Industry

Life insurance may not be the most pursued product, which makes the job of the agent selling it that much more complex as they are required to be very persuasive and patient with their customers to be able to sell them the product (Krishnamurthy et al., 2005). In this background, the role of an agent selling life insurance policies becomes very crucial.

The agents are trained by insurance companies after they pass the IRDAI exam and get their licence. The agents can shift across insurance companies, however training in each company is given depending upon the personnel's requirement. As all the products sold are approved by IRDAI and are very similar, the approach of the agent towards individuals/customers is of huge importance. The *management representative of Company E* said that whenever a new agent comes, he/she is guided on what to stress about to the individuals/customers.

The *management representative of Company F* feels that a lot of time is spent and effort is made in training the agents as they are the core/base of the life insurance industry. He added:

> .....it's difficult to get people on board, hence agents are taught the 'art of selling' through various modules and most importantly through 'experience'.

The *management representative of Company A* talked about internal product training given to the agents in his company through 'Agent Managers' or 'Development Officers' who look after the appointment, training, monitoring, etc. of agents. A lot of training is 'on the field' based on individual/customer dealings. The agent managers/development officers earn incentives that are linked to their performance which is in-turn related to the performance of the agents. This process is represented in Fig. 6.2.

Interviewee 2 elaborated on how 4–5 days (earlier 7) of training is given to the agents wherein the focus is on quality and her company also provides a 'Morning Huddle' session of an hour to discuss about old and new products, give training, tips, etc.

Saha and Dutta (2019) in their study found that largely customers of the Indian life insurance industry while purchasing a new insurance policy preferred insurance agents further pointing to the importance of agents in ensuring life insurance uptake.

4.2 Need Identification/Need Analysis Is the Key

The approach that agents take to address the concerns of individuals and identify the needs of the customers is paramount for the success of the company. It is imperative for agents to get into the psyche of the individuals to be able to sell the right product for the appropriate time especially when they will be more willing to buy the policies/products that matches their requirements. Most of the *management representatives* were of the view that 'Need Identification/Analysis' of individuals/customers is important as it holds the key to success. *Interviewee 5* said:

Fig. 6.2.   Agent Training Process. *Source:* In-depth Interview, Interviewee 1.

.... Need Analysis of the individuals/customers is of the essence for which their full background including details about their income, profession, children, timing of requirement of money, etc. is to be ascertained.....humein dekhna hai kahan pe banda toot jaega. (We need to see where the person breaks down).

As narrated by *Interviewee 6*, the main job is to understand the individual/customer's investment portfolio and identify the gaps in order to pitch in the right product to them. The major problem is that the needs of individuals/customers are not properly analysed and they are often directly approached by agents with the products; this becomes a non-starter and the individual/customer says '........theek hai, main batata hoon' (Ok. I will let you know) which is a sophisticated way of saying- '... .insurance nahi chahiye' (No need of insurance) he adds.

Individual needs are very distinct and profound understanding of the same is a necessary condition for the agents to be able to sell them their products. Customised insurance products are considered as important by consumers and they want those products that complement their specific needs (Suneja & Sharma, 2009). The more people they meet, the more the agents absorb through on-the-field learning. Also, working for years together gives them the required experience to understand the individual's profile, identify the gaps in their investment portfolio, analyse their needs and ultimately fit in the appropriate product that best suits their requirements. Fig. 6.3. sums up the importance of need identification and analysis for selling life insurance.

4.2.1 Apprehensions of Individuals/Customers

While interacting with people, the agents usually stumble upon things that individuals/customers are apprehensive or hesitant about.

Interviewee 2 detailed how some people are apprehensive about non-guaranteed plans as misselling is possible. To which *Interviewee 5* added that misselling of policies is a reality wherein often clear picture about the returns is not shown. He also pointed out the scepticism that individuals/customers have

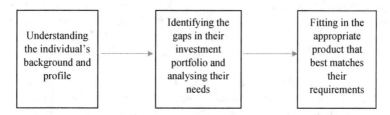

Fig. 6.3.   Need Analysis/Identification of Individuals/Customers.
Source: In-depth Interviews.

about private life insurance companies which impede them from purchasing long-term policies from them as they are worried that the company may go bust or run away with their money.

Interviewee 6 also had a similar response and said that first and foremost people are worried about the safety and security of their money and are anxious that the company may run away with their money. He further suggested that people mustn't be directly approached out of desperation as the agent's efforts may go in vain. He suggested:

> ......we must first understand what people want and fit the product accordingly so that the individual/customer feels that this is a product 'tailor-made' just for him/her. This is how people will develop a trust on the life insurance company.

Individuals have different financial requirements which they wish to fulfil through various financial instruments in the market. When it comes to life insurance, there are all kinds of people as some may depend entirely on the agent for selecting the policy while some may select policies based on referrals, advise of friends, colleagues, etc. Some purchase life insurance for tax savings (Chadha & Kapoor, 2008), others purchase term plans (pure insurance) (Deb et al., 2021), yet others purchase endowment plans (for marriage, education) and some to create a corpus for annuity. A few people also purchase policies based on the return they earn. Comprehending the needs and requirement of individuals/customers is thus very imperative for a life insurance company to succeed.

4.2.2 Product Range

When probed about the kind of products sold, most of the interviewees believed, different kinds of products are sold that most appeals to people. Annuities, ULIPS, Traditional Plans are all equally popular. Even, Term Plans have become popular post the pandemic. The policies taken vary strictly according to the needs of individuals. Employees and business class invest for taxation purpose, service class usually invests for education, pension, corpus fund, while big industries take up policies for employees as revealed by various interviewees in their interviews.

Interviewees 1, 5 and 6 compared pure life insurance to vehicle insurance. *Interviewees 1* and *5* both opined that in the absence of vehicle insurance there is a deterrence of Challan by the police. *Interviewee 5* said:

> .... darr hai ki police pakad legi (There is fear of being caught by the police). Thus, people buy vehicle insurance whether or not they get any return on it. However, when it comes to life insurance, there is no such compulsion.

Interviewee 1 added that lack of compulsion leads to the scenario of expectation of some return on the insurance policies as people feel they are investing in it and paying premiums, hence there must be some return on it as well.

In India, preference is more for investment mixed plans/products feels *Interviewee 6*. He further adds that endowment plans particularly the non-participating ones are the 'flavour of the town' which sell like hot cake as they comprise of guaranteed plans.

Only after thorough understanding and analysis of the individual's background/profile and identification of financial requirements are the agents of various life insurers able to sell their policies to prospective individuals/customers. Fig. 6.4 chalks out the policies that individuals are likely to take based on their educational profile and financial requirements as per the interviewees.

4.3 The Building Blocks for Success Among Individuals/Customers

Insurance is a service offering products that are not inimitable and hence the scope of differentiation gets curbed pushing the focus on innovation, good quality service delivery, etc. to ensure competitive advantage in this market (Krishnamurthy et al., 2005). The life insurance industry involves sale of products

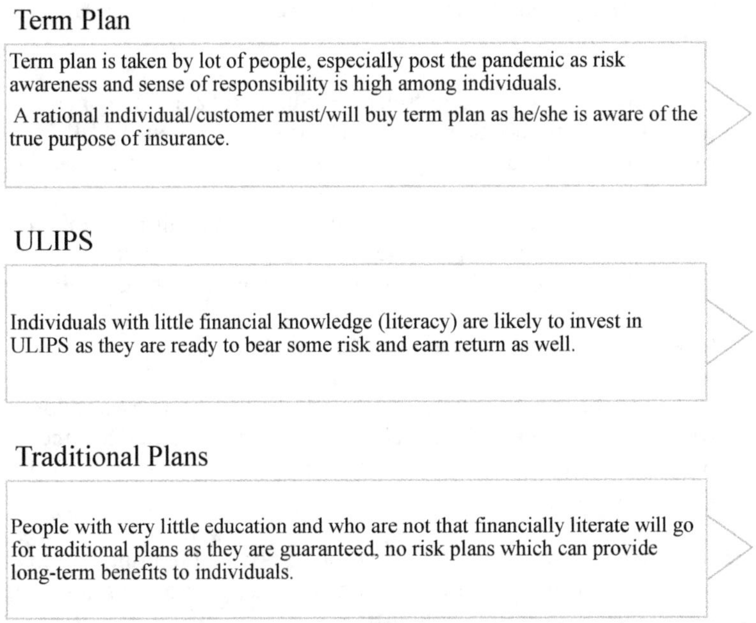

Term Plan

> Term plan is taken by lot of people, especially post the pandemic as risk awareness and sense of responsibility is high among individuals.
>
> A rational individual/customer must/will buy term plan as he/she is aware of the true purpose of insurance.

ULIPS

> Individuals with little financial knowledge (literacy) are likely to invest in ULIPS as they are ready to bear some risk and earn return as well.

Traditional Plans

> People with very little education and who are not that financially literate will go for traditional plans as they are guaranteed, no risk plans which can provide long-term benefits to individuals.

Fig. 6.4.   Life Insurance Uptake and Individual's/Customer's Profile.
Source: In-depth Interview, Interviewee 5.

(policies) which are very similar across companies. The main differentiator among companies is thus not the product alone but also the kind of service provided by them to individuals/customers. The only way the Life Insurers are able to hold on to their share and stay profitable in this business is through ensuring 'trust' and 'brand' which are the two pillars of competitive edge with these companies as explained by a few interviewees.

4.3.1 Trust

Trust plays an important role in the success of any company operating in any domain. While 'trust' has been an area of interest by researchers in many disciplines, it's difficult to establish its precise meaning (Tyler & Stanley, 2007). Trust is developed through correspondence between people in real ways (Panigrahi et al., 2018). Ennew and Sekhon (2007) suggest consumer's trust in an organisation may be cognitive (centred around the idea of reliability and dependability) or affective (centred around the idea of being mindful of the customer's best interests). Trust is the long-term association that a firm builds with its customers and is the primary component for owning of life insurance (Chee & Sin, 2020). Trust is one key factor that shapes an individual's intention to purchase life insurance (Dragos et al., 2020; Masud et al., 2021). Thus, trust on an organisation by individuals/customers is paramount for their success.

An *Interviewee* recalled, how in the interior regions of Haryana and UP, private life insurers would say:

> ...... LIC karane aaye hain Reliance/Sahara ki (We have come to give LIC of Reliance/Sahara) as LIC was synonymous to BIMA (insurance) in the minds of people living in those regions.

This speaks volumes about the trust people had and still have on LIC. The insurance companies strive to gain the trust of people as trust of individuals/customers on the company alone, ensures a long-lasting relationship between them.

Interviewee 6 hit the nail on the wood directly and said:

> ....service we give determines what kind of relationship we develop with our customers; if we build trust, then for years together people will remain connected to us. This is how insurance business works.

The *management representatives* of two other private life insurers were of the opinion that as product differentiation isn't possible, trust and branding are the two key points for success in this industry.

This is also reiterated in the study by Panigrahi et al. (2018) who found service quality factors like reliability and problem-solving skills of insurance agents to be able to increase customer trust; further suggesting, customer trust to be mediating the relationship between service quality factors and purchase intention of life insurance products. Trust in service provider (life insurer) leads to the individual/customer engaging with them (Agyei et al., 2020). Trust of individuals/customers on the agents/insurance companies thus becomes a pre-requisite for success and profitability of the company.

4.3.2 Brand

While trust is one essential pillar of competitive edge, the other important pillar is the Brand that the insurance companies are able to create through their style of working, practices, policies, products, positioning, etc. Branding is essentially concerned with perception and there is increased significance of branding in the competitive financial services market (Chadha & Kapoor, 2008). Yadav and Jain (2014) suggest that brand is a multifaceted programme with the potential to carve out a distinct position for the company in the market and is representative of an emotional and logical bond that the company shares with all interested parties including the individual/customer. Brand is thus the greatest tool through which the company can create, communicate and share anything and everything about itself with the target audience.

Sooner or later, the various stakeholders of the company begin to identify it through the brand that it builds as the idea of that brand resonates with them. This is very crucial in any industry wherein companies face aggressive competition. In services sector, specifically in the life insurance industry, the brand that the companies build are the foundations of their sustainability in the long-run. Due to the opening up of the industry, the life insurers are required to concentrate on individual/customer's needs, inclinations and brand perceptions (Chadha & Kapoor, 2008). A few interviewees threw their weight behind the importance of brand that their organisations have built with grit and sweat.

Interviewee 5 opined that during the initial years of opening up of the industry, all Indian private players required the assistance of well-established, highly reputed foreign companies to enter and sustain in the domestic life insurance market. The brand that the foreign partners had created for their respective companies all over the world was likely to aid their entry and growth in the Indian markets as well.

Similarly, the Indian players too encashed on their own brand as explained by *Interviewee 2* in her interview. She explained how individuals/customers were taken into confidence by talking about the Indian company, its legacy, years of dominance, its nationality (Indian company), having higher stake in the joint-venture and about the brand that it is to shake-off the apprehensions of people regarding private life insurance company.

The views expressed by the interviewees are in line with the literature as Wibowo and Djumarno (2019) in their study found image of the brand had a significantly positive impact on quality perceptions of insurance products. Similarly, Suneja and Sharma (2009) while reviewing factors influencing choice of a life insurance company found that customers of private and public insurers considered Image of company to be very important which included Brand of company.

4.3.3 Internal Process

While Trust and Brand are the two main pillars of competition in life insurance business, there is another pillar which ensures that these two pillars grow strong. The internal processes and working of life insurance companies are equally important as they help the company gain the trust of individuals/customers and ultimately build the brand for their long-term relationship and survival.

Interviewee 6 believed that Trust and Brand are two of the biggest assets of his company which enables them to have an edge over the other players. He opined:

> .... the internal processes are so strong and robust that it aids in building trust among people and ultimately the brand; they are all inter-linked as all three pillars are equally important.

Thus, the trinity of trust, brand and internal processes ensure a sustainable and profitable profile for the life insurance companies in the long run as depicted in Fig. 6.5.

4.4 Reforms, Foreign Participation and the Change in Value System

The opening up of the industry allowed the entry of foreign firms into the country, which has benefitted the Indian insurance market as well. The work culture has also seen some change owing to the increase in the level of competition as summarised by a few interviewees. Foreign participation in the insurance industry leads to increased competition which encourages innovative products, quality in services, choice and value for individuals/customers (Skipper, 1997).

Interviewee 1 feels that foreign participation improved the working environment in the industry for the better as he feels that his company has become more 'customer oriented' in its approach. Even branch managers at times took calls to clear queries of customers. The reforms, thus ensured a working environment that was conducive for individuals/customers.

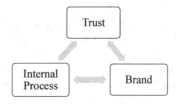

Fig. 6.5.   The Three Pillars of Success in the Insurance Business.
Source: In-depth Interview, Interviewee 6.

Interviewee 2 thinks that FDI policy per se doesn't directly bear any effects on the functioning of the company as the major stake is with the Indian Company which has always stressed on quality of work that has only increased over a period of time.

Interviewee 3 believes that work culture wasn't majorly impacted as the joint-venture set up between Indian and foreign life insurers was mandated by the rules and regulations governing the insurance industry and that the foreign partners usually brought in the much-needed investment while the work was done according to the practices of their Indian counterparts. Then again, he feels that with the foreign participation, mainly came increased job opportunities which boosted the employment levels of labour rich India and instilled better work culture in the industry as a whole.

Interviewee 5 feels that the changes in FDI policies from time to time have allowed many foreign companies to enter the market.

Interviewee 6 opined that life insurance has always been a capital-intensive business which involves huge capital expenditure in the initial 10–12 years before breaking-even and becoming profitable; the foreign partners thus brought in the much-needed 'capital' along with the 'expertise' required to run the insurance business. He further pointed out how over the years even foreign firms wanted increased stake in the insurance companies to be able to run the business the way they want. The low FDI limits forced the foreign firms to hold only minority stake which also hindered their expansion activities. With the increased FDI limits, the exit options for Indian promoters have also opened as they can now hand over the business to their foreign counterparts should they wish so. He added that the major beneficiary of increased competition levels has been the individual/customer as the products have become more 'customer friendly.'

The Indian life insurers benefitted from the foreign participation as they provided their technical and operational expertise (Krishnamurthy et al., 2005), encouraging them to take on practices equivalent to global averages. The reforms in the insurance industry led to a more spirited market which hugely profited the individual policyholder/ultimate customer while FDI-related regulatory changes have taken place from time-to-time for strengthening the insurance industry, making it more robust and affable to individuals/customers as depicted in Fig. 6.6.

4.5 Tactical Approach Towards Individuals/Customers

Life insurance companies deal with the same target market with almost no/negligible product differentiation. Thus, they ought to have some tactics in place to pull individuals towards them and not allow them to move towards their rivals.

Interviewee 1 suggested that agents are trained to convincingly talk to people and take them into confidence by being polite and gentle in their approach.

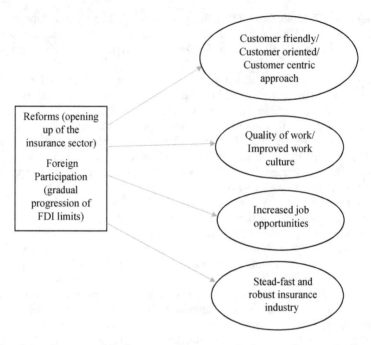

Fig. 6.6.   Impact of Reforms on Insurance Industry. *Source:* In-depth interviews.

Interviewee 2 chalked out a few imperatives such as talking to the customers politely, creating an atmosphere of comfort, striking an emotional chord with them, and then pitching in the product.

Interviewee 5 reasoned that death of a near and dear one causes both financial and emotional loss; while time heals the emotional loss, insurance aids in overcoming the financial loss. He feels people generally don't want to put their hard-earned money in insurance; so, the idea of tapping the inherent fear of an individual to aid the sale of insurance seems plausible. Covid-19 played a catalyst in this process as it heightened the risk awareness levels of an average individual making him/her wonder – 'What if this happens to me?'. Many *management representatives* pointed out the increased sale of term policies post the pandemic.

Interviewee 6 echoed:

> ...our strategy is to build a robust product line for each segment be it pension, children, term policies, etc. and not to spoil the market.

He articulated that giving value to the customers apart from other things is very important for the company and that the customer is always at the top, as they believe in 'customer centricity.'

The different tactics that come in handy to the agents/employees are represented in Fig. 6.7.

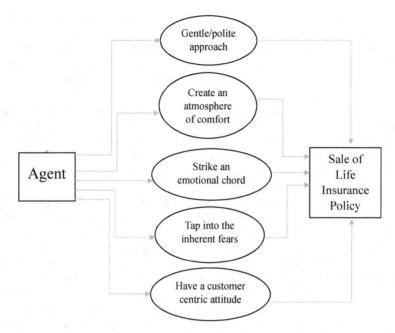

Fig. 6.7.   Tactical Approach Towards Individuals/Customers for Sale of Life Insurance. *Source:* In-depth Interviews.

4.6 Financial Literacy

While people may have different financial requirements, their financial knowledge still seems to play catch up. Financial literacy levels are lower in developing countries in comparison to the developed ones (Lahiri & Biswas, 2022). A survey conducted in 2019 in India, divulged that 27.18% of the respondents (compared to 20% in 2013) have achieved minimum target score in each of the components of financial literacy prescribed by OECD- INFE (RBI, 2021). While these statistics, are heart-warming, the reality is financial literacy is low in India and no one is fully/optimally insured.

The interviewees believe that percentage of people possessing financial knowledge is very low. Financial literacy in India is a mixed bag as there are all kinds of people. There are a few who are very well versed with the financial products right from the basics to the nuanced technicalities, while there are quite a few who are not at par with even the basics. Financial awareness is also low and as a result huge part of the insurable population is under-insured.

Interviewee 1 feels that from the total population approximately 30% people would have taken insurance that too under the pressure of agents who are often relatives/friends.

Interviewee 3 pointed out that financial literacy is definitely low and approximately 60% of people are partially insured.

Interviewee 6 pointed out that almost 65% (approx.) of people are not very well-versed or well-aware about financial products. The growth prospects of this industry are boundless which need to be effectively utilised by the life insurance companies.

The lack of understanding about financial products, their uses and benefits hinder their sale as well. Particularly in the life insurance business, lack of financial knowledge acts as a spoil sport as it affects its uptake by individuals. Low financial literacy is also an indication of lack of awareness among individuals and educative programs by the concerned authorities. Gallery et al. (2011) proposed a theoretical framework suggesting the various factors that affect financial literacy of fund members and its relationship with superannuation investment choice decisions. Likewise, Weedige et al. (2019) in their study found an association between individual/consumer's insurance literacy and behavioural intention to purchase insurance, moderately mediated by perceived product benefits and favourable attitudes suggesting that an individual having high insurance literacy would presumably purchase insurance on the basis of perceived product benefits and favourable attitudes. Lahiri and Biswas (2022) in their study found that with increased financial literacy scores, the chances of insurance uptake increase.

In today's day and age, being financially literate is highly necessary to manage one's own hard-earned wealth. In this background, awareness and educative programmes are the need of the hour to address the inadequacies in financial literacy levels of individuals and aid in the process of increased insurance penetration.

4.7 Grievance Redressal System

While financial knowledge of individuals may be hindering the growth of insurance industry in India, it's equally important to evaluate the industry's customer outreach programmes and grievance redressal mechanisms which reassure the individuals/customers about the safety, security and profitability of their investments in the policies. The regulatory body of insurance companies – IRDAI, is thus responsible for ensuring a vigorous grievance redressal mechanism for the policyholders.

Interviewee 5 opined that replying to the queries of the public is the company's duty as they are answerable to them and if they fail to reply, it is mentioned so in their reports/statements.

Interviewee 1 said, they have a CRM department that handles the grievances and queries. The Integrated Complaint Management System (ICMS) aids in the grievance redressal process. The customer makes his/her complaint on the portal and the company is bound to call back/resolve the complaint within 3 days as their internal system keeps sending reminders for resolution to avoid any pendency. This makes way for a very robust grievance redressal system.

Interviewee 6 emphasised on customer centricity being their top priority which ensures a robust customer redressal system. He said:

> ....the customers can approach us directly or digitally and when we receive a complaint, we are bound to resolve it within 24 hours; if they aren't satisfied, they may approach the Ombudsman as well.

Most of the *management representatives* opined that majority of the problems either get resolved at the office or are resolved by the agents and branch managers by reaching out to the aggrieved individuals/customers. Only when the individual isn't satisfied with the resolution, he/she approaches the IRDAI Ombudsman which then directs the company to take appropriate action.

Yadav and Mohania (2014) point out that there is increase in number of grievances related to life insurance services with the increase in customer base and mandate the necessity of a distinct grievances management system. They further suggest that increase in the number of complaints also indicates the confidence and trust people have on the Ombudsman. Similarly, Sandhu and Bala (2011) in their study found proficiency (in a way depicted through effective customer's grievance redressal procedures and processes) to have a significant impact on customer's perception about life insurance service quality.

Life insurance companies have taken various steps to fast-track redressal of policyholder's complaints and ensure their long-term association with the company. Thus, effective and efficient grievance redressal system is very essential for the growth of the life insurance industry and uptake of life insurance as well.

4.7.1 The Regulatory Body – IRDAI

The role of IRDAI in making the insurance industry robust and efficient cannot be undermined. Though the role of IRDAI is at the macro-level, it's importance can nevertheless be diminished. It acts as an anchor for the entire insurance industry which is reflected in their mission statement –

> To Protect the interests of the policyholders, to regulate, promote and ensure orderly growth of the insurance industry and for matters connected therewith or incidental thereto. (which is reflected in their website namely, www.irdai.gov.in)

Be it reforms, relaxations in complex regulations, flexible and easy processes, fast pace approvals or grievance management, IRDAI has stood the test of time and emerged victorious. It has ensured that insurance reaches every nook and corner of the country. The insurance industry can thus measure greater heights under the umbrella of their regulatory body.

Interviewee 2 equated the role of IRDAI to that of RBI and suggested that both overlook and govern their respective industries.

Interviewee 5 gave the example of how IRDAI increased the lock in period of ULIPS from 3 to 5 years and also reduced the commissions on them to increase the reach of the products and make insurance more affordable.

Interviewee 6 argued that no industry can flourish without a regulator. He added:

> ...although IRDAI might not have been as pro-active as SEBI or RBI, today all life insurance companies have been given the freedom for product innovation and launching as approval timeline has reduced.

As people also go by the merits of the products, he strongly believes that moving ahead, product innovation is of the essence as it helps in achieving success. This industry is likely to grow, provided the life insurers can offer new and innovative products (Chadha & Kapoor, 2008). The individuals/consumers require quality services which life insurers need to be cautious about (Mohamad et al., 2014). The role of IRDAI up-till now and further with respect to the growth of the industry as a whole cannot be undermined. Thus, the journey of India's insurance industry has been complemented by IRDAI through its various policies, actions and programs.

Various dimensions have emerged in the study which the policymakers and life insurers need to note/work upon to be successful and sustain in this business for the long term. Based on the above analysis and discussion of data collected through interviews, the various dimensions having a hold on life insurance uptake are depicted in Fig. 6.8.

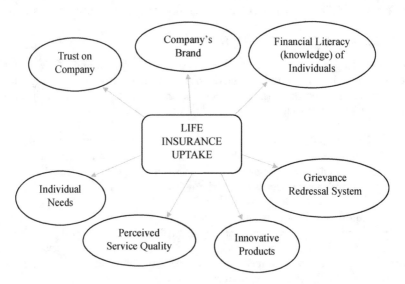

Fig. 6.8.   Dimensions Critical to Life Insurance Uptake. *Source:* Author's compilation.

5. Implications

5.1 Theoretical Contribution

This study contributes to the existing literature by providing a view of the life insurance industry from the standpoint of the management representatives which has been less explored, leaving a gap that this present study has attempted to fill. This study provides the necessary groundwork vital for developing a theory through the suggestion of dimensions that impact life insurance uptake. The dimensions suggested are representative of both – the extant literature and the information acquired from the interviews. The suggested dimensions hold scope for further theoretical expansion, development of a comprehensive model and empirical testing.

5.2 Practical Implication

Life insurance is an unsought product which needs to be sold by matching them with individual requirements. While individuals/customers may be the primary source of information to gain knowledge about life insurance industry, this study nevertheless looks at it from the other side of the table as it attempts to showcase the life insurance industry through the eyes of agents, managers and others representing the management of the companies and adds a new perspective to the way it is comprehended. The study provides a better understanding of the various dimensions which influence life insurance uptake by individuals/customers from the agents/employees' perspective.

6. Conclusion

The life insurance industry in India has long been dominated by LIC, the sole public life insurer. However, the industry has witnessed many changes since it was opened for private participation. The Indian life insurance market with its abundant opportunities provides the perfect environment for investors and companies to reap huge benefits. This study found consumer trust (Agyei et al., 2020; Chee & Sin, 2020; Dragos et al., 2020; Masud et al., 2021; Panigrahi et al., 2018) and brand (Chadha & Kapoor, 2008; Suneja & Sharma, 2009; Wibowo & Djumarno, 2019) of the life insurance company to be key dimensions which have a bearing on life insurance uptake. Individual needs are central among the dimensions which influence life insurance uptake. Perceived service quality also has a bearing on customer trust and satisfaction (Panigrahi et al., 2018; Qureshi & Bhatt, 2015). Service-related attributes are very significant for individuals/ consumers when choosing life insurance services (Mohamad et al., 2014). Financial literacy (knowledge) influences insurance uptake, insurance purchase intention and/or investment decisions (Gallery et al., 2011; Lahiri & Biswas, 2022; Prasad et al., 2021; Weedige et al., 2019) and grievance redressal system too impacts individual's perception about service quality (Sandhu & Bala, 2011). The life insurance companies as reinforced in the various interviews by different *management representatives* are constantly working towards maintaining their image, upholding their trust among the masses and building their brand so as to succeed in the market. Proper training, transparent internal processes and robust work environment act like a feather on the cap and aid the companies achieve success in the life insurance business. The top-level management and policy-makers need to make a note of the key dimensions in this study for better policy formulation and execution. This study only focuses on life insurance industry and cannot expand its findings to the entire insurance industry. Due to paucity of time and resources, the study included seven interviews of management representatives/agents in total which can be increased in future researches.

References

Agyei, J., Sun, S., Abrokwah, E., Penney, E. K., & Ofori-Boafo, R. (2020). Influence of trust on customer engagement: Empirical evidence from the insurance industry in Ghana. *Sage Open, 10*(1), 2158244019899104.

Chadha, S. K., & Kapoor, D. (2008). An attribute based perceptual mapping of the selected private life insurance companies: An empirical study in Ludhiana. *Vision, 12*(3), 53–60. https://doi.org/10.1177/097226290801200305

Chakraborty, J. (2017). Firm performances in Indian life insurance industry: Non-parametric analysis. *SCMS Journal of Indian Management, 14*(4), 95–111.

Chee, L. C., & Sin, T. S. (2020). The significance of personal value, risk attitude and trust on life insurance ownership in the northern regions of Malaysia. *Jurnal Pengurusan, 58*, 67–78. https://doi.org/10.17576/pengurusan-2020-58-06

Deb, R., Nath, K. K., Nepal, M., Chakraborty, S., & Chakraborty, K. S. (2021). Do people choose life insurance for protection or for saving? *Metamorphosis, 20*(1), 35–44.

DPIIT. (2020). *Consolidated FDI policy.* https://dpiit.gov.in/sites/default/files/FDI-PolicyCircular-2020-29October2020_0.pdf. Accessed on December 11, 2021.

DPIIT. (2021). *Press note 2.* https://dpiit.gov.in/sites/default/files/pn2-2021.pdf. Accessed on December 11, 2021.

Dragos, S. L., Dragos, C. M., & Muresan, G. M. (2020). From intention to decision in purchasing life insurance and private pensions: Different effects of knowledge and behavioural factors. *Journal of Behavioral and Experimental Economics, 87*, 101555.

Ennew, C., & Sekhon, H. (2007). Measuring trust in financial services: The trust index. *Consumer Policy Review, 17*(2), 62–68.

Gallery, N., Newton, C., & Palm, C. (2011). Framework for assessing financial literacy and superannuation investment choice decisions. *Australasian Accounting, Business and Finance Journal, 5*(2), 3–22.

Ghauri, P. N., & Grønhaug, K. (2005). *Research methods in business studies: A practical guide* (3rd ed.). Prentice Hall.

Glaser, B. (1978). *Theoretical sensitivity.* Sociology Press.

Glaser, B. G., & Strauss, A. L. (1967). *The discovery of grounded theory.* Aldine.

Insurance Institute of India. (2016). *Insurance agents- life.* https://www.insuranceins tituteofindia.com/downloads/IC38/ALEnglish.pdf. Accessed on December 17, 2021.

IRDAI. (2020). *History of insurance in India.* https://www.irdai.gov.in/ADMINCMS/
cms/NormalData_Layout.aspx?page=PageNo4&mid=2. Accessed on January 15,
2022.

IRDAI. (2021). *Annual report 2020–21.* https://www.irdai.gov.in/ADMINCMS/cms/
frmGeneral_NoYearList.aspx?DF=AR&mid=11.1. Accessed on February 03,
2022.

IRDAI. (2022). *Business figures – Life.* https://www.irdai.gov.in/ADMINCMS/cms/
NormalData_Layout.aspx?page=PageNo4649. Accessed on July 03, 2022.

Krishnamurthy, S., Mony, S. V., Jhaveri, N., Bakhshi, S., Bhat, R., Dixit, M. R., &
Bhat, R. (2005). Insurance industry in India: Structure, performance, and future
challenges. *Vikalpa, 30*(3), 93–120.

Lahiri, S., & Biswas, S. (2022). Does financial literacy improve financial behavior in
emerging economies? Evidence from India. *Managerial Finance, 48*(9/10),
1430–1452. https://doi.org/10.1108/MF-09-2021-0440

Masud, M. M., Ahsan, M. R., Ismail, N. A., & Rana, M. S. (2021). The underlying
drivers of household purchase behaviour of life insurance. *Society and Business
Review, 16*(3), 442–458.

Mohamad, S. S., Rusdi, S. D., Hashim, N. H., & Husin, N. (2014). The influence of
intrinsic brand cues in intangible service industries: An application to life insurance
services. *Procedia-Social and Behavioral Sciences, 130*, 347–353.

Panigrahi, S., Azizan, N. A., & Waris, M. (2018). Investigating the empirical relationship between service quality, trust, satisfaction, and intention of customers
purchasing life insurance products. *Indian Journal of Marketing.* http://doi.org/10.
2139/ssrn.3121509

Prasad, S., Kiran, R., & Sharma, R. K. (2021). Behavioural, socio-economic factors,
financial literacy and investment decisions: Are men more rational and women
more emotional? *Indian Economic Journal, 69*(1), 66–87. https://doi.org/10.1177/
0019466220987023

Qureshi, M. N. Z., & Bhatt, J. (2015). An assessment of service quality, customer
satisfaction and customer loyalty in life insurance corporation of India with special
reference to Srinagar district of Jammu and Kashmir. *Pacific Business Review
International, 7*(8), 60–70.

Rajendran, R., & Natarajan, B. (2009). The impact of LPG on life insurance corporation of India (LIC). *Asia Pacific Journal of Finance and Banking Research,
3*(3).

Rastogi, S., & Sarkar, R. (2007, May). Enhancing competitiveness: The case of the
Indian life insurance industry. In *Conference on global competition & competitiveness of Indian corporate.* Indian Institute of Management Kozhikode. http://hdl.
handle.net/2259/43

RBI. (2021). *National strategy for financial education: 2020–2025.* https://rbidocs.rbi.org.
in/rdocs/PublicationReport/Pdfs/NSFE202020251BD2A32E39F74D328239740D4
C93980D.PDF. Accessed on October 22, 2022.

Saha, S., & Dutta, A. (2019). Factors influencing service quality perception in Indian
life insurance sector. *Global Business Review, 20*(4), 1010–1025.

Sandhu, H. S., & Bala, N. (2011). Customers' perception towards service quality of
Life Insurance Corporation of India: A factor analytic approach. *International
Journal of Business and Social Science, 2*(18), 219–231.

Sinha, T. (2005). *The Indian insurance industry: Challenges and prospects.* Available at SSRN 792166 or http://doi.org/10.2139/ssrn.792166

Sinha, S., & Jain, N. K. (2014). *Did the Indian life insurance industry overlook a key leadership issue? An exploratory study investigating the role of shared leadership with reference to the top management issues.* https://www.anzam.org/wp-content/uploads/pdf-manager/1715_ANZAM-2014-361.PDF. Accessed on May 29, 2022.

Skipper, H. D. (1997). *Foreign insurers in emerging markets: Issues and concerns* (Vol. 1). International Insurance Foundation.

Strauss, A., & Corbin, J. (1998). *Basics of qualitative research: Techniques and procedures for developing grounded theory* (2nd ed.). SAGE.

Suneja, A., & Sharma, K. (2009). Factors influencing choice of a life insurance company. *LBS Journal of Management and Research, 7*(1–2), 44–56.

Swiss Re Institute. (2021). *World insurance: The recovery gains pace.* Sigma. (3). https://www.swissre.com/dam/jcr:ca792993-80ce-49d7-9e4f-7e298e399815/swiss-re-institute-sigma-3-2021-en.pdf. Accessed on December 11, 2021.

The Economic Times. (2022, July 02). *What is 'Bancassurance'.* https://economictimes.indiatimes.com/definition/bancassurance. Accessed on July 03, 2022.

Tyler, K., & Stanley, E. (2007). The role of trust in financial services business relationships. *Journal of Services Marketing, 21*(5), 334–344.

Washid, M., & Kazmi, A. (2000). Strategic investment decisions of transnational corporations in the Indian Insurance Sector. *Paradigmi, 4*(2), 78–87.

Weedige, S. S., Ouyang, H., Gao, Y., & Liu, Y. (2019). Decision making in personal insurance: Impact of insurance literacy. *Sustainability, 11*(23), 6795.

Wibowo, R. Y., & Djumarno, D. P. (2019). Determined brand trust in insurance: The effect of brand image and brand awareness on purchase intention. *International Journal of Innovative Science and Research Technology, 4*(7), 1352–1359.

Yadav, R., & Jain, R. (2014). "Brand building through corporate social responsibility"-A case study of SBI life insurance. *International Letters of Social and Humanistic Sciences, 29*, 34–38. https://www.learntechlib.org/p/176629/. Accessed on October 22, 2022.

Yadav, R. K., & Mohania, S. (2014). Role of insurance ombudsman and grievance management in life insurance services in Indian perspective. *International Letters of Social and Humanistic Sciences, 31*, 9–13.

Zikmund, W. G. (2000). *Business research methods* (6th ed.). The Dryden Press.

Chapter 7

Research on Economic Policy Uncertainty: A Bibliometric Analysis

Sukhmani Bhatia Chugh and Archana Goel

Chitkara University, India

Abstract

With the increase in uncertainty around the globe, an intensifying interest is seen in Economic Policy Uncertainty (EPU) as a topic of research. Researchers worldwide understand the significance of the impact of EPU on the country's development. EPU has a far-reaching impact as uncertainty shocks in one part of the world resonate worldwide due to the level of interconnectivity, globalization and quick communication. In order to facilitate these researchers, this study presents a bibliometric analysis of the existing research in this field using VOS viewer software, by consolidating all the studies from Scopus indexed journal articles, conference proceedings and review papers published in English language from 2006 to 2022. Bibliometric analysis on EPU has rarely been performed. The analysis identifies the publication trends, journal-wise citation, most influential authors, countries, institutions, keyword co-occurrence and authors of different countries who have collaborated for the research in the field. Finally, 1,055 papers were used for bibliometric analysis. The findings depicted that the most cited article on EPU is 'Measuring economic policy uncertainty' by Baker et al. (2016) and the most prolific author appears to be Rangan Gupta from University of Pretoria which as an institution also has the maximum publications on this topic. The Journal Finance Research Letters has published the greatest number of researches on EPU. This chapter also summarizes the limitations of the study along with new areas of research.

Keywords: Economic policy uncertainty; bibliometric analysis; EPU; global EPU; global economic policy uncertainty

Modeling Economic Growth in Contemporary India, 109–135
Copyright © 2024 Sukhmani Bhatia Chugh and Archana Goel
Published under exclusive licence by Emerald Publishing Limited
doi:10.1108/978-1-80382-751-320241007

1. Introduction About EPU

Research on Economic policy uncertainty (EPU) has seen a whirlwind of activity in the recent past. The number of studies exploring the effect of EPU on currency exchange rates (Abid, 2020), mergers and acquisitions (Bonaime et al., 2018), financial institutions (Caglayan & Xu, 2019), imports (Sharma & Paramati, 2021), investment (Chen et al., 2020; Dejuán & Ghirelli, 2018; Wang et al., 2014), stock returns (Phan et al., 2018), financial stability (Phan et al., 2021), banks (Tran et al. 2021), capital structure (Zhang et al., 2015), cash holdings (Li, 2019), bank valuations (He & Niu, 2018) and stock markets (Li et al., 2020) is growing dramatically. But various studies have presented conflicting results. By going through the available literature, we find that a study consolidating all the research on the topic of EPU is rarely available. There is hardly any study that utilizes bibliometric analysis to consolidate the research available in this area. This chapter enables to fill this research gap and provide analysis of the existing research to propose new avenues of research. Baker et al. (2016) explain EPU as 'the probability of changes in future policies compared to the existing condition and how these changes affect the micro and macro ecosystems.' Brogaard and Detzel (2015) define EPU as 'the uncertainty regarding fiscal, regulatory, or monetary policy.'

EPU refers to uncertainty in the country, financial markets, investments, etc., due to uncertainty in the policymaking by the government. When the road ahead in terms of the government's policy decisions is unclear, or the impact of various policy changes on business is ambiguous, it leads to uncertainty, impacting multiple facets of an economy. EPU has significant ramifications for how a firm conducts business and the country's economic development (Baker et al., 2016). Li et al. (2020) explains that economic uncertainty has been on a sharp incline in the United States since the financial crisis and the next recession. EPU has a far-reaching impact as uncertainty shocks in one part of the world resonate worldwide due to the level of interconnectivity, globalization and quick communication. EPU is an essential topic for research as it has substantial implications for households and businesses. Unforeseen events lead to unpredictability and uncertainty about the future, making the investors nervous. Households and businesses go into the precautionary saving mode to prepare for the uncertainty in the economy. As the consumption by the households decrease, the corporate investment reduces, leading to lower production and higher unemployment, ultimately leading to an economic slowdown. The policymakers need to keep the policies transparent and flexible so that companies and households are better equipped to deal with such issues. They need to be aware of the effects of global events on their economy and take timely action to understand and mitigate the risks.

The main aim of this study is to infer the relevance and increasing importance of EPU as a research topic by examining the bibliometric matrix encapsulating the top articles, publication trends, authors, citations, keywords, countries, variables and the top journals. The study intends to contribute to the existing knowledge of the academicians and managers and provide them with the potential trajectories for the future research. Due to the rapid growth in the research in this area, a structured and integrated analysis is needed to obtain clarity.

Bibliometric analysis helps in understanding the existing research available, comprehending research trends and facilitating the future scope of research in new frontiers. Bibliometric analysis has gained rapid and immense popularity to research and analyse large volumes of data and create a prominent research impact, this can be ascribed to the accessibility and availability of softwares like VOS Viewer, Gephi and Leximancer for analysis. Bibliometric analysis is being employed by scholars and researchers to explore emerging trends in publication, journal performance, comprehend collaborative patterns and research components (Donthu et al., 2021). Bibliometric analysis if done in a meaningful way can immensely contribute to the research field by providing a precise overview, discovering knowledge gaps, deriving new and innovative ideas for further research and positioning the intended contributions (Arora et al., 2023; Gupta et al., 2024).

This study makes important contribution in the upcoming field of EPU. Most of the studies have explored the relationship of EPU with various important variables. This paper consolidates all the studies from 2006 to 2022 from the Scopus databases.

The research questions that we attempt to answer in this study are as follows:

- What are the publication trends in this field?
- Which journal published the maximum articles on EPU?
- Who are the most eminent authors in this field?
- Which are the authors who have co-authored the most with other experts?
- What are the countries in which the maximum research on this topic has been explored?
- Which are the countries that have the maximum number of co-authorship?
- Which articles have obtained the maximum citations?
- What keywords have been used the most?
- Which keywords have co-occurred with each other the most?

The rest of this paper is organized in the following way. The next section discusses the research design, focusing on the methodology of data collection and data cleaning employed to conduct this bibliometric analysis. In Section three, we discuss and analyse the findings of the analysis conducted. Finally, we conclude with the discussion of the limitations and future possibilities of the research.

2. Research Design

To conduct a bibliometric analysis a step-by-step approach was adopted. In order to find answers to the research questions, the data was collected from the Scopus database from time period of 2006–2022 as the search generated no results before 2006. In fact, the majority of results generated were from the year 2013 onwards. This gives evidence to the fact that EPU as a research topic has garnered attention in the recent times only and there is a vast scope of future research in the field. The

Scopus database has been extensively used by various previous researchers. Scopus is the database that offers widest coverage of peer-reviewed research in finance (Pattnaik et al., 2020). As compared to the Web of Science database, Scopus is much more extensive (Valtakoski, 2020). The major sources of data selected were journals and books and the initial studies identified were numbered at 1,148 comprising of articles, review papers and conference papers. The keywords used included 'Economic policy Uncertainty' and 'EPU' as that was the main variable under scrutiny. Also, the areas of field included for data collection were 'Economics' and 'Business Management' (Table 7.1).

Data obtained from any search engine is prone to various errors which might produce erroneous bibliometric findings (Baker et al., 2021). As a result, direct processing of this information without data cleaning might lead to incongruous inferences. The data cleaning was done in the excel datasheet first by checking for duplicates in the doi column and then the entire sheet. Two duplicates were observed and removed. Four papers with missing abstracts were also removed. Final content cleaning was done by going through the keywords, titles and abstracts and manually screening the data for any irrelevance and unrelatedness which led to elimination of 86 papers from the data collected. This took the final reading of documents to 1,055 where articles were numbered at 1,040, conference papers at 7 and review papers at 8.

3. Findings

3.1 Publication Trend Analysis of EPU

The trend of publication of the studies related to EPU has been depicted in Fig. 7.1 where the year of publication is charted along with the number of publications. The figures propound that the research in the area of EPU is fairly new and

Table 7.1. Search Criteria and Article Selection.

Filtering Criteria	Reject	Accept
Search Criteria	875	2,023
Search engine: Scopus		1,148
Search term: 'economic policy uncertainty' OR 'EPU' OR 'policy uncertainty'		
Subject area: 'economics' and 'business management'.		
Document type: "articles", "conference papers", and "review papers"		
Language screening: included documents in English only		
Article Selection		6
Erroneous records screening:		
Content Screening:	86	1,055
Manually screened the title, abstracts and keywords and included the ones that are relevant to EPU		

Source: Author's compilation.

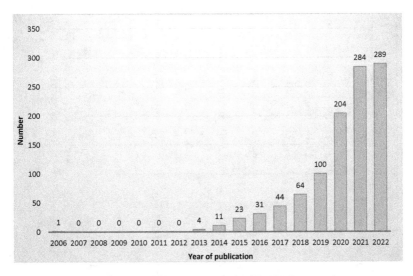

Fig. 7.1.   Publication Trend of EPU Research.

it has proliferated only after the year 2013. The most prolific years have been 2022 (289 articles), 2021 (284 articles), 2020 (204 articles) and 2019 (100 articles). This trend is expected to escalate in the year 2022 as 289 publications have already been made by the mid of third quarter of the year.

3.2 Top Authors, Institutions and Countries of EPU Research

The top authors in EPU research in Finance, alongside their institutions and countries at the time of authorship have been summarized in Table 7.2. The author with the most impact based on the number of citations turns out to be Rangan Gupta with 1929 citations. Rangan Gupta is currently a professor at University of Pretoria, South Africa and his main research interests are in the field of Monetary policy and theory and time series econometrics. The second and third most impactful authors appear to be Wensheng Kang with 940 and Mehmet Balcilar with 595 citations. Wensheng Kang is currently working at Kent State University and his main research interests are in the field of Monetary policy, Bayesian analysis and asset pricing to name a few. Mehmet Balcilar is currently working as a professor and department head of economics at Eastern Mediterranean University in North Cyprus. He also worked as an Extraordinary professor at University of Pretoria, Pretoria, South Africa. His main interests lie in macroeconomics, forecasting and financial markets to name a few.

Rangan Gupta also appears to be the most productive author with 40 publications followed by Xiao-Lin Li (Ocean University of China) and Jiqian Wang (Southwest Jiaotong University, China) with 16 publications each.

Table 7.2. Top Authors, Institutions and Countries of Economic Policy Uncertainty.

TC	Author	TP	TC	Organization	TP	TC	Country	TP
1929	Gupta R.	40	1,596	Department of Economics, University of Pretoria, Pretoria, South Africa	31	5,983	China	371
940	Kang W.	10	346	Montpellier Business School, Montpellier, France	7	4,993	United States	192
595	Balcilar M.	15	322	Istanbul Medeniyet University, Turkey	7	2,614	France	83
553	Demir E.	12	309	IPAG Business School, Paris, France	11	2,341	United Kingdom	95
545	Hammoudeh S.	11	300	School of Public Policy and Management, University of Chinese Academy of Sciences, Beijing, China	5	2,203	Australia	70
540	Gozgor G.	13	196	School of Finance, Central University of Finance and Economics, Beijing, China	6	1,980	South Africa	52
309	Li X.	16	152	School of Economics and Management, Southwest Jiaotong University, Chengdu, China	14	1,612	Turkey	81
293	Zhang X.	11	141	School of Economics & Management, Southwest Jiaotong University, Chengdu, China	6	956	Pakistan	40
285	Zhu H.	10	139	Department of Economics, Helmut Schmidt University, Hamburg, Germany	5	871	Vietnam	62
201	Ma F.	12	121	College of Business Administration, Northern Border University, Saudi Arabia	8	810	South Korea	38
175	Wang J.	16	109	Institut sup‚rieur de gestion de gabšs, gabšs university, gabšs, Tunisia	7	764	Germany	49

TC	Author	TP		Institution		TC	Country	TP
173	Tiwari A. K.	10	98	School of Business, Central South University, Changsha, China	7	722	New Zealand	41
142	Wu T.-P.	11	91	School of Economics and Finance, Massey University, New Zealand	6	579	Taiwan	32
141	Li Y.	14	89	Manouba University, Manouba, Tunisia	5	554	Canada	36
113	Wu H.-C.	10				515	India	50

Notes: TC, total citations; *TP*, total publications. The table has been sorted according to the number of citations and the author, institution and the country are arranged based on the number of citations only.

Also based on the number of citations, the most influential institution appears to be University of Pretoria, Pretoria, South Africa with total citations of 1,596. The most productive institution in terms of the number of publications is also the University of Pretoria, Pretoria, South Africa with 31 publications. As far as the country is concerned, China is the most intellectual at 371 publications and 5,983 citations followed by United States with 192 publications and 4,993 citations in the field of EPU. Figs. 7.2–7.4 represent the total number of publications author wise, institution wise and country wise respectively.

3.3 Top Journals for EPU Research

Table 7.3 represents the top journals that publish the research for EPU in finance. Based on the number of citations Finance Research letters and Economics letters are the most influential journals with 2,249 and 1,565 citations respectively. Fig. 7.5 presents the top journals in terms of the total number of publications. The most productive journals are Finance Research Letters and Resources Policy with the total number of publications as 56 and 42 respectively. The top five journals with the most citations are published by Elsevier's. The top three journals with the most publications namely finance research letters, e-source policy and International review of financial analysis are also Elsevier's publications.

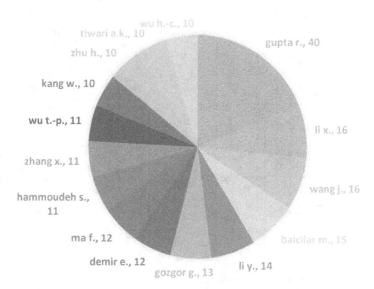

Fig. 7.2.   Total Publications by the Authors.

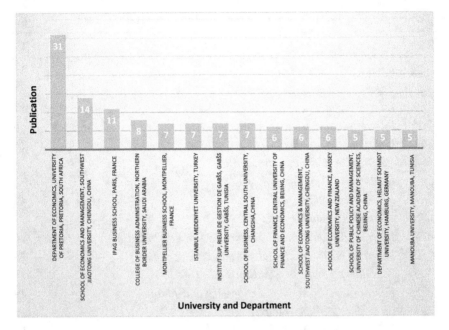

Fig. 7.3.   Total Publications University Wise.

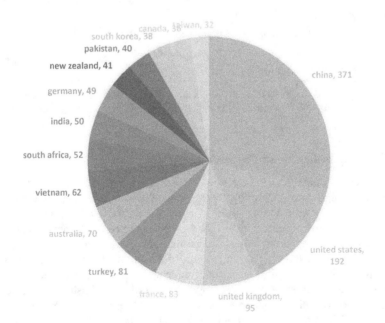

Fig. 7.4.   Total Publications Country Wise.

Table 7.3. Top Journals for Economic Policy Uncertainty Research.

TC	Source	TP
2,249	*Finance Research Letters*	56
1,565	*Economics Letters*	31
1,288	*Energy Economics*	27
1,190	*International Review of Financial Analysis*	35
853	*Economic Modelling*	26
688	*Pacific Basin Finance Journal*	27
547	*North American Journal of Economics and Finance*	30
547	*Resources Policy*	42
496	*Applied Economics*	32
478	*Journal of International Financial Markets, Institutions and Money*	15
472	*Research in International Business and Finance*	28
409	*Journal of Financial Stability*	11
338	*International Review of Economics and Finance*	29
293	*Emerging Markets Finance and Trade*	25
235	*Tourism Economics*	15
224	*Journal of Corporate Finance*	13
219	*Applied Economics Letters*	30
142	*International Journal of Finance and Economics*	19
138	*Quarterly Review of Economics and Finance*	13
72	*Economics Bulletin*	13

Note: TC, total citations; TP, total publications. The research constituent (i.e., author, institution, country) appear according to total citations in this table.

3.4 Top Cited Articles on Economic Policy Uncertainty

The top cited articles on EPU have been summarized in the Table 7.4. 'Measuring economic policy uncertainty' by Baker et al. (2016) is the most influential and impactful article with a total of 2,834 citations and 'COVID-19 pandemic, oil prices, stock market, geopolitical risk and policy uncertainty nexus in the US economy: Fresh evidence from the wavelet-based approach' by Sharif et al. (2020) with 535 citations. Baker et al. (2016) proposes a unique index for measuring the economic policy uncertainty using the frequency of newspaper-based references. This index has been extensively used by various authors publishing in the field of EPU. Various studies (Abakah et al., 2021; Arbatli et al., 2017; Bermpei et al., 2022; Goodell et al., 2021; Ioannidis & Ka, 2021; Jiang et al., 2021; Jin & Wu, 2021; Lee et al., 2022; Lei & Song, 2022; Li et al., 2022; Naidenova, 2021; Nonejad, 2021, 2022; Padungsaksawasdi et al., 2023; Smales, 2021, 2022; Ur Rehman et al., 2022; Vo et al., 2021; Wen et al., 2022) to name a few, have

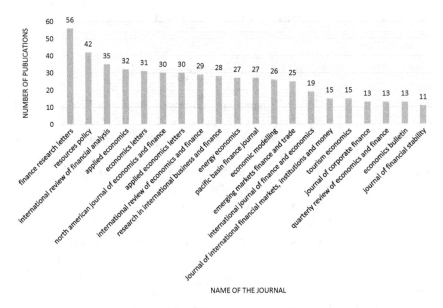

Fig. 7.5.   Journal-Wise Total Publications.

employed Baker's index for measuring EPU, supporting its popularity and extensive use.

The second most cited paper 'COVID-19 pandemic, oil prices, stock market, geopolitical risk and policy uncertainty nexus in the US economy: Fresh evidence from the wavelet-based approach' by Sharif et al. (2020) examines the relationship between COVID-19 pandemic, geopolitical risk, stock market, oil price volatility and EPU using wavelet analysis in the United States. The third most cited article 'The asset-pricing implications of government economic policy uncertainty' by Brogaard and Detzel (2015) captures EPU in the United States using Baker's newspaper-based index and finds that EPU is positively able to forecast excess market returns. The fourth most cited article 'Oil shocks, policy uncertainty and stock market return' by Kang and Ratti (2013) examines the relation between EPU and oil price changes and their impact on stock returns. With an increase in concerns about future oil prices, EPU increases and it negatively impacts stock returns.

The fifth most cited article 'Do global factors impact BRICS stock markets? A quantile regression approach' 'was by Mensi et al. (2014) and it analyses the impact of global factors on the stocks markets of the BRICS countries. The study concludes that global stock and commodity markets, volatility in the US stock market changes create an impact on the stock markets of the BRICS countries.

3.5 Keyword Co Occurrence

Table 7.5 summarizes the top 15 author keywords that are prominent in the publications. The analysis of keywords helps in understanding the key themes and

Table 7.4. Top Cited Articles on Economic Policy Uncertainty.

Author(s)/Year	Title	TC
Baker S. R. (2016)	Measuring economic policy uncertainty	2,834
Sharif A. (2020)	COVID-19 pandemic, oil prices, stock market, geopolitical risk and policy uncertainty nexus in the US economy: Fresh evidence from the wavelet-based approach	535
Brogaard J. (2015)	The asset-pricing implications of government economic policy uncertainty	511
Kang W. (2013)	Oil shocks, policy uncertainty and stock market return	278
Mensi W. (2014)	Do global factors impact BRICS stock markets? A quantile regression approach	275
Colombo V. (2013)	Economic policy uncertainty in the US: Does it matter for the Euro area?	268
Demir E. (2018)	Does economic policy uncertainty predict the bitcoin returns? An empirical investigation	266
Wang Y. (2014)	Economic policy uncertainty and corporate investment: Evidence from China	263
Liu L. (2015)	Economic policy uncertainty and stock market volatility	229
Kang W. (2014)	Economic policy uncertainty and firm-level investment	224
Antonakakis N. (2014)	Dynamic spillovers of oil price shocks and economic policy uncertainty	212
Arouri M. (2016)	Economic policy uncertainty and stock markets: Long-run evidence from the US	191
Bordo M. D. (2016)	Economic policy uncertainty and the credit channel: Aggregate and bank level US evidence over several decades	174
Ko J.-H. (2015)	International economic policy uncertainty and stock prices: Wavelet approach	158
You W. (2017)	Oil price shocks, economic policy uncertainty and industry stock returns in China: Asymmetric effects with quantile regression	156

Table 7.5. Cluster-Wise List of Keywords With the Number of Occurrences.

S.No	Keywords	Cluster	Occurrences
1	epu	1	46
2	covid-19		36
3	Vix		16
4	stock markets		15
5	gold		12
6	partisan conflict		8
7	precious metals		8
8	implied volatility		7
9	safe haven		7
10	spillover index		7
11	brexit		6
12	brics		6
13	hedge		6
14	global financial crisis		5
15	green bonds		5
16	Markov-switching		5
17	real exchange rate		5
18	risk management		5
19	economic policy uncertainty	2	605
20	policy uncertainty		68
21	China		41
22	investment		17
23	cash holdings		12
24	firm value		11
25	corporate governance		10
26	financial constraints		10
27	corporate social responsibility		9
28	panel data		9
29	information asymmetry		8
30	innovation		8
31	cost of capital		5
32	firm performance		5
33	inflation		5
34	risk		5

(Continued)

Table 7.5. *(Continued)*

S.No	Keywords	Cluster	Occurrences
35	trade credit		5
36	global economic policy uncertainty		26
37	wavelet analysis	3	17
38	oil price		16
39	Garch-Midas		12
40	volatility forecasting		12
41	exchange rate		8
42	monetary policy		8
43	gold price		7
44	stock price		6
45	tourism activities		6
46	frequency domain		5
47	frequency domains		5
48	political risk		5
49	stock market returns		5
50	time domains		5
51	time-varying		5
52	volatility spillover		5
53	geopolitical risk	4	23
54	volatility		22
55	economic policy uncertainty (epu)		20
56	granger causality		14
57	causality		12
58	connectedness		10
59	economic growth		10
60	wavelet coherence		9
61	earnings management		7
62	tourism demand		7
63	wavelet		7
64	crude oil		6
65	reits		6
66	systemic risk		6
67	commodities		5
68	tourism		5

Table 7.5. *(Continued)*

S.No	Keywords	Cluster	Occurrences
69	uncertainty	5	76
70	asymmetry		14
71	economic policy		12
72	political uncertainty		12
73	emerging markets		11
74	nardl		11
75	epu index		8
76	spillover effects		8
77	emerging economies		7
78	exchange rates		7
79	financial crisis		6
80	Europe		5
81	monetary policy uncertainty		5
82	nonlinear ardl model		5
83	panel var		5
84	economic uncertainty	6	22
85	investor sentiment		13
86	realized volatility		10
87	cryptocurrencies		8
88	economic policy uncertainty index		8
89	financial uncertainty		8
90	corporate investment		7
91	covid-19 pandemic		7
92	US		7
93	dynamic connectedness		6
94	financial stress		6
95	predictability		6
96	tvp-var		6
97	svar		5
98	bitcoin	7	33
99	stock market		23
100	forecasting		15
101	spillovers		11
102	cryptocurrency		10

(Continued)

Table 7.5. *(Continued)*

S.No	Keywords	Cluster	Occurrences
103	spillover		10
104	spillover effect		8
105	business cycles		7
106	garch-midas model		7
107	stock market volatility		6
108	macroeconomic variables		5
109	uncertainty index		5
110	vector autoregression		5
111	quantile regression	8	29
112	stock returns		22
113	oil prices		18
114	structural var		8
115	oil price shocks		7
116	asymmetric effects		6
117	oil shocks		5
118	India	9	6
120	Chinese stock market	10	5

topics that have been examined by various authors frequently. A total of 2,261 keywords were obtained during the research out of which we have utilized 120 and listed the top 15 in the table below. EPU is the top keyword that is used by the authors with 605 occurrences which is obvious since that was our search keyword. It means that out of 1,055 studies, EPU has been used by 605 studies. Uncertainty has also been used by authors with 76 occurrences. Other major keywords include policy uncertainty, EPU, Covid-19 and Bitcoin. Keywords like economic uncertainty, stock returns, volatility and economic policy uncertainty (epu) have almost equal occurrences in the research. The various keywords are sorted cluster wise and keywords in a single cluster represent strongly related terms. Clusters 1 and 2 are the biggest clusters consisting of 18 keywords each, which have a strong co-relation.

Keyword co-occurrence analysis is mainly done in order to analyse which keywords have been studied together to understand their relatedness. This map provides an insight in various topics and areas which have been analysed by the researchers in connection with EPU. Fig. 7.6 has been prepared by using VOS viewer and the various coloured nodes represent different keywords. The size of the node represents the number of occurrences of the keyword, larger the size and more is the frequency of occurrence. Various keywords are joined together with

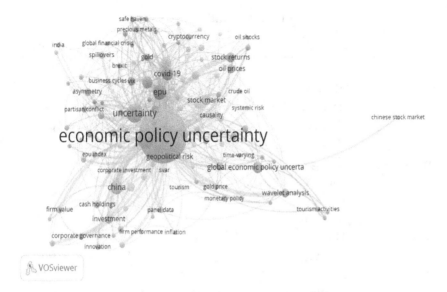

Fig. 7.6.   Network Map of Keyword Co-occurrence Analysis.

lines which represent the co-occurrences. The width and depth of the line represent the strength of the connection. The co-occurrence of 'Economic policy uncertainty' with China suggests that 'Economic policy uncertainty' has been studied in China a lot. The co-occurrence of the word 'Economic policy uncertainty' with firm value and stock returns suggest that the impact of 'Economic policy uncertainty' has been studied very frequently on firm value and stock returns, though separately. 'Economic policy uncertainty' also shows a strong co-occurrence with wavelet analysis, cash holdings, investment, corporate governance, meaning that various studies have focussed on the relation between these above-mentioned areas.

3.6 Co-Authorship Analysis

To make the analysis in the study more extensive, co-authorship analysis is done using VOS viewer software. VOS basically means Visualization of Similarities and is a software that is used to create a network map of journals and authors, etc. Researchers collaborate with other experts in same or different countries in order to acquire new knowledge and expertise and it is interesting to analyse this collaboration.

3.6.1 Co-Authors

Table 7.6 shows the list of top 74 authors who have co-authored with atleast five authors. The total authors numbered at 1788 out of which 74 were identified and

Table 7.6. Cluster-Wise List of Co-Authors.

S.No	Authors	Cluster	No. of Documents
1	Li X.	1	16
2	Ma F.		12
3	Zhang X.		11
4	Zhu H.		10
5	Wei Y.		8
6	Zhang Y.		8
7	Chen Y.		7
8	Li Z.		7
9	Su C.-W.		7
10	Umar M.		7
11	Liu Y.		6
12	Ren Y.		6
13	Zhang L.		6
14	Chen W.		5
15	Qin M.		5
16	Liu J.	2	9
17	He F.		8
18	Wang Z.		8
19	Liu Z.		8
20	Wang X.		6
21	Wu J.		6
22	Yin L.		6
23	Xiong x.		5
24	Wu s.		5
25	Zhang J.		5
26	Li R.		5
27	Balli F.	3	8
28	Shahzad S.J.H.		8
29	Uddin G.S.		8
30	Bekiros S.		7
31	Nguyen D.K.		7
32	Vo X.V.		7
33	Mensi W.		6
34	Shahbaz M.		6

Table 7.6. *(Continued)*

S.No	Authors	Cluster	No. of Documents
35	Ji Q.		5
36	Gupta R.	4	40
37	Balcilar M.		15
38	Roubaud D.		9
39	Fang L.		7
40	Lee C.-C.		7
41	Wohar M.E.		7
42	Yu H.		7
43	Bouri E.		6
44	Gozgor G.	5	13
45	Demir E.		12
46	Hammoudeh S.		11
47	Tiwari A.K.		10
48	Mokni K.		8
49	Ajmi A.N.		6
50	Das D.		5
51	Naifar N.		5
52	Li Y.	6	14
53	Wang Y.		9
54	Jiang Y.		7
55	Zhang B.		7
56	Zhao Y.		6
57	Wang H.		5
58	Zhang H.	7	8
59	Chen J.		6
60	Demirer R.		6
61	Huang J.		5
62	Yang C.		5
63	Wang J.	8	16
64	Chiang T. C.		9
65	Chen X.		8
66	Sun X.		5
67	Kang W.		10
68	Lee K.	9	8

(Continued)

Table 7.6. *(Continued)*

S.No	Authors	Cluster	No. of Documents
69	Ratti R. A.		8
70	Jeon Y.		5
71	El ghoul S.	10	5
72	Guedhami O.		5
73	Antonakakis N.	11	6
74	Filis G.		5

Fig. 7.7.   Network Map of Co-Authorship.

sorted into 11 clusters. Fig. 7.7 presents a map of co-authorship among various authors and the nodes with same colours represent same clusters. Bigger sized nodes represent greater number of collaborations in documents and inter connecting lines represent the collaboration between various authors. Authors in the same cluster connote that they are related to each other in terms of their co-authorship with each other. The biggest cluster is the first one with 15 authors and cluster 2 has 11 authors and cluster 3 has nine authors. Rangan Gupta, Mehmet

Balcilar and David Roubaud form a part of same cluster 4, where Rangan Gupta has the maximum number of collaborative documents as evidenced from the map also. Rangan Gupta also has the maximum number of publications and the greatest number of citations as previously explained.

3.6.2 Inter-Country Co-Authorship Analysis

Table 7.7 lists down the top countries with respect to the number of citations. Fig. 7.8 presents the network map of inter country co-authorship for research on EPU. This map aids in understanding that authors in which countries have co-authored with the maximum number of co-authors with the other countries. Total number of countries identified were 84 of which 47 met the criteria. The nodes in the figure symbolizes the countries whose authors have co-authored with the authors of other countries and the lines represent the connections between various countries. Bigger the node size, more are the number of authors of that country who have co-authored with other countries and the depth of the connecting lines increase with the increase in the number of documents the authors have published. The map generated by VOS viewer shows that the authors of China have co-authored with the maximum number of authors of other countries. In fact, they have co-authored with authors of almost all the other countries as shown by the connecting network of lines. The authors of The United States, France, United Kingdom and Australia have co-authored with the maximum authors of other countries. In total six clusters have been formed, where countries in a single cluster are represented by the same colour in the map. The largest cluster is the first one having 11 countries that are strongly collaborating with each other followed by cluster 2 with 10 countries and cluster 3 with 9 countries.

4. Discussion and Conclusions

The results of this study reveal that EPU has been studied in relation to a lot of variables and a lot of research has already been generated. But this topic is still relatively new and a lot of areas of research can be explored for future scope. Based on the research questions it was found that the journal with the maximum number of publications on EPU is Finance Research Letters from the Elsevier publication. The publications in this field started only recently in 2013 and in fact picked up pace only after 2018. It can be inferred that the topic of EPU has caught the attention of researchers due to its significant and far-reaching impact on the households, businesses and the economy as a whole. The top most cited paper is Measuring Economic policy Uncertainty by Baker et al. (2016) which proposes a unique index that quantifies the EPU and has been used by almost all the new studies. The most prolific author who has received the maximum citations is Gupta R. Moreover, he has also co-authored the maximum times for research studies. The most influential institution based on the number of citations and having the maximum number of publications is the University of Pretoria, Pretoria, South Africa. China has secured the maximum number of publications and

Table 7.7. Cluster-Wise List of Countries.

S.No	Label	Cluster	No of Documents
1	Turkey	1	81
2	South Africa		52
3	Germany		49
4	Saudi Arabia		30
5	Tunisia		29
6	Nigeria		20
7	Lebanon		12
8	United Arab Emirates		10
9	Belgium		8
10	Cyprus		8
11	Ghana		8
12	China	2	371
13	Australia		70
14	India		50
15	New Zealand		41
16	Pakistan		40
17	Malaysia		25
18	Bangladesh		9
19	Thailand		9
20	Macau		6
21	Singapore		6
22	France	3	83
23	Viet Nam		62
24	Russian federation		18
25	Sweden		11
26	Ireland		7
27	Finland		6
28	Norway		6
29	Poland		6
30	Oman		5
31	United States	4	193
32	South Korea		38
33	Canada		36
34	Japan		12

Table 7.7. *(Continued)*

S.No	Label	Cluster	No of Documents
35	Brazil		6
36	Kuwait		6
37	United Kingdom	5	94
38	Spain		29
39	Greece		23
40	Italy		20
41	Austria		10
42	Portugal		6
43	Taiwan	6	32
44	Hong Kong		15
45	Denmark		6
46	Indonesia		6
47	Iran		6

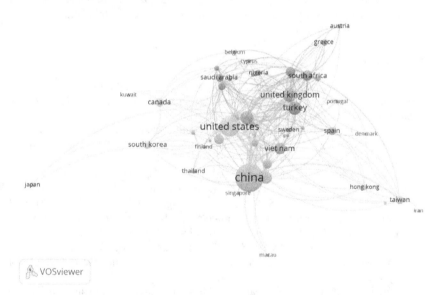

Fig. 7.8.   Network Map of Inter-Country Co-Authorship Analysis.

citations among all the other countries. Moreover, it has been observed that China is the country that has maximum number of inter country co-authorships also. Also, from keyword co-occurrence analysis, we can deduce that 'Economic policy Uncertainty' has readily co-occurred with 'China' in the studies. Other important keywords that have been investigated by researchers include 'EPU', 'Covid-19', 'Investment', 'firm value', 'stock returns' etc. which leads to an inference that the impact of EPU has been studied on these variables in the past studies.

It is needless to say that our study is not devoid of limitations. Firstly, we have explored only the Scopus database for our analysis that implies that studies published in journals not indexed in Scopus were excluded from the studies. We have been able to search only a single study in the year 2006 and thereafter no published study till 2013. Possibly we could have obtained a different result if we could have included other databases like Web of Science for our analysis as research including a number of different databases encompasses a larger picture, which presents a scope for future studies. Secondly only papers published in the English language were included for our analysis which excludes the work done in other languages. Thirdly we have not included PHD thesis, unpublished papers, masters and doctoral dissertations on EPU for our analysis. For future analysis, data can be collected from all these areas and a comparative study can be made. Accepting all the above limitations, it is nevertheless believed that an extensive data has been collected and a comprehensive and novice study on bibliometric analysis has been presented that would contribute in the research for EPU in future.

To conclude it is safe to say that the topic EPU has been presented in a new light and it would open new and novel arenas of research in this field.

References

Abakah, E. J. A., Caporale, G. M., & Gil-Alana, L. A. (2021). Economic policy uncertainty: Persistence and cross-country linkages. *Research in International Business and Finance, 58*, 101442.

Abid, A. (2020). Economic policy uncertainty and exchange rates in emerging markets: Short and long runs evidence. *Finance Research Letters, 37*, 101378. https://doi.org/10.1016/j.frl.2019.101378

Arbatli, E. C., Davis, S. J., Ito, A., & Miake, N. (2017). *Policy uncertainty in Japan (No. w23411)*. National Bureau of Economic Research.

Arora, M., Prakash, A., Dixit, S., Mittal, A., & Singh, S. (2023). A critical review of HR analytics: Visualization and bibliometric analysis approach. *Information Discovery and Delivery, 51*(3), 267–282. https://doi.org/10.1108/IDD-05-2022-0038

Baker, S. R., Bloom, N., & Davis, S. J. (2016). Measuring economic policy uncertainty. *Quarterly Journal of Economics, 131*(4), 1593–1636. https://doi.org/10.1093/qje/qjw024

Baker, H. K., Kumar, S., & Pattnaik, D. (2021). Research constituents, intellectual structure, and collaboration pattern in the Journal of Forecasting: A bibliometric analysis. *Journal of Forecasting, 40*(4), 577–602. (in this issue). http://doi.org/10.1002/for.2731

Bermpei, T., Kalyvas, A. N., Neri, L., & Russo, A. (2022). Does economic policy uncertainty matter for financial reporting quality? Evidence from the United States. *Review of Quantitative Finance and Accounting, 58*(2), 795–845.

Bonaime, A., Gulen, H., & Ion, M. (2018). Does policy uncertainty affect mergers and acquisitions? *Journal of Financial Economics*, *129*(3), 531–558. https://doi.org/10.1016/j.jfineco.2018.05.007

Brogaard, J., & Detzel, A. (2015). The asset-pricing implications of government economic policy uncertainty. *Management Science*, *61*(1), 3–18. https://doi.org/10.1287/mnsc.2014.2044

Caglayan, M., & Xu, B. (2019). Economic policy uncertainty affects the credit and stability of financial institutions. *Bulletin of Economic Research*, *71*(3), 342–347. https://doi.org/10.1111/boer.12175

Chen, X., Le, C. H. A., Shan, Y., & Taylor, S. (2020). Australian policy uncertainty and corporate investment. *Pacific-Basin Finance Journal*, *61*, 101341. https://doi.org/10.1016/j.pacfin.2020.101341

Dejuán, D., & Ghirelli, C. (2018). *Policy uncertainty and investment in Spain*. https://papers.ssrn.com/sol3/papers.cfm?abstract_id=3306560

Donthu, N., Kumar, S., Mukherjee, D., Pandey, N., & Lim, W. M. (2021). How to conduct a bibliometric analysis: An overview and guidelines. *Journal of Business Research*, *133*, 285–296.

Goodell, J. W., Goyal, A., & Urquhart, A. (2021). Uncertainty of uncertainty and firm cash holdings. *Journal of Financial Stability*, *56*, 100922.

Gupta, K., Kumar, C., Deshpande, A., Mittal, A., Chopade, P., & Raut, R. (2024). Internet gaming addiction–A bibliometric review. *Information Discovery and Delivery*, *52*(1), 62–72.

He, Z., & Niu, J. (2018). The effect of economic policy uncertainty on bank valuations. *Applied Economics Letters*, *25*(5), 345–347. https://doi.org/10.1080/13504851.2017.1321832

Ioannidis, C., & Ka, K. (2021). Economic policy uncertainty and bond risk premia. *Journal of Money, Credit, and Banking*, *53*(6), 1479–1522.

Jiang, Y., Wu, L., Tian, G., & Nie, H. (2021). Do cryptocurrencies hedge against EPU and the equity market volatility during COVID-19?–New evidence from quantile coherency analysis. *Journal of International Financial Markets, Institutions and Money*, *72*, 101324.

Jin, X., & Wu, H. (2021). Economic policy uncertainty and cost stickiness. *Management Accounting Research*, *52*, 100750.

Kang, W., & Ratti, R. A. (2013). Oil shocks, policy uncertainty and stock market return. *Journal of Intentional Financial Markets, Institutions and Money*, *26*, 305–318.

Lee, K., Joen, Y., & Kim, M. (2022). Which uncertainty measures matter for the cross-section of stock returns? *Finance Research Letters*, *46*, 102390.

Lei, A. C., & Song, C. (2020). Economic policy uncertainty and stock market activity: Evidence from China. *Global Finance Journal*, 100581.

Li, X. (2019). Economic policy uncertainty and corporate cash policy: International evidence. *Journal of Accounting and Public Policy*, *38*(6), 106694. https://doi.org/10.1016/j.jaccpubpol.2019.106694

Li, R., Li, S., Yuan, D., & Yu, K. (2020). Does economic policy uncertainty in the U.S. influence stock markets in China and India? Time-frequency evidence. *Applied Economics*, *52*(39), 4300–4316. https://doi.org/10.1080/00036846.2020.1734182

Li, W., Su, Y., & Wang, K. (2022). How does economic policy uncertainty affect cross-border M&A: Evidence from Chinese firms. *Emerging Markets Review*, 100908.

Liu, L., & Zhang, T. (2015). Economic policy uncertainty and stock market volatility. *Finance Research Letters, 15*, 99–105.

Mensi, W., Hammoudeh, S., Reboredo, J. C., & Nguyen, D. K. (2014). Do global factors impact BRICS stock markets? A quantile regression approach. *Emerging Markets Review, 19*, 1–17.

Naidenova, I. (2021). Economic policy uncertainty and company's human capital. *Journal of Economic Studies, 49*(5).

Nonejad, N. (2021). Predicting equity premium using news-based economic policy uncertainty: Not all uncertainty changes are equally important. *International Review of Financial Analysis, 77*, 101818.

Nonejad, N. (2022). Predicting equity premium out-of-sample by conditioning on newspaper-based uncertainty measures: A comparative study. *International Review of Financial Analysis, 83*, 102251.

Padungsaksawasdi, C., Treepongkaruna, S., & Jiraporn, P. (2023). LGBT-supportive corporate policies, risk aversion and mitigation and economic policy uncertainty. *Review of Behavioral Finance, 15*(2), 240–256.

Pattnaik, D., Kumar, S., & Vashishtha, A. (2020). Research on trade credit – A systematic review and bibliometric analysis. *Qualitative Research in Financial Markets, 12*(4), 367–390.

Phan, D. H. B., Iyke, B. N., Sharma, S. S., & Affandi, Y. (2021). Economic policy uncertainty and financial stability–Is there a relation? *Economic Modelling, 94*, 1018–1029. https://doi.org/10.1016/j.econmod.2020.02.042

Phan, D. H. B., Sharma, S. S., & Tran, V. T. (2018). Can economic policy uncertainty predict stock returns? Global evidence. *Journal of International Financial Markets, Institutions and Money, 55*, 134–150. https://doi.org/10.1016/j.intfin.2018.04.004

Sharif, A., Aloui, C., & Yarovaya, L. (2020). COVID-19 pandemic, oil prices, stock market, geopolitical risk and policy uncertainty nexus in the US economy: Fresh evidence from the wavelet-based approach. *International Review of Financial Analysis, 70*, 101496.

Sharma, C., & Paramati, S. R. (2021). Does economic policy uncertainty dampen imports? Commodity-level evidence from India. *Economic Modelling, 94*, 139–149. https://doi.org/10.1016/j.econmod.2020.09.019

Smales, L. A. (2021). Policy uncertainty in Australian financial markets. *Australian Journal of Management, 46*(3), 523–547.

Smales, L. A. (2022). The influence of policy uncertainty on exchange rate forecasting. *Journal of Forecasting, 41*(5), 997–1016.

Tran, D. V., Hoang, K., & Nguyen, C. (2021). How does economic policy uncertainty affect bank business models? *Finance Research Letters, 39*, 101639. https://doi.org/10.1016/j.frl.2020.101639

Ur Rehman, M., Raheem, I. D., Al Rababa'a, A. R., Ahmad, N., & Vo, X. V. (2022). Reassessing the predictability of the investor sentiments on US stocks: The role of uncertainty and risks. *The Journal of Behavioral Finance*, 1–16.

Valtakoski, A. (2020). The evolution and impact of qualitative research in Journal of Services Marketing. *Journal of Services Marketing, 34*(1), 8–23.

Vo, H., Trinh, Q. D., Le, M., & Nguyen, T. N. (2021). Does economic policy uncertainty affect investment sensitivity to peer stock prices? *Economic Analysis and Policy, 72,* 685–699.

Wang, Y., Chen, C. R., & Huang, Y. S. (2014). Economic policy uncertainty and corporate investment: Evidence from China. *Pacific-Basin Finance Journal, 26,* 227–243. https://doi.org/10.1016/j.pacfin.2013.12.008

Wen, J., Khalid, S., Mahmood, H., & Yang, X. (2022). Economic policy uncertainty and growth nexus in Pakistan: A new evidence using NARDL model. *Economic Change and Restructuring, 55*(3), 1701–1715.

Zhang, G., Han, J., Pan, Z., & Huang, H. (2015). Economic policy uncertainty and capital structure choice: Evidence from China. *Economic Systems, 39*(3), 439–457. https://doi.org/10.1016/j.ecosys.2015.06.003

Chapter 8

Indian Teens Buying Behaviour Towards E-Commerce

Ruchika Dawar, Sonika Siwach and Sapna Sehrawat

National Institute of Fashion Technology, India

Abstract

E-commerce in India has been experiencing remarkable growth, successfully changing the way people transact. The pandemic has accelerated the shift towards a more digital world and triggered changes in online shopping behaviours that are likely to have lasting effects. Social media has become integral to the teen market online shopping experience. Food and clothing are the primary sources of expenditure in teenagers, followed by health and personal care for girls and video games for boys. 42% of adolescent spending is directed to social uses, such as food, video games, music, movies, events and books. 38% of their expenses are related to clothing, accessories or shoes and 15% to beauty and personal care. The research was conducted to study factors that affected the teen age group in shopping online. This inquisitiveness led to the formation of a questionnaire which focuses on collecting information on the current e-commerce trends of Indian teenagers. The study was conducted online in the age group ranging between 13 years and 19 years over a period spanning two weeks. The study focuses on determining gaps in the Indian Market for teenagers in order to cater them in a better way.

Keywords: Teen market; online shopping; market gap; shopping experience; buying behaviour

1. Introduction

E-commerce is the process of buying and selling tangible products and services online. It involves more than one party along with the exchange of data or currency to process a transaction. Young demography, increasing Internet and

Modeling Economic Growth in Contemporary India, 137–150

Copyright © 2024 Ruchika Dawar, Sonika Siwach and Sapna Sehrawat

Published under exclusive licence by Emerald Publishing Limited

doi:10.1108/978-1-80382-751-320241008

smartphone penetration, and relatively better economic performance are some key drivers of this sector.

The growth story of India continues – a big growth story. To the extent of being as conservative as one can, the GDP is seen increasing from 6% to 7% a year with consumption expenditures expected to rise by a factor of three to reach $4 trillion by 2025. With a nominal year-over-year expenditure growth of 12% which is more than double the anticipated global rate of 5%, India will make the third-largest consumer market by 2025.

E-commerce has transformed the way business is done in India. The Indian E-commerce market is expected to grow to US$ 188 billion by 2025 from US$ 46.2 billion as of 2020. By 2030, it is expected to reach US$ 350 billion. Propelled by rising smartphone penetration, launch of 4G network and increasing consumer wealth, the Indian E-commerce market is expected to grow to US$ 200 billion by 2026 from US$ 38.5 billion in 2017. IBEF (2022) E-commerce industry in India. Retrieved from https://www.ibef.org/industry/ecommerce.

A *teenager*, or *teen*, is someone who is between 13 and 19 years old.

The life of a teenager seems to change daily. Constantly exposed to new ideas, social situations and people, Teenagers work to develop their personalities and interests during this time of great change. Before their teenage years, these adolescents focused on school, play and gaining approval from their parents.

The perception of teenagers as cool, trend-setting and influential was – and still is – just as much a creation of commerce and media as a reflection of reality. Teenage music, fashion and language ripples across the rest of society, supercharged by industries established to profit from them.

2. Objectives

The objectives of the study were:

- to evaluate the Teens Market and Buying Behaviour towards E-Commerce in India and
- to evaluate the Brand choices, Trends, Price Points, Competition Mapping, White Gaps and Shopping Challenges for Teens.

3. Scope of the Study

The study can be used to understand the current e-commerce trends of Indian teenagers. The findings of the study can also help gauge the popular sites teenagers prefer to engage in, for online shopping. Based on the preferences of teenage buyers, these websites can fine tune their services to improve their online business prospects.

4. Limitations of the Study

The study was limited only to those teenagers who directly engage in shopping online, and those people who buy on behalf of teenagers were not included.

5. Literature Review

Teenagers are brand conscious but not necessarily brand loyal. Friends, whose opinions they value, heavily influence buying behaviour. Peer approval of purchases is very important, especially to girls. The Piper Jaffray report states that friends had the most influence over teen purchase decisions and about 50% of both males and females said social media influenced them. Shopping is a core social activity for teenage girls who are more likely to be swayed by celebrities than boys. Email: Almost 40% of teenage girls sign up for emails from their favourite brands to receive information about sales and promotions. Sharing is common: 65% say when their favourite brand has a sale, they want to share the information with their best friend or sister, and 57% say when they find a new brand or trend, they tell a best friend or sister. About 80% prefer to share the information by texting or calling rather than posting to social media platforms. Celebrities influence 43% are influenced by the style of celebrities. Teens have short attention spans, especially regarding advertisements. They filter out a good deal of the messages and are often doing several other things while shopping online, especially if they are on a mobile device. Messaging that is concise, transparent and has a point is necessary to garner their attention. It can be time-consuming to keep up with the changing inclinations of teenagers but they do have substantial purchasing power (Kaplan, 2013).

The term 'digital natives' has been used to describe Generation Z. They are the first generation to always have the Internet at their disposal. They grew up in a world that is seamlessly connected. 41% of teens identify an athletic apparel brand as their preferred clothing brand with Nike topping the list (Kaplan, 2017); 70% of teens prefer to shop at their favourite stores online. Teens are shopping more via the Internet and brick and mortar outlet stores and less at specialty stores. Teens have to come up with more of their own resources, which may account for teens shopping less at pricier specialty stores. When it comes to online shopping, teens are outspending their parents. Shoppers aged between 13 and 18 years old spent at twice the rate of adults. Teen confidence in online shopping for consumer goods extends across the retail landscape. Amazon.com is the most frequented site. Teens also frequent specialty retailers looking for discounts and unique items – sites their parents may not be familiar with (Amato-McCoy, 2017).

Gen Z. Loosely defined as people born between the mid-1990s and the early 2010s, this generation has never known a world without the Internet or smartphones. For them, social media is second nature. And according to marketing experts, that very much shapes how they buy things, even in real life. The way that teenagers shop now is totally different than before – brands and trends mostly gain steam over social media – and yet still very much the same. They're into clothes, makeup and getting pizza with their friends.

Gen Z considers the brands they support to be a reflection of their values, and the products they buy a way of telling the world how they wish to be perceived. Teens: They're just like us (Brooke, 2018).

6. Methodology

6.1 Research Design

The study is both quantitative and qualitative in nature. The nature of the research is both descriptive as it clearly defines the demographics segment and our analysis is based on the data derived from various sources to perform competitor analysis and understand market trends, also to launch Teens-specific platform in the market. It is exploratory as a few assumptions have been made to analyse market sizing for potential growth and sales.

Method of Data Collection: Primary and Secondary Method

- Primary Data: Conducted primary research (Group discussions, Personal Interview & Questionnaire) for knowing customer preferences and top performing e-commerce platform for the age group 13–19.
- Secondary Data: Conducted detailed analysis of the Teens Market by reviewing brand websites, journals, case studies, papers, research databases, etc.

Sample Size: 200 teenagers in the age group of 13 years–19 years.

7. Analysis

The concerned demographics for this research amounted to a total of 105 respondents. Out of the 105 teens who took the survey 67.3% were Girls and 28.8% were Boys. The age group considered for the survey was 13–19 years, where 13–15 years accounted for 32.7% and 16–19 accounted for 67.3% (Figs. 8.1 and 8.2).

The teen segment shopped the most on the basis of requirement, i.e. during occasions/festivals followed by once or twice a month. Assuming the average basket size as two to three articles, Teens spending power ranges between Rs. 1000 and Rs. 2000 the most while shopping followed by more than Rs. 3000 and

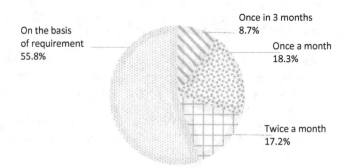

Fig. 8.1.   Frequency of Shopping. *Source:* Researcher's own work.

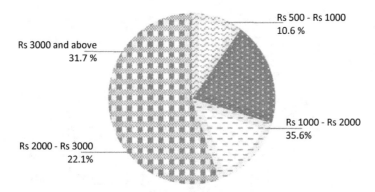

Fig. 8.2.   Amount Spent in One Time on Shopping. *Source:*
Researcher's own work.

Rs. 2000–Rs. 3000. It can be inferred that the teenage segment is willing to spend somewhere between Rs. 500 and Rs. 800 per product.

Most teenagers prefer to shop offline from local stores or flea markets in their area, followed by E-commerce platforms and Multi-brand outlets like Shopper Stop and Lifestyle. It can be inferred that teens look for options under one roof. One major factor influencing the selection decision is the ease of trial and selection (Fig. 8.3).

As of now, Teens mostly prefer Amazon followed by Myntra and Urbanic to shop online (Fig. 8.4).

Teens have a strong inclination towards E-Commerce and would want to have a dedicated platform to shop from considering the ease of navigation (Fig. 8.5).

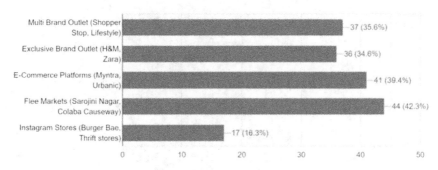

Fig. 8.3.   Most Preferred Shopping Destination. *Source:* Researcher's
own work.

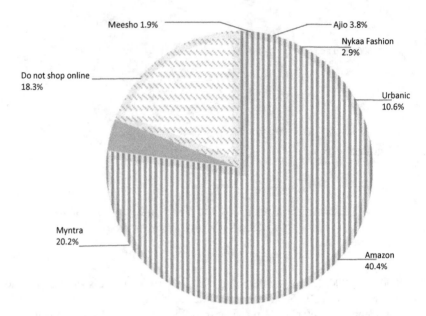

Fig. 8.4.   Most Preferred E-Commerce Platform. *Source:* Researcher's own work.

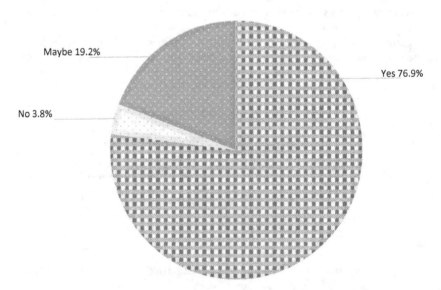

Fig. 8.5.   Requirement of Teen-Specific Category on E-Commerce Application. *Source:* Researcher's own work.

7.1 Teens Online Presence

Teens segment is an underserved segment in the market with limited brands/labels catering to the market. Teenage is a phase of transitioning from kid to adulthood in the process of taking control. This is a period of transitioning with physical and sociological change converging. This is the time when the child acquires a smartphone and gets on social media. The pandemic accelerated the virtual lifestyle and transitioned the shopping culture to virtual. The transition of virtual source of education during the pandemic had forced parents to give access to smartphones to their kids as early as 12/13 years of age.

Different Facets of Teens

- *Augmented Reality:* An average teen spends 3–6 hours of social media everyday with Instagram and YouTube being the most used apps for Entertainment, Socialization, Expression and Information. YouTube and Instagram, being the highly used and influential apps for teens, are used for general browsing, songs, entertainment videos and informative videos. Both the platforms provide awareness of fashion trends. Instagram provides more insights since it gives easy access to communication and also explores new stores and shopping experiences. Followed by Snapchat, Pinterest and Facebook as we move towards the older teens.
- *Amalgamated Identity:* Social media acts as a way of expression for teens, therefore they present a layered personality. A layered personality does not mean having a fake, but rather a kind of identity that shows off the best version of oneself to the world.
- *Gocal Existence:* Indian and International Influences through OTT, Music, Food, Fashion. International Influence has rather more impact on the Indian Teens with Content including Korean, Japanese and American and a huge impact from the Westernized and Fusion Wear styles and Body Image. This, however, generates inter-generational tension in small towns and conservative families. Parents are unable to fathom the depth of impact of global exposure. With time, both parents and teens are striving to compromise, adapt and bridge the gap.
- *Privileged and Pragmatic:* Teens expect quick gratification of the immediacy of their online lives impatient and quick to consume and move on. They believe in making informed choices like checking reviews before buying anything and are in a data-rich environment where they're aware of their needs and wants.
- *Vulnerability:* Teens tend to not trust easily and are privacy conscious. Teens on social media of age 12/13 are prone to being hurt by comments that impact self-image. They feel the pressure to project a positive confident powerful picture to the world through their social media.

8. Teens Fashion Evolution Analysis

Male and Female Teens have different need sets arising from attitude and environment. Therefore, it was important to study the choices for both Girls and Boys with further segregation into Early Teens (12–14) and Late Teens (15–19) (Tables 8.1 and 8.2).

Table 8.1. Evolution of Teenage Girl's Fashion Identity.

	12–14 Years	**15–19 Years**
Traits	The age group represents an under confident and confused state of mind with lifestyle choices regulated largely going to school, connecting with friends in the vicinity and occasional partying or sleepover.	The age group represents a freer and more independent lifestyle with increased time spent with friends and more occasions.
Goal	The goal is to become confident, express emotions and be accepted by peers and parents.	The goal is now to experiment and try new things and be different from the peer group in order to make an impact on society.
Media	It plays a crucial role in shaping decisions, from cartoons like Doremon, Sinchan to daily soaps and movies like family man, Squid games, Emily in Paris.	The consumption choices changed from cartoons to content with reality shows like MTV Roadies, Splits villa and other OTT shows.
Fashion inspiration	The constant need for validation and attention comes as a life challenge during this phase in life. Fashion inspiration comes from self-assured older siblings, cousins and friends and are at the stage to discover influencers on social media.	Fashion inspiration comes from fashion Icons and Influencers, brand websites, shopping fashion apps, peers and Instagram.
Fashion trends	The age group is considered as a beginner in the fashion world and is a learning stage where they experiment with different styles appropriate for different occasions. Mix and match and Experimentation to find the appropriate fit.	The age group is considered as an adopter of fashion. The stage revolves around adopting trends and creating a unique style for self.
Demands	The girls of the age group search for the right fit and for comfort and do not focus on budget.	The girls of this age group are more concerned with the trends and fit of the garment. The budget thus becomes more important.

Table 8.1. (*Continued*)

	12–14 Years	**15–19 Years**
Shopping behaviour	Browse online for info range. The age group mainly prefer buying offline after ensuring the right fit. Online purchases are supervised by mothers.	Purchases are still skewed offline. The age group usually browses and buys online and the payment is usually done by mothers.
Shopping apps	Usually browses Instagram and Facebook stores. Very limited access and use of e-commerce stores like Amazon and Myntra. Shopping apps are usually used on parent's mobile phones.	Multiple shopping apps on mobile to trace the best deal on different brands. Family influence accounts for shopping on Amazon. Spending power still rests on parents.
Brands	The relationship with brands is nascent but evolving. They are more focused on styles than brands but leading brands like Zara and H&M set their fashion taste. They begin to explore portals like Amazon, Myntra, Meesho and Urbanic.	Brands like Zara and H&M, Westside, lifestyle and Forever 21 drive their style concept. These are largely offline. Online brands like Myntra, Ajio, Urbanic and Nykaa become default online options.

Source: Researcher's own work.

Table 8.2. Evolution of Teenage Boys Fashion Identity.

	12–14 Years	**15–19 Years**
Traits	The age group represents itself as boys with a limited lifestyle revolving around school and playing cricket/football as a hobby. The media accessible and enjoyed by the age group revolves around gaming and sports.	The age group represents itself as man when the body starts growing. The attitude grows more responsible and self-aware. Life choices are more fitness oriented. Social media starts playing a major role in order to socialize with interests in more adventurous and funny content.
Fashion	The fashion interest is more sports driven. The age group is physically underdeveloped and aspires to be taller/muscular.	The interest in fashion and experimenting with looks starts to interest them. The body transitions making them feel

(Continued)

Table 8.2. *(Continued)*

	12–14 Years	15–19 Years
	They aspire to look older and therefore emulate their favourite sports star. They do not bother about fashion as they're unsure of what would suit them according to colours and body type.	more self-assured. The occasions to go out expand and thus, fashion helps create an identity and helps feel inclusive.
Demands	For younger teens, comfort is non- negotiable. They are more inclined towards sports and therefore unconcerned about looks.	The older teens would trade comfort for fit. Tradeoff in semi-formal/smart casuals in order to attract the opposite sex or to settle in with the group of friends.
Fashion inspiration	Influenced by sports stars, young movie actors and singers like Virat Kohli, Tom Holland.	Influencer set expands with more style-based icons like Zayn Malik, Harry Styles.
Shopping apps	Very low use of shopping apps. May browse occasionally in search of particular shoes. Seeks approval of parents to make a purchase if the right product is found.	More into browsing on apps like Amazon/Myntra. Takes purchasing power in their hands if the product is on budget, otherwise convinces siblings/ parents to buy for them.
Brands	Brand understanding is tenuous. They seek comfort over brands. Parents and older cousins/siblings are key sources of information and therefore, the choices are influenced by them instead of peers.	Connects with brands in order to provide a sense of class, status and identification. Influenced by celebrities and peers in making purchasing decisions about brand choices.

Source: Researcher's own work.

9. Pain Points

9.1 Size and Fit

Issue: The body is growing and body curves are not fully developed therefore, finding the right fit becomes a challenge. The transition of size chart from Age Group to Adult sizing chart creates confusion. The body falls between sizes and lack of size consistency across brands creates lack of options.

Current Workaround: Shopping offline to be able to try from across the kids and adult section makes decision-making easy.

9.2 Style Gaps

Issue: Taste matures fast but retains some child element. Therefore, toggling between child and adult styles creates confusion. The brands with right sizing usually end up not being able to cater to the trend.

Current Workaround: Tries both adult and kids' sections to find the appropriate style.

9.3 Culture Clashes

Issue: Convincing mothers on more forward styles in smaller towns/conservative families. Generation Gap creates acceptance of the choices made by the teens difficult to the parents.

Current Workaround: Educating mothers about the changing trends and styles. Gives decision-making to mothers on traditional outfits.

10. Pain Points

10.1 Finding the Balance Between Comfort and Fit

Issue: They are constantly playing sports and involved in other activities and therefore the body keeps changing. A Good Fit is therefore the closest to fashion. They're unsure of colours, styles and what works on their changing body types.

Current Workaround: They tend to buy clothes that are a size large to make do with the outfit or completely rely on the choice of parents.

10.2 No Say in Buying Decision-Making

The buying decision relies on parents and the teens has no say. With little pocket money, they would rather spend it on food than buying clothes. Buying decisions goes from mothers for boys aged 12–14 to fathers for boys aged 15 and above with change in dynamics and ease of communication.

11. Competitive Brand Analysis and Gap Mapping

11.1 Customer Profile

The analysis helped study the customer profile in order to cater to the segment better. The age group includes 13–19 years both Girls and Boys with Student as a profession. The style revolves around Streetwear, Casual Wear, Y2K and Sporty. The fashion Role Model for the age are celebrities like Khushi Kapoor, Ananya Pandey, Justin Bieber and Influencers like Komal Pandey. The hobbies post pandemic revolve around accessing Internet Content like series (Euphoria, Emily in Paris, K-Drama) and K-pop Music. The consuming habits include shopping once or twice a month accompanied and taking parents approval for age up to 15 years or E-Commerce platforms and Instagram stores with COD options with peer group approvals for the age group beyond 15.

11.2 Brands Catering to Indian Teen Market

The Indian Teens market is very niche and has limited brands that cater to the segment. The brands are divided into Established and Emerging brands. Where Established brands further divide into Pocket Friendly and Expensive. Established Brands are Brands that hold credibility in the Indian Market and are widely accepted by teens. Where Pocket Friendly depicts Brands that are Budget Friendly to Teens Spending power. Emerging Brands include brands that are tapping into the Indian Teens specific market. The brands fit the criteria for affordability and trend savvy (Fig. 8.6).

11.3 Established Brands

Pocket Friendly: Urbanic, H&M (Divided), Forever 21, Aeropostale, UCB, American Eagle.

Expensive: Nike, ZARA, Mango Teens, Tommy Hilfiger, Hollister, Superdry, Abercrombie & Fitch, Gap.

11.4 Emerging Brands

Freakins, Burger Bae, Bonkers, BlueBrew, HerSheInbox, Off Duty, Nomad, Madish.

12. Learnings and Suggestions

There is a need for a special platform that addresses the needs of the teenager as: They have a different set of needs from the mainstream audience.

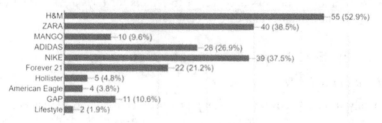

Fig. 8.6.   Brands Preferred by Teens. *Source:* Researcher's own work.

Beginner mindset: Beginners in fashion + beginners in online shopping, hence special needs. The target segment would therefore be a 12–16-year-old mindset since they're in a transitional phase and do not readily find styles and sizes for themselves.

Different aesthetic/fashion needs: tastes informed by the fact that they are in the cusp of childhood and adulthood-designs, ensembles, accessories they want are slightly different.

Different purchase dynamics: Associative purchase with parents or siblings.

The range of merchandize for boys revolves around athleisure and sports driven while for girls, the range revolves around specific aesthetic-based styles. While boys radiate towards Athletic brands like Nike, Adidas and HRX, Girls radiate towards brands like H&M, Zara and Shein.

The teen segment gravitates towards ease of navigation of products, therefore the use of simple and efficient filters, search bars with appropriate tagging for age groups. Use of Visual and Icon-Driven navigation.

The age group of 12–16 is inquisitive and therefore are seeking knowledge. They love to experiment and mix and match in order to find their own sense of style. They are therefore, building and learning about ensembles. Providing them with knowledge alongside the options to purchase makes their purchasing decision easier.

The need for a strong communication method, prominently Social Media Platforms like Instagram and Influencer marketing to push forward the Teens Store and highlight its presence to the target market.

With the study and gap analysis, it is observed that there is an opportunity for e-commerce platforms to have a separate store or category to cater teenagers.

A Teens store with styling tips and fashionable look books would be a shopping heaven for the Gen-Z shoppers, to cater to their specific fashion and style needs and to offer unique and absorbing experiences to this customer cohort. This platform needs to have a different vibe. It should be a young and playful store.

13. Conclusion

The study reveals the way teenagers think and behave while going to shop online. In online shopping platforms, a digital market is presented before them in place of the real market. They do not make impulsive purchases, rather their decisions are affected by a number of reasons. Their buying decision-making is therefore influenced by one major factor that is ease of navigation. Teenagers in today's time want quick responses to their problems and therefore switch between different e-commerce platforms that cater according to their requirements. The study has proved that if these factors are not considered seriously by the company, their decision may be changed. The study analysed the gaps in the market for the teenage segment after careful analysis of their requirements and brand choices that cater to the segment.

Although some will argue that tailoring e-commerce sites to attract the teen market isn't as valuable because teens don't have direct buying power when it comes to online shopping, they are extremely influential when it comes to the consumption levels of their parents.

References

Amato-McCoy, D. M. (2017, October 15). *Study: Teens twice as likely to shop online than adults.* https://chainstoreage.com/technology/study-teens- twice-likely-shop-online-adults

Brooke, E. (2018, September 24). *Teen shopping habits, explained by teens.* https://www.vox.com/the-goods/2018/9/24/17861398/gen-z-shopping-habits-juul-glossier

IBEF. (2022, April). *E-commerce industry in India.* https://www.ibef.org/industry/ecommerce#:~:text=In%202022%2C%20the%20Indian%20e,in%20internet%20and%20smartphone%20penetration

Kaplan, M. (2013, June 13). *Teenage online shopping trends.* https://www.practicalecommerce.com/Teenage-Online-Shopping-Trends

Kaplan, M. (2017, May 11). *Teen shopping habits and trends.* https://www.practicalecommerce.com/teen-shopping-habits-and-trends

Chapter 9

Impossible Trinity: Deepening Capital Flows and Converging Exchange Rate Regimes

Shilpa Ahuja and Puja Padhi

Indian Institute of Technology, India

Abstract

Making monetary policy decisions is a fine line to tread, always seeking to balance the needs of the domestic economic conditions with the need to keep events in the outside world under check. It is impossible to overstate the significance of monetary Trilemma in this context. This study aims to test the presence of monetary Trilemma and the contrasting dilemma hypothesis in India. The study is conducted over a considerable long span of time (1996–2022) to understand the evolution and changes in the management of Trilemma. In order to ascertain the changes in the existence of dilemma in India, this study analyses pre- and post-global financial crisis time periods. The relevance of exchange rate regimes in transforming Trilemma into a dilemma in the Indian context is assessed by providing for capital account restrictions. This evaluation helps to comprehend the impact of spillovers caused by monetary policy shocks in the United States and the resulting global financial cycle in India. The study provides evidence in favor of Trilemma and the relevance of exchange rate regimes as well as capital controls in determining monetary policy independence. The prevalence of more flexible exchange rate regimes favors a gradual shift toward dilemma, in situation of low capital controls.

Keywords: Monetary Trilemma; dilemma; exchange rate regime; monetary independence; exchange rate stability; capital flows; spillovers

1. Introduction

Monetary policy frameworks are crucial to the economic performance of an economy. The monetary policy decisions made by a country's central bank at the

Modeling Economic Growth in Contemporary India, 151–174

Copyright © 2024 Shilpa Ahuja and Puja Padhi

Published under exclusive licence by Emerald Publishing Limited

doi:10.1108/978-1-80382-751-320241009

appropriate time determine the course of its economic growth trajectory. How-ever, the issue is not as straightforward as it looks. There are various limits that policymakers must consider when evaluating what may be the optimal policy option given the economic situation. These include several domestic economic objectives – inflation control, GDP growth, capital formation, employment generation, and global factors like foreign capital flows, exchange rate stability, foreign monetary policy, and global investor sentiments (i.e., volatility).

Mundell–Fleming were the first to moot the phenomenon of the monetary Trilemma. Mundell (1963) mentions the tradeoff between the three phenomena of monetary independence, capital mobility, and exchange rate stability. The pres-ence of the Trilemma has been investigated in several studies. The results have, however, been quite mixed. Aizenman et al. (2013), Obstfeld et al. (2005) support the existence of Trilemma in the set of countries under study. Additionally, some studies tend to draw a bifurcation between results for developing and developed economies like Hsing (2012) and Lee (2021). Further, a continuous debate exists on different methodologies that appropriately capture the phenomenon. Aizenman et al. (2008) used three indices with values ranging from 0 to 1 to define the impossible trinity. A weighted average of these indices sum up to a constant in a simple linear form of regression. This methodology suffers from two major weaknesses. First, considering the correlation of interest rates between domestic and base country and secondly measuring the volatility of exchange rates with one base country (US) only. This study borrows from Durán-Vanegas (2019), which uses predictions from Taylor's Rule to forecast interest rates based on domestic conditions determined by Inflation and GDP to test the presence of Trilemma in India.

The role of global factors in affecting domestic monetary policy is a significant concern in maintaining monetary policy independence. After Rey's (2015) argument on the issue of global financial cycles, a breakthrough was attained in the study of trilemma literature. The study claimed that the "Trilemma has morphed into a dilemma in the wake of Global Financial Cycles" and that exchange rate systems are irrelevant. In the Indian context, several studies (Grewal & Trivedi, 2021b; Prabheesh et al., 2021) have established the existence of synchronization of the domestic financial cycle with the global financial cycle. The presence of US monetary spillovers in India has been suggested by several studies (Ghosh et al., 2014; Reinhart & Reinhart, 2009). We proceed based on the methodology provided by Han and Wei (2018) and consider changes in US interest rates and volatility index to assess impact on domestic monetary policy. This is done by providing the necessary controls to adjust exchange rate regimes and India's capital controls.

Studies (Aizenman, 2010; Hutchison et al., 2012; Obstfeld et al., 2005) conducted in the area comprise developed countries that are considerably different from India in terms of economic development, and capital flows. The policies or actions determined by developed countries based on these studies are not applicable in the Indian sce-nario. Thus, this study aims to fill this gap. The main aim of the study is to test the presence and evolution of monetary Trilemma in India. This is done using ACI methodology and a narrow and broad definition of Trilemma (Han & Wei, 2018).

The study also compares the findings of Trilemma with contrasting hypotheses of dilemma over the period from 1996q2 to 2022q1. The study incorporates the impact of global financial spillovers through changes in US interest rates and Volatility Index on interest rates in India. This provides for testing dilemma constraint, the second hypothesis of this study.

The ensuing portions of the study are organized as follows. The literature review of studies on the Trilemma and dilemma is included in Section 2. Section 3 and 4 provides a description of the variables under consideration, along with their sources. Additionally, Section 5 describes the estimation strategy. The results and findings are provided in Section 6. The conclusion and policy suggestions are presented in portion 7, and the final portion, Section 8, describes the research's limitations and future directions.

2. Literature Review

In the extension of the IS–LM model, Fleming (1962) proposed that a monetary expansion in a flexible exchange rate regime significantly influences income more than a fixed exchange rate regime. The model proposed by R. A. Mundell (1963) is among the first papers to raise the issue of the Trilemma. It dealt with increased capital mobility across borders and its implications for domestic policies. Mundell (1963) claims that if flexible exchange rates are assumed, monetary policy substantially impacts the income level by influencing the interest rate and inducing capital flows. Under a fixed exchange rate regime, corresponding capital outflows do not occur; hence, the balance of payments worsens. Thus, the exchange stabilization process initiated by the central bank reverses its function, and thus the monetary policy is rendered ineffective.

The Trilemma holds that a country may select any two of the three policy objectives of monetary autonomy, exchange rate stability, and capital mobility, but not all three (Fig. 9.1). In the figure, each side of the triangle represents – monetary independence, financial integration and exchange rate stability, which are desirable policy goals. All three cannot be accomplished at once.

In the Neo-Keynesian open economy model, perfect capital mobility in a fixed exchange rate regime is "denoted by the policy pair" on the right side of the "Trilemma" triangle (Fig. 9.1). The monetary base and interest rates are unaffected by attempts to expand the money supply; they simply change the balance sheet's mix of domestic and foreign assets. Thus, the economy must relinquish its monetary policy to achieve perfect capital mobility and a fixed exchange rate. Hence, the Trilemma. Similarly, a small open economy that wants to retain financial integration might reclaim its monetary independence by giving up fixed exchange rates. With flexible exchange rates, a rise in the money supply lowers interest rates, which results in capital outflows that raise the demand for foreign currency and drive the exchange rate down. The trade balance improves when exports rise as a result of the currency's depreciation. Hence, this case denotes the left side of the triangle (Fig. 9.1). In yet another case, a country may choose exchange rate stability and monetary independence and compromise on the financial integration process. This implies that capital

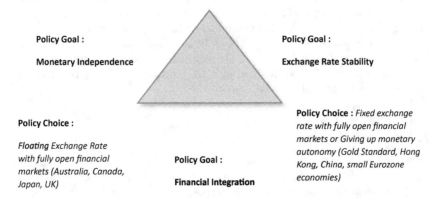

Policy Choice : *Fixed exchange rate with Closed Financial Markets (Bretton Woods, PRC in pre-1990s, etc.)*

Policy Goal :

Monetary Independence

Policy Goal :

Exchange Rate Stability

Policy Choice :

Floating Exchange Rate with fully open financial markets (Australia, Canada, Japan, UK)

Policy Goal :

Financial Integration

Policy Choice : *Fixed exchange rate with fully open financial markets or Giving up monetary autonomy (Gold Standard, Hong Kong, China, small Eurozone economies)*

Fig. 9.1.   The Trilemma.
Source: Ito and Kawai (2014).

flows are restricted across borders and hence central bank exercises full control and the model resembles that of a closed economy in this scenario. This policy is associated with the top vertex of the trilemma triangle (Fig. 9.1). Thus, we can say that the problem of the "impossible trinity" persists.

Okina et al. (1999) highlight the idea of the policy trilemma; a nation can only accomplish two of the three objectives at once. Before World War I, industrialized nations opted for gold standard-based currency stability and unrestricted capital movement. While maintaining stable exchange rates and independent monetary policies under the Bretton Woods arrangement, industrialized nations sacrificed global capital mobility. Following the demise of the Bretton Woods system, the domestic economy's stability and unrestricted capital mobility were prioritized. As a result, capital mobility has progressively expanded once more under the floating exchange rate regime.

2.1 Monetary Trilemma

The problem assumes complexity, as countries prefer to choose a certain degree of each. Thus, rather than the polar Trilemma located at the vertex of the triangle, the problem is concentrated in the middle. Measurement of the degree of capital mobility, exchange rate flexibility (various intermediate exchange rate regimes), and monetary autonomy in robust ways is also a challenge.

McKinnon and Schnabl (2004) highlight the phenomenon of pegging currencies to the US dollar in the aftermath of the East Asian crisis. International Monetary Fund (IMF) recommends a free float system. However, due to the "fear of floating", many developing economies accumulate currency reserves to stabilize exchange rates. Mohanty and Scatigna (2005) propose that an optimum exchange rate regime choice is crucial. Discussing the bipolar view, they suggest that soft exchange rate pegs make countries prone to currency attacks and thus recommend a hard peg or fully floating regime. For emerging countries, Goldstein (2002) proposes a "managed floating plus regime with three main goals: inflation targeting, exchange rate smoothing, and regulatory and market development policies." This may result in a credible exchange rate system with significant monetary autonomy. This study borrows from Ilzetzki et al. (2019) for the exchange rate classification into two exchange rate regimes under the flexible arrangement.

Traditionally, measures of legislative limits on cross-border capital flows, such as controls on inflows versus controls on outflows, quantity controls versus price controls, restrictions on foreign stock ownership, etc., have been used to gauge financial openness. The Annual Report on Exchange Rate Arrangements and Exchange Restrictions (AREAER) published by IMF tracks over 60 distinct kinds of restrictions. These types of measures are called de jure measures. An alternative approach (Prasad et al., 2003) is de facto measures that undertake how much a country is integrated into international capital markets in practice. Many countries have strict capital controls but are toothless in practice; as such their actual levels of financial integration are considerable. In our study, we restrict this to de facto measures proxied by total foreign inflows and outflows arising in the capital account of India.

Aizenman and Sengupta (2013), Aizenman et al. (2013), Hutchison et al. (2012), Arora and Kaur (2019), and Majumder and Nag (2021) support the existence of Trilemma in the Indian scenario. Others like Hofmann and Takáts (2015) and Edwards (2015) invalidate the Trilemma. Gupta and Manjhi (2011) report that the international trinity is valid in India, and India has adopted middle solutions. Mohan and Kapur (2009) state, "The impossible trinity was managed by preferring middle solutions of open but managed capital account and flexible exchange rate but with the management of volatility." Hutchison et al. (2012) note that increased capital account openness, particularly in the 2000s, has been accompanied with a decline in the independence of monetary policy or restrictions on exchange rate stability.

2.2 Dilemma

A study by Rey (2015) claimed that "the trilemma has morphed into a dilemma" in the wake of the Global Financial Cycles. The author describes global financial cycles as "characterized by large common movements in asset prices, gross flows, and leverage." The study asserts that whenever there is free capital mobility, the global financial cycle restricts monetary policy regardless of the exchange rate regime. As such, the tradeoff is with only two constraints presenting a dilemma as against a trilemma, given global financial cycles.

Aizenman and Ito (2016) highlight the fact that there is considerable increase in capital flows across borders in order to achieve higher economic growth. According to Reinhart and Reinhart (2009) and Ghosh et al. (2014), the US monetary policy is one of the major factors influencing the global capital flow waves, which are then transmitted all over the world. In another study, Grewal and Trivedi (2021b) established a statistically significant relation of spillovers between exchange rate of USD-INR and capital flows in India, originating from US monetary policy decisions.

Tica et al. (2016) test Mundell–Fleming's "trilemma" hypothesis against the "dilemma" and "quadrilemma" hypothesis by building wealth into consumption function and using two threshold variables – exchange rate stability index and measure of financial integration simultaneously to solve the basic open macroeconomic model. They conclude that "international business cycle is transmitted to developing and emerging countries due to choice of exchange rate regimes and not because of the ineffectiveness of monetary policy per se." Further analysis shows that government expenditure and international reserves are less significant in a fixed exchange rate regime, while a high level of financial integration renders strikingly different results under two exchange rate regimes. A study published by ECB states that a global financial cycle can transform the problem of Trilemma into a dilemma as opening a capital account automatically sets the tone for interest rates, irrespective of the prevalent exchange rate regime and central bank's policy stance. Durán-Vanegas (2019) report that when threshold levels are considered, Trilemma morphs into dilemma. Cerutti et al. (2019) as well as find evidence for global financial cycle and its ability to transmit to credit supply in domestic economy through exchange rate channel of transmission. Bernanke (2017) argues that the existence of a world financial cycle does not render Mundellian Trilemma invalid.

By using the technique of IV estimations, Majumder and Nag (2021) conclude that the dilemma does not hold in the Indian context. While several studies have been conducted in panel set up for testing of dilemma hypothesis, there is shortage of literature to testing dilemma hypothesis in Indian context. This research aims to fill this gap by building the impact of monetary policy spillovers on Indian monetary policy independence against the backdrop of Trilemma. The study tests two pre- and post-crisis models to test the dilemma's hypotheses and finds proof for the existence of the dilemma in India.

3. Variables and Data Sources

The study is focused on time period ranging from 1996q2 to 2022q1. This considerable long period has been chosen to provide for impact of major economic events – capital account convertibility, rise in global financial flows, rapid economic growth, global financial crisis and taper tantrum.

For testing of trilemma hypothesis, we construct a monetary policy index based on Taylor's rule prediction which uses domestic interest rates, inflation gap and output gap. Further, exchange rate stability index and capital openness index are constructed based on REER and net capital outflows as percent of GDP. For the study of dilemma, two more variables depicting global uncertainties are added – foreign interest rates, provided by US effective federal funds rate and CBOE Volatility Index. The variables used in the analysis are described in Table 9.1 along with sources.

Table 9.1. Variables Description and Data Source.

Variable of Interest		Variable	Time Period	Data Source	Frequency
Interest rates	Domestic	Weighted average call money rates	1996q2–2020q1	RBI	Quarterly (averaged from monthly data)
	Foreign	Effective funds rate	1996q2–2020q1	Fed	Quarterly (averaged from monthly data)
Inflation		WPI	1996q2–2020q1	Ministry of commerce	Quarterly (averaged from monthly data and adjusted for base year 2011–12)
Output	Nominal	GDP	1996q2–2020q1	RBI	Quarterly
	Real	GDP	1996q2–2020q1	RBI	Quarterly (base year 2011–12)
REER		Real effective exchange rate (basket of 36 currencies)	1996q2–2020q1	RBI	Quarterly (averaged from monthly data)
Capital flows	India	Capital flows	1996q2–2020q1	RBI	Quarterly
Volatility		VIX	1996q2–2020q1	CBOE	Quarterly (averaged from daily closing price data)
Exchange rate regime		ERR	1996q2–2020q1	https://www.ilzetzki.com/irr-data	Quarterly (calculated from annual)

4. Variables Description[1]

Indian Monetary Independence Index (MI) is constructed using weighted average call money rate. This rate is chosen for Taylor's rule estimation following several studies (Grewal & Trivedi, 2021b; Nair & Anand, 2020) and due to its close relation with repo rate and considerable volatility. WACR has been quite volatile, rising and falling sharply before 2008 crisis, after which it became comparatively stable, before a gradual decline again due to COVID-19 (Fig. 9.2a).

Wholesale Price Index (WPI) is used as proxy for Inflation (Fig. 9.2b). It is important to note that RBI adopted CPI as a measure of Inflation since 2014, however WPI remains a crucial tool to measure headline inflation for considerable part of our study. Target inflation rate is calculated using Hodrick–Prescott filter as against the default rate of 2%, defined in Taylor (1993). Inflation has remained considerably stable over significant part of the study, peaking only in 2007 and 2014. It remained substantially within the targeted framework and suddenly peaking in 2021, in the aftermath of Covid crisis.

Real Gross Domestic product is used to estimate the output gap (Fig. 9.2c). Considerable deviations in output gap have been reduced after 2008 crisis recovery. Impact of Covid first and second wave is observed in 2020 and 2021 as sharp fall (negative values) of output gap (Table 9.2).

Log values of Real Effective Exchange Rate (REER) (Fig. 9.2d) based on 36-currency basket is used to calculated Exchange Rate Stability (ERS) index. A rising trend in the values of real effective exchange rate is observed over the period. There was a sharp fall in index value in 2008, after which it has continued to rise, following minor dips in 2020 and 2021.

Capital Openness (KO) index is based on net capital flows (Outflows – Inflows) as percentage of GDP. Net capital flows as percentage of GDP have been quite fluctuating, but remaining in a considerable positive range, except for two periods marked by sudden capital outflows in 2014 and 2019, owing to taper tantrum and rise in US monetary policy rates, respectively.

US monetary policy rates are proxied by Effective Federal Funds Rate (EFFR) (Fig. 9.2e) which is the counterpart of WACR in India. EFFR had been considerably stable before 2000, when it experienced a sudden fall following the burst of dotcom bubble. Soon after recovery, it fell sharply again due to collapse of Lehman Brothers in 2008. The rates have remained considerably low thereafter at least till 2015, when Fed announced to raise the rates marking the end of financial stimulus provided after global financial crisis. The rates again dipped low following Covid crisis in 2019.

In addition to monetary policy spillovers, global volatilities are captured using log values of Volatility Index (Fig. 9.2f). Volatility index saw a dip in 2005 when markets were considerably stable and investor sentiments were high. It peaked in 2008 with global financial crisis and remained quite volatile again stabilizing only around 2015. A sharp increase in volatility is also observed toward the end of 2019, due to outbreak of corona virus. The volatility seems to be rising up since 2017.

---

[1]Summary statistics for variables under consideration is provided in Table AIII in Appendix.

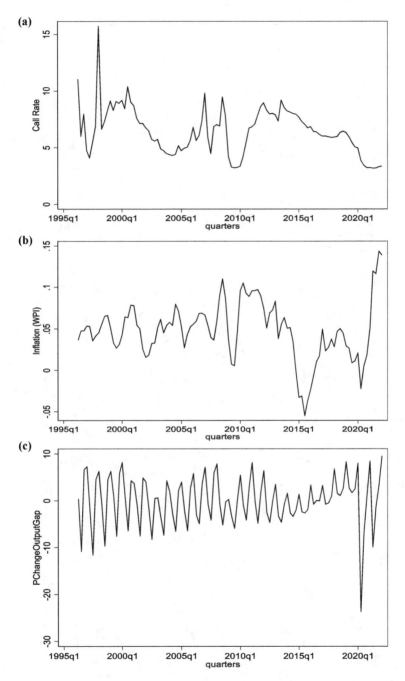

Fig. 9.2.   Major Variables and Their Trend. (a) Weighted average call money rate. (b) Wholesale price index. (c) Change in output gap (percent). (d) Real effective exchange rate. (e) Effective federal funds rate. (f) Volatility index. (g) Gross capital flows.

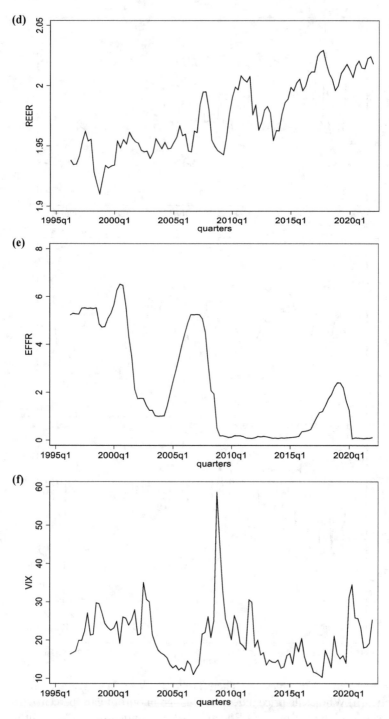

Fig. 9.2. *(Continued)*.

(g)

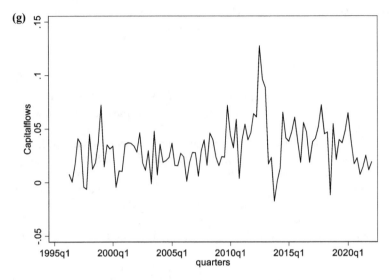

Fig. 9.2. *(Continued).*

Table 9.2. Correlation Between Variables.

Variables	WACR	EFFR	Inflation Gap	Output Gap	Capital Flows	REER	Volatility Index
WACR	1.0000						
EFFR	0.3677	1.0000					
Inflation gap	0.1421	0.0474	1.0000				
Output gap	0.1733	0.0957	0.1959	1.0000			
Capital flows	−0.2861	−0.6444	0.0483	0.0882	1.0000		
REER	−0.3405	−0.5616	0.0294	0.0879	0.8803	1.0000	
Volatility index	−0.0415	−0.0049	−0.1625	−0.1008	−0.2090	−0.2691	1.0000

Source: Author calculations.

5. Methodology

Hsing (2012), Arora and Kaur (2019), Grewal and Trivedi (2021a), Hutchison et al. (2012), Majumder and Nag (2020), Padhan et al. (2021) have tested trilemma configurations in various regions and periods based on metrics developed by Aizenman et al. (2010). This is described below:

- *Monetary Independence Index* – This is defined as the reciprocal of market interest rate in home country j and base country i.

$$\text{MI} = 1 - \frac{\text{corr}(i_i - i_j) - (-1)}{1 - (-1)} \tag{9.1}$$

The value of MI index is bound to lie between 0 and 1; higher value indicates greater monetary independence. Base country is defined as the country with which country i's policies are most closely linked.

A major shortcoming of this measure of monetary independence is that it considers only two interest rates – home country and base country. Secondly, it measures the degree of correlation between these interest rates, which might emerge as a matter of sheer coincidence or similarity due to economic conditions that are analogous in the two countries under question. This method fails to internalize changes in interest rates due to domestic factors. For the purpose of our analysis, we modify Monetary Independence Index by predicting domestic interest rates based on Taylor's rule (Taylor, 1993), and as suggested by Durán-Vanegas (2019) as:

$$i_t = \alpha_0 + \alpha_1 i_{t-1} + \alpha_2(\pi_t - \pi_t^*) + \alpha_3(y_t - \tilde{y}_t) + \mu_t \tag{9.2}$$

where i_t is the estimated policy rate at time t;
i_{t-1} is the interest rate in previous period;
$(\pi_t - \pi_t^*)$ is the inflation gap, that is, the gap between observed and targeted Inflation;
$\dfrac{(y_t - y_t)}{y_t}*100$ is the output gap, that is, the difference between the observed and long-run potential value of the gross domestic product; and
μ_t is the error term

Quarterly GDP estimates at constant prices and WPI data are base adjusted to the year 2011–2012. Further, both series are seasonally adjusted using X-13 ARIMA SEATS procedure. In the next step, y_t or potential output and targeted inflation are estimated using Hodrick–Prescott Filter. The estimated interest rates are used to calculate absolute deviations from actual interest rates and inserted in the formula below to calculate Monetary Independence Index:

$$\text{MI}_t = \frac{0.01}{0.01 + |i_t - i_t|} \tag{9.3}$$

where $|i_t - i_t|$ measures the absolute difference between the actual policy rate of the country and its estimate as calculated in Eq. (9.2). This measure has several advantages over the previous one:

- It encompasses all external factors and developments that might affect domestic interest rate movements and is not restricted to Indian and US call money rates.

- The measure is superior as compared to the ACI methodology. This index measures deviations in interest rates rather than measuring a correlation to provide a measure of independence. This eliminates the coincidence factor and brings objectivity to the variable under consideration.
- Using Taylor's rule to predict interest rates effectively helps provide for all domestic factors that may impact short-term interest rates. Thus, the differential now indicates movement only due to external factors.

- *Exchange Rate Stability* – This measure uses the standard deviation of log change in the exchange rate between home and base country as indicated below:

$$\text{ERS} = \frac{0.01}{0.01 + \text{stdev}(\triangle \log(\text{Exch}_{\text{rate}}))} \quad (9.4)$$

This index is also bound to lie between 0 and 1 by construction. Further, the higher the index value, the higher the stability of exchange rates.

This measure is also modified to encompass a broader basket of goods to provide for changes in exchange rates among major currencies. Hence, instead of the USD-INR exchange rate, the new variable used is REER, which comprises a basket of 36 currencies and is reflective of broader exchange rate movements.

$$\text{ERS} = \frac{0.01}{0.01 + \text{stdev}(\triangle \log(\text{REER}))} \quad (9.5)$$

- *Capital Openness/Financial Integration* – Capital openness is measured as Net Capital flows over GDP based on the framework defined in Grewal and Trivedi (2021), and Arora and Kaur (2019):

$$\text{KO} = \text{Net Capital Outflows/ GDP} \quad (9.6)$$

This is not an index and hence is not range bound, thus, we normalize the values obtained to lie between 0 and 1.[2] Higher value indicates greater financial integration of capital markets.

Using the exchange rate stability index, MI index and KO index as the explanatory factors and a constant as the dependent variable, OLS regression is conducted in the following regression equation:[3]

$$2 = \alpha_t \text{MI} + \beta_t \text{ERS} + \gamma_t \text{KO} + \varepsilon_t \quad (9.7)$$

---

[2]Normalized Value $= X - X_{\min}/X_{\max} - X_{\min}$.

[3]Maximum value of 2 in the regression equation as 2 is the maximum value that this equation can obtain if the trilemma/trade-off exists between the three measures. Let us suppose MI and ERS attain their maximum values of 1 each then KO must be 0 if the trilemma hypothesis holds true.

5.1 Dilemma

According to Rey (2015), one of the major factors influencing the global financial cycle is US monetary policy. Thus, any movements in US interest rates leading to shift in Indian interest rates indicate global financial spillovers. We also consider CBOE Volatility Index to provide for global spillover effects. Han and Wei (2018) conclude that flexible exchange rate systems do not provide monetary policy autonomy. Aizenman et al. (2016) provide for exchange rate stability and financial openness to determine that economies experiencing high exchange rate stability and financial openness have more interdependencies between center and peripheral economies. This study combines the aspect of both capital controls and exchange rate regimes into one variable.

Han and Wei (2018) establish that change in domestic interest rates is provided by four main factors: lagged interest rates (i_{t-1}), changes in estimated interest rates, Δi_t^*, change in US interest rates, Δi_t^{US} (center country) and global financial cycle factor are given by the change in Volatility Index, VIX_t. This can be expressed as:

$$\Delta i_t = \gamma_1 i_{t-1} + \gamma_2 \Delta i_t^* + \gamma_3 \Delta i_t^{US} + \gamma_4 VIX_t + \varepsilon_t \qquad (9.8)$$

Change in estimated interest rate is calculated using the Taylor's rule model (differentiating (Eq. 9.2)):

$$\Delta i_t^* = \alpha_0 + \varnothing_1 {}^* \Delta\left(\pi_t - \pi_t^*\right) + \varnothing_2 {}^* \Delta(y_t - \tilde{y}_t) + \mu_t \qquad (9.9)$$

Further, ERR that is exchange rate regime provided based on coarse classification of exchange rate arrangements as described in Ilzetzki et al. (2019) for India. This study period pertaining to 1996–2022 contains two regimes – de facto crawling band within $+/-2\%$ and de facto crawling band within $+/-5\%$ or moving band.[4]

Secondly, to classify the capital account restrictions, this paper uses the methodology as described in Forbes and Warnock (2012). The episodes of "surges" or "stops" are based on total capital flows beyond the limits of two standard deviations of its quarterly moving average. The periods in which India experienced heavy capital flows (inflows/outflows and surges/stops) are classified as periods of low capital account restrictions.[5] In contrast, all other periods are classified as periods of capital account restrictions. This provides a good proxy

---

[4]For India, Ilzetzki et al. (2019) classify two exchange rate regimes. From 1996 to 2009(M2), coarse classification categorizes India as "de facto crawling peg" or "de facto crawling band that is narrower than or equal to $+/-2\%$" and 2009(M3) onwards as second category of "de facto crawling band that is narrower than or equal to $+/-5\%$" or "moving band that is narrower than or equal to $+/-2\%$" or "Managed floating." Fine classification provides for four intermediate regimes during the same period as 1996M4–2005M7 as "de facto crawling peg", 2005M8–2009M2 as "de facto crawling band that is narrower than or equal to $\pm 2\%$", 2009M3–2012M11 as "de facto crawling band that is narrower than or equal to $\pm 5\%$", and finally 2012M12–2019M12 as moving band that is narrower than or equal to $\pm 2\%$.

[5]Description of "surges" and "stop" episodes identified is provided in Table AIV in Appendix.

based on a de facto measure of capital account openness. Next, we combine the different regimes as:

$$\gamma_3 = \beta_1 D_{\text{peg,NCC}} + \beta_2 D_{\text{peg,CC}} + \beta_3 D_{\text{band,NCC}} + \beta_4 D_{\text{band,CC}} \tag{9.10}$$

where $D_{\text{peg,NCC}} = 1$ if India is in pegged exchange rate regime without capital control restrictions (surges/stops) and 0 otherwise. Similarly, $D_{\text{peg,CC}} = 1$, if India chooses pegged exchange rate with capital controls and 0 otherwise. Correspondingly in the band framework, we classify $D_{\text{band,NCC}} = 1$ if India follows a band exchange rate regime without capital controls and 0 otherwise; $D_{\text{band,CC}} = 1$, if there is a band exchange rate regime with capital controls. We denote the time period before 2009 as "pegged" and after 2009 as "band" within floating exchange rate regime (as per de jure classification of RBI). This is important to understand and analyse the shift in exchange rate regime using de facto classification as per Ilzetzki et al. (2019) and Patnaik and Sengupta (2021). The analysis is carried out using the ordinary least squares regression. Replacing Eqs. (9.9) and (9.10) in Eq. (9.8), we obtain:

$$\Delta i_t = \alpha_1 + \gamma_1 i_{t-1} + \emptyset_1 {}^* \Delta(\pi_t - \pi_t^*) + \emptyset_2 {}^* \Delta(y_t - \bar{y}_t) + \beta_1 D_{\text{peg,NCC}} \Delta i_t^{\text{US}} \\ + \beta_2 D_{\text{peg,CC}} \Delta i_t^{\text{US}} + \beta_3 D_{\text{band,NCC}} \Delta i_t^{\text{US}} + \beta_4 D_{\text{band,CC}} \Delta i_t^{\text{US}} + \gamma_4 \text{VIX}_t + \varepsilon_t \tag{9.11}$$

6. Results

6.1 Trilemma

The estimation shows that coefficients pertaining to exchange rate stability and capital openness are positive and highly significant, while the third coefficient to monetary independence is also positive although not significant, indicating tradeoff. As such, we conclude that there is a tradeoff in the relationship and Trilemma holds in the Indian scenario. Table 9.3 presents OLS regression results from Eq. (9.7) for Trilemma. Before proceeding to trilemma estimations, all the variables are tested for unit root stationarity, using Augmented Dickey–Fuller Test and Phillips–Perron Test.[6] Fitted values of weighted average call money rates are obtained from the Taylor's rule as described in Eq. (9.2). Regression results for Taylor's rule estimation are provided in Table AII in Appendix.

Average of three indices multiplied with coefficient values indicates policy weights attached to each variable. Maximum policy weight is attached to maintaining exchange rate stability (1.67), followed by capital openness (0.25) and monetary autonomy (0.01). Clearly, exchange rate stability is India's most important policy choice as it places maximum emphasis on exchange rate stability, followed by capital openness and monetary independence.

A deeper study on evolution of trilemma indicates that exchange rate stability has been the major thrust among the three policy goals in India (Fig. 9.3).

---

[6]The results for stationarity are provided in Table AI in Appendix. All the variables are stationary at levels except US effective federal funds rate.

Table 9.3. Regression Results Based on $2 = \alpha_t MI + \beta_t ERS + \gamma_t KO + \varepsilon_t$.

Variable		Mean	Policy Weights
MI	0.2745	0.0504	0.0138
	(0.2285)		
ERS	2.9515***	0.5662	1.6713
	(0.1021)		
KO	0.9722***	0.2615	0.2542
	(0.1699)		
N	103		
R-square	0.97		
DW statistic	1.0659		
ARCH[a]	0.0202		

Robust standard errors are indicated in parentheses. *Significant for $p < 0.10$, ** for $p < 0.05$ and * for $p < 0.01$.

[a]ARCH provides p-values for Lagrange multiplier up to 4 lags. DW statistic refers to Durbin–Watson statistic for test of serial correlation.

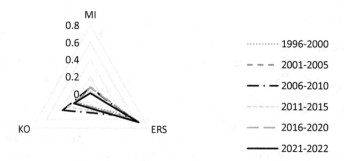

Fig. 9.3.   Trilemma in India (With Reference to Ito and Kawai (2014)). *Source:* Author's calculations.

Exchange rate stability has been the major thrust among the three policy goals in India. Capital openness received consideration from policymakers in 2006–2010, which declined with outbreak of global financial crisis in 2011–2015. Monetary independence has been emphasized thereafter in addition to exchange rate stability. This aligns with central bank's objective of Inflation targeting framework and macroprudential policies. Overall, we can conclude that India lies toward the right vertex as defined by Ito and Kawai (2014).

Composition of Index

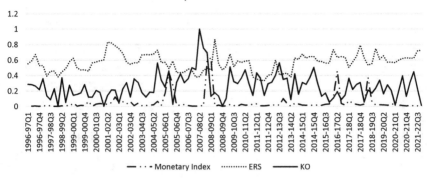

Fig. 9.4.   Trilemma Policy Indices – Composition. *Source:* Author's calculations.

Fig. 9.4 provides a compositional variation of indices over time in India. This depicts the policy stance of the management of Trilemma. The top priority in India has been assigned to exchange rate stability, followed by capital openness. There is a change observed after 2005–06q1 when capital restrictions were relaxed, and hence exchange rate stability was compromised to some extent. Monetary independence was also emphasized for a short duration, but by the end of the financial year 2005–2006, there was a spurt in capital flows to India, until the onset of the global financial crisis. The period from 2008–09q3 saw an increased emphasis on exchange rate stability and controlled capital mobility, with a compromise on monetary policy independence.

India soon recovered from the aftermath of the global financial crisis, with the capital openness index again rising in 2011–12q1 until 2016–17q3, when the monetary independence index rose, coinciding with the Inflation targeting framework announced by the Reserve Bank of India. A further rise in the monetary independence index was observed in 2018–19q2 pertaining to high inflation rates, compromising the other two goals of exchange rate stability and capital account openness.

Further, the period after COVID-19, when achieving a high growth rate and controlling inflation are the primary targets, the policymakers are fueling this through foreign capital flows and maintaining exchange rate stability.

6.2 Dilemma

Table 9.4 provides results relating to dilemma estimation. It is observed that lagged call rate is significant and has a negative coefficient. This is in line with the literature as there is a tendency for interest to not increase after a period of expansionary stance. The output gap and inflation gap both have the necessary positive sign. Inflation gap is measured using Wholesale Price Index in our study,

Table 9.4. Regression Results for Dilemma.

Variable	Model 1	Model 2 Pre-Crisis	Model 2 Post-Crisis
Constant	2.2337** (0.8911)	4.188207*** (1.153839)	0.3325 (0.2433)
Call rate (lagged)	−0.3553** (0.1478)	−0.6116*** (0.1766)	−0.0739 (0.0456)
Output	0.0554 (0.0355)	0.1024* (0.0554)	−0.0090 (0.0150)
Inflation	0.0710 (0.0465)	0.1274 (0.1425)	0.0895*** (0.0292)
VIX	−0.3060 (0.4396)	−1.1009 (1.6017)	0.4317 (0.2716)
$D_{peg,NCC}*\Delta EFFR$	0.0342 (0.2392)	−0.1358 (0.3057)	
$D_{peg,CC}*\Delta EFFR$	−0.1483 (0.5482)	−0.0966 (0.7275)	
$D_{band,NCC}*\Delta EFFR$	−12.4859 (11.0108)		−12.4321* (6.3660)
$D_{band,CC}*\Delta EFFR$	−0.0715 (0.5465)		0.4204* (0.2389)
N	103	49	53
R-square	0.24	0.39	0.30
DW statistic	2.201509	2.059411	1.252216
ARCH[a]	0.0094	0.8446	0.7382

Source: Authors' calculation.

Robust standard errors are indicated in parentheses. *Significant for $p < 0.10$, ** for $p < 0.05$ and * for $p < 0.01$.

$\Delta i_t = \alpha_1 + \gamma_1 i_{t-1} + \emptyset_1*\Delta(\pi_t - \pi_t^*) + \emptyset_2*\Delta(y_t - y_t^*) + \gamma_4 VIX_t + \beta_1 D_{peg,NCC}\Delta i_t^{US} + \beta_2 D_{peg,CC}\Delta i_t^{US} + \beta_3 D_{band,NCC}\Delta i_t^{US} + \beta_4 D_{band,CC}\Delta i_t^{US} + \varepsilon_t$

ARCH provides p value for Lagrange multiplier up to 4 lags. DW statistic refers to Durbin–Watson statistic for test of serial correlation.

which could be the reason for an insignificant coefficient. This becomes significant in post-crisis results. Volatility Index has an expected negative sign, indicating the negative relationship between domestic interest rates and global volatility. Post-crisis Indian interest rates are displaying a positive trend with volatility. The impact due to US spillovers is not observed in our data, as none of the coefficients related with change in US interest rates is significant in Model 1. All the variables except the period of no capital controls during pegged exchange rate regime (prior to 2009) have a negative sign. This prompts us to further analyze the relationship in pre- and post-crisis period to understand the change in spillover effects.

In Model 2, the coefficients β1 and β2 are negative and statistically insignificant denoting that during pegged exchange rate regime, an increase in US interest rates is associated negatively with interest rate movement in India.[7] The impact is reduced when capital controls are employed indicating partial effectiveness of capital control measures. Thus, we can say that relatively fixed exchange rate regime and restricted capital mobility help maintain monetary policy independence. Further, β3 and β4 are both significant, however they are opposite in signs. This implies that shift towards a more flexible exchange rate regime restrict monetary policy independence in a significant way. This is consistent with trilemma hypothesis in broad sense that loss of monetary policy independence is accompanied with more flexible exchange rate regime and no capital controls. The impact turns less severe when capital controls are placed. Hence, as India moves towards a more flexible exchange rate regime, capital controls are only effective way of managing monetary policy independence. This indicates shift towards a "dilemma".

7. Conclusion

The study validates the trilemma hypothesis in the Indian scenario in line with the findings of Aizenman and Sengupta (2013), Hutchison et al. (2012), Arora and Kaur (2019), and Majumder and Nag (2020). Our model displays quite similar results, and hence the validity of Trilemma is re-emphasized in the Indian context in contemporary times. Estimation of the monetary index using Taylor's rule predictions renders robust results. The relevance of the new monetary independence index can be established from the study, in line with the findings of Durán-Vanegas (2019) for Latin American countries. Further, this approach also combines exchange rate volatility calculated as a measure of REER, which is also not conventionally observed in Indian trilemma literature. This study, thus, adds a newer dimension to measuring Trilemma.

Exchange rate regimes, as well as capital controls, both, play a significant role in India in determining monetary policy independence. Combining exchange rate regime classification based on Ilzetzki et al. (2019) helps in identifying time periods of

---

[7]For the purpose of narrow and broad definitions of trilemma, the authors interpret pegged exchange rate regime as closer to fixed exchange rate system and band system as comparatively flexible exchange rate regime within floating regime framework in India. This is consistent with the terminology as used by Patnaik and Sengupta (2021).

various intermediate exchange rate regimes and their relevance in determining monetary policy independence. Additionally, a de facto measure of capital mobility based on total capital outflows effectively segregates the time horizons when capital account restrictions were rendered ineffective. The findings of this study are in line with literature establishing global spillovers on India's monetary policy (Grewal & Trivedi, 2021a, 2021b; Prabheesh et al., 2021). However, the findings are in contrast with Majumder and Nag (2021), who do not find sufficient evidence in favor of the dilemma. The spillover effects are evidently visible in the time period after the global financial crisis. One visible contributing factor to this is a change in the exchange rate regime. Monetary independence is continuously being compromised in view of global developments, irrespective of capital control restrictions. Further, considering the adjustment to more fluctuating exchange rate regimes in the future, it can be said that the relevance of the dilemma cannot be denied in the Indian context.

8. Limitations/Further Scope

This study assumes only two versions of the exchange rate regime classification. This may be further analyzed on the basis of fine classification based on Ilzetzki et al. (2019). There is also a scope to provide for methodological improvement. Macro-prudential policies are used by countries to curb exchange rate volatility, in addition to the piling of foreign exchange reserves. This could serve as other potential areas to extend the research.

References

Aizenman, J. (2010). *The impossible trinity (aka the policy trilemma): The encyclopedia of financial globalization (No. 666)*. Working paper.

Aizenman, J., Chinn, M. D., & Ito, H. (2008). *Assessing the emerging global financial architecture: Measuring the Trilemma's configurations over time (No. w14533)*. National Bureau of Economic Research.

Aizenman, J., Chinn, M. D., & Ito, H. (2010). The emerging global financial architecture: Tracing and evaluating new patterns of the trilemma configuration. *Journal of International Money and Finance, 29*(4), 615–641.

Aizenman, J., Chinn, M. D., & Ito, H. (2013). The "impossible trinity" hypothesis in an era of global imbalances: Measurement and testing. *Review of International Economics, 21*(3), 447–458.

Aizenman, J., Chinn, M. D., & Ito, H. (2016). Monetary policy spillovers and the Trilemma in the new normal: Periphery country sensitivity to core country conditions. *Journal of International Money and Finance, 68*, 298–330.

Aizenman, J., & Ito, H. (2016). *East Asian economies and financial globalization in the post-crisis world*. NBER Working Paper No. 22268.

Aizenman, J., & Sengupta, R. (2013). Financial trilemma in China and a comparative analysis with India. *Pacific Economic Review, 18*(2), 123–146.

Arora, N., & Kaur, R. (2019). Modeling international trinity and policy choices for India. *Indian Journal of Industrial Relations, 54*(4).

Bernanke, B. S. (2017). Federal reserve policy in an international context. *IMF Economic Review, 65*, 1–32.

Cerutti, E., Claessens, S., & Rose, A. K. (2019). How important is the global financial cycle? Evidence from capital flows. *IMF Economic Review, 67*(1), 24–60.

Durán-Vanegas, J. D. (2019). Making hard choices: Trilemmas and dilemmas of macroeconomic policy in Latin America. *Economia Chilena, 22*(2).

Edwards, S. (2015). Monetary policy independence under flexible exchange rates: An illusion? *The World Economy, 38*(5), 773–787.

Fleming, J. M. (1962). Domestic financial policies under fixed and under floating exchange rates. *Staff Papers-International Monetary Fund*, 369–380.

Forbes, K. J., & Warnock, F. E. (2012). Capital flow waves: Surges, stops, flight, and retrenchment. *Journal of International Economics, 88*(2), 235–251.

Ghosh, A. R., Qureshi, M. S., Kim, J. I., & Zalduendo, J. (2014). Surges. *Journal of International Economics, 92*(2), 266–285.

Goldstein, M. (2002). *Managed floating plus*. Peterson Institute.

Grewal, H. S., & Trivedi, P. (2021a). The path of impossible trinity in India: 1991–2018. *Global Business and Economics Review, 24*(4), 382–408.

Grewal, H. S., & Trivedi, P. (2021b). Spillover effects of the US monetary policy on the Indian Trilemma. *International Journal of Emerging Markets, 18*(1).

Gupta, A. S., & Manjhi, G. (2011). *Capital flows and the impossible trinity: The Indian experience (No. 11-02)*. Centre for International Trade and Development, Jawaharlal Nehru University.

Han, X., & Wei, S. J. (2018). International transmissions of monetary shocks: Between a trilemma and a dilemma. *Journal of International Economics, 110*, 205–219.

Hofmann, B., & Takáts, E. (2015, September). International monetary spillovers. *BIS Quarterly Review*, 105–118.

Hsing, Y. (2012). Test of the trilemma for five selected Asian countries and policy implications. *Applied Economics Letters, 19*(17), 1735–1739.

Hutchison, M., Sengupta, R., & Singh, N. (2012). India's trilemma: Financial liberalisation, exchange rates and monetary policy 1. *The World Economy, 35*(1), 3–18.

Ilzetzki, E., Reinhart, C. M., & Rogoff, K. S. (2019). Exchange arrangements entering the twenty-first century: Which anchor will hold? *Quarterly Journal of Economics, 134*(2), 599–646.

Ito, H., & Kawai, M. (2014, January 30). *Determinants of the trilemma policy combination*. ADBI Working Paper No. 456.

Lee, D. (2021). Global financial integration and monetary policy spillovers. *Economics Letters, 202*, 109820.

Majumder, S. B., & Nag, R. N. (2021). India facing the macroeconomic policy tradeoff–is it dilemma, Trilemma or quadrilemma? *Macroeconomics and Finance in Emerging Market Economies, 14*(1), 24–44.

McKinnon, R., & Schnabl, G. (2004). The East Asian dollar standard, fear of floating, and original sin. *Review of Development Economics, 8*(3), 331–360.

Mohan, R., & Kapur, M. (2009). *Managing the impossible trinity: Volatile capital flows and Indian monetary policy*. Available at SSRN 1861724.

Mohanty, M. S., & Scatigna, M. (2005). Has globalisation reduced monetary policy independence. *BIS Papers*, 23.

Mundell, R. A. (1963). Capital mobility and stabilization policy under fixed and flexible exchange rates. *Canadian Journal of Economics and Political Science, 29*(4), 475–485.

Nair, A. R., & Anand, B. (2020). Monetary policy and financial stability: Should central bank lean against the wind? *Central Bank Review, 20*(3), 133–142.

Obstfeld, M., Shambaugh, J. C., & Taylor, A. M. (2005). The Trilemma in history: Tradeoffs among exchange rates, monetary policies, and capital mobility. *The Review of Economics and Statistics, 87*(3), 423–438.

Okina, K., Shirakawa, M., & Shiratsuka, S. (1999). Financial market globalization: Present and future. *Monetary and Economic Studies, 17*(3), 1–40.

Padhan, H., Sahu, S. K., & Dash, U. (2021). Non-linear analysis of international reserve, trade and trilemma in India. *The Journal of Economic Asymmetries, 23*, e00191.

Patnaik, I., & Sengupta, R. (2021). Analysing India's exchange rate regime. *India Policy Forum, 2021* (pp. 53–86). Sage Publications.

Prabheesh, K. P., Anglingkusumo, R., & Juhro, S. M. (2021). The dynamics of global financial cycle and domestic economic cycles: Evidence from India and Indonesia. *Economic Modelling, 94*, 831–842.

Prasad, E., Rogoff, K., Wei, S. J., & Kose, M. A. (2003). Effects of financial globalization on developing countries: Some empirical evidence. In *India's and China's recent experience with reform and growth* (pp. 201–228). Palgrave Macmillan UK.

Reinhart, C. M., & Reinhart, V. R. (2009, January). Capital flow bonanzas: An encompassing view of the past and present. *NBER International Seminar on Macroeconomics, 5*(1), 9–62. Chicago, IL: The University of Chicago Press.

Rey, H. (2015). *Dilemma not trilemma: The global financial cycle and monetary policy independence (No. w21162)*. National Bureau of Economic Research.

Taylor, J. B. (1993, December). Discretion versus policy rules in practice. In *Carnegie-Rochester conference series on public policy* (Vol. 39, pp. 195–214).

Tica, J., Globan, T., & Arčabić, V. (2016). Monetary policy effectiveness, net foreign currency exposure, and financial globalisation. *EFZG Working Paper Series*, (03), 1–23.

Appendix 1

Table AI. Estimation Result – Taylor's Rule.

Variable	
Lagged interest rate	0.6411*** (0.1376)
Output gap	0.0533* (0.0319)
Inflation gap	0.0673 (0.0433)
Constant	2.2638*** (0.8430)
N	103
R-square	0.47
DW statistic	2.182379
ARCH[a]	0.0114

Source: Authors calculation.

Robust standard errors are indicated in parentheses. *Significant for $p < 0.10$, ** for $p < 0.05$ and * for $p < 0.01$.

[a]ARCH provides p-values for Lagrange multiplier up to four lags. DW statistic refers to Durbin–Watson statistic for test of serial correlation.

Table AII. Stationarity Test (ADF and PP).

Variable	ADF Test Statistic	PP Test Z(rho)	Z(t)
WACR	−4.734	−38.344	−4.847
	(0.000)		(0.000)
Inflation gap	−3.687	−31.086	−4.033
	(0.004)		(0.001)
Output gap	−9.784	−81.465	−9.943
	(0.000)		(0.000)
Monetary index	−6.634	−55.465	−6.428
	(0.000)		(0.000)
Exchange rate stability index	−4.722	−38.710	−4.746
	(0.000)		(0.000)
Capital openness index	−6.654	−69.091	−6.818
	(0.000)		(0.000)
EFFR (first diff)	−4.680	−39.498	−4.824
	(0.000)		(0.000)
VIX (log)	−3.607	−22.187	−3.499
	(0.005)		(0.008)

Source: Authors calculation.

^p-values are reported in parentheses.

Table AIII. Summary Statistics.

Variable	Mean	Standard Deviation	Min	Max	Number of Observations
WACR	6.490	2.060	3.173	15.717	104
Inflation gap	0.000	2.609	−7.114	5.512	104
Output gap	0.017	5.318	−23.686	9.530	104
Monetary independence index	0.050	0.111	0.001	0.628	103
Exchange rate stability index	0.566	0.113	0.334	0.868	104
Capital openness index	0.262	0.165	0.003	1.000	104
Effective federal funds rate	2.150	2.167	0.060	6.520	104
Volatility index	2.959	0.328	2.333	4.071	104

Source: Authors calculation.

Table AIV. Capital Control Episodes.

Event		
Surges	**Stops**	**Duration**
1999-00Q4–2001-02Q1	2001-02Q3–2002-03Q2	6/4
2003-04Q3–2004-05Q4		6
2005-06Q3–2008-09Q3	2008-09Q4–2009-10Q3	13/4
2010-11Q3–2011-12Q3		5
2013-14Q2–2014-15Q1		4
2021-22Q2–2021-22Q4		3

Source: Authors calculation.

Chapter 10

Assessing Progress Made by Indian States and UTs for the Attainment of Sustainable Development Goals

Pratham Parekh and Bhajan Lal

Nirma University, India

Abstract

The study compares all three versions of sustainable development goal (SDG) India index and assess the pace and direction of each State/UT for the attainment of SDGs by 2030. The study is an attempt to scrutinise performance of each indicator of every State and UT of India across 16 SDGs from 2018 to 2020. For this purpose, 13 SDGs with 56 indicators for first version, 16 SDGs with 101 indictors from second version and 115 indicators across 16 SDGs from third version of SDG India Index are investigated. Instead of relining NITI Aayog's indexing methodology, the study uses the same dataset to assess the distance of each state from national target for SDG. Cursorily, it also derives statistical projections of duration required by each State/UT for achieving particular indicator and goal at large. The investigation derives statistical projections of duration required by each State/UT for achieving a particular indicator and goal at large.

Based on the progress made by each State/UT, distance from present conditions are categorised as a Very far (distance less than 0%), Far (distance from 1% to 25%), Near (distance from 26% to 50%), Very Near (distance from 51% to 75%), Achieving target (76%–100%).

The conclusion of the study intends to highlight the benefits and challenges for adopting indexing or ranking approach to monitor the subnational level progress made for attainment SDGs.

Keywords: Sustainable development; national development; NITI Aayog; economic growth; indexing

Modeling Economic Growth in Contemporary India, 175–186
Copyright © 2024 Pratham Parekh and Bhajan Lal
Published under exclusive licence by Emerald Publishing Limited
doi:10.1108/978-1-80382-751-320241010

1. Introduction and Background

The 17 Sustainable Development Goals (SDGs) declared by UN wholesomely present optimistic vision for future of humankind. These goals are designed for cultural, social and political customisation depending on national development priorities. Linkages of national development strategies with SDG in recent times have witnessed emergence of huge discourse at National and Global levels of governance. But there exists a scarce scientific literature on nation and sub-nation specific progress attainment for achieving SDGs.

Latest global report on sustainable development (2022) provides an estimate how every country is far from attaining each goal. This report measures a distance of country's progress from 0% to 100%, it is not surprising that all countries of the world are moving towards fulfilment of SDGs. Unfortunately, India is nowhere near 100% completion of SDGs by 2030. Reasons for such lag is a subject for deeper research. According to data published in the said report, achievement of all goals will remain unfulfilled by 2030. As per predications made, India can set majority of SDGs by 2059, though the country has performed better among its 'grouped' countries (Lomborg et al., 2022). It's clear from Fig. 10.1 that India is no near to best category in terms of achievement of SDGs.

In India, deriving SDG specific indicators that can be linked with national development priorities and monitoring the progress at various regional/ administrative levels (like block level, district level or state level) has been a mammoth task. In order to carry out such task, the Ministry of Statistics and Programme Implementation (MoS&PI) devised National Indicator Framework (NIF) that aligns Indian National Development Agenda with SDGs. The progress against each indicator derived by MoS&PI is traced at state and national level resulting in development vital database that can be used by state and non-state agencies for monitoring not only progress made but also direction and pace of development. Based on this database, the apex planning body of India, NITI Aayog monitors and ranks every State and Union Territory (UT) in terms of progress made for achievement of 17 SDGs through the SDG India Indexes.

The Index developed by NITI Aayog ranks States and UTs based on their performance calculated by using composite score across 16 SDGs. The first version of SDG India Index 2018 includes 13 SDGs having 39 targets composed of 62 indicators. The second version of this index released in 2019 consists of 100 indicators, 54 targets across 16 SDGs and the latest available version of index released in 2020 ranks States/UTs across 16 SDGs having 70 targets and 115 indictors. Majority of indicators used in preparing these indices are rooted in NIF (Table 10.1).

Attainment of SDGs remains a long way ahead for country like India. The journey of India for attaining SDGs remains noteworthy but from impeccable. With half of the time remaining to attain SDGs since 2016, it becomes utmost necessary to trace the progress of each goals, targets and indicators since 2016 at sub-national level. Ample of data and literature available for cross country comparison for such progress monitoring but there exists severe lag in terms of

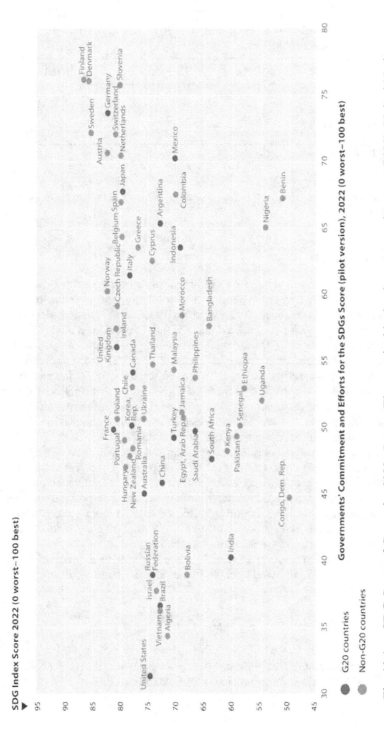

Fig. 10.1. SDG Score of Countries 2022. *Source:* The sustainable development goals report (2022), United Nations.

Table 10.1. Number of Goals, Targets and Indicators in all Three Versions of NITI Aayog's SDG India Index.

Year	Goals	Targets	Indicators
2018	13	39	62
2019	16	54	100
2020	16	70	115

Source: NITI Aayog, Government of India.

reliable data and scientific literature that provides fair picture of progress made by Indian States and UTs.

2. About the Study

The study applies comparative approach to investigate all three versions of SDG India Index that is prepared in collaboration with UN Systems in India, Indian Sates/UTs and Non-Government Organisations. These indexes are considered as important policy monitoring tool at national and sub-national in India.

The selection of indicators for indexes and its mapping with national development priorities is based on criteria like relevance of SDGs with national priority, statistically feasible alignment with NIF, and availability of data at national and sub national levels, consent of concerned ministries/departments/local governments, ownership of data, data collection techniques and sufficiency of data. Following such criteria, indicators are selected and data available for these indicators are then used for developing composite score.

Based on the composite scores, an index is devised wherein a score of State/UTs presents its overall position among others. Comparison of present version of index with previous version (or baseline index) provides a picture about the progress made by each State/UT. After rounding off this composite score the State/UT is classified into four categories 'Achiever' (having index score of 100), 'Front Runner' (having index score of 65–99), 'Performer' (having index score-50–64) and 'Aspirant' (having index score less than 50).

Following normalisation formula (Eq. 1) was adopted with normalisation of indicators with a positive trend (for example improvement in institutional delivery)

$$\delta = \frac{x - \text{Min}(x)}{T(x) - \text{Min}(x)} \times 100$$

Eq. 1: Normalisation of indicators for which positive trend is the best trend

While for normalisation of indicators with a negative trend (for example reduction in MMR) following formula (Eq. 2) was adopted.

$$\delta = \left| 1 - \frac{x - T(x)}{\text{Max}(x) - T(x)} \right| \times 100$$

Eq. 2: Normalisation of indicators for which negative trend is the best trend

Since targets of indicator under SDG14 are not used for normalisation, ideal values were not static but it falls within a range. So for this goal, raw data were separately normalised with the following formula (Eq. 3)

$$\delta = \frac{x - \text{Min}(x)}{\text{Max}(x) - \text{Min}(x)} \times 100$$

Eq. 3: Normalisation of SDG no. 14

where x = actual value of raw data
$\text{Min}(x)$ = Minimum value observed in the dataset of an indicator
$\text{Max}(x)$ = Minimum value observed in the dataset of an indicator
$T(x)$ = Value of Target set for Indicator
δ = Normalised value.

After normalising raw data, it computed scores for each state against each goal with the following formula (Eq. 4). Estimation is based on the arithmetic mean of normalised values under each goal for every state. Equal weightage was given to each indicator.

$$I_{ij}\left(N_{ij}, I_{ijk}\right) = \sum_{k=1}^{N_{ij}} \frac{1}{N_{ij}} I_{ijk}$$

Eq. 4: Providing weightage to every indicator

where,
state = i
Specific SDG = j
Indicator value = k
I_{ij} = score of goal for given state i under SDG j
N_{ij} = non-null SDG indicator j for given state i
I_{ijk} = normalised value of state I of indicator k under SDG j.

For computing composite index, arithmetic means of goal score for every state. The score represents the overall position of the state and its comparison with the previous version of the index provides an idea about their progress. After rounding off the scores, all Indian States and UTs were categorised into performance categories (Table 10.2).

Table 10.2. Progress Categories Defined Based on a Composite Score Range.

Category	Index Score
Achiever	100
Front runner	65–99
Performer	50–64
Aspirant	Less than 50

82 (78.10%) of indicators under study contains data values from the year 2019 to 2021, while 22 (20.95%) indicators contain data values ranging from 2016 to 2018 followed by 1 (0.95%) indicator that contains a value from 2005.

The objective of the study is to compare all three versions of SDG India index and assess the pace and direction of each State/UT for attainment of SDGs by 2030. The study is an attempt to scrutinise performance of each indicator of every state and UT of India across 16 SDGs from 2018 to 2020. For this purpose, 13 SDGs with 56 indicators for first version, 16 SDGs with 101 indictors from second version and 115 indicators across 16 SDGs from third version of SDG India Index are investigated. Instead of relining NITI Aayog's indexing methodology, the study uses the same dataset to assess the distance of each state from national target for SDG. The study intends to highlight the benefits and challenges for adopting indexing or ranking approach to monitor the sub-national level progress made for attainment SDGs. The investigation derives statistical projections of duration required by each State/UT for achieving particular indicator and goal at large. Based on the progress made by each State/UT, distances from present conditions are categorised as a Very far (distance less than 0%), Far (distance from 1% to 25%), Near (distance from 26% to 50%), Very Near (distance from 51% to 75%), Achieving target (76%–100%).

3. Data Analysis

At national level, 124 (74%) indicators are forecasted to miss their targets by 2030 while only 23(14%) are falling into category ranging from 76% to 100% of achievement. 3(2%) indicators are predicated to have no change (Table 10.3) based on NITI Aayog's SDG India Indices data. Sub-national data of 30 states suggest similar pattern of achievement of 167 indicators. 72.04% of total indicators at state level falls into very far and far categories stating progress made up

Table 10.3. No. of Indicators Moving Towards Targets by 2030 at National Level.

Goals	Very Far	Far	Near	Very Near	Achieving Target	No Change	Can't Determine
SDG1	2	3			1	2	
SDG2	3	5			2		1
SDG3	4	6	1		1		1
SDG4	5	9		1	1		4
SDG5	3	5			3		1
SDG6	1	5	1	2			2
SDG7	1	1			1		1
SDG8	4	5	1	1			

Table 10.3. *(Continued)*

Goals	Very Far	Far	Near	Very Near	Achieving Target	No Change	Can't Determine
SDG9		4	2		1		1
SDG10	5	6				1	2
SDG11	3	7	1				
SDG12	5	7					
SDG13	1	5					
SDG14	3						2
SDG15	4	5					2
SDG16	4	3	1		2		
Total	48	76	7	4	12	3	17

to 25% by the Indian States. Only 4.55% of indicators at states would be able to make achievement from 76% to 100% (Table 10.4). States like Andhra Pradesh, Gujarat, Haryana, Himachal Pradesh, Karnataka, Odisha, Rajasthan, West Bengal and Tamil Nadu have most indicators falling into achieving target category, i.e. these states can be assumed to achieve SDGs faster compared to other states, while north-eastern states like Manipur, Meghalaya, Nagaland, Sikkim

Table 10.4. No. of Indicators Moving Towards Targets by 2030 at State Level.

States	Very Far	Far	Near	Very Near	Achieving Target	No Change	Can't Determine
Andhra Pradesh	48	79	8	2	11	5	15
Arunachal Pradesh	38	67	6	4	5	5	40
Assam	45	75	4	5	9	5	24
Bihar	44	78	7	3	7	6	21
Chhattisgarh	47	78	1	3	9	7	21
Delhi	42	72	7	3	7	2	31
Goa	43	79	4	2	6	6	27
Gujarat	48	79	5	3	11	8	15

(Continued)

Table 10.4. *(Continued)*

States	Very Far	Far	Near	Very Near	Achieving Target	No Change	Can't Determine
Haryana	44	75	7	2	11	6	22
Himachal Pradesh	45	74	9	3	10	4	22
Jammu and Kashmir	46	72	6	1	8	5	28
Jharkhand	49	76	9	2	5	4	21
Karnataka	47	80	7	5	10	4	15
Kerala	46	80	6	4	8	8	16
Madhya Pradesh	44	76	7	4	9	5	22
Maharashtra	48	81	4	7	7	6	16
Manipur	40	71	7	4	4	4	34
Meghalaya	41	74	8	1	4	4	32
Mizoram	41	71	5	2	6	4	36
Nagaland	40	70	4	6	2	4	36
Odisha	49	78	7	3	10	4	17
Punjab	45	76	9		7	8	22
Rajasthan	46	76	7	2	11	5	20
Sikkim	38	71	4	4	3	9	34
Tamil Nadu	48	84	4	3	12	3	15
Telangana	36	81	6	2	8	3	31
Tripura	41	76	6	4	4	4	28
Uttar Pradesh	47	76	11	3	5	5	20
Uttarakhand	46	75	9	3	7	5	22
West Bengal	48	79	8	1	12	4	17

and Tripura are lagging in attainment of goals. In terms of achievement, States of India is forecasted to achievement indicators listed in Table 10.6. In terms of Union Territories, only Andaman and Nicobar and Puducherry are observed having more indicators moving towards target achievement as compared to other UTs (Table 10.5). Detailed data regarding performance of each state are annexed as Annexure-1. The forecasted detailed data for each indicator for each state are annexed as Annexure-2.

Table 10.5. No. of Indicators Moving Towards Targets by 2030 at Union
Territories Level.

Union Territories	Very Far	Far	Near	Very Near	Achieving Target	No Change	Can't Determine
Andaman and Nicobar Islands	32	62	4		5	5	59
Chandigarh	37	61	5	4	1	5	54
Dadra and Nagar Haveli	32	59	3	2	2	5	64
Daman and Diu	36	58	3	2	1	5	62
Lakshadweep	26	47	2	1	2	2	87
Puducherry	36	68	5	2	4	5	47

Table 10.6. Goal Wise of List of Indicators in Which Indian States Are
Predicated to Achieve Targets by 2030.

SDG No.	Indicator
1	Percentage of households with any usual member covered by a health scheme or health insurance (Goal 1)
	Persons provided employment as a percentage of persons who demanded employment under Mahatma Gandhi National rural Employment Guarantee Act (MGNREGA) (Goal 1)
2	Percentage of children under 5 years who are stunted (Goal 2)
	Percentage of pregnant women aged 15–49 years who are anaemic (Goal 2)
3	HIV incidence rate (Goal 3)
	Maternal mortality ratio (Goal 3)
	Total case notification rate of tuberculosis (Goal 3)
	Total physicians' nurses and midwives (Goal 3)
	Under 5 mortality rate (Goal 3)
4	Adjusted Net Enrolment Ratio (ANER) in elementary education (class 1–8) (Goal 4)
	Average annual dropout rate at secondary level (class 9–10) (Goal 4)

(Continued)

Table 10.6. *(Continued)*

SDG No.	Indicator
5	Percentage of elected women over total seats in the state legislative assembly (Goal 5)
	Ratio of female to male average wage/salary earnings received among regular wage/salaried employees (Goal 5)
	Sex ratio at birth (Goal 5)
6	Percentage of individual household toilets constructed against target (SBM(G)) (Goal 6)
	Percentage of rural population getting safe and adequate drinking water within premises through Pipe Water Supply (PWS) (Goal 6)
7	Percentage of households electrified (Goal 7)
8	Annual growth rate of GDP (constant prices) per capita (Goal 8)
	Ease of Doing Business (EODB) score (feedback score) (Goal 8)
9	Number of mobile connections (mobile tele density) (Goal 9)
11	Wards with 100% door-to-door waste collection (%) (Goal 11)
13	Number of human lives lost due to extreme weather events (Goal 13)
15	Number of wildlife crime cases detected and reported annually (Goal 15)
16	Cognisable crimes against children (Goal 16)
	Murder rate (Goal 16)
	Percentage of births registered (Goal 16)

4. Conclusion

Since 2018, NIIT Aayog in India is considered as a prime agency for tracking progress of Indian states and UTs in terms of attainment of SDGs. For this purpose, NITI Aayog has formulated an SDG India Index. This index reports data and experiences of Indian States and UTs. The paper uses indicators from all three indexes published from 2018 to 2020. Technically, these indexes pinpoint actual status of the goal attainment. The actual status is then calculated to form a composite score and ranking States and UTs. This ranking for States and UTs serves as important parameter of designing policy interventions and promoting Cooperative Federalism among States (NITI Aayog, 2018). The latest version of SDG India Index released on 2021 is a collaborative effort of Indian States and UTs; United Nations Systems of India; Ministry of Statistics and Programme Implementation and the concerned Ministries of Government of India. The number of indicators used for measuring progress is increased from 62 across 39 targets in 2018 to 115 (an increase of 167%) across 70 (increase of 203%) targets in 2020 (NITI Aayog, 2021b). The previous two versions of index used 68 and 76 (66.09% of total indicators used in the 2020 index) indicators in 2019 and 2020 respectively from National Indicator Framework (NIF) (NITI Aayog, 2021a). This implies that second version of the index had 88% of total indicators while the third version of the Index had 93.04% of indicators derived from NIF, stating increasing inclination towards NIF. But looking at the larger picture, it can be observed that the share of SDG indicators in the second version of the Index in NIF is 29.14%, i.e. 88 SDG Indicators against 302 NIF indicators. Similarly, in the third version of the index, the share of SDG indicators has derived at 34.74%, i.e. 107 indicators against 308 NIF indicators. With less than half of indicators from NIF, the claim of measuring the holistic progress of states for all SDGs becomes sceptical (Parekh, 2021).

The categorisation of composite presents a scenario that few states with high differences in data value are part of similar category. For example, Jharkhand under SDG 2 scored 19, while West Bengal Scored 46 but both states were considered as 'Aspirants'. It is not wrong to comment that performance score range devised by NITI Aayog is too broad (Parekh, 2021). A need for critical analysis of absolute values of each indicator for every state and UTs across three versions of SDG India is posed.

The study attempts to chart out the progress made by Indian states and UTs towards attainment of 16 Goals. The data discussed herewith obviously comes from NITI Aayog's SDG India Indexes but with no marrying methodology. The study uses absolute values rather than a composite score for forecasting. Simple forecasting method with Exponential Smoothing (ETS) algorithm is used to determine value of each indicator for every state and UT until 2030. The last year, i.e. 2030 values are juxtaposed with target and distance is derived. This distance in percentage terms categorised as Very far (distance less than 0%), Far (distance from 1% to 25%), near (distance from 26% to 50%), Very Near (distance from 51% to 75%), Achieving target (76%–100%). Country, states and UTs then assessed with number of indicators under each derived category.

The major challenge posed to such study is data gaps that persists over a period. Some indicators selected by NITI Aayog and in this study are survey based. Thus, data values of some indicators are not very recent. Average of 14.23% indicators falls in category of 'can't determine' due to such data gaps. As data suggest, on an average only 4.55% indicators across States and UTs are achieving SDG targets by 2030. Forecasting of these values presents a picture that almost no Indian State and UT will attain SDGs fully by 2030. The reasons for slow progress towards attainment of SDGs in India offer a wide avenue for multi-disciplinary research.

References

Lomborg, B., Debroy, B., & Sinha, A. (2022, October 2). Sustainable development goals: How India and the world are doing. https://www.livemint.com/opinion/online-views/sustainable-development-goals-how-india-and-the-world-are-doing-11664731506364.html

NITI Aayog. (2018, December). *SDG India index: Baseline report 2018*. https://niti.gov.in/writereaddata/files/SDX_Index_India_21.12.2018.pdf

NITI Aayog. (2021a, June). *SDG India index & dashboard 2020–21: Partnerships in the decade of action*. Government of India.

NITI Aayog. (2021b, June 3). *NITI Aayog releases SDG India index and dashboard 2020–21*. [Press release]. https://pib.gov.in/PressReleasePage.aspx?PRID=1723952

Parekh, P. (2021). Assessing prospects and retrospect of progress monitoring of sustainable development goals in India. *The Journal of Oriental Research Madras*, 92(5), 94–109. https://doi.org/10.13140/RG.2.2.12677.06881

Sustainable Development Report. (2022). *Sustainable development report*. https://www.sustainabledevelopment.report/reports/sustainable-development-report-2022/

Chapter 11

Assessing Financial Inclusion, Skill Development and Basic Infrastructure in 112 Aspirational Districts of India

Pratham Parekh

Nirma University, India

Abstract

The apex planning body of India, NITI Aayog launched an Aspirational District Programme (ADP) in January 2018. The programme aimed to the quick and effective transformation of 112 (14%) districts of the country. This programme is considered as world's biggest result-based governance initiative having reached up to 250 million people. It is based on a ranking that is done on monthly basis. This ranking is based on 49 KPIs across six broad socio-economic themes.

The study attempts to inquire and assess the progress made by 112 Aspirational Districts under Financial Inclusion, Skill Development and Basic Infrastructure theme from the inception of the programme to June 2022 (i.e. 54 months). Instead of ranking districts with delta rank or composite scores, the study divorce from NITI Aayog's methodology of monthly delta ranking. The study explores 8 indicators under the basic infrastructure theme and 16 indicators under the financial inclusion and skill development themes. For this purpose, the study explores the availability of individual household latrines, drinking water, electricity and road connectivity. Districts are also tracked for the number of Internet-connected Gram Panchayats, and panchayats with Common Services. Every district is provided with the target as per national development priority, the study makes an effort to grasp the distance of each district from the national target. This allows researchers to develop a scale Very Far, Far, Near, Very Near, Achieved with descriptive statistics techniques. Juxtaposing the scale with timelines results in a pattern of progress made by these 112 districts.

Modeling Economic Growth in Contemporary India, 187–213
Copyright © 2024 Pratham Parekh
Published under exclusive licence by Emerald Publishing Limited
doi:10.1108/978-1-80382-751-320241011

Keywords: Aspirational districts; sustainable development goals; social policy; governance; economic growth

1. Introduction and Background

Economic growth of the India since 1950s has remained noteworthy with colossal scope in terms of translating economic progress into social development. The exhaustive and extensive geographical, cultural and demographic diversity of country makes such translation difficult task. Even administrative efforts for translating economic growth into social development experiences limitations to address to socio-economic and regional inequalities.

Long-lasting colonial effects on society and economy on Indian states and districts engrained in culture are still posing unique challenge to development. While on other side, many states and districts, mostly coastal states, gained advantages from colonial economic policy are presenting picture of rapid economic growth. However, in both kind of states and districts translation of economic growth into development remains sceptical.

The post-colonial Indian development strategies were inclined towards Planning Commission of India's perception of development. This perception of development was designed, planned and executed through Five-Year Plans has remained vacillating over different periods with changes in Prime Ministers and their political willingness (Mukherji, 2009). Though these plans differ over periods, a singular though dominates the Five-Year Plan, i.e. economic growth. Almost all five-year plans considered economic growth as prime indicator of development (Shaban, 2016). Until date, this though dominates India's development planning discourse. It's in 1990s, planning discourse of India presents a challenge for achieving holistic development because of urges to address regional disparities, deprivations, elimination of social inequalities, etc. these efforts are reflected in objectives and targets of 11th five-year plan that was carry forwards in last five-year plan of the country. Though country have attempted to accelerate economic growth, its translation into human well-being and human development has proven mammoth challenge evidently observed in poor performance of country in several global social indices.

All attempts to analyse development are mostly made at global, national level or sub-national levels. There exists very scarce academic and scientific literature that grasps efforts made for development at local or district levels.

1.1 Development of Districts

After independence, an idea of empowering local governments through planning emerges in a report by Grow More Food (GMF) Enquiry Committee in 1952. This report recommended to consider the Community Development Blocks as a solution to the challenges posed to variety of local governments that are observed to be working in silos or without any common shared objective (Mehta, 1957). These recommendations paved a way for a Community Development

Programme. This programme on first hand focused on the development of agriculture and allied economic activities which can led to rural development while addressing issues linked with rural health, communication, rural education, etc. The concept was enthusiastically adopted and implemented in the newly independent country. The Balwant Rai Mehta Committee, in 1957 recommended to establish three-tire Panchayati Raj Institutions. These institutions were to be considered as an agencies of local governance organizations at the village, block(taluka) and district levels of administration. By 1964, coverage of Community Development Block was extended over the entire country, such vast coverage created a need for resource allocation at the local level of administration. This need was addressed by the Administrative Reforms Commission in 1967 by making recommendations that purposeful planning has to be undertaken for resource allocation for local-level administrations (Parekh, 2022). In the new century, the country's decentralized planning efforts started inclining towards allocation of financial resources to micro administrative departments and expenditure through local governments diluting the very objective decentralized planning. Brief details about efforts made to consider districts as pivot of development planning in India are listed below:

Committee & Year	Major Decision
1964	Coverage of Community Development Block was extended over the entire country, such vast coverage created a need for resource allocation at the local level of administration
Prof. M. L. Dantwala Committee (1978)	Recommended that block level planning must serve as a link between village plans and district plans.
The Reserve Bank of India (RBI) (1984)	Steps into development discourse by developing a credit plan for district-level planning.
Hanumantha Rao Committee (1984)	Recommended the decentralization of administrative functions, powers and finances through specialized district planning agencies and district planning cells.
G. V. K. Rao Committee (1985)	Made an effort for making district panchayats as managing and monitoring units for all development programs at a rural level.

(Continued)

(Continued)

Committee & Year	Major Decision
7th Five-Year Plan (1985–1990)	Focused on decentralization before which planning processes, decision-making and strategy formulation remain concentrated at the state and union levels.
	After recommendations of the Balwant Rai Committee though some states constituted panchayats, the panchayat remained a non-permanent feature government system. Development programs/schemes formulated by the central government (known as Centrally Sponsored Schemes or CSS) and were implemented through line departments, making the district-level planning process collapse or irrelevant.
74th amendment acts in 1992 (implemented in 1993)	Decentralized planning where districts became key units (known as Urban Local Bodies or ULBs) for regional as well as national planning processes. This constitutional amendment recognized districts as a planning unit for urban local demography. This 74th amendment also mandated the formation of District Planning Committees that would be responsible for draughting district plans based on plans received from panchayats and municipalities.
8th Five-Year Plan (1992–1997)	Stressed building and strengthening peoples' institutions and generating active participation within liberalization and privatization frameworks. During plan period, district plans focused on population control, environment preservation and

(Continued)

Committee & Year	Major Decision
	development of infrastructure at the local level.
9th Five-Year Plan (1997–2002)	Focused on themes related to social justice and equity.
10th Five-Year Plan (2002–2007)	Advocated area approach and policy priorities for strengthening decentralized planning.
2nd Administrative Reform Commission (2004)	Decentralized planning mandated the preparation of village plans based on the development needs of the village at block levels and was finally consolidated at the district level for preparing district plans. Such activity though mandated, remained merely paperwork in several states, resulting in regional imbalances in development. Regional developmental imbalances remained the major priority of planning in India (Mohan, 2005). Such mechanism created a confusing scenario that was studied.
Group of Ministers (GoM) constituted in 2007	Accepted recommendations for devolution of power to urban local governments under themes like school education, public health (administration of community health centres or area hospitals), traffic management, civil policing, urban environment, heritage maintenance, land management and registration.
Ministry of Panchayati Raj (2008)	Constituted an expert group that made recommendations on developing district and sub-district plans at all levels of Panchayats aimed to deliver basic needs to citizens at grass root levels. Based on this report by Shri V. Ramachandran-led expert group, the Planning Commission issued detailed

(Continued)

(Continued)

Committee & Year	Major Decision
	guidelines for developing district plans in the 11th Five-Year Plan (Ministry of Panchayati Raj, 2008).
Planning Commission initiated Integrated District Planning in 2008	For transforming vertical planning processes into the horizontal process. This initiation ensured the participation of district administration in the preparation of sectoral plans like a district health plan, district watershed plan, district education plan, etc. this effort confirmed sectoral thrusts in development that fine-tuned the planning processes with increased specializations to address local problems (Planning Commission of India, 2014).
	Integrated District Planning since 2008 focused on specific roles of local bodies and line departments. This framework aimed to ensure that sectoral specialization is efficiently and responsibly utilized. In such a context, urban planning is left with scattered sub-optimal planning agencies and processes. The local governments then were empowered to be part of actual decision-making in district planning assuming them as a vital layer connecting regional planning and national planning.

Source: (Parekh, 2022).

The apex planning body of India, NITI Aayog launched an Aspirational District Programme (ADP) in January 2018. The programme aimed to the quick and effective transformation of 112 (14%) districts of the country that are historically claimed as backward districts. The UNDP in recent times acclaimed this programme for enabling local, state and national governments to achieve significant milestones in terms of health, nutrition and education. This programme is considered as world's biggest result-based governance initiative having reached up to 250 million people. It is based on three dimensions, i.e. (a) Convergence of Central and State schemes, (b) Collaboration of 'Prabhari' officers of States with District Collectors and (c) Competition among districts through a ranking that is done on monthly basis. This ranking is based on 49 KPIs across six broad socio-economic themes.

Data are a pivotal aspect of ADP wherein districts are ranked based on their monthly progress captured against key indicators across six themes, i.e. Health & Nutrition, Education, Agriculture, Basic Infrastructure, Financial Inclusion and Skill Development. Monthly data provided by district administration and ministries provide the in-depth perception of progress made by districts for each indicator. These data trends not only enable policymakers to design policy intervention strategies but also allows them to assess the effectiveness of executed interventions.

2. Objective and Purpose of Study

To inquire and assess the progress made by 112 Aspirational Districts under Financial Inclusion, Skill Development and Basic Infrastructure theme from the inception of the programme to June 2022 (i.e. 54 months).

3. Method

Instead of ranking districts with delta rank or composite scores, the study divorce from NITI Aayog's methodology of monthly delta ranking. The study explores 8 indicators under the basic infrastructure theme and 16 indicators under the financial inclusion and skill development themes.

For this purpose, the study explores the availability of individual household latrines, drinking water, electricity and road connectivity. Districts are also tracked for the number of Internet-connected gram panchayats, and panchayats with Common Services.

Every district is provided with the target as per national development priority, the study makes an effort to grasp the distance of each district from the national target. This allows researchers to develop a scale Very Far, Far, Near, Very Near, Achieved with descriptive statistics techniques. Juxtaposing the scale with time-lines results in a pattern of progress made by these 112 districts (Fig. 11.1).

Achievements made under each indicator are grasped at two levels, i.e. at the state level and the district level as such status indicates the progress made by state and district for achieving sustainable development goals at local levels (Table 11.1).

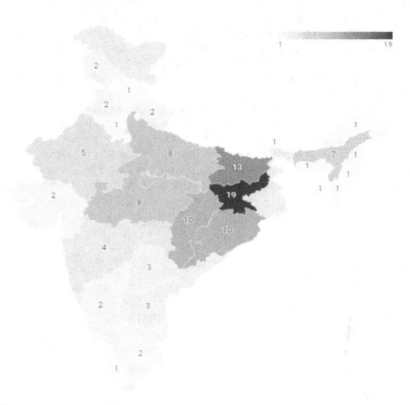

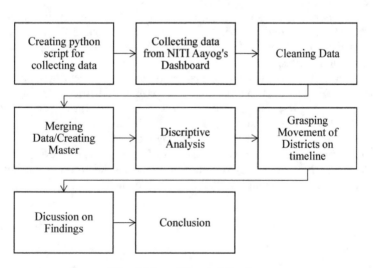

Fig. 11.1.   Flow of Study.

Table 11.1. Indicators Under Inquiry.

Code	Indicator
Theme: Financial Inclusion and Skill Development	
264	Total disbursement of Mudra loan (in crore rupees) per 1 lakh population
267	Pradhan Mantri Jeevan Jyoti Bima Yojana (PMJJBY): Number of enrolments per 1 lakh population
269	Pradhan Mantri Suraksha Bima Yojana (PMSBY): Number of enrolments per 1 lakh population
271	Atal Pension Yojana (APY): Number of beneficiaries per 1 lakh population
273	Percentage of accounts seeded with Aadhaar to total bank accounts
360	Number of accounts opened under Pradhan Mantri Jan Dhan Yojana per 1 lakh population
276	Percentage of youth certified in short-term or long-term training schemes to no. of youth in district in age group 15–29
279	Percentage of certified youth employed# to no. of youth trained under short-term or long-term training
281	Number of apprenticeships completing to total number of trainees registered on the portal
284	No. of people certified under recognition of prior learning to non-formally skilled workforce
287	Percentage certified trained: Women
289	Percentage certified trained: SC
291	Percentage certified trained: ST
293	Percentage certified trained: OBC
295	Percentage certified trained: Minorities
297	Percentage certified trained: Differently abled
264	Total disbursement of Mudra loan (in crore rupees) per 1 lakh population
267	Pradhan Mantri Jeevan Jyoti Bima Yojana (PMJJBY): Number of enrolments per 1 lakh population
Theme: Basic Infrastructure	
299	Percentage of households with electricity connection
302	Percentage of gram panchayats with Internet connection
304	Percentage of habitations with access to all weather roads under PMGSY

(Continued)

Table 11.1. *(Continued)*

Code	Indicator
361	Cumulative number of kilometres of all-weather road work completed as a percentage of total sanctioned kilometres in the district under PMGSY
307	Percentage of households with individual household latrines
309	Percentage of rural habitations with access to adequate quantity of potable water (40 lpcd) drinking water
311	Percentage coverage of establishment of Common Service Centres at gram panchayat level
314	Percentage of pucca houses constructed for households who are shelterless or have one room with kuchha wall and roof or have two rooms with kuchha wall and roof
299	Percentage of households with electricity connection
302	Percentage of gram panchayats with Internet connection
304	Percentage of habitations with access to all weather roads under PMGSY
361	Cumulative number of kilometres of all-weather road work completed as a percentage of total sanctioned kilometres in the district under PMGSY
307	Percentage of households with individual household latrines
309	Percentage of rural habitations with access to adequate quantity of potable water (40 lpcd) drinking water
311	Percentage coverage of establishment of Common Service Centres at gram panchayat level
314	Percentage of pucca houses constructed for households who are shelterless or have one room with kuchha wall and roof or have two rooms with kuchha wall and roof
299	Percentage of households with electricity connection
302	Percentage of gram panchayats with Internet connection

The achievements made under each indicator is grasped at two levels, i.e. at state level and at districts as such status indicates progress made for achieving sustainable Development goals at local levels.

Out of 112 Aspirational Districts, majority districts are from Eastern zone (37.50%) followed by Central India districts (25%) and North-eastern districts (12.50%) and least districts are from Western zone of India (5.36%). Jharkhand has highest number of aspirational districts, i.e. 19 districts (16.96% of total aspirational districts). Goa do not have any aspirational districts while districts of West Bengal have been 'dropped off' by NITI Aayog.

4. Literature Survey

There exists a significant gap in terms of literature regarding aspirational districts (Fig. 11.2). Among existing literature majority of literature exists in terms of a specific sector or state. The comprehensive data analysis is generally provided by literature emerging from the NITI Aayog itself.

5. Result and Finding

It is clearly observed that the majority districts fall in category of 'far' to 'very far' when it comes to achieving targets (Fig. 11.3). Careful observations suggest that very districts could attain set targets. Each district attaining target against number of indicators is shown in annexure 2. Very few districts are observed under 'target achieved' category. It is also observed that districts were able to achieve targets only for 10 indicators given in Table 11.2. Majority of districts are missing targets in 25 indicators, i.e. less than 0% achievement have been made for indicators listed in Table 11.3. Out of 112 districts, half of the districts falls under 'far' category, stating their achievement up to 25% against targets of 25 indicators as shown in Table 11.4. Similarly, only one-third number of districts were able to achieve targets up to 50% for only 20 indicators that is evident from Table 11.5. Districts are able to reach near achievement for 18 indicators which can be seen from Table 11.6, in which there are less than 10% districts are observed.

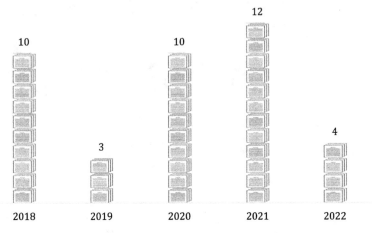

Fig. 11.2.   Number of Research Papers Available Related to Aspirational Districts. *Source*: Google Scholar and Scopus.

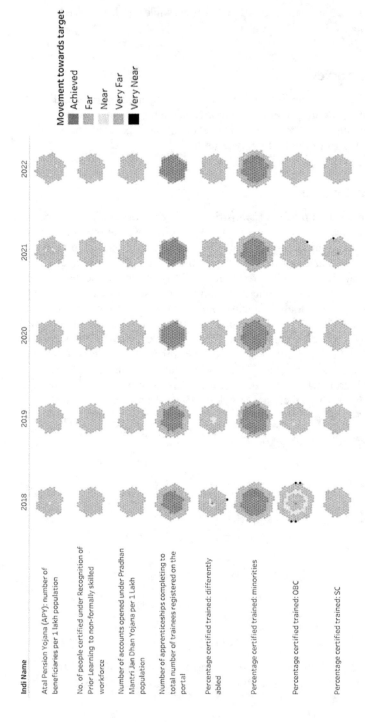

Fig. 11.3.   Distance of Districts From the Benchmark/Target Set in March 2018.

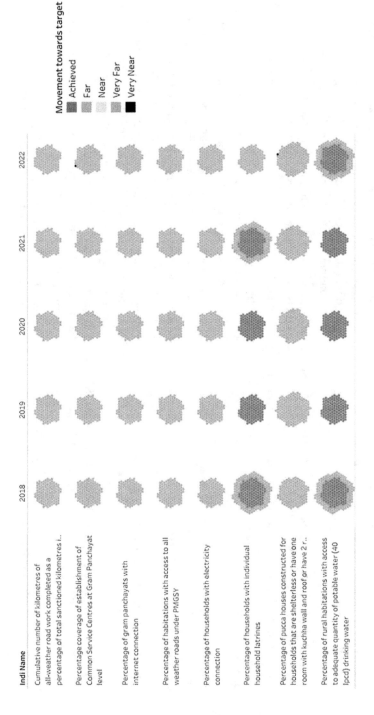

Fig. 11.3. (*Continued*).

Table 11.2. Publications Surveyed for Review of Literature.

Authors	Title
A Kumar, JC Jeeva, A Sarkar, B Sahoo, SK Srivastava	Nutritional status of children in the aspirational districts of Odisha, India
	Women in agriculture in aspirational districts of Odisha
A Kumar, JC Jeeva, DN Sarangi, AK Panda…	Analysis of the socio-economic status of people in aspirational districts of Odisha for inclusive growth:
Adarsh Kumar, J. Jeeva, D. Sarangi, A. Panda, S. Srivastava	Socioeconomic status of aspirational districts of Odisha Analysis of socio-economic status of people in aspirational districts of Odisha for inclusive growth
Anil. Kumar, J. Jeeva, A. Sarkar, B. Sahoo, S. Srivastava	Nutritional status of children in the aspirational districts of Odisha
B. Komow	Urbanization of the aspirational districts of India: Namsai – The Eastern divisional headquarter of Arunachal Pradesh
Bikash Santra, A. Goswami, K. Dhara, S. Biswas, D. P. Swain	Knowledge index of women goat farmers in various aspirational districts of Niti-Ayog in West Bengal, India
Dr Amulya Kumar Acharya	Social adjustment of tribal girls of aspirational districts of Odisha in relation to their socio-economic status
E Sarin, N Bisht, JS Mohanty…	Putting the local back into planning experiences and perceptions of state and district health functionaries of seven aspirational districts in India on an innovative …
E. Sarin, D. Bajpayee, Arvind Kumar, S. Dastidar, Subodh Chandra, Ranjan Panda, G. Taneja, Sachin Gupta, H. Kumar	Intrapartum foetal heart monitoring practices in selected facilities in aspirational districts of Jharkhand, Odisha and Uttarakhand
E. Sarin, N. Bisht, J. Mohanty, Naresh Chandra Joshi, Arvind Kumar, Surajit Dey, H. Kumar	Putting the local back into planning experiences and perceptions of state and district health functionaries of seven

Author	Title
	aspirational districts in India on an innovative planning capacity-building approach.
G. ArunKumar, M. S. Nain, Rashmi Singh, N. V. Kumbhare, R. Parsad, Shiv Kumar	Training effectiveness of skill development training programmes among the aspirational districts of Karnataka
I Pradhan, B Kandapan, J Pradhan	Age-appropriate feeding practices and their association with undernutrition among children aged 6–23 months in aspirational districts of India: A multinomial analysis
Itishree Pradhan, Binayak Kandapan, J. Pradhan	Age-appropriate feeding practices and their association with undernutrition among children aged 6–23 months in aspirational districts of India: A multinomial analysis.
J. Mohanty, Anil Prabhanjan, P. Saboth, H. Kumar, E. Sarin, A. Minz, S. Chourasia, Sachin Gupta	Integrated approach for survival and development during first 1,000 days of life: Assessing health systems readiness in three aspirational districts of Jharkhand (India)
JS Mohanty, AK Prabhanjan, PK Saboth...	... approach for survival and development during first 1,000 days of life: Assessing health systems readiness in three aspirational districts of Jharkhand (India)
K Anil, JC Jeeva, DN Sarangi, AK Panda...	Analysis of the socio-economic status of people in aspirational districts of Odisha for inclusive growth.
KS Das, SK Mondal, S Das, SS Singh	Krishi Kalyan Abhiyan: Towards agricultural development in aspirational districts
N Aayog	Aspirational districts Programme
	Aspirational districts: Unlocking potentials
	Deep dive: Insights from champions of change, the aspirational districts dashboard
	Government of India. Deep dive: Insights from champions of change, the aspirational districts dashboard. [Internet] New Delhi: NITI Aayog, Government ...

(Continued)

Table 11.2. (*Continued*)

Authors	Title
	Transformation of aspirational districts
	Transformation of aspirational districts baseline rankings and real-time monitoring dashboard
	Transformation of aspirational districts: A New India by 2022
N Puri	A review of the Aspirational Districts Programme of The National Institute of Transforming India, Government of India
N Uddin, MH Qadri	… adequacy and optimization of antenatal quality of care and client satisfaction during pregnancy: A cross-sectional study of two aspirational districts of Jammu & …
R Jain, P Chand, P Agarwal, S Rao…	Determination of agricultural infrastructural suitability in aspirational districts: A case study of Bundelkhand
R. Singh	Impact of COVID-19 pandemic on aspirational districts from Kerala and Maharashtra
RV Krishnaveni, N Pandey	Empowering women at grassroots–A case study analysis on aspirational districts
S Kumaravel	CDB's initiatives under Krishi Kalyan Abhiyan as part of the Aspirational districts Programme.
S Satyam	Agricultural produces, marketing and supportive mechanism: A study in aspirational districts of Telangana

S Sharma, V Sharma	Efficiency assessment of maternal health services in the aspirational districts of EAG States in India: A data envelopment analysis approach
S Sinha	Is the Aspirational Districts Programme merely a political device?
Sreetama Bhattacharjee, K. Dhara, S. Kesh, S. Ghosh, Purnabha Dasgupta, A. Giri, B. Sarkar, S. Roy, S. Bose, A. Dey	Study on socio-economic status and constraints faced by the livestock farmers of the aspirational districts of West Bengal, India
Sreetama Bhattacharjee, K. Dhara, Shilpa Ghosh, Paramita Das, Asim Giri, Biman Sarkar, S. Roy, S. Bose	Study on knowledge level of the livestock farmers of aspirational districts of West Bengal, India
T Haque, PK Joshi	a. Agricultural transformation in aspirational districts of India: A comparative analysis of districts in Bihar Agricultural transformation in aspirational districts of India
T Sarkar, M Mishra, RB Singh	Managing the regional inequalities in India with particular reference to the transformation of Aspirational Districts Programme
V Bhatia, RS Rath, AK Singh	Developing the underdeveloped: Aspirational Districts Programme from a public health point of view

Table 11.3. Districts Under 'Target Achieved' Category.

Indicators	No. of Districts that have achieved 75% to 100% targets				
	2018	2019	2020	2021	2022
No. of people certified under Recognition of Prior Learning to non-formally skilled workforce	1	2	1		
Number of Soil Health Cards distributed		1	1		1
Percentage certified trained: differently abled			1		1
Percentage certified trained: OBC		1	3	2	2
Percentage certified trained: SC	5	4	1	6	1
Percentage coverage of establishment of Common Service Centres at Gram Panchayat level	1				
Percentage increase in agricultural credit		4	3	1	
Percentage of gram panchayats with internet connection			1		
Percentage of pucca houses constructed for households that are shelterless or have one room with kuchha wall and roof or have 2 rooms with kuchha wall and roof	3			2	
Total disbursement of Mudra loan (in Crore rupees) per 1 lakh population	5	2	1	2	1

It is observed under each theme at majority of districts are failing to reach at least near to the set targets over a span of 54 months (Table 11.7).

6. Conclusion

As a sub-discipline of sociology, public sociology emphasizes the expansion of disciplinary boundaries and allowing non-academic audiences (Burawoy, 2005). Public sociology advocates engaging sociology with issues of public policies, governance and political activism. This stem of sociology leverage over empirical methods (mostly statistics, mathematics or computational) linked with sociological theoretical frameworks to grasp not just 'what is' or 'what has been' but also 'what might be'. The majority of versions of public sociology have remained normative and political (Piven, 2007). The study grounds its rationale on such a theoretical perspective.

Table 11.4. Districts Under 'Very Far' Category.

Indicators	No. of Districts that have achieved less than 0% targets				
	2018	2019	2020	2021	2022
Atal Pension Yojana (APY): number of beneficiaries per 1 lakh population	98	107	106	112	112
Number of accounts opened under Pradhan Mantri Jan Dhan Yojana per 1 Lakh population	111	111	112	112	112
Percentage of rural habitations with access to adequate quantity of potable water (40 lpcd) drinking water	111	112	112	112	112
Pradhan Mantri Jeevan Jyoti Bima Yojana (PMJJBY): number of enrolments per 1 lakh population	110	112	112	112	112
Pradhan Mantri Suraksha Bima Yojana (PMSBY): number of enrolments per 1 lakh population	110	112	112	112	112
Percentage of youth certified in short term or long-term training schemes to no. of youth in district in age group 15-29*	100	111	111	105	108
Cumulative number of kilometres of all-weather road work completed as a percentage of total sanctioned kilometres in the district under PMGSY	104	110	109	110	107
Percentage of habitations with access to all weather roads under PMGSY	103	110	109	110	107
Percentage coverage of establishment of Common Service Centres at Gram Panchayat level	95	104	106	107	105
Percentage of accounts seeded with Aadhaar to total bank accounts	103	103	104	104	104
Percentage certified trained: minorities	102	111	110	102	101
Percentage certified trained: ST	89	109	107	103	100
Number of apprenticeships completing to total number of trainees registered on the portal	64	78	85	93	98
Percentage of gram panchayats with internet connection	59	77	92	104	93

(Continued)

Table 11.4. *(Continued)*

Indicators	No. of Districts that have achieved less than 0% targets				
	2018	2019	2020	2021	2022
Percentage of pucca houses constructed for households that are shelterless or have one room with kuchha wall and roof or have 2 rooms with kuchha wall and roof	65	95	94	92	74
Percentage of certified youth employed# to no. of youth trained under short term or long-term training	46	106	106	105	71
Percentage certified trained: women	39	105	43	55	59
Wheat: Percentage change in Price Realization (defined as the difference between Farm Harvest Price (FHP) and Minimum Support Price (MSP))	65	70	73	62	56
Percentage certified trained: OBC	53	77	21	28	14
Percentage of area under micro-irrigation	13	21	22	26	14
Crop Insurance - Kharif: Percentage of net sown area under Pradhan Mantri Fasal Bima Yojana (PMFBY)	19	29	21	26	6
Percentage certified trained: SC	1	13	2	9	5
Total disbursement of Mudra loan (in Crore rupees) per 1 lakh population			3	2	2
No. of people certified under Recognition of Prior Learning to non-formally skilled workforce		1			
Percentage certified trained: differently abled	3				

It is well known that the economic growth of India since its independence presents an applauding picture. This economic growth also comes with a shadowing cost of socio-economic inequalities and regional imbalances attaining development. Post-independence period Indian governments made attempts to get rid of colonial exploitative effects on the economy and society which is still observed as an ongoing project. India's adoption of Five-Year Plans always had economic growth, national development and regional development as dominating agendas. The role and priorities of the Planning Commission of India have remained fluctuated with changing political scenarios. By the 1990s, it became

Table 11.5. Districts Under 'Far' Category.

Indicators	No. of Districts that have achieved 1% to 25%targets				
	2018	2019	2020	2021	2022
Total disbursement of Mudra loan (in Crore rupees) per 1 lakh population	43	89	98	95	81
Percentage certified trained: SC	52	79	62	54	65
Percentage certified trained: OBC	45	25	62	53	64
Percentage of area under micro-irrigation	34	46	45	45	49
Percentage certified trained: women	56	6	65	48	43
Percentage of certified youth employed# to no. of youth trained under short term or long-term training	36	3	4	6	40
Percentage of pucca houses constructed for households that are shelter less or have one room with kuchha wall and roof or have 2 rooms with kuchha wall and roof	33	13	14	14	30
Percentage of gram panchayats with internet connection	30	20	17	8	18
Number of Mandis in the District linked to Electronic Market	10	19	23	29	11
Percentage of accounts seeded with Aadhaar to total bank accounts		5	6	8	8
Percentage coverage of establishment of Common Service Centres at Gram Panchayat level	12	6	5	4	7
Cumulative number of kilometres of all-weather road work completed as a percentage of total sanctioned kilometres in the district under PMGSY	7	1	3	1	5
Percentage of habitations with access to all weather roads under PMGSY	8	1	3	2	5
Percentage certified trained: differently abled	3	10			1
Atal Pension Yojana (APY): number of beneficiaries per 1 lakh population	10	4	3		
No. of people certified under Recognition of Prior Learning to non-formally skilled workforce		3			
Number of accounts opened under Pradhan Mantri Jan Dhan Yojana per 1 Lakh population		1			

(Continued)

Table 11.5. *(Continued)*

Indicators	No. of Districts that have achieved 1% to 25%targets				
	2018	2019	2020	2021	2022
Paddy (Common): Percentage change in Price Realization (defined as the difference between Farm Harvest Price (FHP) and Minimum Support Price (MSP)		1	1	2	
Pradhan Mantri Jeevan Jyoti Bima Yojana (PMJJBY): number of enrolments per 1 lakh population	1				
Pradhan Mantri Suraksha Bima Yojana (PMSBY): number of enrolments per 1 lakh population	1				

clear to governments that a narrow vision of linear economic planning and growth is not going to address the developmental issues of the country. Issues like social deprivation, regional disparities, evaluation of social inequalities, etc. became priority issues during the 11th Five-Year Plan that continued till the last five-year plan. Though the country is adopting and continuing with rigorous development planning at all levels of governance, India is fairly unable to translate economic growth into human well-being.

The study thus turns its face to regional development assuming national development as an accumulation of regional development and focuses on district-level governance (assuming districts as an aggregated unit of blocks and villages). Districts have always remained an important part of development planning in India. Districts as planning units have been debated a lot since independence, such debates can be traced from (1) Grow More Food (GMF) Enquiry Committee in 1952; (2) community development programme by planning commission 1952; (3) Administrative Reforms Commission in 1967; (4) Prof. M. L. Dantwala Committee in 1978; (5) Strengthening of district plan/District Credit Plan by Reserve Bank of India (RBI) in 1984; (6) Hanumantha Rao Committee in 1984; (7) G. V. K. Rao Committee in 1985; (8) 7th Five-Year Plan (1985–1990) focused on decentralization; (9) The enactment of the 74th amendment acts in 1992; (10) 8th Five-Year Plan (1992–1997) stressing on building and strengthening peoples' institutions and generating active participation within liberalization and privatization frameworks; (11) 10th Five-Year Plan (2002–2007) advocating area approach and policy priorities for strengthening decentralized planning; (12) 2nd Administrative Reform Commission in 2004; (13) Group of Ministers (GoM) constituted in 2007; (14) Expert group constituted by Ministry of Panchayati Raj;

Table 11.6. Districts Under 'Near' Category.

Indicators	No. of Districts that have achieved 26% to 50%targets				
	2018	2019	2020	2021	2022
Total disbursement of Mudra loan (in Crore rupees) per 1 lakh population	22	12	6	2	13
Percentage certified trained: SC	7	5	11	8	10
Percentage certified trained: OBC	1	1	5	6	4
Percentage increase in agricultural credit	9	8	5	8	4
Percentage of gram panchayats with internet connection	3				2
Percentage of pucca houses constructed for households that are shelterless or have one room with kuchha wall and roof or have 2 rooms with kuchha wall and roof	4	1		1	2
Percentage certified trained: differently abled	1	4			1
Percentage certified trained: women	5		2	4	1
Cumulative number of kilometres of all-weather road work completed as a percentage of total sanctioned kilometres in the district under PMGSY	1			1	
Percentage coverage of establishment of Common Service Centres at Gram Panchayat level	1				
Percentage of accounts seeded with Aadhaar to total bank accounts	1	2	2		
Percentage of certified youth employed# to no. of youth trained under short term or long-term training		1	1		

(15) 11th Five-Year Plan providing detailed guidelines for developing district plans.

An important milestone in district-level development planning is observed in 2008 when the planning commission made an attempt to streamline previously recommended measures and initiated Integrated District Planning that focused on specific roles of local bodies and line departments to sectoral specialization. Due

Table 11.7. Districts Under 'Very Near' Category.

Indicators	No. of Districts that have achieved 51% to 75% targets				
	2018	2019	2020	2021	2022
Percentage of area under micro-irrigation	3	1	9	4	5
Percentage certified trained: OBC		1	1	1	4
Percentage certified trained: SC	6	2	4	5	4
Total disbursement of Mudra loan (in Crore rupees) per 1 lakh population	14	3		3	4
Number of Mandis in the District linked to Electronic Market	1	1	6	5	2
Percentage certified trained: women	2				1
No. of people certified under Recognition of Prior Learning to non-formally skilled workforce	1	5			
Percentage certified trained: differently abled			2		
Percentage of accounts seeded with Aadhaar to total bank accounts		2			
Percentage of certified youth employed# to no. of youth trained under short term or long-term training	2				
Percentage of gram panchayats with internet connection	1				

Table 11.7. *(Continued)*

Indicators	No. of Districts that have achieved 51% to 75% targets				
	2018	2019	2020	2021	2022
Percentage of pucca houses constructed for households that are shelterless or have one room with kuchha wall and roof or have 2 rooms with kuchha wall and roof	1				

to this urban planning is left with scattered sub-optimal planning agencies and processes. The local governments then were empowered to be part of actual decision-making in district planning assuming them as a vital layer connecting regional planning and national planning.

A new political regime replaced the planning commission with a new body called National Institute for Transforming India (NITI) Aayog. NITI Aayog, in January 2018 launched the Transformation of Aspirational Districts Programme focused on the rapid transformation of districts lagging in various development parameters. This programme makes Prabhari Officer and District Collector/ Magistrates accountable for improving socio-economic indicators through competitive federalism.

Achievements of districts under this programme are monitored through quantifiable outcomes through sophisticated MIS across six thematic areas. These thematic areas have been narrowed down into 49 key performance indicators.

After analysing public data of NITI Aayog on Aspirational Districts, the study attempts to grasp the distance of districts from the set benchmark/target and compounded annual growth rate of districts' indicators. Overall, it is observed that more than 45% districts are missing their annual targets for all indicators. Districts are observed to perform weakly in terms of indicators related to agriculture and basic infrastructure while indictors related to financial inclusion and water resources are observed to be moving forward as compared to other themes. It can be assumed that aspirational districts are doing well in terms of road and water accessibility. While household infrastructure like house and electricity needs reasonable focus at the implementation level. District-wise movement can be visualised on the dashboard developed by researchers and made available at url: https://public.tableau.com/app/profile/pratham.parekh/viz/alls/Dashboard1.

In addition to describing data and gauging the progress of districts, the study also observed qualitative insights. The data-driven governance model demonstrated by the Aspirational Districts Programme on first look appears to be a vital initiative for a country like India. But such systems tend to face several miss-management hurdles due to the cultural and political inclination of the scheme. The majority of indicators are receiving data directly from Districts. These districts focusing on competition may ascent on extravagating monthly data. The lack of granular data on selected monitoring indicators has to face impediments to administrative efficiency. Further, the indicators that are selected by NITI Aayog require more meticulous attention for instance from data captured for any given indicator is difficult to distinguish between output and outcome. The output may not necessarily accumulate into the outcome, for example, an output indicator like 'Percentage coverage of establishment of Common Service Centres at Gram Panchayat level' cannot represent the 'quality of service' (outcome indicator) provided to citizens through such common service centres. This limitation can serve as an inception point for outcome-based monitoring and management systems. Another important drawback of data-driven transformation reforms is that such reforms may miss the opportunity to pay detailed attention to the quality of implementation. Considering the Aspirational Districts Programme as a district database that enables and encourages district and state administration to diagnose needs and customise solutions for targeted interventions fails to align with an idea ranking districts. Competition rather creates a psyche of focusing on targets rather than focusing on solutions. Even while considering competition as a better mechanism for development, one needs to look at the incentives attached to competition. The induced competition of improving district ranks is forced on IAS officers serving as District Development Officers, District Collectors and District Magistrates. These officers serve their office generally for three years dealing with more than 100 ongoing schemes/programs. Such a scenario creates a sceptical viewpoint on the improvement of implementation quality as focussing on visible political priority rather than competing with fellow districts may be a rational choice for such officers. Additionally, a centralized monitoring system that aligns with politically inclined target settings is being monitored closely and realistically resisted. The Aspirational District Programme in such a sense also fails to promote decentralization as rural local bodies as panchayats have not been given any role. It is clear that developing such systems takes the planning process to new levels but assuming data as a substitute for engrained administrative failures can rise an urgent need to focus on actual administrative reforms and developing implementation capacity. Many such intriguing questions raised during studying open an arena for undertaking sociologically driven research.

References

Burawoy, M. (2005, February). For public sociology. *American Sociological Review*, *70*(1), 4–28.

Mehta, A. C. (1957). *Report of the Foodgrains Enquiry Committee*. Ministry of Food and Agriculture, Government of India.

Ministry of Panchayati Raj. (2008). *Framework for preparation of block and district development plan for rural area* [E-book]. Government of India. https://www.

panchayat.gov.in/bddpra/mobile/index.html#p=26. Accessed on September 1, 2022.

Mohan, K. (2005). *Addressing regional backwardness: An analysis of area development programmes in India*. Manak Publications.

Mukherji, R. (2009). The state, economic growth, and development in India. *India Review*, *8*(1), 81–106.

Parekh, P. (2022). Evaluating performance of Pradhan Mantri MUDRA Yojana in 112 backward districts of India. In S. Kalil (Ed.), *National conference on emerging business innovations and trends in India* (1st ed., pp. 153–163). Department of Corporate Secretaryship, Quaide Milleth College for Men.

Piven, F. F. (2007). From public sociology to politicized sociologist. In *Public sociology: Fifteen eminent sociologists debate politics and the profession in the twenty-first century* (pp. 158–166). University of California Press.

Planning Commission. (2014). *Manual for integrated district planning: Report of the Task Force of the Planning Commission (no. id: 5626)*. Government of India.

Shaban, A. (2016). Development strategies in India. In *Economic geography: Urbanisation, industry and development*. Oxford University Press.

Chapter 12

Advertisement Expenditure and Stock Returns: Evidence From India

Priya Mandleshwar

Indian Institute of Management, India

Abstract

According to the efficient market hypothesis, a company's advertising expenditures are fully reflected in its stock price. If so, then future abnormal stock returns should not be correlated to advertising spending. Nonetheless, this chapter explores the impact of advertising spending on the abnormal stock returns using portfolio sort based on both the advertising intensity and change in advertising intensity. Using data from 2000 to 2019, the results suggest that larger advertising intensity is coupled with negative abnormal stock returns in India. The study suggests that market is penalizing the firms for spending more on advertising. Hence, it suggests that advertising budgets should be allocated with caution by marketing managers.

Keywords: Advertising; abnormal stock returns; efficient market hypothesis; India; consumer economics

1. Introduction

There is a growing interest among researchers to uncover the role of advertising expenditure on stock returns. Anecdotal evidence suggests the growth of advertising expenditure is estimated at 10.8% in 2021. India, being one of the fastest-growing advertising sectors, with revenues of over 800 billion rupees in 2019. Similar to other global marketplaces, the advertising sector in India plays a significant influence in molding customer attitudes toward products and services. Therefore, it is essential to investigate the advertising industry in India. The marketing managers show the development of advertisement from profit motive to the marketing–sales relationship. Hence, it develops a new direction to know the benefit realized by increasing the expenditure. The following procedure can explain the cycle of advertising

Modeling Economic Growth in Contemporary India, 215–231

Copyright © 2024 Priya Mandleshwar

Published under exclusive licence by Emerald Publishing Limited

doi:10.1108/978-1-80382-751-320241012

expenditure on stock return. There is a budget assigned for the advertisement expenditure, which increases the sales, followed by the increase in profit. The increased profit will ultimately enhance the stock price of the company and hence, provide a higher return. Prior studies have explored the role of advertising spending and the stock market reactions. Joshi and Hanssens (2010) exhibited that the advertising spending of the firm has a direct influence on the stock returns, exceeding its influence on profits and earnings. Lou (2014) finds that advertising spending leads to short-term abnormal stock returns followed by a decrease in a future return. Chemmanur and Yan (2019) also provide evidence that investor attention is associated with the short-term increase in abnormal returns and small future returns. Similarly, Srinivasan et al. (2009) cite a positive impact of advertising spending on innovation and firm's financial performance. On the other side, Erickson and Jacobson (1992) find an inverse relationship between advertising and stock returns. Few studies (Bublitz & Ettredge, 1989; Tuli et al., 2012) found no positive significant reaction by the stock market on an increase in advertising expenditure. Core et al. (2003) find no significant association between advertising spending and firm value. Therefore, the relationship between advertising spending and stock return is still not conclusive. With these previous studies and anecdotal evidence suggesting the mixed link between advertising spending and abnormal stock returns, the research on the impact of advertising on a developing country like India is still to draw roots. Oh et al. (2016) find an anomaly involved in increased advertising spending and show the stock market undervaluation of the firms investing in advertising expenditure. In contrast to the Oh et al. (2016) paper, this study mainly focuses on whether advertising spending has a positive or negative abnormal stock return. This chapter uses the CAPM model and "Fama and French's (1993)" three-factor model to study the effect of advertising intensity on the stock returns and find a negative association between advertising spending and stock return. Most importantly, the study finds that a high level of advertising spending leads to a lower level of negative stock return when compared with low advertising spending. For example, the results from Fama–French three-factor model show that low advertising spending (d1) will result in 24.23% decrease in stock return, whereas the high advertising spending (d10) will result in 15.01% decrease in stock return.

2. Literature Review

Advertising spending provides signal to the investors and attract customers. Thus, helps to increase sales (Tellis, 2009), stock price and stock returns (Joshi & Hanssens, 2009, 2010), systematic risk (McAlister et al., 2007) and profit (Erickson & Jacobson, 1992). "McAlister et al. (2007)" find an inverse relationship between advertising spending and systematic risk, particularly when the companies are supported by pioneering innovation (Srinivasan et al., 2009). Prior studies have found anomalies in various intangible expenses and investments. For example, Oh et al. (2016) explore the firm's spending in advertising, Chan et al. (2001) explore firms spending in R&D expenditure, etc. Literature on various domains of finance, marketing and accounting posits that advertising expenditure affects the sales and firm value directly or indirectly. Essentially, advertising spending creates greater consumer awareness (Barroso & Llobet, 2012), quality competitiveness (Tellis & Fornell, 1988) and brand value (Eng & Keh, 2007). West et al. (2008) state that advertising spending increases customer attention and increases brand so firms are under constant pressure to increase their brand value by delivering creative ads and spending more on advertising. Moreover, advertising increases the customer response. "Srinivasan et al. (2009)" indicate that "advertising helps develop instant awareness of new products that may accelerate the diffusion process," implying that advertising spending generates cash flows rapidly. All the above factors help the firm to attain greater financial value. The finance and accounting literature also studies the impact of advertising spending. For instance, "Grullon et al. (2004)" find that firms with relatively higher advertising spending creates increased visibility and awareness among investors and therefore have more individual and institutional investors. Moreover, they found that firms engaging more on advertising spending have more liquid stocks. Hence, improves the firm's liquidity. "Joshi and Hanssens (2010)" exhibited that the advertising spending of the firm has a direct influence on the stock returns, exceeding its influence on profits and earnings. They proposed two mechanisms, i.e., spillover effect and signaling effect. Firms use advertising spending to signal the quality and brand image to the customer. Prior studies have talked about the signaling effect to attain long-term visibility. Higher advertising spending signals about firms present as well as future financial strength in terms of sales, profit and cash flow (Erickson & Jacobson, 1992; Joshi & Hanssens, 2010). Another mechanism was the spillover effect. Studies have suggested that investors are more attracted to the familiar firms (Joshi & Hanssens, 2009). For instance, stock investors are more confident to invest in companies having products familiar to investors (Frieder & Subrahmanyam, 2005), shareholders prefer to invest in the companies of similar place of origin (Feldstein & Horioka, 1980). Media decisions is also one of the factors along with the advertising spending affecting the sales, brand value and profitability of the firm. Further, advertising spending decreases the investor's cost of gathering information related to the firm's products and signals firm's present as well as future projects, growth and profitability. However, the impact of advertising spending on firm value is challenged in various studies. For instance, Joshi and Hanssens (2009) advertising spending impacts "nonlinearly" with "negative" marginal returns. Similarly, "Ali Shah and Akbar (2008)" find conflicting evidence of positive as well as negative relationship between advertising spending and stock return. They could not find any conclusive results. There are studies of negative relationships (Bublitz & Ettredge, 1989; Erickson & Jacobson, 1992; Tuli et al., 2012) as well as no significant relationship (Core et al., 2003).

3. Data and Variable

This study has extracted non-financial firm's data listed in NSE from the year 2000–2019. Data on the firm's sales, advertising spending, market capitalization and monthly stock returns are obtained from ProwessIQ. The data regarding the Fama–French model (Rm, Rf, SMB, HML) have been extracted from the IIM-A library with adjusting survivorship bias. SMB and HML factors are computed based on the portfolio generated using the data from IIM-A library (Agarwalla et al., 2013).

This chapter has excluded datasets with missing sales, market capitalization, advertising spending and returns with more than 3 months of data missing. The advertising intensity is estimated as the fraction of advertising spending scaled by total sales. The description of variables and sources are shown below in Appendix.

Table 12.1 summarizes the year-wise sample distribution. It shows that as we move across the sample period, firms have started reporting the advertisement spending, i.e., the number of firms with the missing advertisement is declining, which results in an increase in the sample size of final firms. Similarly, we observe the number of firms with zero or missing market capitalization is also declined.

Table 12.2 summarizes the descriptive statistics of value-weighted and equal-weighted portfolios. It is observed that in an equal-weighted portfolio construction, decile1 maximum return (8.26%) is more than the decile10 maximum return

Table 12.1. Year-Wise Sample Distribution.

Year	No. of Firms	No. of Firms With Missing Advertisement	No. of Firms With Missing Sales	No. of Firms With Zero or Missing Market Cap	Firms With More Than 3 Blank Returns	Final Firms
2000	1,993	1,323	54	293	24	299
2001	1,993	1,309	52	320	17	295
2002	1,993	1,317	55	329	18	274
2003	1,993	1,269	53	380	2	289
2004	1,993	1,240	57	381		315
2005	1,993	1,197	67	388	2	339
2006	1,993	1,155	70	359		409
2007	1,993	1,113	74	293	1	512
2008	1,993	1,073	76	269		575
2009	1,993	1,045	77	283	2	586
2010	1,993	1,016	79	261	2	635
2011	1,993	1,047	81	220		645
2012	1,993	1,037	79	210	4	663
2013	1,993	1,015	87	223		668
2014	1,993	972	83	258	4	676
2015	1,993	946	83	253		711
2016	1,993	942	84	219	1	747
2017	1,993	934	82	182	4	791
2018	1,993	923	89	104	7	870
2019	1,993	936	80	83		894
						11,193

Table 12.2. Equal Weighted.

Variable	Obs	Mean	Std.Dev	Min	Max
decile1	232	−0.19108	1.505044	−4.96026	8.261861
decile2	232	−0.16159	1.494153	−4.09945	7.232206
decile3	232	−0.22952	1.395423	−4.77059	4.644705
decile4	232	−0.18268	1.420557	−4.42858	4.410481
decile5	232	−0.19026	1.3691	−5.58159	5.682539
decile6	232	−0.1893	1.422926	−5.17392	4.512206
decile7	232	−0.24878	1.322632	−4.60122	3.743705
decile8	232	−0.23205	1.290332	−4.87592	4.286206
decile9	232	−0.18081	1.197516	−4.30358	4.340482
decile10	232	−0.11803	1.166132	−3.65626	2.692409
decile10−1	232	0.073053	1.061757	−7.42366	5.095988

(2.69%). It means firms spending less (decile1) in advertising generate more returns (8.26%) as compared to firms spending more (decile10) on advertising.

This relationship reverses when we use a value-weighted portfolio. The results based on a value-weighted portfolio (Table 12.3) state that firms spending more (decile10) advertising will generate more returns (7.988%) as compared to firms spending less (decile1) in advertising. Along with that, the chances of getting negative returns are low (−4.26%) when firms spend more on advertising.

Table 12.3. Value-Weighted.

Variable	Obs	Mean	Std.Dev	Min	Max
decile1	232	−0.1292	1.600296	−7.29726	5.066796
decile2	232	−0.0918	1.961504	−8.21593	11.20244
decile3	232	−0.15034	1.490796	−4.9255	4.684635
decile4	232	−0.13365	1.718563	−6.66407	7.661891
decile5	232	−0.10343	1.505974	−7.11465	3.667547
decile6	232	−0.17759	1.573645	−5.63804	5.880221
decile7	232	−0.08722	1.89379	−6.20351	11.08691
decile8	232	−0.1782	1.289312	−5.29625	3.779402
decile9	232	−0.13185	1.580101	−8.05338	7.382937
decile10	232	−0.06224	1.483468	−4.26572	7.988198
decile10−1	232	0.00669	1.584167	−4.60409	6.83085

4. Empirical Model

Firstly, we have removed the firms with missing sales, advertising expenses, and market capitalization. Then, the advertising intensity is calculated as a fraction of advertising spending to sales. The change of advertising intensity is calculated by subtracting previous advertising intensity from the current. The portfolio is then sort in deciles based on the advertising intensity and change in advertising intensity. The portfolio is constructed using the equal-weighted and value-weighted methods. The value-weight is assigned on the basis of market capitalization. For the look-ahead bias, we have matched the advertising intensity of March to returns of September. For example, for the construction of the portfolio of 2000, we take the advertising intensity of March 2000 and the returns from September 2000 to August 2001, and so on. By this process, monthly time-series data is constructed from September 2000 to December 2019. This study follows Fama and French's (1993) and CAPM model to study whether advertising spending can forecast future stock returns.

This chapter uses the following equation:

$$R_{pt} - R_{ft} = \alpha_p + \beta_p \left(R_{mt} - R_{ft} \right) + \epsilon_{pt}$$

$$R_{pt} - R_{ft} = \alpha_p + \beta_p \left(R_{mt} - R_{ft} \right) + s_p \, \mathrm{SMB}_t + h_p \, \mathrm{HML}_t + \epsilon_{pt}$$

R_{pt} represents the raw return on the monthly portfolio p for month t; R_{ft} represents risk-free rate, computed using the rate of 91-days Treasury bill in month t; SMB_t represents size factor, computed using small-stock portfolio returns minus big-stock portfolios return in month t; HML_t represents value factor, computed using high minus low book-to-market ratio in month t. The α_p is the abnormal returns of the deciles. Following the efficient market hypothesis, market is efficient, and all the information is reflected in the market. Hence, there are no abnormal returns (α_p is zero).

Table 12.4(a), Panel A shows the abnormal stock returns sorted by advertising intensity using an equal-weighted portfolio, following CAPM and the three-factor model. Portfolio d1 shows the least advertising spending by the firm, whereas portfolio d10 shows the highest advertising spending by the firm. The explanatory power increased to some extent using the three-factor model. The results show a significantly negative relationship between stock returns and advertising spending.

Both CAPM and the three-factor model suggest economic loss to the firm, i.e., more advertising spending will decrease the stock returns.

Table 12.4(b), Panel B shows the abnormal stock returns sorted by change in advertising intensity using an equal-weighted portfolio. The negative relationship between advertising spending and abnormal stock returns remains the same as Panel A, even by changing advertising spending. Additionally, Panel B suggests a high degree of loss when firms follow high advertising spending. Tables 12.5(a) and 12.5(b) show the abnormal stock returns sorted by advertising intensity using a value-weighted portfolio. Only firms with portfolios d6 and d8 have significant results at a 5% significance level, although negative relationship.

Table 12.4(a). CAPM and Equal Weighted (Panel A).

| | CAPM | | | Equal-Weighted | | | | | |
| | Panel A | | | Panel A | | | | | |
Portfolio	Alpha	$R_m R_f$	Adj R^2	Portfolio	Alpha	$R_m R_f$	SMB	HML	Adj R^2
d1	-0.23526	0.052282	0.0619	d1	-0.24233	0.047317	0.031113	0.005324	0.0606
	(-2.44)**	(3.90)***			(-2.50)**	(3.33)***	-1.41	0.34	
d2	-0.2065	0.053154	0.0608	d2	-0.22619	0.041666	0.048236	0.020284	0.0912
	(-2.16)**	(4.00)***			(-2.39)**	(3.00)***	(2.23)**	(1.34)	
d3	-0.2752	0.054065	0.077	d3	-0.28938	0.046354	0.025509	0.015919	0.0816
	(-3.10)***	(4.38)***			(-3.25)***	(3.56)***	(1.26)	(1.12)	
d4	-0.22372	0.048574	0.06	d4	-0.23582	0.041687	0.026816	0.012868	0.062
	(-2.45)**	(3.83)***			(-2.58)**	(3.11)***	(1.29)	(0.88)	
d5	-0.23468	0.052566	0.0716	d5	-0.24068	0.048252	0.028045	0.004288	0.074
	(-2.69)***	(4.34)***			(-2.75)***	(3.76)***	(1.4)	(0.31)	
d6	-0.2348	0.053852	0.0694	d6	-0.2382	0.050889	0.024409	0.001218	0.0678
	(-2.59)**	(4.27)***			(-2.61)***	(3.80)***	(1.17)	(0.08)	
d7	-0.28629	0.044392	0.0537	d7	-0.29532	0.039121	0.02216	0.009299	0.0558
	(-3.37)***	(3.76)***			(-3.45)***	(3.13)***	(1.14)	(0.68)	
d8	-0.26682	0.041162	0.0522	d8	-0.26028	0.04355	0.00744	-0.01007	0.0422
	(-3.21)***	(-3.56)			(-3.10)***	(3.54)***	(0.39)	(-0.75)	

(Continued)

Table 12.4(a). (*Continued*)

| | CAPM | | | | Equal-Weighted | | | | |
| | Panel A | | | | Panel A | | | | |
Portfolio	Alpha	R_mR_f	Adj R^2	Portfolio	Alpha	R_mR_f	SMB	HML	Adj R^2
d9	−0.21909	0.04531	0.0694	d9	−0.22119	0.04335	0.01723	0.000444	0.0657
	(−2.87)***	(4.27)***			(−2.87)***	(3.85)***	0.98	0.04	
d10	−0.14922	0.036911	0.0473	d10	−0.15017	0.035695	0.013158	−0.00055	0.054
	(−1.98)**	(3.53)***			(−1.98)**	(3.21)***	(0.98)	(0.04)	
d10−d1	0.086039	−0.01537	0.0064	d10−d1	0.092153	−0.01162	−0.01796	−0.00588	0.007
	(−1.23)	(−1.58)			(1.31)	(−1.13)	(−1.12)	(−0.52)	

Note: $*p < 0.1$; $**p < 0.05$; $***p < 0.01$ the parentheses shows *t*-value.

Advertisement Expenditure and Stock Returns *223*

Table 12.4(b). CAPM and Three-Factor Model (Panel B).

	CAPM			Three-Factor Model					
	Panel B				Panel B				
Portfolio	Alpha	$R_m R_f$	Adj R^2	Portfolio	Alpha	$R_m R_f$	SMB	HML	Adj R^2
d1	−0.23541	0.045668	0.051	d1	−0.23856	0.044374	0.023355	−0.0031	0.048
	(−2.59)**	(3.57)***			(−2.61)***	(3.23)***	−1.13	(−0.21)	
d2	−0.18468	0.037419	0.0352	d2	−0.19272	0.032783	0.031624	0.003804	0.0405
	(−2.08)**	(3.00)***			(−2.17)**	(2.45)**	(1.57)	(0.26)	
d3	−0.19048	0.048219	0.0566	d3	−0.1963	0.044949	0.024526	0.002049	0.0554
	(−2.09)**	(3.76)***			(−2.14)**	(3.26)***	(−1.18)	(0.14)	
d4	−0.25922	0.055945	0.061	d4	−0.27222	0.047649	0.033983	0.013284	0.0702
	(−2.54)**	(3.90)***			(−2.67)***	(3.11)***	(1.47)	(0.81)	
d5	−0.22135	0.056981	0.0936	d5	−0.22896	0.053472	0.048472	−0.00415	0.1143
	(−2.65)***	(4.86)***			(−2.77)***	(4.30)***	(2.59)**	(−0.31)	
d6	−0.30141	0.039262	0.036	d6	−0.31367	0.030731	0.01706	0.018779	0.042
	(−3.27)***	(3.03)***			(−3.40)***	(2.21)**	−0.82	(1.26)	
d7	−0.23194	0.047397	0.0558	d7	−0.24125	0.042696	0.050728	−0.00149	0.0766
	(−2.57)**	(3.73)***			(−2.69)***	(3.17)***	(2.50)**	(−0.10)	
d8	−0.20579	0.053083	0.0862	d8	−0.20993	0.050779	0.01805	0.001222	0.0827
	(−2.54)**	(4.65)***			(−2.57)**	(4.14)***	−0.98	(0.09)	

(Continued)

Table 12.4(b). *(Continued)*

| | CAPM | | | Three-Factor Model | | | | | |
| | Panel B | | | Panel B | | | | | |
Portfolio	Alpha	R_mR_f	Adj R^2	Portfolio	Alpha	R_mR_f	SMB	HML	Adj R^2
d9	−0.22837	0.0419	0.048	d9	−0.23185	0.04057	0.027893	−0.0043	0.0483
	(−2.66)***	(3.47)***			(−2.69)***	(3.13)***	(1.43)	(−0.31)	
d10	−0.216	0.039534	0.0434	d10	−0.21507	0.040918	0.01447	−0.00798	0.0375
	(−2.54)**	(3.31)***			(−2.51)**	(3.18)***	−0.75	(−0.58)	
d10−d1	0.019416	−0.00613	−0.0007	d10−d1	0.023482	−0.00346	−0.00888	−0.00488	−0.0024
	(−0.41)	(−0.92)			(−0.49)	(−0.48)	(−0.82)	(−0.63)	

Note: $*p < 0.1$; $**p < 0.05$; $***p < 0.01$ the parentheses show *t*-value.

Table 12.5(a). CAPM and Three-Factor Model.

| | CAPM | | | Three-Factor Model | | | | | |
| | Panel A | | | Panel A | | | | | |
Portfolio	Alpha	R_mR_f	Adj R^2	Portfolio	Alpha	R_mR_f	SMB	HML	Adj R^2
d1	-0.16451	0.041798	0.0308	d1	-0.15849	0.043055	0.2223	-0.01145	0.0267
	(-1.58)	(2.89)***			(-1.51)	(2.80)***	(0.93)	(-0.68)	
d2	-0.13319	0.048989	0.0278	d2	-0.1578	0.039325	-0.0166	0.036242	0.0324
	(-1.04)	(2.76)***			(-1.23)	(2.09)**	(-0.57)	(1.76)*	
d3	-0.17233	0.026029	0.0114	d3	-0.16919	0.027144	0.004091	-0.00491	0.0031
	(-1.76)*	(1.91)*			(-1.71)*	(1.87)*	(0.18)	(-0.31)	
d4	-0.14171	0.009536	-0.0028	d4	-0.14499	0.008816	-0.01151	0.006145	-0.0105
	(-1.25)	(0.6)			(-1.26)	(0.52)	(-0.44)	(0.33)	
d5	-0.14855	0.053406	0.0604	d5	-0.14021	0.055091	0.031753	-0.016	0.0622
	(-1.54)	(3.94)***			(-1.45)	(3.88)***	(1.44)	(-1.03)	
d6	-0.22594	0.057228	0.0638	d6	-0.2184	0.058762	0.028503	-0.01442	0.0629
	(-2.24)**	(4.09)***			(-2.16)**	(3.96)***	(1.23)	(-0.89)	
d7	-0.11085	0.027963	0.0069	d7	-0.12162	0.024914	-0.0266	0.018597	0.0038
	(-0.89)	(1.61)			(-0.97)	(1.35)	(-0.93)	(0.92)	
d8	-0.2045	0.031124	0.0257	d8	-0.19195	0.037473	-0.01481	-0.01519	0.0285
	(-2.43)**	(2.66)***			(-2.27)**	(3.03)***	(-0.77)	(-1.12)	

(Continued)

Table 12.5(a). (*Continued*)

| | CAPM | | | Three-Factor Model | | | | | |
| | Panel A | | | Panel A | | | | | |
Portfolio	Alpha	R_mR_f	Adj R^2	Portfolio	Alpha	R_mR_f	SMB	HML	Adj R^2
d9	-0.15597	0.028551	0.0125	d9	-0.16224	0.026873	-0.01706	0.011046	0.0069
	(-1.5)	(1.98)**			(-1.55)	(1.75)*	(-0.71)	(0.66)	
d10	-0.05972	-0.00298	-0.0041	d10	-0.08018	-0.00873	-0.05117	0.035426	0.0209
	(-0.61)	(-0.22)			(-0.82)	(-0.61)	(-2.30)**	(2.26)**	
d10-d1	0.104792	-0.04478	0.0368	d10-d1	0.078312	-0.05179	-0.07341	0.046872	0.0851
	(1.02)	(-3.13)**			(0.78)	(-3.51)***	(-3.20)***	(2.90)***	

Note: *$p < 0.1$; **$p < 0.05$; ***$p < 0.01$ the parentheses show *t*-value.

Table 12.5(b). CAPM and Three-Factor Model.

| | CAPM | | | Three-Factor Model | | | | | |
| | Panel B | | | Panel B | | | | | |
Portfolio	Alpha	$R_m R_f$	Adj R^2	Portfolio	Alpha	$R_m R_f$	SMB	HML	Adj R^2
d1	−0.0526	0.015422	0.0005	d1	−0.04881	0.016452	−0.03939	0.008422	0.004
	(−0.50)	(1.05)			(−0.47)	(−1.05)	(−1.66)*	(−0.50)	
d2	−0.09683	0.028844	0.0154	d2	−0.097	0.029735	0.021601	−0.00866	0.0108
	(−0.99)	(2.10)**			(−0.99)	(2.01)**	(−0.97)	(−0.54)	
d3	−0.19243	0.034782	0.0213	d3	−0.18465	0.039964	−0.01585	−0.00984	0.0178
	(−1.87)*	(2.40)**			(−1.78)*	(2.57)**	(−0.68)	(−0.59)	
d4	−0.12901	0.018179	0.0016	d4	−0.13882	0.011727	0.021499	0.011741	0.0005
	(−1.16)	(1.16)			(−1.25)	(0.70)	(0.85)	(0.65)	
d5	−0.22525	0.042399	0.0464	d5	−0.22434	0.043808	0.015238	−0.00827	0.0406
	(−2.55)**	(3.41)***			(−2.52)**	(3.28)***	(0.76)	(−0.57)	
d6	−0.19653	0.051971	0.0522	d6	−0.1999	0.049328	−0.00173	0.007828	0.0444
	(−1.92)*	(3.61)***			(−1.94)*	(3.18)***	(−0.07)	(0.47)	
d7	−0.15274	0.00521	−0.004	d7	−0.151	0.007544	0.021391	−0.0126	−0.0086
	(−1.45)	(0.35)			(−1.43)	(0.47)	(0.89)	(−0.74)	
d8	−0.15609	0.043742	0.0459	d8	−0.1571	0.044352	0.029349	−0.0101	0.046
	(−1.70)*	(3.40)***			(−1.71)*	(3.21)***	(1.41)	(−0.68)	

(Continued)

Table 12.5(b). (Continued)

| | CAPM | | | Three-Factor Model | | | | | |
| | Panel B | | | Panel B | | | | | |
Portfolio	Alpha	R_mR_f	Adj R^2	Portfolio	Alpha	R_mR_f	SMB	HML	Adj R^2
d9	−0.18852	0.035935	0.0364	d9	−0.18862	0.036613	0.016003	−0.00647	0.0308
	(2.25)**	(3.05)**			(−2.23)**	(2.88)***	(0.84)	(−0.47)	
d10	0.20017	0.0000401	−0.0046	d10	−0.2006	−0.0005	−0.01211	0.005956	−0.0125
	(−1.93)*	(0.03)			(−1.92)*	(−0.03)	(−0.51)	(0.35)	
d10−d1	−0.14756	−0.01502	0.0018	d10−d1	−0.15179	−0.01695	0.027285	−0.00247	0.0011
	(−1.63)	(−1.18)			(−1.67)*	(−1.24)	(1.32)	(−0.171)	

Note: *$p < 0.1$; **$p < 0.05$; ***$p < 0.01$ the parentheses show t-value.

5. Results and Future Scope

Firms spend on advertising with a view that it will generate abnormal returns (Joshi & Hanssens, 2009, 2010). The results of the negative coefficient imply that stock market reacts adversely to advertising spending. It means that the stock market is not positively rewarding firms spending in advertising. Interestingly, the market perceives advertising spending as the factor of reducing the firm's profitability. One reason for the negative reaction could be that firms are spending more on advertising than the optimal level, hence being penalized. Also, it suggests that the firm's higher level of advertising spending signifies access of funds (Erickson & Jacobson, 1992).

Abnormal returns can be obtained with a unique product or a strategy that cannot be imitated easily. Advertising spending can be easily imitated. Hence, it could not be treated as a means to achieve excess returns (Erickson & Jacobson, 1992).

Future study can investigate advertising expenditures based on industries such as fast-moving consumer goods (FMCG), e-commerce, automotive, consumer durables, education, retail, pharmaceutical, and media and entertainment. In addition, advertising expenditures can be categorized by advertising medium, such as television, digital, print, radio, and cinema.

6. Conclusion

This chapter attempts to address whether advertising spending has an abnormal stock return in India. Using non-financial firms' data, the result suggests a negative stock return generated with the increase in advertising spending. However, the level of negative returns decreases when firm moves from low advertising spending to high advertising spending. The study has sorted the portfolio using both the equal-weighted and value-weighted method. The results were nearly the same.

The study suggests that market is penalizing the firms for spending more on advertising. Hence, it suggests that advertising budgets should be allocated with caution by marketing managers.

References

https://www.exchange4media.com/advertising-news/indias-ad-spend-to-grow-at-108-per-cent-in-2021-to-reach-us-9-billion-dentsu-report-114251.html

Agarwalla, S. K., Jacob, J., & Varma, J. R. (2013). *Four factor model in Indian equities market*. Working Paper W.P. No. 2013-09-05, Indian Institute of Management, Ahmedabad. http://www.iimahd.ernet.in/~iffm/Indian-Fama-French-Momentum/four-factors-India-90s-onwards-IIM-WP-Version.pdf

Ali Shah, S. Z., & Akbar, S. (2008). Value relevance of advertising expenditure: A review of the literature. *International Journal of Management Reviews*, *10*(4), 301–325. https://doi.org/10.1111/j.1468-2370.2007.00228.x

Barroso, A., & Llobet, G. (2012). Advertising and consumer awareness of new, differentiated products. *Journal of Marketing Research*, *49*(6), 773–792. https://doi.org/10.1509/jmr.11.0045

Bublitz, B., & Ettredge, M. (1989). The information in discretionary outlays: Advertising, research, and development. *The Accounting Review*, *64*(1), 108–124. http://www.jstor.org/stable/248131

Chan, L. K. C., Lakonishok, J., & Sougiannis, T. (2001). The stock market valuation of research and development expenditures. *The Journal of Finance*, *56*(6), 2431–2456. https://doi.org/10.1111/0022-1082.00411

Chemmanur, T. J., & Yan, A. (2019). Advertising, attention, and stock returns. *Quarterly Journal of Forestry*, *09*(03), 1950009. https://doi.org/10.1142/S2010139219500095

Core, J. E., Guay, W. R., & Buskirk, A. Van. (2003). Market valuations in the new economy: An investigation of what has changed. *Journal of Accounting and Economics*, *34*(1), 43–67. https://doi.org/10.1016/S0165-4101(02)00087-3

Eng, L. L., & Keh, H. T. (2007). The effects of advertising and brand value on future operating and market performance. *Journal of Advertising*, *36*(4), 91–100. https://doi.org/10.2753/JOA0091-3367360407

Erickson, G., & Jacobson, R. (1992). Gaining comparative advantage through discretionary expenditures: The returns to R&D and advertising. *Management Science*, *38*(9), 1264–1279. https://doi.org/10.1287/mnsc.38.9.1264

Fama, E. F., & French, K. R. (1993). Common risk factors in the returns on stocks and bonds. *Journal of Financial Economics*, *33*(1), 3–56. https://doi.org/10.1016/0304-405X(93)90023-5

Feldstein, M., & Horioka, C. (1980). Domestic saving and international capital flows. *The Economic Journal*, *90*(358), 314–329. https://doi.org/10.2307/2231790

Frieder, L., & Subrahmanyam, A. (2005). Brand perceptions and the market for common stock. *Journal of Financial and Quantitative Analysis*, *40*(1), 57–85. https://doi.org/10.1017/S0022109000001745

Grullon, G., Kanatas, G., & Weston, J. P. (2004). Advertising, breadth of ownership, and liquidity. *Review of Financial Studies*, *17*(2), 439–461. https://doi.org/10.1093/rfs/hhg039

Joshi, A., & Hanssens, D. M. (2010). The direct and indirect effects of advertising spending on firm value. *Journal of Marketing*, *74*(1), 20–33.

Joshi, A. M., & Hanssens, D. M. (2009). Movie advertising and the stock market valuation of studios: A case of 'great expectations?'. *Marketing Science*, *28*(2), 239–250.

Lou, D. (2014). Attracting investor attention through advertising. *Review of Financial Studies*, *27*(6), 1797–1829. https://doi.org/10.1093/rfs/hhu019

McAlister, L., Srinivasan, R., & Kim, M. (2007). Advertising, research and development, and systematic risk of the firm. *Journal of Marketing*, *71*(1), 35–48. https://doi.org/10.1509/jmkg.71.1.035

Oh, Y. K., Gulen, H., Kim, J.-M., & Robinson, W. T. (2016). Do stock prices undervalue investments in advertising? *Marketing Letters*, *27*(4), 611–626. https://doi.org/10.1007/s11002-016-9411-4

Srinivasan, S., Pauwels, K., Silva-Risso, J., & Hanssens, D. M. (2009). Product innovations, advertising, and stock returns. *Journal of Marketing, 73*(1), 24–43. https://doi.org/10.1509/jmkg.73.1.024

Tellis, G. J. (2009). Generalizations about advertising effectiveness in markets. *Journal of Advertising Research, 49*(2), 240–245. https://doi.org/10.2501/S00218499 09090357

Tellis, G. J., & Fornell, C. (1988). The relationship between advertising and product quality over the product life cycle: A contingency theory. *Journal of Marketing Research, 25*(1), 64–71. https://doi.org/10.1177/002224378802500106

Tuli, K. R., Mukherjee, A., & Dekimpe, M. G. (2012). On the value relevance of retailer advertising spending and same-store sales growth. *Journal of Retailing, 88*(4), 447–461. https://doi.org/10.1016/j.jretai.2012.07.001

West, D. C., Kover, A. J., & Caruana, A. (2008). Practitioner and customer views of advertising creativity: Same concept, different meaning? *Journal of Advertising, 37*(4), 35–46. https://doi.org/10.2753/JOA0091-3367370403

Appendix: Description of Variables and Sources

Variable	Description	Data Source
Advertising intensity	Ratio of advertising spending to total sales	ProwessIQ
Market capitalization	Market capitalization	ProwessIQ
R_{pt}	Raw return	ProwessIQ
R_{ft}	Risk-free rate: Estimated using 91-days Treasury bill rate	IIM-A
R_{Mt}	Market portfolio return	IIM-A
SMB_t	Size factor: Small-stock portfolio returns minus big-stock portfolios return	IIM-A
HML_t	Value factor: High minus low book-to-market ratio	IIM-A

Chapter 13

Ownership Structure and CO_2 Emission-Adjusted Efficiency of Coal-Fired Power Plants: Evidence From India

Varsha Singh Dadia and Rachita Gulati

Indian Institute of Technology Roorkee, India

Abstract

Using the most recent dataset from 2013–2014 to 2017–2018, the study examines the efficiency of 75 coal-fired power plants in the Indian thermal power sector. The authors obtained robust estimates of efficiency scores by employing Seiford and Zhu's (2002) DEA-based classification invariance technique to account for CO_2 emissions as an undesirable output. Meta-frontier analysis and the Tobit regression are used to compute technology heterogeneity across power plants belonging to public and private groups and investigate the factors driving carbon-adjusted efficiency, respectively. The results reveal that, on average, the efficiency of power plants during the study period is 78.26%, showing significant room for reduction in CO_2 emissions alongside augmentation in electricity generation. Private plants are more efficient than public ones, and relative performance inefficiency is the primary source of inefficiency in the thermal power sector. Regression analysis indicates that domestic-equipped plants perform with lesser levels of efficiency, and plants with more units are more inefficient than plants with fewer units. Carbon productivity significantly improves efficiency since fewer fossil fuels with high carbon will generate more electricity.

Keywords: Electricity generation; CO_2 emissions; ownership structure; technology heterogeneity; thermal power plants; data envelopment analysis

Modeling Economic Growth in Contemporary India, 233–260
Copyright © 2024 Varsha Singh Dadia and Rachita Gulati
Published under exclusive licence by Emerald Publishing Limited
doi:10.1108/978-1-80382-751-320241013

1. Introduction

Global warming has become a big concern in recent years due to the persistent rise in greenhouse gas (GHG) emissions. Carbon dioxide (CO_2), chlorofluoro-carbons (CFCs), methane (CH_4) and nitrous oxide are all GHG contributors. CO_2 emissions are the primary cause of the greenhouse effect, which must be reduced to avert a dangerous shift in climate. Power plants, oil refineries, fertilizers, cement and steel mills are the key sources of carbon emissions. Around 50% of all CO_2 emissions in India come from coal power stations, which produce 70% of the country's total electricity (International Energy Agency, 2020).

The Indian coal-fired electricity generation segment concerns include coal production and shortage, new emissions norms, weak inter-ministry synchronization, social opposition, coal prices, supply logistics, climate change, installation of 'Flue Gas Desulphurization,' poor functioning of distribution companies, etc. Furthermore, fewer coal projects are being approved due to increased focus on renewable energy, thus reflecting the priority towards achieving 'net-zero' emission targets. India's power sector is the leading source of carbon emissions, with coal power plants accounting for most emissions, followed by transportation, manufacturing and construction, and agriculture (International Energy Agency, 2021).

Carbon emissions are not explicitly controlled in India; however, other pollutants are. Emission reduction attempts have been focused on the command and control policy methods but are blamed for diminishing economic effectiveness in India (Jain & Kumar, 2018). Thus, India pioneered market-based initiatives to maximize efficiency and lower emission levels. In 2010–2011, a 'Clean Energy Cess' of INR 50 per tonne of coal was established. In 2015 and 2016, the coal cess was hiked to INR 200 and INR 400 per tonne, respectively. The 'GST Compensation Cess' replaced the 'Clean Energy Cess' in July 2017, with INR 400 for every metric tonne. These estimations will be useful in functioning market-based initiatives like carbon pricing, trading, etc.

The present study on the carbon performance of coal power stations has piqued our interest for the following reasons. First, climate change is dramatically worsening, and carbon emissions are the main contributor to greenhouse gases. The electrical industry of India, which is predominantly made up of coal power plants, is responsible for more than half of the nation's CO_2 emissions. Second, thermal power plants create more than 79% of India's electricity, and coal generates substantially more electricity than other energy sources in India, i.e. about 72% of total electricity (Central Electricity Authority (CEA), 2018). Despite India's recent switchover to clean energy sources such as wind and solar power, thermal power retains the most consistently successful source of electricity production. Thus, there is a need to understand how well power plants are doing in terms of efficiency adjusted for carbon emissions.

In light of the above context, we have developed the following research questions: (i) Are there efficiency differences between public and private coal-fired thermal power producers in India? Alternatively, we can say, does ownership matter in coal-fired thermal power generation in India? (ii) What drives the carbon-adjusted performance of thermal power plants? The three specific objectives were developed to provide answers to these crucial questions. First, to examine the carbon-adjusted efficiency of thermal power plants in India by accounting for the role of CO$_2$ emissions as an undesirable output.[1] Second, to explore the ownership variations and account for technology heterogeneity in the carbon-adjusted efficiency of coal-fired plants, and third, to explore the contextual factors determining the carbon-adjusted efficiency.

The novelties of the study are manifolds. First, this study uses a recent dataset from 2013–2014 to 2017–2018[2] to examine the efficiency performance in the thermal power industry. Even the most recent study by Jindal and Nilakantan (2022) could not present a clear picture of this sector as they included data up to 2014. Second, the study accounts for carbon emissions by employing the data transformation technique of Seiford and Zhu (2002); despite India's rigorous research on power plants' efficiency, only a few studies consider carbon emissions as a bad output in the electricity generation process (for instance, Jain & Kumar, 2018; Jindal & Nilakantan, 2022; Murty & Nagpal, 2019; Yadav et al., 2014). Perhaps no study adopted Seiford and Zhu's transformation procedure to treat carbon emissions in the Indian thermal power sector. Only a few studies consider carbon emissions a bad output in the electricity generation process. Third, previous studies mainly considered meta-frontier analysis from the perspective of centre and state; while this is perhaps the first attempt to consider the heterogeneity across public and private plants, we expect ownership variations to occur because of institutional environments, regulations, technology, management, resources endowments, financial capital stock, etc. Further, 40% of the electricity generation comes from private power plants, and they must be included while estimating efficiency performance. Therefore, the adoption of meta-frontier holds. Fourth, our study considers carbon productivity as a second-stage regressor, which perhaps no other studies have taken.

The remaining portions of the essay are organized as follows. Section 2 discusses India's power generation sources and regulatory framework and reforms. An overview of relevant literature on the topic is included in Section 3. The methodology and database are apparently in Sections 4 and 5, respectively. The results of the current study are described in Section 6. The last Section 7 summarizes and provides some policy implications.

2. Coal-Fired Electricity Generation in India: Stylized Facts

2.1 Sources and Trends

Electricity can be generated from different sources of energy. The major sources of electricity generation are renewable and non-renewable sources. The total electricity generation from conventional or traditional, i.e. 1,330.00 billion units (BU), and non-conventional, i.e. 138.337 BU, was 1,468.337 BU during 2019–2020. Table 13.1

---

[1] Undesirable output can be referred as bad output and desirable output can be referred as good output.

[2] The study follows the Indian financial year; 2013–2014 refers to the fiscal year ending 31 March 2014.

Table 13.1. Year-Wise Generation From 2015 to 2020 (in Billion Units).

| Years | Generation From Non-renewable Energy Sources (RES) | | | | Generation From Renewable Energy Sources (RES) | | | | | Total |
| | Subtotal | Major Non-RES | | | Subtotal | Major RES | | | | |
		Coal	Lignite	Gas		Wind	Solar	Small Hydro	Biopower	
2014–2015	1,048.67	800.33	35.5	40.09	61.71	33.76	4.59	8.05	14.49	1,110.39
2015–2016	1,107.82	862.02	34.24	46.97	65.78	33.02	7.44	8.35	16.68	1,173.60
2016–2017	1,160.14	910.14	34.73	49.07	81.54	46.00	13.49	7.67	14.15	1,241.68
2017–2018	1,206.30	951.75	34.83	50.20	101.83	52.66	25.87	7.69	15.25	1,308.14
2018–2019	1,265.00	1,008.29	36.00	49.83	126.75	62.03	39.26	8.70	16.32	1,391.75
2019–2020	1,330.00	1,058.97	36.00	48.44	138.33	64.64	50.13	9.45	13.74	1,468.33

Source: Central Electricity Authority (Compiled from annual reports).

shows that electricity generation from traditional sources, especially coal, has increased in absolute terms over the years. Thermal plants (including coal, lignite and gas) contribute the most significant proportion, i.e. 87.30% of electricity generation in conventional energy sources and 77.78% in total generation. Coal power plants constitute 80.95% of thermal power generation and 79.44% of generation in traditional sources. In addition, the coal plants generated 72.12% of total electricity generation in 2019–2020. Lignite and gas power plants have contributed 2.45% and 3.29% to total electricity generation during 2019–2020, respectively. However, waste to energy holds a small proportion in generating electricity from renewables, so this study has not included them in Table 13.1. However, liquid fuel and diesel are part of non-renewables, but they generate less electricity, which is why they are not shown in Table 13.1. There has been a continuous rise in renewable fonts from 2014–2015 to till-date. Fig. 13.1 shows that the electricity generation from non-renewable sources is much higher than renewables.

2.1.1 Renewable Sources

Renewable sources, including solar, wind, hydro, biomass, biodiesel, tidal waves and geothermal, are unlimited in supply and can be recycled. Renewables' percentage in power generation has grown over time, and out of these sources, wind power is the main source (64,646 BU), followed by solar (50,131 BU), biopower (13,742 BU) and small hydro (9,451 BU) for 2019–2020 (see Fig. 13.2). Wind

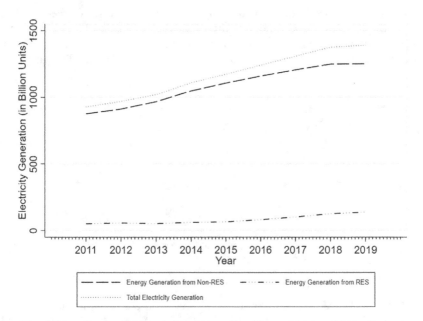

Fig. 13.1.   Annual Electricity Generation From 2011 to 2019. *Source:* Authors' elaboration based on data from CEA.

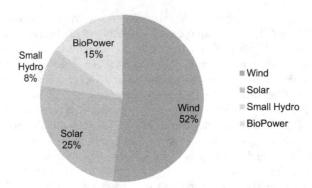

Fig. 13.2.   Generation Share of Various Sources of Renewable Energy Sources as of 31st March 2018. *Source:* Authors' elaboration using the data from the annual report of MNRE (2018).

power generates around 52% of electricity, solar power generates 25%, biopower generates 15% and small hydro plants generate 8% (Annual Report of Ministry of New and Renewable Energy (MNRE), 2018).

2.1.2 Non-renewable Sources

Non-renewable sources are limited in supply and cannot be replenished quickly; examples of non-renewable sources are coal, lignite, oil, diesel, naphtha, high-speed diesel and natural gas. Out of non-renewable sources, coal is the dominant source and generates around 79% of electricity. Lignite generates 3%, gas plants

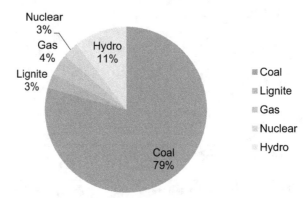

Fig. 13.3.   Generation Share of Various Sources of Non-renewable Energy Sources as of 31st March 2018. *Source:* Authors' elaboration based on data from CEA (2018).

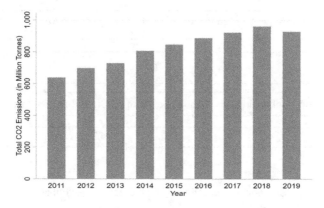

Fig. 13.4. CO_2 Emission in the Indian Power Sector. *Source:* Authors' elaboration based on data from CEA (2021).

generate 4%, nuclear generates 3% and hydro generates 11% among non-renewable sources (see Fig. 13.3).

Thus, coal remains the dominant source even after the increased share of wind, solar and hydro in electricity generation. The CO_2 emission from power plants is continuously growing and is expected to reach approximately 3,700 million tonnes by 2035. Fig. 13.4 indicates the power sector's increasing level of total emissions over the last few years.

2.2 Regulatory Structure and Reforms in the Power Sector

2.2.1 Present Regulatory Structure

India has a federal structure, and electricity is a concurrent subject, i.e. central and state governments are jointly responsible for its development. The current regulatory framework consists of the central electricity regulatory commission at the center, with state electricity regulatory commissions in each state, as shown in Fig. 13.5.

2.2.2 Reforms in the Power Sector

The Electricity Supply Act of 1948 regulated the Indian power industry after independence, resulting in vertically integrated companies, known as State Electricity Boards, in each state. Implementing reforms in the power industry throughout the 1990s was spurred by difficulties such as electricity board debts, inadequate rates for non-industrial subscribers, severe technical and commercial deficits, insufficient investment for capacity building, etc. The revision of 1991 with the 1910 and 1948 statutes was the initial step of the

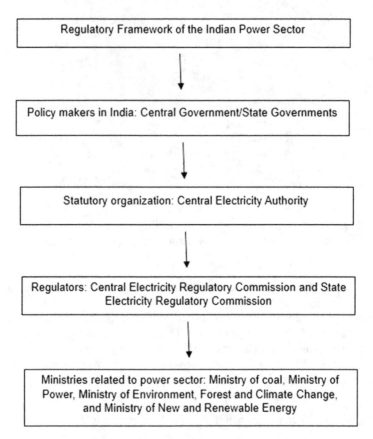

Fig. 13.5.   Regulatory Framework of Electricity Sector. *Source:*
Authors' compilation.

reform effort. The Road to Electricity Regulatory Commissions Act of 1998 authorized the formation of regulatory organizations at both state and central levels. The act intended to isolate tariff setting from state govt operations because their involvement in tariff determination made vertically integrated companies weak and financially unsound. Phase 2 occurred between 1998 and 2003; many states formed state power regulating commissions. Some states separated their state electrical boards into separate companies in phase 2. The Electricity Act 2003 was adopted in the third phase, superseding all previous acts. The law also mandated that state electricity regulatory commissions dismantle state electricity boards' corporatization. The passage of the historic act of 2003 ushered in a new chapter in the power industry's transformation. The major episodes of the Indian electricity sector throughout the pre/post periods are given in Table 13.2.

Table 13.2. Timeline for Significant Power Sector Reforms – Pre-and Post-independence.

Year	Act/Policy	Main Features
Post-independence Era		
1887	Indian Electricity Act	• To safeguard persons and property from harm and dangers related to the supply and usage of electricity for illumination and other purposes
1903	Indian Electricity Act	• Replaced the 1887 act
		• First effort to regulate the power sector comprehensively
		• Did not acknowledge bulk electricity sales, and the authority of local govts and central govt was not clearly delimited
1910	Indian Electricity Act	• Delegated licensing authority to local govts, and issue of bulk supply was implemented
Post-independence Era		
1948	Electricity Supply Act	• Mandated creation of State Electricity Boards with complete authority for electricity generation, transmission and distribution in each state
		• Constituted Central Electricity Authority
		• Revised in 1975, 1985, 1991 and 1998
1956	Indian Electricity Rules	• Strengthened the EA 1910
1991	Power sector reforms	• Allowed private companies in the generation
		• Permit 100% foreign investment and establish Regional Load Dispatch Centres
1998	Electricity Regulatory Commissions Act	• Creation of State Electricity Regulatory Commissions (SERCs) and the Central Electricity Regulatory Commission (CERC)
		• Allowed both CERCs and SERCs to decide on the electricity supply pricing
2003	Electricity Act	• Replaced 1910, 1948 and 1998 acts
		• State Electricity Boards unbundled and the establishment of State Electricity Regulatory Commissions mandatory

(Continued)

Table 13.2. *(Continued)*

Year	Act/Policy	Main Features
		• Rationalize rate-based cost coverage, reduce subsidies and provide third parties with open access to the network
2014	EA (Amendment) Bill, 2014	• Separation of retail supply and distribution • Multiple supply licensees
2015	Ujwal DISCOM Assurance Yojana (UDAY)	• The states will take on 75% of the DISCOM debt • States support Discoms' efforts to become more effective
2020	Electricity (Amendment) Bill 2020-(Draft)	• Direct Benefit Transfer of Consumer Subsidy • Encourages mitigation of cross-subsidization • National Renewable Policy and tighter Renewable Purchase Obligations • Establishes Electricity Contract Enforcement Authority • Ensure round-the-clock supply to consumers across the country

Source: Authors' Compilation from Different Sources.

3. Literature Review

3.1 Studies on the Efficiency of Thermal Power Plants in the International Context

The well-known literature reviews on the efficiency of the power sector by Zhou et al. (2008), Meng et al. (2016) and Sueyoshi et al. (2017) serve convincing arguments that empirical literature on this topic is extensive and covers a wide range of research topics. Some noteworthy studies on thermal power station efficiency strand include Lam and Shiu (2004), Vaninsky (2006), Barros and Peypoch (2008), Nakano and Managi (2008), Liu et al. (2010) and See and Coelli (2012). Research is mainly confined to the United States, South Korea, China, other East Asian nations and very few EU nations. Many efficiency-related studies in power plants are concentrated in China using distinct methods, samples and pollutants (e.g. Du et al., 2016; Kaneko et al., 2010; Nakaishi, 2021; Wei et al., 2013; Yu et al., 2017; Zhang et al., 2013). We find that the issue of accounting for carbon emissions and group heterogeneity in power plant efficiency is relatively understudied, particularly in developing economies.

3.2 Studies on the Efficiency of Thermal Power Plants in the Indian Context

The literature on thermal power plant efficiency in India is substantial (e.g. Ghosh & Kathuria, 2016; Khanna et al., 1999; Shanmugam & Kulshreshtha, 2005; Shrivastava et al., 2012; Singh, 1991; Singh & Bajpai, 2013; Sugathan et al., 2019). Interestingly, Kumar and Rao (2003), Murty et al. (2007), Ghosh (2010), Yadav et al. (2014), Sahoo et al. (2017), Jain and Kumar (2018), Kumar and Jain (2019), Murty and Nagpal (2019), Sengupta and Mukherjee (2021) and Jindal and Nilakantan (2022) acknowledge the presence of CO_2 emissions as a bad output in power generating process. In evaluating the performance of diverse Indian thermal plants, limited studies considered group variations by applying a meta-frontier approach. Kumar and Jain (2019) assessed the performance of 56 publicly owned (center and state) coal power plants in India from 2000 to 2013. Jindal and Nilakantan (2022) used the directional distance function (DDF) in a meta-frontier approach to determine the effect of regulatory autonomy on the efficiency of Indian coal power stations from 2005 to 2014 and how other conceivable variables and regulatory autonomy affect efficiency. The literature on plant efficiency currently available in India highlights the lack of studies that permit the generation of good and bad outputs. As a result, there are insufficient accurate estimates of carbon-adjusted efficiency for Indian plants considering technology heterogeneity. Table 13.3 depicts the efficiency studies that incorporate undesirable outputs in the thermal power sector.

After evaluating previous research on coal power plants in India, we identified some significant components and will enhance the literature in several ways. First, extensive literature is available that assesses the performance of coal power plants, but very few of them account for the effect of the bad output, *viz.* carbon *emissions in the production process.* Since these plants are the major emitter of carbon emissions in India, special emphasis must be given to bad outputs with traditional inputs–outputs while evaluating the carbon-adjusted performance. *In Indian* power plants, *limited studies have included* carbon *emissions; thus, our study will look at the performance of power units with both good and bad outputs.*

Second, power plants' functioning differs in *business practices*, production *technology, adherence to governance norms, etc.* As a result, considering heterogeneity between plants is critical, as examining the performance of power plants with the same production frontier appears impractical. Previous studies used non-parametric or parametric methods to assess performance, ignoring technological heterogeneity by assuming all power plants had the standard production function. The firms can differ in capital, financial and human stocks, resource endowments, etc. (O'Donnell et al., 2008). The failure to account for the deviations results in distorted estimation results. One such method for looking at power plant disparities is the meta-frontier analysis. Only two studies in India have used a meta-frontier framework to estimate efficiency levels. Kumar and Jain (2019) did not include the private sector in their research; our study would consider variations in ownership types across power plants. Third, a research vacuum arises because most recent published studies have analysed the carbon-adjusted performance of power plants until 2014. The proposed research would rely on the most recent

Table 13.3. Studies on the Efficiency Performance in the Indian Thermal Power Sector.

Author (Year)	Sample (Period of Study)	Estimation Methodology			Treatment of Pollutants
		Efficiency and Productivity Measure	Estimation Method	Technological Heterogeneity	
Kumar and Rao (2003)	33 thermal power plants (1991)	Parametric linear programming	Output distance function	No	SPM
Murty et al. (2007)	5 thermal power plants in Andhra Pradesh (1996–2003)	Stochastic frontier analysis	Directional output distance function	No	SO_2, NO_x and SPM
Ghosh (2010)	Thermal power plants (2004–2007)	Indexing- composite weighted index	-	No	CO_2
Yadav et al. (2014)	65 coal-based thermal power plants (2008)	Multi-criteria data envelopment analysis and cross-efficiency analysis	-	No	CO_2
Sahoo et al. (2017)	71 thermal power plants (2010)	Multiple data envelopment analysis	-	No	CO_2
Jain and Kumar (2018)	56 coal-fired thermal power plants (2000–2013)	Linear programming approach	Directional output distance function	No	CO_2
Kumar and Jain (2019)	56 coal-based thermal power plants (2000–2013)	Stochastic meta-Luenberger productivity indicator	Directional output distance function	By ownership	CO_2
Murty and Nagpal (2019)	48 coal-fired thermal power plants (2008–2014)	Data envelopment analysis	By-production approach	No	CO_2

Sengupta and Mukherjee (2021)	74 coal-fired thermal power plants (2002–2014)	Non-radial Data Envelopment Analysis	By-production approach	No	SPM
Jindal and Nilakantan (2022)	129 coal-based thermal power plants (2005–2014)	Meta-data envelopment analysis	Non-radial directional distance function	By regulatory independence	CO_2
This study	75 coal power plants (2013–2014 to 2017–2018)	Meta-frontier data envelopment analysis	Seiford and Zhu	By ownership	CO_2

Source: Authors' elaboration.

data to present the clearest picture of the Indian thermal power industry. Lastly, the study will investigate the possible contextual factors that impact power plants' carbon-adjusted performance by including plant, fuel and location characteristics.

4. Methodology

4.1 Treatment of Undesirable Output for Carbon-Adjusted Efficiency

We used linear monotone decreasing transformation on CO_2 emissions (bad output) in standard data envelopment analysis (DEA) suggested by Seiford and Zhu (2002) to compute the scores for each power plant; they considered the translated vector of undesirable output as desirable. The following steps are conducted to acquire efficiency scores of power plants by allowing increasing y_r^g and decreasing: y_p^b

  Step 1: Multiply each undesirable output y_p^b by (-1).
  Step 2: Find $v_r = \max\{y_p^b\} + 1$; where v_r is the translation vector, which lets all negative bad outputs to be positive.
  Step 3: Create a new variable $\bar{y}_{pj}^b$

$$\bar{y}_{pj}^b = -y_{pj}^b + v_r > 0$$

  Step 4: Use $\bar{y}_{pj}^b$ as output and estimate the full model.

  Linear programming for plant 'o' is defined as follows:

$$\max_{\phi\lambda} \phi_o$$

$$s.t.$$

$$\sum_{j=1}^{n} \lambda_j x_{ij} \leq x_{io}, i = 1, 2, .., m$$

$$\sum_{j=1}^{n} \lambda_j y_{rj}^g \geq \phi y_{ro}^g, r = 1, 2, ..s$$

$$\sum_{j=1}^{n} \lambda_j \bar{y}_{pj}^b \geq \phi \bar{y}_{po}^b, p = 1, 2, .., b$$

$$\lambda_j \geq 0, j = 1, 2, ..n$$

  Where $x_{io}, y_{ro}^g, \bar{y}_{po}^b$ denotes input used (s), good output(s) and bad output(s) produced by power plant k, respectively. ϕy_{ro}^g and $\phi \bar{y}_{po}^b$ indicate the proportionate rise and shrinkage in good and bad outputs, respectively, using 'm'. λ_j is a vector of $n \times 1$ weight that allows for the convex combination of input(s) and output(s). ϕ indicate potential improvement of the specified decision-making units (DMUs) j (Note: 'n' connotes the number of DMUs; 'm' connotes the number of inputs; 's' connotes the number of good, and 'b' connotes bad outputs.)

4.2 Meta-Frontier Framework

Charnes et al. (1978) revised Farrell's (1957) single input–output to multiple input–output radial measures of technical efficiency. The CCR model makes the long-term ideal scale assumption of constant returns to scale (CRS), but the BCC study given by Banker et al. (1984) has an additional convexity constraint to allow for variable returns to scale (VRS). The efficiency scores for the sample are used to gauge how well the power plant is operating. Businesses make decisions based on a variety of possible input–output combinations. Due to differences in the stocks of readily available human, financial, physical capital and economic bases in which firms operate, these input–output combinations or technology sets may differ across geographical regions. Therefore, the meta-production frontier's function is a frontier function that encompasses all frontiers of specific groups.

Meta-frontier analysis helps account for group heterogeneity and improves the decomposition of inefficiency sources. It makes it possible to compare efficiency across several heterogeneous groups concerning a single meta-frontier. O'Donnell et al. (2008) introduced the meta-frontier approach into the DEA framework. Battese and Rao (2002) suggested meta-frontier-stochastic frontier analysis to measure the efficiency performance by handling single output on individual and meta-technology frontiers. Therefore, our case has multiple outputs, so employing this method may be ineffective. The efficiency scores are calculated using a meta-frontier (encompasses all frontiers of separate groups) and a group frontier. The scores are obtained from the below models (Gulati, 2022):

$$\text{Groupfrontier } (E_{\text{Own}}) \quad \text{Metafrontier } (E_{\text{Meta}})$$

$$
\begin{array}{ll}
\max\limits_{\phi,\lambda} \phi_o^k & \max\limits_{\phi,\lambda} \phi_o^m \\[4pt]
s.t. & s.t. \\[4pt]
\sum\limits_{j=1}^{N_k} \lambda_j^k x_{ij}^k \le x_{io}^k, \, i = 1,2,..,m & \sum\limits_{j=1}^{N_k}\sum\limits_{k=1}^{K} \mu_j^k x_{ij}^k \le x_{io}^k, \, i = 1,2,..,m \\[8pt]
\sum\limits_{j=1}^{N_k} \lambda_j^k y_{rj}^{gk} \ge \phi^k y_{ro}^{gk}, \, r = 1,2,..s & \sum\limits_{j=1}^{N_k}\sum\limits_{k=1}^{K} \mu_j^k y_{rj}^{gk} \ge \phi^m y_{ro}^k, \, r = 1,2,..s \\[8pt]
\sum\limits_{j=1}^{N_k} \lambda_j^k \bar{y}_{pj}^{bk} \ge \phi^k \bar{y}_{po}^{bk}, \, p = 1,2,..,b & \sum\limits_{j=1}^{N_k}\sum\limits_{k=1}^{K} \mu_j^k \bar{y}_{pj}^{bk} \ge \phi^m \bar{y}_{po}^{bk}, \, p = 1,2,..,b \\[8pt]
\lambda_j^k \ge 0, j = 1,2,...n & \mu_j^k \ge 0, j = 1,2,...n
\end{array}
$$

The overall technological inefficiency (OTIE) is divided into two components: technology gap inefficiency (TGIE), i.e. technical differences, and relative inefficiency (RIE), i.e. excess input consumption or output shortfall; therefore, OTIE = TGIE + RIE. The technology gap ratio (TGR) for a power plant 'o' in group k is thus defined as follows:

$$TGR_k^o = \frac{E_{\text{Meta}}^o}{E_{\text{public}}^o}.$$

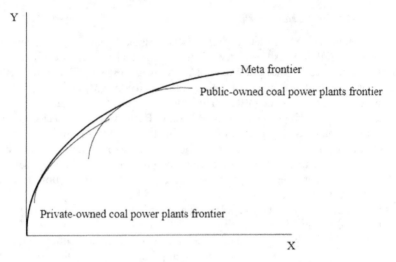

Fig. 13.6.   Meta-Frontier Model. *Source:* Authors' elaborations.

The study determines the efficiency using group frontier and assumed two groups ($k = 2$) representing public and private power plants (see Fig. 13.6). Since we have two groups, we define $TGR^o_{public} = \frac{E^o_{Meta}}{E^o_{public}}$ and $GR^o_{private} = \frac{E^o_{Meta}}{E^o_{private}}$. Note that TGR measures how near a plant is to the meta-frontier on a group frontier and ranges from zero to one; TGIE is calculated as $E_{Own} - E_{Meta}$, and relative inefficiency is calculated as $1 - \theta_{Own}$. The meta-frontier framework for ownership groups, i.e. for public and private power plants, is shown in Fig. 13.6.

4.3 Tobit Regression

Tobit regression investigates determinants that are beyond management control but have the potential to impact power plants' efficiency. The dependent variable, the DEA-CCR meta-efficiency score, is regressed against postulated efficiency drivers known as independent variables. The bias will be estimated using ordinary least square regression because the DEA efficiency score can only be zero when the data is left-censored and one when it is right-censored. When the dependent variable is constrained, as in this situation, the Tobit model is used; the censored regression model is best suited to eliminate this potential bias. The Tobit model is stated in its simplest form:

$$y_j^* = \beta X_j + u_j$$
$$y_j = y_j^*, \text{if } y_j^* > 0$$
$$y_j = 0, \text{otherwise}$$

Where y_j^* is a limited dependent variable; β is the unknown parameter vector that governs the link between X_j and y_j^*; and X_j is the explanatory variables vector.

5. Database

The study is based on a balanced panel dataset of 75 coal power plants operating in India from 2013–2014 to 2017–2018. Data on the power plant is extracted from the Central Electricity Authority (CEA) of India: (1) 'Review of Performance of Thermal Power Stations,' an annual publication of CEA and (2) 'User Guide of CO2 Baseline Data,' an annual publication of CEA. The description of inputs and outputs is given in Table 13.4. To lessen the impact of random noise brought on by measurement errors in input and output variables, we divide all input and output variables except ratio ones-by units of individual coal plants for the given year. All input and output variables aside from ratio ones are divided by the units of specific coal plants for the given year to reduce the impact of stochastic terms caused by measurement mistakes in variables.

The following critical elements are taken into consideration. First is ownership type (denoted by Public Ownership); power plants are classified into public and private. If a public organization owns the power plant (central or state-owned), then the dummy is set to 1; otherwise, 0. Second, location (denoted by location); regional growth in India is imbalanced, and the productivity of power plants in different regions may vary. So, power plants are located in five zones: northern, western, southern, eastern and northeastern. Third, the type of coal (denoted by

Table 13.4. Specification of Input(s), Desirable and Undesirable Output(s).

Variables	Unit	Definition
Input(s)		
Installed Capacity	Megawatts	Maximum amount of electricity a power plant can produce under specific conditions set by the manufacturer
Operating Availability	Per cent	Percentage of time for which a power plant is actually available to generate electricity
Plant Load Factor	Per cent	Ratio of actual electricity production to maximum possible electricity production
Coal Consumption	Million Tonnes	Quantity of coal consumed in a power plant for electricity production in one year
Desirable Output (s)		
Net Electricity Generation	Gigawatt Hours	Gross electricity generation minus auxiliary consumption of electricity that the power plant uses for electricity generation
Undesirable Output (s)		
CO_2 Emissions	Million Tonnes	Emissions released due to the burning of coal for electricity production

Source: Authors' Elaboration.

DOMESTIC Coal) discloses whether a power plant is using domestic coal or imported from another nation. Fourth, make (denoted by BHEL), whether equipment comes from a native (BHEL Ltd.) or a foreign manufacturer (Russia, China, Britain, etc.). BHEL MAKE (denoted by BHEL) is coded as a dummy variable for domestic equipment with the value 1. Fifth, carbon productivity (denoted by CP) is the ratio of electricity produced to CO_2 emissions. Sixth, the number of units (denoted by Units); a power plant comprises various units that may or may not run simultaneously. Lastly, the age of a power plant (denoted by Plant Age) is the discrepancy between the year a plant started operating and the year it was commissioned. It is calculated using a weighted average basis by unit capacity and the year it was put into service. Therefore, we estimated the following Tobit regression:

$$OTE = \beta_0 + \beta_1 Public + \beta_2 North + \beta_3 West + \beta_4 South + \beta_5 Domestic\ Coal + \beta_6 BHEL + \beta_7 CP + \beta_8 Units + \beta_9 Age + \beta_{10} AgeSquare$$

The descriptive statistics of each input and output variable, along with explanatory are presented in Table 13.5.

Table 13.5. Descriptive Statistics of Variables.

	Obs	Mean	Std. Dev.	Min	Max
All Plants					
Installed Capacity (MW)	375	309.497	167.695	45	800
Operating Availability (%)	375	78.379	16.138	24.04	98.96
Plant Load Factor (%)	375	66.733	17.263	16.83	97.25
Coal Consumption (Million tonnes)	375	1,244.345	850.300	69	9,218.3
Net Electricity Generation (Gigawatts hours)	375	1,693.226	1,044.97	75.476	5,060.6
CO_2 Emissions (tonnes)	375	6,070,079	4,358,821	0.076	23,000,000
Public-Owned Plants					
Installed Capacity (MW)	250	306.260	134.185	76.666	600
Operating Availability (%)	250	80.869	14.000	24.04	98.96
Plant Load Factor (%)	250	69.499	15.453	16.83	93.9
Coal Consumption (Million tonnes)	250	1,324.97	815.112	253.666	9,218.3
Net Electricity Generation (Gigawatts hours)	250	1,699.45	865.8777	344.712	4,504.4

Table 13.5. *(Continued)*

	Obs	Mean	Std. Dev.	Min	Max
CO_2 Emissions (tonnes)	250	4,909,725	4,092,472	0.076	23,000,000
Private-Owned Plants					
Installed Capacity (MW)	125	315.972	220.450	45	800
Operating Availability (%)	125	73.398	18.826	26.64	97.66
Plant Load Factor (%)	125	61.203	19.315	18.56	97.25
Coal Consumption (Million tonnes)	125	1,083.094	898.443	69	5,742.72
Net Electricity Generation (Gigawatts hours)	125	1,680.779	1,337.061	75.476	5,060.6
CO_2 Emissions (tonnes)	125	8,390,787	3,940,685	0.111	13,800,000
Explanatory Variables					
Public Ownership	375	0.666	0.472	0	1
North	375	0.306	0.461	0	1
West	375	0.266	0.442	0	1
South	375	0.2	0.400	0	1
Domestic Coal	375	0.906	0.291	0	1
BHEL	375	0.693	0.461	0	1
Age	375	14.010	10.440	0.5	44.666
Carbon Productivity	375	7,522.988	52,147.96	0.0000124	487,444.5
Units	375	4.349	2.254	1	13

Source: Authors' Elaboration.

6. Empirical Results

6.1 Trends in Carbon-Adjusted Efficiency of Coal-Fired Plants Across Ownership Structure

Using meta-frontier analysis, year-wise efficiency scores for coal-fired power plants from 2013–2014 to 2017–2018 were determined. Table 13.6 shows the annual mean efficiency scores for the Indian power sector and its various ownership groups employing CRS technology during the study period. This section details the study to provide carbon-adjusted TGR, meta-frontiers and group frontier-based efficiency estimates. TGRs show how close or far a plant is from the industry (meta) frontier. Table 13.6 presents the estimations of the yearly means, and Fig. 13.7 shows trends in carbon-adjusted efficiency levels.

Table 13.6. Yearly Mean Carbon-Adjusted Efficiency in India (2013–2014 to 2017–2018).

Year	Industry	Public	Private
2013–2014	0.854	0.863	0.951
2014–2015	0.825	0.858	0.964
2015–2016	0.857	0.918	0.920
2016–2017	0.863	0.900	0.949
2017–2018	0.856	0.891	0.921
Average	0.851	0.886	0.941

Source: Authors' calculation.

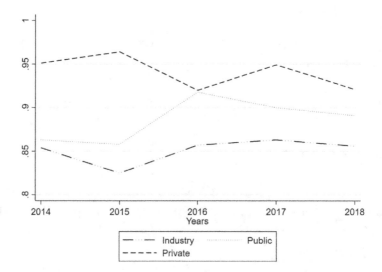

Fig. 13.7.   Efficiency Trends in Coal Power Plants. *Source:* Authors' elaboration based on estimated efficiency scores.

Private plants outperformed public plants because later are smaller, older and less technologically advanced and burn additional fuel to produce electricity compared to former. The bigger power stations use superior technology, viz., supercritical steam generators, thus enhancing efficiency. The industry efficiency also shows a downward trend due to regulatory patterns in this segment. The downward trend caused by the regulator's limited ability to influence or penalize plants for performance improvement, notably SERCs; the current regulatory framework that bases performance norms for electricity generation on historical power station performance rather than a station with the highest performance;

and the regulatory agencies' negligence in norm-setting. The efficiency levels show almost a decreasing pattern, but some sort of convergence was observed in 2016. After that, they again started parting. We now concentrate on the most recent year, 2018, which shows tremendous space for efficiency improvement at the lower end of the range, with TE scores ranging significantly from 0.476 to 1. The results show only three out of 75 had one efficiency score, whereas 29 plants were performing with efficiency levels from 0.80 to 1, and the remaining 43 were considered laggards as their efficiency was below 0.80.

6.2 Carbon-Adjusted Efficiency Variations Across Ownership Groups

The inefficiency of a plant within the meta-frontier (OTIE) may result from managerial failure (RIE), which is a failure to make the best use of the group-specific technology available to that power plant, or it may result from a technology gap (TGIE), which is the differences between the meta-technology (best practice technology) and the group technology for that plant. Table 13.7 shows the results for carbon-adjusted performance under group frontier technologies.

In terms of public plants, the group carbon-adjusted efficiency ranges from 0.4583 to 1 (average = 0.7843), indicating that, on average, public-owned electricity generators can increase their efficiency by approximately 21.57% if they operate on the boundary of group production technologies. Eleven power plants have carbon-adjusted efficiency equal to unity, indicating these plants are on the best practice group frontier. For private plants, efficiency ranges from 0.5438 to 1 (average = 0.8842), indicating that, on average, private plants are not efficient in energy use or emission reduction and thus have the potential to improve their energy efficiency (by 11.58%) substantially. The standard deviation for public generators is higher than that for private ones, indicating a more significant gap in CO_2-adjusted efficiency for the public group. That is to say that private generators operate under relatively uniform conditions in terms of efficiency. The performance levels measured for one frontier cannot be directly compared with those for another frontier. In this regard, we compute the carbon emission efficiency performance under meta-frontier technologies. The average efficiency under meta-technology efficiency value for the private-owned plant group is higher than that for the public-owned plant group, indicating that, on average, private generators are more efficient than public ones.

Table 13.7. Carbon Emission Adjusted Performance Under Group-Frontier Technologies.

Group (Type)	Average	Standard Deviation	Maximum	Minimum
Public Sector Plants	0.7843	0.1307	1	0.4583
Private Sector Plants	0.8842	0.1123	1	0.5438

Source: Authors' calculations.

6.3 Top Performers in Coal Power Plants

In the public-owned power plants group, KODARMA TPP (2014–2016); SIPAT STPS (2016–2018); and DR N.TATA RAO TPS (2016–2018) are efficient in the public plant group. Conversely, the most efficient public sector plants are RIHAND STPS (2014) and VINDHYACHAL STPS (2018), with less than 1% inefficiency. These are 11 power plants in the public sector group, viz. BHILAI TPS (in 2018); Dr N.TATA RAO TPS (2015); IB VALLEY TPS (2018); KAKATIYA TPS (2014, 2015); KODARMA TPP (2015–2017); RAJIV GAN-DHI TPS (2015–2018); SIPAT STPS (2016–2018); TALCHER (OLD) TPS (in 2018); TALCHER STPS (in 2014); TANDA TPS (2018); TENUGHAT TPS (2017, 2018) whose carbon-adjusted efficiency is equal to unity. It is also observed that among the sample plants in the private-owned power plant group, MAHATMA GANDHI TPS, MAQSOODPUR TPS, MUNDRA UMTPP and UTRAULA TPS are the most efficient plants, i.e. having the efficiency score of one across the sample period. However, DAHANU TPS (in 2016); BARKHERA TPS (in 2017); KHAMBARKHERA TPS, BARKHERA TPS and MAITHON RB TPP (in 2018) observed inefficiency of less than 1% in the private sector group. In private sector groups, ANPARA C TPS (2014, 2016); BARKHERA TPS (2015, 2016); BINA TPS (2017); BUDGE BUDGE TPS (2014); KHAM-BARKHERA TPS (2016); MAHATMA GANDHI TPS (2016, 2017); MAQ-SOODPUR TPS (2015–2018); MUNDRA UMTPP (2016–2018); SOUTHERN REPL. TPS (2014, 2015); TORANGALLU TPS (SBU-II) (2014, 2015); UDUPI TPP (2016); UTRAULA TPS (2015, 2016) have an efficiency score of one. In the overall industry group, Dr N.TATA RAO TPS (in 2015), KAKATIYA TPS (in 2014, 2015), RAJIV GANDHI TPS (in 2018), SIPAT STPS (in 2017), TALCHER STPS (in 2014), BARKHERA TPS (in 2015, 2016), BINA TPS (in 2017), BUDGE BUDGE TPS (in 2014), KHAMBARKHERA TPS (in 2016), MAHATMA GANDHI TPS (in 2016, 2017), MAQSOODPUR TPS (2015–2018), MUNDRA UMTPP (2016–2018), SOUTHERN REPL. TPS (in 2014, 2015), TORANGALLU TPS (SBU-II) (in 2014, 2015), UDUPI TPP (in 2016) and UTRAULA TPS (2015, 2016) all have efficiency scores of one and thus perform to the best of their capacity.

6.4 Technology Heterogeneity Across Ownership Groups

Out of 25.16% of the inefficiency of public plants between 2014 and 2018, 21.56% is attributable to poor management and 3.60% is attributable to a lack of technology. Out of 14.86% of the inefficiency of private plants, 11.57% is attributable to poor monitoring and 3.29% is due to technology failure (see Table 13.8). As a result, RIE bears a heavy share of responsibility for both public and private plant inefficiency. A bigger (smaller) TGR value indicates a less (more) technology gap between the individual and the meta-frontiers. A TGR score of 100% corresponds to the intersection of a regional frontier and a meta-frontier. The private plants have the highest TGR average (0.961), indicating they are closer to the meta-frontier than public plants (0.956).

Table 13.8. Carbon-Adjusted Efficiency Across Ownership Groups From 2013–2014 to 2017–2018.

Panel A: Public Sector Plants			
Model Specifications	$\bar{E}_{\text{Meta}}$ (OIE)	$\bar{E}_{\text{Own}}$ (RIE)	$\bar{E}_{\text{TGR}}$ (TGIE)
Period: 2013–2014 to 2017–2018	0.7483 (25.16)	0.7843 (21.56)	0.956 (3.601)
Panel B: Private Sector Plants			
Model Specifications	$\bar{E}_{\text{Meta}}$ (OIE)	$\bar{E}_{\text{Own}}$ (RIE)	$\bar{E}_{\text{TGR}}$ (TGIE)
Period: 2013–2014 to 2017–2018	0.8513 (14.86)	0.8842 (11.57)	0.961 (3.292)
Panel C: All Plants			
Model Specifications	$\bar{E}_{\text{Meta}}$ (OIE)	$\bar{E}_{\text{Own}}$ (RIE)	$\bar{E}_{\text{TGR}}$ (TGIE)
Period: 2013–2014 to 2017–2018	0.7826 (21.79)	0.8176 (18.23)	0.957 (3.498)

Source: Authors' calculations.

Efficiency under the meta-frontier for all plants from 2013–2014 to 2017–2018 is 78.26%. DMUs could do this while maintaining the same input level, resulting in a proportionate 21% increase in electricity production and a 21% reduction in carbon emissions. Our findings imply that the plants have not been sufficiently encouraged by India's power generation ownership structure to improve their performance. The performance of government and privatized plants can be compared to determine the impact of ownership structure on plant performance. Public plants were more inefficient (25.16%) than private plants (14.86%). The important ramifications that follow are as follows. Private plants are advancing into the meta-frontier faster than public equivalents to fulfil their purpose. According to this study, private plants employ the most advanced or creative technologies to increase electricity production. The lower technology gap inefficiency (TGIE) for public plants is observed, indicating that they operate away from the meta-frontier. India's public plants use older production technology to generate more electricity.

6.5 Factors Influencing Carbon-Adjusted Efficiency of Power Plants

In this study, we look at the impact of ownership, region, coal quality, make, carbon productivity, units and age effects on the efficiency of power stations. The Tobit model in our study explains efficiency rather than inefficiency, and Table 13.9 presents the Tobit regression findings. The coefficient signs indicate the

Table 13.9. Results of Tobit Analysis.

Variable-Efficiency	Model 1	Model 2	Model 3	Model 4
Public Ownership	−0.068** (0.043)	−0.063* (0.080)	−0.065* (0.081)	−0.070* (0.063)
Northern			−0.003 (0.918)	−0.001 (0.956)
Western			−0.012 (0.729)	−0.011 (0.753)
Southern			0.011 (0.771)	0.014 (0.710)
Domestic Coal		−0.017 (0.717)	−0.014 (0.785)	−0.012 (0.816)
BHEL	−0.061** (0.050)	−0.059* (0.058)	−0.052* (0.091)	−0.060* (0.060)
Carbon Productivity	0.000*** (0.000)	0.000** (0.012)	0.000** (0.015)	0.000*** (0.010)
Units	−0.026*** (0.000)	−0.026*** (0.000)	−0.023*** (0.000)	−0.025*** (0.000)
Plant Age	0.003 (0.364)	0.003 (0.370)		0.003 (0.354)
Plant Age Square	−0.000 (0.497)	−0.000 (0.505)		−0.000 (0.490)
Constant	1.040*** (0.000)	1.053*** (0.000)	1.063*** (0.000)	1.050*** (0.000)

Notes: Figures in parentheses are the *p*-values. ***, ** and * indicate that the value is statistically significant at 1%, 5% and 10% significance levels, respectively.
Source: Authors' Calculations.

direction of efficiency. Positive results show that efficiency decreases as the variable's value decreases. A negative coefficient, on the other hand, denotes a rising efficiency as the variable's value falls.

Using the Tobit model, four different regression specifications are estimated. Models 1, 2 and 3 test the sensitivity of variable coefficients by removing the insignificant variables from Model 4. Publicly owned plants are less effective than privately owned ones, as shown by the negative and significant coefficient for public ownership across all specifications. Public plants are inefficient because bureaucrats and politicians exert excessive control over them. The BHEL manufacturing equipment coefficient is negative and statistically significant in all regressions, demonstrating that BHEL-equipped stations are less effective than foreign-equipped ones. This outcome supports the Indian government's choice to permit foreign investment in the power sector. The **BHEL MAKE** power plant has lower efficiency ratings than other foreign companies because of poor boiler design, ineffective BTG component synchronization and slower maintenance by BHEL engineers (Singh & Bajpai, 2013). Because the coefficient for the number of units is negative and significant in all four models, it is obvious that a plant's efficiency decreases as the power plant units increase. Our findings support power plants' presumption that auxiliary power consumption follows suit as the unit count rises. In other words, having more units increases the cost of operation and maintenance because more personnel are required to coordinate between and among the units and monitor the equipment.

7. Conclusion and Policy Implications

The study employed the meta-frontier data envelopment analysis model to evaluate the CO_2-adjusted efficiency in coal power stations in India. While examining the performance of the thermal power sector, special attention must be paid to the coal power stations because they are the primary source of electricity and CO_2 emissions. This paper undertakes carbon emission as undesirable/bad output and electricity generation as good output. The average efficiency score is 78.26%; power plants may produce proportionately more electricity and cut CO_2 emissions by 21% while maintaining the same input levels. When carbon emissions are excluded from electricity production, efficiency is misinterpreted, whereas including emissions leads to more realistic results. The efficiency comparisons across plant ownership groups show that plants in the public sector are more inefficient than plants in the private sector. The major chunk for higher inefficiency in public and private plants is due to relative performance compared to the technology gap. The lower efficiency of public plants can be attributed to the advanced age, excessive coal consumption, severe emissions, electricity generation deficit, etc. Furthermore, inefficiency levels during the study period varied from around 13%–18%, indicating that electricity regulators have sufficient scope to push the plants to improve their performance. Fourth, according to the Tobit model, estimated results, ownership, BHEL, carbon productivity and units impact the efficiency of power plants. The age and age-squared positive and negative coefficients show that efficiency levels peak between 20 and 25 years, after which they decline. Those using foreign equipment perform more efficiently than plants with Indian equipment. Plants with fewer units are more effective than plants with fewer units.

These findings imply that the government can narrow the technology gap by investing in generating equipment and encouraging technical innovation to improve the CO_2-adjusted performance of electricity-producing power plants. This will help to change the environment of laggard power plants and thus enable them to generate more electricity and reduce emissions. Improved environmental compliance may spur innovation, reducing the net cost of compliance and resulting in a net benefit in the power sector, consistent with the Porter hypothesis.

The electricity regulators can direct plants to comply with Perform Achieve and Trade (PAT) objectives. Well-designed climate strategy, adopting worldwide managerial and O&M standards, switching to ultra-supercritical technology and strengthening coal management to ensure timely supplies. Deploying supercritical technologies might boost sector efficiency and help manage growing input costs while preserving ecological harmony, employing better operating procedures, periodic repair and frequent maintenance inspections. Lastly, promoting the installation of 'Flue Gas Desulphurization' in power plants may aid in reducing emissions of solid particulate matter.

References

Banker, R. D., Charnes, A., & Cooper, W. W. (1984). Some models for estimating technical and scale inefficiencies in data envelopment analysis. *Management Science*, *30*(9), 1078–1092.

Barros, C. P., & Peypoch, N. (2008). Technical efficiency of thermoelectric power plants. *Energy Economics*, *30*(6), 3118–3127.

Battese, G. E., & Rao, D. P. (2002). Technology gap, efficiency, and a stochastic metafrontier function. *International Journal of Business and Economics*, *1*(2), 1–7.

Central Electricity Authority. (2018). *Review of performance of thermal power station 2018*. https://cea.nic.in/wpcontent/uploads/opm_grid_operation/2020/07/thermal_review-2018%20(1).pdf

Central Electricity Authority. (2021). *CO_2 baseline database for the Indian power sector*. https://cea.nic.in/wpcontent/uploads/tpe___cc/2022/02/User_Guide__ver_17_2021.pdf

Charnes, A., Cooper, W. W., & Rhodes, E. (1978). Measuring the efficiency of decision making units. *European Journal of Operational Research*, *2*(6), 429–444.

Du, L., Hanley, A., & Zhang, N. (2016). Environmental technical efficiency, technology gap and shadow price of coal-fuelled power plants in China: A parametric meta-frontier analysis. *Resource and Energy Economics*, *43*(C), 14–32.

Farrell, M. J. (1957). The measurement of productive efficiency. *Journal of the Royal Statistical Society: Series A*, *120*(3), 253–281.

Ghosh, S. (2010). Status of thermal power generation in India – Perspectives on capacity, generation and carbon dioxide emissions. *Energy Policy*, *38*(11), 6886–6899.

Ghosh, R., & Kathuria, V. (2016). The effect of regulatory governance on efficiency of thermal power generation in India: A stochastic frontier analysis. *Energy Policy*, *89*(C), 11–24.

Gulati, R. (2022). Global and local banking crises and risk-adjusted efficiency of Indian banks: Are the impacts really perspective-dependent? *The Quarterly Review of Economics and Finance*, *84*(C), 23–39.

International Energy Agency. (2020). World Energy Outlook 2020. https://www.iea.org/reports/world-energy-outlook-2020

International Energy Agency. (2021). World Energy Outlook 2021. https://www.iea.org/reports/india-energy-outlook-2021

Jain, R. K., & Kumar, S. (2018). Shadow price of CO_2 emissions in Indian thermal power sector. *Environmental Economics and Policy Studies*, *20*(4), 879–902.

Jindal, A., & Nilakantan, R. (2022). Regulatory independence and thermal power plant performance: Evidence from India. *Journal of Regulatory Economics, 61*(1), 32–47.

Kaneko, S., Fujii, H., Sawazu, N., & Fujikura, R. (2010). Financial allocation strategy for the regional pollution abatement cost of reducing sulfur dioxide emissions in the thermal power sector in China. *Energy Policy, 38*(5), 2131–2141.

Khanna, M., Mundra, K., & Ullah, A. (1999). Parametric and semi-parametric estimation of the effect of firm attributes on efficiency: The electricity generating industry in India. *Journal of International Trade & Economic Development, 8*(4), 419–430.

Kumar, S., & Jain, R. K. (2019). Carbon-sensitive meta-productivity growth and technological gap: An empirical analysis of Indian thermal power sector. *Energy Economics, 81*(C), 104–116.

Kumar, S., & Rao, D. N. (2003). Estimating marginal abatement costs of SPM: An application to the thermal power sector in India. *Energy Studies Review, 11*(1), 76–92.

Lam, P. L., & Shiu, A. (2004). Efficiency and productivity of China's thermal power generation. *Review of Industrial Organization, 24*(1), 73–93.

Liu, C. H., Lin, S. J., & Lewis, C. (2010). Evaluation of thermal power plant operational performance in Taiwan by data envelopment analysis. *Energy Policy, 38*(2), 1049–1058.

Meng, F., Su, B., Thomson, E., Zhou, D., & Zhou, P. (2016). Measuring China's regional energy and carbon emission efficiency with DEA models: A survey. *Applied Energy, 183*(C), 1–21.

Ministry of New and Renewable Energy. (2018). Annual Report 2017–2018. https://mnre.gov.in/annual-reports-2017-18/

Murty, M. N., Kumar, S., & Dhavala, K. K. (2007). Measuring environmental efficiency of industry: A case study of thermal power generation in India. *Environmental and Resource Economics, 38*(1), 31–50.

Murty, S., & Nagpal, R. (2019). Measuring output-based technical efficiency of Indian coal-based thermal power plants: A by-production approach. *Indian Growth and Development Review, 13*(1), 175–206.

Nakaishi, T. (2021). Developing effective CO$_2$ and SO$_2$ mitigation strategy based on marginal abatement costs of coal-fired power plants in China. *Applied Energy, 294*(C), 1–17.

Nakano, M., & Managi, S. (2008). Regulatory reforms and productivity: An empirical analysis of the Japanese electricity industry. *Energy Policy, 36*(1), 201–209.

O'Donnell, C. J., Rao, D. S., & Battese, G. E. (2008). Metafrontier frameworks for the study of firm-level efficiencies and technology ratios. *Empirical Economics, 34*(2), 231–255.

Sahoo, N. R., Mohapatra, P. K., Sahoo, B. K., & Mahanty, B. (2017). Rationality of energy efficiency improvement targets under the PAT scheme in India – A case of thermal power plants. *Energy Economics, 66*(1), 279–289.

See, K. F., & Coelli, T. (2012). An analysis of factors that influence the technical efficiency of Malaysian thermal power plants. *Energy Economics, 34*(3), 677–685.

Seiford, L. M., & Zhu, J. (2002). Modeling undesirable factors in efficiency evaluation. *European Journal of Operational Research, 142*(1), 16–20.

Sengupta, D., & Mukherjee, D. (2021). By-production of electricity and particulates: Efficiency of Indian thermal power plants revisited. *International Journal of Energy Sector Management, 16*(2), 265–283.

Shanmugam, K. R., & Kulshreshtha, P. (2005). Efficiency analysis of coal-based thermal power generation in India during post-reform era. *International Journal of Global Energy Issues, 23*(1), 15–28.

Shrivastava, N., Sharma, S., & Chauhan, K. (2012). Efficiency assessment and benchmarking of thermal power plants in India. *Energy Policy, 40*(C), 159–176.

Singh, J. (1991). Plant size and technical efficiency in the Indian thermal power industry. *Indian Economic Review, 26*(2), 239–252.

Singh, S. K., & Bajpai, V. K. (2013). Estimation of operational efficiency and its determinants using DEA: The case of Indian coal-fired power plants. *International Journal of Energy Sector Management, 7*(4), 409–429.

Sueyoshi, T., Yuan, Y., & Goto, M. (2017). A literature study for DEA applied to energy and environment. *Energy Economics, 62*(C), 104–124.

Sugathan, A., Malghan, D., Chandrashekar, S., & Sinha, D. K. (2019). Downstream electric utility restructuring and upstream generation efficiency: Productivity dynamics of Indian coal and gas based electricity generators. *Energy, 178*(C), 832–852.

Vaninsky, A. (2006). Efficiency of electric power generation in the United States: Analysis and forecast based on data envelopment analysis. *Energy Economics, 28*(3), 326–338.

Wei, C., Löschel, A., & Liu, B. (2013). An empirical analysis of the CO_2 shadow price in Chinese thermal power enterprises. *Energy Economics, 40*(C), 22–31.

Yadav, V. K., Kumar, N., Ghosh, S., & Singh, K. (2014). Indian thermal power plant challenges and remedies via application of modified data envelopment analysis. *International Transactions in Operational Research, 21*(6), 955–977.

Yu, Y., Qian, T., & Du, L. (2017). Carbon productivity growth, technological innovation, and technology gap change of coal-fired power plants in China. *Energy Policy, 109*(C), 479–487.

Zhang, N., Zhou, P., & Choi, Y. (2013). Energy efficiency, CO_2 emission performance and technology gaps in fossil fuel electricity generation in Korea: A meta-frontier non-radial directional distance function analysis. *Energy Policy, 56*(C), 653–662.

Zhou, P., Ang, B. W., & Poh, K. L. (2008). A survey of data envelopment analysis in energy and environmental studies. *European Journal of Operational Research, 189*(1), 1–18.

Chapter 14

Interlinkages Between Technological Progress, Unemployment and Labour Productivity: Insights From the Solow Residual Model on Sustainable Economic Development

Anuradha S Pai[a], Ananya Sarkar[b], Atreyee Sengupta[b], Anuja Kure[b], Bhumika Goswami[c] and Shilpa Deo[d]

[a]PES University, India
[b]Dr Vishwanath Karad MIT-WPU University, India
[c]Riga Technical University, Latvia
[d]DES Pune University, India

Abstract

This study finds whether there exists any correlation between the rates of technological progress, unemployment and labour productivity among a total of 21 world economies that are categorized as developed, developing and least developed by the United Nations. An attempt has also been made to check the reliability of the model through regression analysis. Time series analysis has been conducted over 19 years, from 2000 to 2018. The Solow Residual Method based on the Cobb Douglas Production function has been used and modified to find the rate of contribution of technological progress towards Gross Domestic Product (GDP) for each country. Correlation analysis has been conducted to measure the degree of correlation between the variables and trend analysis has been used to identify the exact directions in which the variables are moving. Further, regression analysis has been conducted to check whether the identified strength of the relationship between the dependent and the independent variables can be well justified or not. There is an unsustainable economic development when the contribution of technology to a nation's GDP increases in tandem with an increase in the

Modeling Economic Growth in Contemporary India, 261–279
Copyright © 2024 Anuradha S Pai, Ananya Sarkar, Atreyee Sengupta, Anuja Kure, Bhumika Goswami and Shilpa Deo
Published under exclusive licence by Emerald Publishing Limited
doi:10.1108/978-1-80382-751-320241014

rate of unemployment. A country is said to have sustainable economic development when the rate of contribution of technical advances to GDP growth drops or if it grows but with a lower unemployment rate.

Keywords: Technological progress; unemployment; labour productivity; Solow residual growth model; developed countries; developing countries; least developed countries; sustainable development

1. Introduction

Broad Theme and Topic – Technological Progress, Unemployment, Labour Productivity, Sustainable Economic Development. In 1983, Wassily Leontief, the Russian-born American Economist, suggested that when machines and equipment are made to execute functions that are performed by human muscles, the indispensability of labour as a factor of production increases as more labourers are required to operate the machines. However, when advancing technology starts performing functions that are performed by the human mind, the indispensability of labour as a factor of production decreases leading to involuntary unemployment (Leontief, 1983).

While some experts feel that automation or artificial intelligence will have a favourable impact on future employment, others believe that it will have a detrimental effect, especially in the Least Developed Countries (LDCs), which are predominantly labour-intensive. As a result, the paradigm maintains that automation will lead to joblessness, especially among low-skilled workers who lack technological knowledge.

This study broadly attempts to find whether there exists any correlation between the rates of technological progress, unemployment and labour productivity among a total of 21 world economies that are categorized as developed, developing and least developed by the United Nations. Further, an attempt has also been made to check the reliability of the model through regression analysis.

Time series analysis has been conducted over 19 years, from 2000 to 2018. The selected developed economies are Italy, Japan, the United Kingdom (UK), the United States of America (USA), Australia, Spain and the Netherlands. The selected developing economies are Brazil, The Russian Federation, India, Thailand, South Africa, Mexico and Indonesia. The selected LDCs are Bangladesh, Angola, Tanzania, Uganda, Nepal, Cambodia and Sudan. The Solow Residual Method based on the Cobb Douglas Production function has been used and modified to find the rate of contribution of technological progress towards Gross Domestic Product (GDP) for each country. Correlation analysis has been conducted to measure the degree of correlation between the variables and trend analysis has been used to identify the exact directions in which the variables are moving. Further, regression analysis has been conducted to check whether the identified strength of the relationship between the dependent and the independent variables can be well justified or not.

The impact of automation and artificial intelligence (AI) on future job opportunities is a topic of substantial interest. Although there are significant differences in opinion regarding the potential net employment impacts of these technologies, most scholars agree that almost all industries will be affected at some point in time (Korinek & Stiglitz, 2018). Concerns about technological unemployment have long accompanied mechanization and growing worker productivity.

However, automation not only replaces but also complements human work. According to economic history, the loss of some jobs and industries gives rise to others. The notion that automation causes joblessness is contradicted by the fact that the world has seen significant and ongoing technological progress for many decades without consistently growing unemployment (Mutascu, 2021).

Here the question is whether technological progress boosts employment opportunities or increases unemployment. This paper aims to investigate this paradoxical viewpoint for countries categorized as developed, developing and least developed by the United Nations. The aggregate GDP of the selected developed nations in the study accounts for about 35% of the global economy in nominal terms (2018). According to the latest OECD projections, developing nations would account for approximately 60% of global GDP by 2030. Even though the LDCs account for only 1.26% of the global GDP, this study examines these countries to ensure the model's inclusive ability.

Although the selected developed, developing and least developed economies have been studied for technological advancement in the past, there is essentially less research that examines the correlation between technological development and unemployment and labour productivity in these three groupings of countries (Bastos, 1996; Crane, 1977; da Motta e Albuquerque, 2004; Miah & Omar, 2012; Molnar & Clonts, 2019; Renu, 2021; Shahidullah, 1999). As a result, this comparative study should contribute significantly to the field's current body of knowledge. The Sustainable Development Goals (SDGs), viz; goal 8 – Decent work and economic growth and 10 – Reduced inequalities can be achieved by 2030 by understanding the interlinkages between technology, unemployment and labour productivity and by suggesting policy recommendations to reduce the unemployment and resulting inequalities. Therefore, the key findings of the research indicate that advancing technology is assisting labour and capital in the production process and increasing their proportions of contribution to the total GDP of the country when the contribution of technological progress to the GDP of a country decreases over time along with a decrease in the rate of unemployment (as observed in the developed economy of Japan and in the developing economies of Russia, South Africa and Indonesia) also we could see that over time, the technological growth rate in emerging nations has seen a downward trend except in India and Mexico.

Given this background, this study attempts to explore the following relationship.

This study is divided into the following major parts: Literature Review, Research Gap, Research Methodology, Results and Discussions, Implications for Theory and Practice, References and Appendix.

1.1 Objectives of the Study

- To analyse the relationship between the rate of technological progress, rate of unemployment and labour productivity among a total of 21 world economies that are categorized as developed, developing and least developed by the United Nations, over a period of 19 years, i.e. from 2000 to 2018.
- To find out if technological growth promotes sustainable economic development.

2. Review of Literature

Solow (1956) through the Growth Model describes the factors of growth and demonstrates that it is not just capital and labour that contribute to it, but that there is an unaccounted part that is not accounted for by capital and labour increases. The Solow residual –attributed to technical progress – is the unaccounted fraction of economic growth. Robert Solow and Trevor Swan developed the Solow model in 1956, and it is widely regarded as one of the most important contributions to economic growth theory. This model depicts the economy in a simplified manner and aids in understanding the sources of economic growth as well as the reasons for wealth disparities between countries. The growth model explains that an increase in production is a function of capital accumulation and is influenced exogenously by labour expansion and technical innovation. Hence, in the Solow model, the technology factor is the most important. Leontief (1983) analyses how technology has evolved over the past three centuries and how it has influenced the rate of unemployment and income distribution in developed and less-developed economies. During the Great Industrial Revolution, technology was changing rapidly, and new equipment was being invented that performed muscle functions and increased the total output. However, technology could not operate itself and thus required labourers and their skills. Hence, the indispensability of labour increased, which immensely decreased the rate of unemployment and increased the national income.

However, from the late 20th century, technology has started performing mental functions which means that labour and its human skills are not required to operate technology; the indispensability of labour as a factor of production has decreased significantly and is projected to decrease further. It has been universally projected by economists that as technology increasingly overthrows labour in the agricultural and manufacturing sectors, the demand for labour will shift and increase in the service sector. Yet the shift of demand from commodities into services is bound to slow down, while the displacement of labour by increasingly efficient machines seems to have no limits. The ability of the service sector to absorb displaced workers will diminish. All this will lead to involuntary unemployment and reduce national income, increasingly over the coming years. The less-developed countries tend to have a comparative advantage in the labour-intensive production process. However, modern technology has been replacing labour in these countries and making the unemployment rate and national income more unfavourable.

Aba et al. (2016) explained a theoretical Cobb–Douglas production function and compared Philippine development patterns and productivity to those of other ASEAN countries. The development of the Cobb–Douglas production function, as advocated by Samuelson, is highlighted in the derivation of the aggregates of growth and productivity. Cobb and Douglas's theoretical boundaries are followed when considering data. The experimentally tested Solow Growth model is used to extend the derivation. The total output of a country is also affected by technical change aside from labour and capital input. This is evident from the empirical examples of Singapore, the Philippines and Thailand. Singapore's labour and capital have significantly lower contributions towards growth, but thanks to industrialization, it managed to cope up to such heights. Although the Philippines is a developing country, its physical capital expansion indicates great potential for economic progress.

Ozdemir (2017) discusses that Solow has built his model based on a production function in the absence of an investment function. Further, he argues that technological change was to make capital and labour more productive, but the main difference between the Solow growth model and the post-Keynesian approach (Harrod–Domar model) is that they argue that capital is independent of price income distribution and there is no physical measure of aggregate capital. The Solow model could not provide a role for prices in adjusting output changes in demand. Solow also assumed that there would be diminishing returns and marginal productivity would be there even if there is no price flexibility but, marginal costs do not rise, they are either constant or falling, so involuntary unemployment could not be related. Solow assumed that the supply side determines the adjustment but according to Nell this works out in the craft-based economy and not in the mass production economy, because here employment depended only on effective demand, so the argument that the growth of supply will generate equivalent growth in demand could not be held true.

In reality, total factor productivity, the best overall measure of the rate of technical progress, has been stagnant in the United States and across advanced economies since 2005. Matuzeviciute et al. (2017) examined the theoretical and empirical literature on the impact of technological innovation on unemployment in 25 European nations from 2000 to 2012, using long-term productivity and economic growth as the major indicators. For technological development and unemployment controls, panel data were used, and unemployment control was determined using (SYSTEM GENERALISED METHOD OF MOMENTS) using triadic patent families per million people. With or without the lagged numbers, the findings indicated that there was no link between technological advancement and unemployment.

2.1 Research Gap

Most studies have not used the Solow Residual Growth Model to calculate the rate of technological progress, with the motive of conducting its multiple correlation and regression with the variables – unemployment rate and labour productivity. Further, comparative correlation and regression analysis with the selected variables among the developed, the developing and the least developed world economies are relatively understudied.

3. Methodology

The data for this study have been collected from secondary sources to analyse the rates of technological progress, unemployment and labour productivity in the world's developed, developing and least developed economies (see Table 14.1). The data have been collected for a period of 19 years, i.e. from 2000 to 2018, primarily from the data bank of the World Bank. The Solow residual model has been used for calculating technological progress in the selected economies over the selected period. The study tries to improvise the model by eliminating the following two main assumptions of the Solow Residual model: 1. There is perpetual full employment of labour. 2. There is also full employment of the available stock of capital. The following is how the study has attempted to improve on the Solow residual model: $Y(t) = A(t)$.

$$K^*(t)a\ H(t)1 - a \qquad\qquad (14.1)$$

Here,

$Y(t)$ = output of the economy

$A(t)$ = the residual representing technological progress

$K^*(t)$ = capital formation-idle capital stock

$H(t) = L(t)$. $G(t)$; $L(t)$ = total number of workforce-unemployed workforce and $G(t)$ = amount of human capital per worker.

$G(t)$= (Health Expenditure + Education Expenditure)/Total Workforce a = capital share towards output

$1 - a$ = labour share towards output

Further, the above econometric model (14.1) has been decomposed into a logarithmic function,

$$\mathrm{Log}\,Y\ =\ A + a\mathrm{log}K(t) + (1 - a)\mathrm{log}[L(t){\cdot}G(t)]$$

$$\mathrm{Log}\,Y\ =\ A + a\mathrm{log}K + (1 - a)[\mathrm{log}\ L(t) + \mathrm{log}\ G(t)] \qquad (14.2)$$

Multiple regression analysis has been then run-on equation (14.2) to establish a relationship between output (GDP at current USD), technological progress (intercept variable), capital formation in the economy and human capital (including employed labour force and amount of human capital per worker). The intercept A (residual, representing technological progress) has been calculated as:

$$A\ =\ \mathrm{log}\ [Y(t)/\{L(t){\cdot}G(t)\} - a\{\ \mathrm{log}(K(t)/L(t){\cdot}G(t))\} \qquad (14.3)$$

The regression analysis has also been used to determine the goodness of fit of the model. Correlation analysis has then been run to determine the degree of correlation between technological progress and unemployment.

Table 14.1. Correlation Analysis for Developed, Developing and Least Developed Countries.

Sr. No.	Country	Technological Progress and Unemployment Rate	Technological Progress and Labour Productivity
1	Italy	0.81	−0.86
2	Japan	0.75	−0.82
3	United Kingdom	−0.20	−0.79
4	United States	0.05	−0.94
5	Australia	0.42	−0.82
6	Spain	0.85	0.85
7	Netherlands	−0.57	−0.77
8	Brazil	0.32	−0.95
9	Russia	0.80	−0.78
10	India	0.00	0.40
11	South Africa	0.85	−0.70
12	Mexico	0.17	0.11
13	Indonesia	0.74	−0.87
14	Thailand	0.13	0.10
15	Bangladesh	−0.26	−0.86
16	Angola	0.27	0.13
17	Tanzania	0.22	−0.57
18	Uganda	−0.29	0.12
19	Nepal	−0.64	−0.87
20	Cambodia	0.22	0.02
21	Sudan	−0.41	0.29

Source: Author's calculation based on World Bank data.

Note:

Developed Economies	Developing Economies	Least Developed Economies

Additionally, correlation analysis has been used to correlate labour productivity with technological progress to capture any relation between the two. The formula for labour productivity is considered as follows:

Labour productivity = GDP at constant prices/Number of employed persons
(as per International Labour Organization)

4. Results and Discussion

For simplicity, the following countries are selected from each category of developed, developing and least developed, to represent the entire group of selected nations.

4.1 Japan: A Developed Nation

Correlation Analysis:
From 2000 to 2018, it is found that there is 0.75394 degree of positive correlation between technological progress and unemployment in Japan, indicating that the pace of technological progress significantly affects the country's unemployment rate positively. The trends illustrate (see Appendix Fig. A1.1) that over 19 years, the Unemployment rate and Technological Progress both have declined.

From 2000 to 2018, there is a high degree of negative correlation of 0.82126 between technological progress and labour productivity in Japan, indicating that technological progress influenced Labour Productivity. The trends illustrate (see Appendix Fig. A1.2) that labour productivity has increased over time while technological progress has declined.

Regression Analysis:
For Japan, R square and adjusted R square is high which suggests that the dependent and independent variables have a very strong association. The low significance (F −1.4E-05) value and the widening gap between residual and total SS imply that the model is relatively reliable for Japan. When the other variables are zero, the negative intercept of 3.24311 indicates there is almost zero degree of technological development in the economy (see Appendix Figs. A1.3 & A1.4).

4.2 Brazil: A Developing Nation

Correlation Analysis:
From the year 2000–2018, there existed a low degree of positive correlation of 0.32, between technological progress and unemployment in Brazil (see Appendix Fig. A1.5), implying that the rate of technological progress doesn't influence the rate of unemployment in the country. The trend lines show that the rate of technological progress has declined over the period of 19 years while unemployment has been stable.

From the year 2000–2018, there existed a high degree of negative correlation of −0.95 between the rates of technological progress and labour productivity in Brazil (see Appendix Fig. A1.6), implying that the rate of technological progress highly influenced the rate of labour productivity in the country and that the variables moved in opposite directions. The trend lines show that labour productivity increased over the years while technological progress decreased over the years.

Regression Analysis:
The regression analysis is conducted to check the reliability of the Solow Residual model after adding human capital. The R squared and the adjusted R square indicate an extremely strong relationship between the dependent and independent variables. The significance (F) value being very small, at 8.86535E-23, and the widened gap between residual and total SS suggests strong reliability on the model for Brazil. The positive intercept of 1.579602932 suggests that when the other variables are at zero, there still exists a level of technology in the economy. The coefficients of all the independent variables are positive, suggesting as the variables increase, there will be an increase in the output/GDP of the nation (see Appendix Figs. A1.7 & A1.8).

4.3 Angola: A Least Developed Nation

Correlation Analysis:
From the year 2000 to 2018, there existed a low degree of positive correlation of 0.274011588, between technological progress and unemployment in Angola (see Appendix Fig. A1.9), implying that the rate of technological progress doesn't influence the rate of unemployment in the country. The trend lines show that the rate of technological progress has remained stable over the period of 19 years while unemployment has increased.

From the year 2000 to 2018, there existed a low degree of positive correlation of 0.131007816 between the rates of technological progress and labour productivity in Angola (see Appendix Fig. A1.10), implying that the rate of technological progress does not influence the rate of labour productivity in the country. The trend lines show that labour productivity increased over the years while technological progress was stable.

Regression Analysis:
The regression analysis is conducted to check the reliability of the Solow Residual model after adding human capital. The R squared and the adjusted R square indicate an extremely strong relationship between the dependent and independent variables. The significance (F) value being very small, at 7.63E-17, and the widened gap between residual and total SS suggest strong reliability on the model for Angola. The negative intercept of -1.028452878 suggests that when the other variables are at zero, there does not exist a level of technology in the economy (see Appendix Figs. A1.11 & A1.12).

According to the data analysis, adding human capital as an explanatory variable to the existing Solow residual model increases the R square value. This value is 0.98 in the case of most of the selected countries.

The correlation analysis performed for the developed countries suggests no generalized conclusion about the relationship between the rates of technological progress and unemployment. Although, countries like Italy, Japan and Spain, out of the seven selected countries, suggest a high degree of correlation between the two variables. In Italy and Spain, the rates of technological progress and unemployment have experienced an uptrend over the past 19 years, suggesting that as there has been an increase in the contribution of technology to the output, the unemployment rate has also risen. In Japan, both variables have seen a downward trend over the years, implying that as the contribution of the rate of technological progress towards GDP declined, the unemployment rate also declined.

Similarly, the developing economies – Russia, South Africa and Indonesia show a high degree of correlation between the rates of technological progress and unemployment, suggesting that the rate of technological progress has been affecting the rate of unemployment in these countries. In these developing countries, as the rate of growth in technological progress slows down, so does the growth rate in unemployment. One of the reasons can be the lagging pace of technological progress with respect to the high rate of output growth in developing countries. Over time, the technological growth rate in emerging nations has seen a downward trend except in India and Mexico. However, due to the contribution of capital and labour factors, GDP continues to rise.

In the case of LDCs, except for Nepal (to a moderate degree), none of the selected nations depicts a correlation between the rates of technological progress and unemployment.

Further, it has been found that there is a strong negative correlation between the rate of technological progress and labour productivity in developed nations. Among the seven selected developing nations, only Brazil, Russia, South Africa and Indonesia show a strong negative correlation. However, it is difficult to theorise a relationship between technological progress and labour productivity in developing countries and LDCs.

Similarly, among the least developed nations, Bangladesh, Tanzania and Nepal have shown a considerable degree of correlation. It is difficult to theorize a relationship between the rate of technological progress and labour productivity for the least developed nations too as these variables in Bangladesh, Tanzania and Nepal show a high degree of correlation whereas, in Angola, Uganda and Cambodia, the variables do not correlate.

The statistical significance of the variables is shown by the fact that all the countries' significance (F) values in Table 14.2 are less than 0.05. Additionally, the fact that the R square and Adjusted R square values are quite high shows that the data are the strong fit for the model because the independent variables are dependable and can explain the variability of the data.

The estimated regression results reflect the following facts:

When the contribution of technological progress to the GDP of a country increases along with an increase in the rate of unemployment over time (as observed in the developed economies of Italy and Spain), as per Wassily Leontief's theory, it implies that the advancing technology has started performing the functions of the human mind, decreasing the indispensability of labour as a factor of production increasing involuntary unemployment. It also implies that economic development in these countries is not sustainable as the increasing rate of

Table 14.2. Regression Analysis for Developed, Developing and Least
Developed Countries.

Sr.No.	Country	R Squared	Adjusted R Squared	p Value
1	Italy	0.995	0.994	1.42E-17
2	Japan	0.805	0.766	1.40E-05
3	United Kingdom	0.805	0.766	1.14E-14
4	United States	0.998	0.998	3.33E-21
5	Australia	0.999	0.999	6.22E-22
6	Spain	0.997	0.996	4.19E-19
7	Netherlands	0.996	0.995	3.26E-18
8	Brazil	0.999	0.999	8.87E-23
9	Russia	0.998	0.998	6.30E-21
10	India	0.998	0.998	1.09E-20
11	South Africa	0.990	0.988	3.06E-15
12	Mexico	0.906	0.887	6.42E-08
13	Indonesia	0.999	0.999	4.85E-22
14	Thailand	0.991	0.989	1.58E-15
15	Bangladesh	0.997	0.997	2.38E-19
16	Angola	0.996	0.995	7.63E-17
17	Tanzania	0.996	0.995	9.68E-17
18	Uganda	0.995	0.994	1.24E-16
19	Nepal	0.996	0.995	2.45E-18
20	Cambodia	0.995	0.994	1.23E-16
21	Sudan	0.977	0.971	1.23E-11

Source: Author's calculation based on World Bank data.

Note:

Developed Economies	Developing Economies	Least Developed Economies

unemployment means that the public at large is unable to afford a sustainable lifestyle.

When the contribution of technological progress to the GDP of a country decreases along with a decrease in the rate of unemployment over time (as observed in the developed economy of Japan and in the developing economies of Russia, South Africa and Indonesia), it implies that advancing technology is assisting labour and capital in the production process and increasing their proportions of contribution to the total GDP of the country. In these developing countries, as the rate of growth in technological progress slows down, so does the growth rate in unemployment. One of the reasons can be the lagging pace of technological progress with respect to the high rate of output growth in developing countries. Over time, the technological growth rate in emerging nations has seen a downward trend except in India and Mexico. However, due to the contribution of capital and labour factors, GDP continues to rise. As per Wassily Leontief's theory, when machines and equipment are made to execute functions that are performed by human muscles, the indispensability of labour as a factor of production increases as more labourers are required to operate the machines.

When the contribution of technological progress to the GDP of a country increases, decreasing the unemployment rate in the country since technology advances at a faster rate in a country, it necessitates fewer workers because it assists the existing workforce in increasing their efficiency. With an increase in labour productivity, income rises, reducing poverty and promoting sustainable economic development.

5. Conclusion

5.1 Implications for Theory and Practice

This study validates the modified version of the Solow Residual Model, and it also substantially supports Wassily Leontief's theory of technological advancement and its relationship with unemployment.

Future research can use other methodologies available to compare results with our data to test the validity of the current findings. The researchers can take up more countries, as an increase in the sample size enables them to gain more accurate mean values and helps in better identification of outliers. Due to the limited time and missing data, forecasting was not achievable, therefore, further research can forecast the data. Lastly, the period before 2000 can also be included in later research.

5.2 Policy Implications

The present study holds significance amidst the changing current global scenario. The world economies are facing many challenges like recession, mass tech layoffs, supply chain disruptions, Russia–Ukraine war, China's dominance in neighbouring countries and other geopolitical tensions. The study also throws light on the policy implications of technological advancement on unemployment and growth of the countries selected. From the government's or policymakers' perspective, it holds importance since the study points out that there is an unsustainable economic development when the contribution of technology to a nation's GDP increases in tandem with an increase in the rate of unemployment. It also concludes that a country is said to have sustainable economic development when the rate of contribution of technical advances to GDP growth drops or if it grows but with a lower unemployment rate. This means the countries must decide how best to balance between investing in technological development and targeting a lower unemployment rate and customize their policies accordingly. The study's findings can aid the policymakers in designing sustainable development policies for their countries.

References

Aba, P., Maglanoc, D., & Garoy, E. (2016, October). Measuring growth residual: Empirical evidence on total factor productivity test and Solow growth model. In *13th National Convention on Statistics* (pp. 3–4).

Bastos, M. I. (1996). Science and technology policies in developing countries: A political analysis of Latin American practice and prospects. *Science Technology & Society, 1*(2), 225–248. https://doi.org/10.1177/097172189600100203

Crane, D. (1977). Technological innovation in developing countries: A review of the literature. *Research Policy, 6*(4), 374–395. https://doi.org/10.1016/0048-7333(77)90013-0

da Motta e Albuquerque, E. (2004). Science and technology systems in less developed countries. In H. F. Moed, W. Glänzel, & U. Schmoch (Eds.), *Handbook of quantitative science and technology research*. Springer. https://doi.org/10.1007/1-4020-2755-9_35

Korinek, A., & Stiglitz, J. E. (2018). Artificial intelligence and its implications for income distribution and unemployment. In *The economics of artificial intelligence: An agenda* (pp. 349–390). University of Chicago Press.

Leontief, W. (1983). Technological advance, economic growth, and the distribution of income. *Population and Development Review, 9*(3), 403–410. https://doi.org/10.2307/1973315

Matuzeviciute, K., Butkus, M., & Karaliute, A. (2017). Do technological innovations affect unemployment? Some empirical evidence from European countries. *Economies, 5*(4), 48.

Miah, M., & Omar, A. (2012). Technology advancement in developing countries during digital age. *International Journal of Science and Applied Information Technology, 1*(1), 30–38.

Molnar, J. J., & Clonts, H. A. (2019). Technology as a source of economic and social advancement in developing countries. In *Transferring food production technology to developing nations* (pp. 1–15). Routledge.

Mutascu, M. (2021). Artificial intelligence and unemployment: New insights. *Economic Analysis and Policy, 69*, 653–667. https://doi.org/10.1016/j.eap.2021.01.012

Ozdemir, D. (2017). A post-Keynesian criticism of the Solow growth model. *Journal of Economics Business and Management, 5*(3), 134–137.

Renu, N. (2021). *Technological advancement in the era of COVID-19* (Vol. 9, p. 20503121211000912). SAGE Open Medicine.

Shahidullah, M. (1999). Science and technology development in the third world: Competing policy perspectives. *Knowledge, Technology & Policy, 12*, 27–44. https://doi.org/10.1007/s12130-999-1012-6

Solow, R. M. (1956). A contribution to the theory of economic growth. *Quarterly Journal of Economics, 70*(1), 65–94. https://doi.org/10.2307/1884513

Appendix

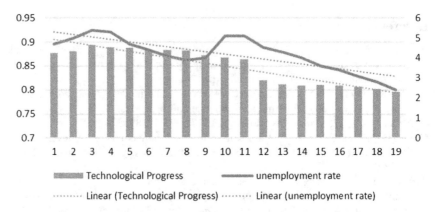

Fig. A1.1.   Technological Progress and Unemployment Rate in Japan.

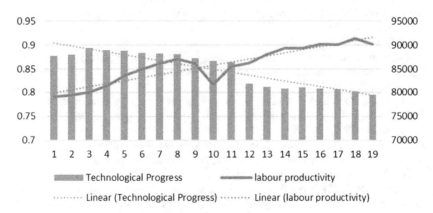

Fig. A1.2.   Technological Progress and Labour Productivity in Japan.

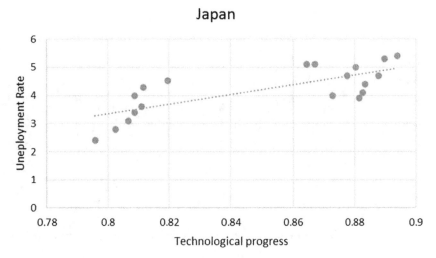

Fig. A1.3.   Regression Line – Technological Progress and
Unemployment Rate in Japan.

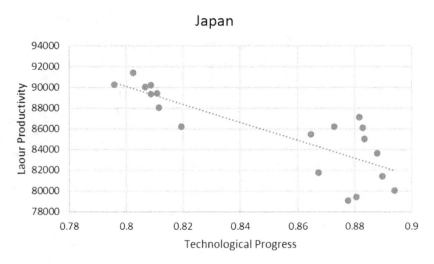

Fig. A1.4.   Regression Line – Technological Progress and Labour
Productivity in Japan.

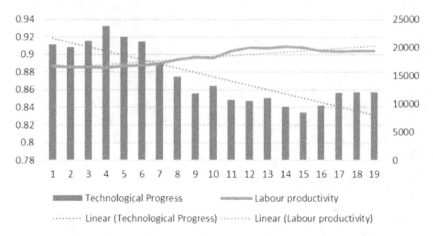

Fig. A1.5.   Technological Progress and Labour Productivity in Brazil.

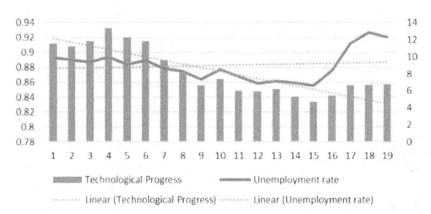

Fig. A1.6.   Technological Progress and Unemployment Rate in Brazil.

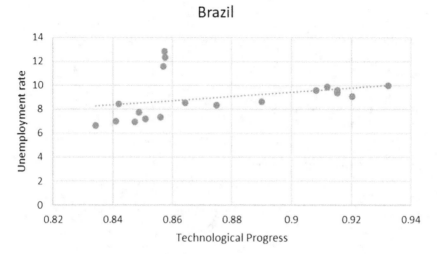

Fig. A1.7.   Regression Line – Technological Progress and
Unemployment Rate in Brazil.

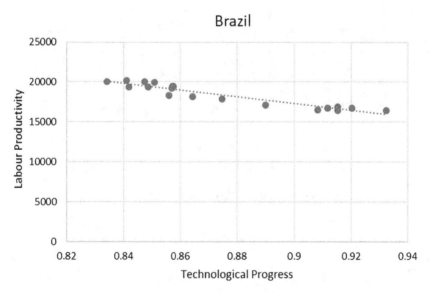

Fig. A1.8.   Regression Line – Technological Progress and Labour
Productivity in Brazil.

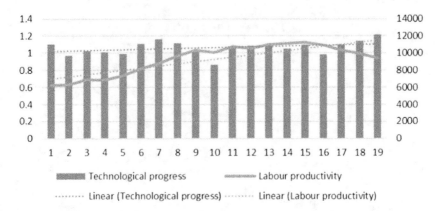

Fig. A1.9.   Technological Progress and Labour Productivity in Angola.

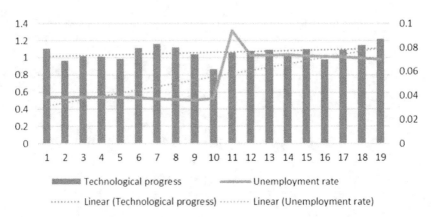

Fig. A1.10.   Technological Progress and Unemployment Rate in Angola.

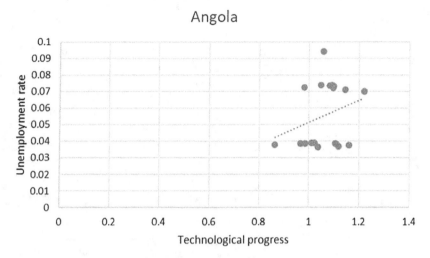

Fig. A1.11.   Regression Line – Technological Progress and
Unemployment Rate in Angola.

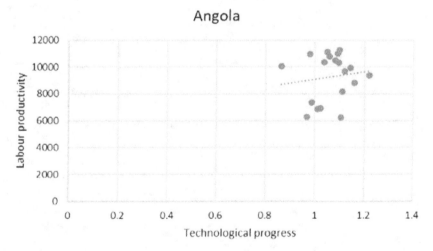

Fig. A1.12.   Regression Line – Technological Progress and Labour
Productivity in Angola.

Chapter 15

Intra-industry Trade in Tourism Services in Emerging Economies: A Study of India and BRICS Countries

Bharti Singh[a] *and Anusuya Biswas*[b]

[a]Institute of Management Technology Centre for Distance Learning, India
[b]Alliance University, India

Abstract

Since 1960s it has been realized that the bilateral trade at international level cannot be explained solely by the classical and neoclassical models of trade based on inter-industry trade. There is an existence of export and import within the same industry among the trading partners. Intra-industry trade (IIT) for products and product groups has been empirically observed by several studies. However, there is not much literature available on IIT in services. So also, from country perspective many studies are based on IIT for advanced countries. There is not much empirical evidence available for IIT among the emerging economies. The study aims to analyze the IIT in tourism services for five major emerging economies constituting BRICS – Brazil, Russia, India, China, and South Africa. The group constitutes 41% of world population with 24% of world GDP and 16% share in world trade. The study used both static and dynamic approaches to measure the IIT between India and other BRICS nations between 2018 and 2020. To empirically estimate the IIT, the study employs Grubel and Lloyd index and Brülhart index (MIIT). The study reveals that India had a very high level of intra-tourism trade with Brazil and South Africa. While with China and Russian Federation it was moderate. Results denote a correlation between the theory of international trade and tourism. There is two-way trade in BRICS tourism flows.

Keywords: Intra-industry trade (IIT); BRICS; intra-tourism; Grubel and Lloyd index; Brülhart index (MIIT)

Modeling Economic Growth in Contemporary India, 281–294
Copyright © 2024 Bharti Singh and Anusuya Biswas
Published under exclusive licence by Emerald Publishing Limited
doi:10.1108/978-1-80382-751-320241015

1. Introduction

Since 1960s numerous studies have concluded that, export and import occur within the same industry between the countries. This was contrary to the erstwhile thought that bilateral inter-industry trade is significant at international level, that is, flows of different products(s) and product groups dominate the trade. Intra-industry trade refers to simultaneous import and export within the same industry at a given time period. This intra-industry trade (IIT) is among the developed countries with similar factor endowments, income level and geographical conditions. The new models are based on imperfect competition, economies of scale and product differentiation in quality and/or variety (Helpman & Krugman, 1985; Krugman, 1979, 1981). Pre-1960s models were based on perfect competition and comparative advantage (Heckscher, 1919; Ohlin, 1933; Ricardo, 1817; Smith, 1776).

Horizontal and vertical differentiation are the two aspects of intra-industry trade. Horizontal IIT (HIIT) refers to economies of scale wherein products are differentiated based on variety. Like export and import of similar type of electronic items of similar price range for a product variety. On the other hand, Vertical IIT (VIIT) involves trade of products at industry level with vertical differentiation in the production process. Firms are located in countries that are trading partners and specialization is based on cost and quality at different levels of the production chain. Global supply chains are created to produce/assemble final product in one country by incorporating a component/intermediate product manufactured in another country. For instance, the battery produced in country A is exported to country B that assembles the mobile phone and exports it to country A.

The study aims to derive empirical evidence about the intra-tourism between the BRICS – Brazil, Russia, India, China, and South Africa. Static and dynamic analysis has been undertaken to find out the level of economic integration between Brazil, Russia, India, China, and South Africa.

The chapter is structured as follows: section 2 comprises literature review, section 3 specifies the research methodology, section 4 constitutes analysis of results, and section 5 provides conclusions followed by section 6 with limitations.

2. Literature Review

Numerous studies have been conducted on the IIT for a product(s) and product group(s). Likewise, studies pertain to IIT between a country and its trading partner(s), IIT among members of a regional group and IIT of a country with a regional group(s). For instance, studies on IIT in automobile manufacturing are for Austria (Turkcan, 2009), Portugal (Leitao et al., 2010), Romania (Razvan & Camelia, 2015) and between NAFTA countries (Montout et al., 2002). In a similar vein, studies on manufacturing include IIT between Australia and its trading partners (Sharma, 2002), Portugal and European Union (Faustino & Leitao, 2007), Iran and G-8 member countries (Nonejad & Haghjoo, 2012), and India with its trading partners (Agarwal & Betai, 2021). Literature on IIT in commodities and manufacturing is abundant. But studies on the IIT in services are scarce. One of the initial studies was on IIT in transportation services (Keirkowski, 1989). Another study was on IIT in international telephone services between US and foreign destinations (Tang, 1999, 2003). Studies undertaken on specific service(s) include IIT in insurance services for United States (Li et al., 2003), financial services for seven OECD countries (Moshirian et al., 2005) and for some European countries (Webster & Hardwick, 2005), financial and business services between China and Hong Kong (Zhao-yi, 2012), and air transport for United States (Blaskova & Skultety, 2015).

A study on IIT on services sector as per OECD classification was conducted for advanced economies (Lee & Llyod, 2002). The study is an empirical analysis of IIT between 20 OECD countries for nine services namely, transportation, travel, communication, insurance, personal, cultural and recreational, financial, and other. Lee and Lloyd concluded that intra-industry trade in services is uniformly high and stable overtime in 20 OECD countries for the nine service industries. It was observed that IIT was significant between Portugal and the trading partners Spain, USA, Italy, Greece, Turkey, and Canada. They also examined the effect on IIT when trade of goods and services is combined. It was found that trade imbalance decreased in 17 out of 20 countries. Studies on IIT in services sector are for South Africa and United States (Sichei et al., 2005), China and Australia (Hongbo, 2012; Qing-bo, 2013), and China and Japan (Wei, 2013).

Few studies have been conducted on IIT in tourism services exclusively. A study on tourism services comprising 44 countries was undertaken to ascertain IIT for both developing and developed countries (Webster et al., 2007). Data comprising trading partners of a country for the duration 2000–2003 were grouped to derive empirical evidence. It showed that Indonesia, Greece, and Mexico among developing countries; Canada, Netherlands and US among the advanced countries have highest values of IIT. This means that IIT is not specifically a feature of the high-income developed countries. It was found that countries specialize as exporters and importers of international tourism naturally. There is no need to create differentiation as required in the international trade in goods. Empirical evidence of relevance of the new trade models in comparison to the traditional trade theory was observed in IIT for USA and its trading partners (Hu et al., 2008). Significant IIT in tourism was observed for Portugal and trading partners for the period 2008–2009 (Leitao, 2011, 2012). It was found that there is an association between product differentiation, economies of scale and can be explained with monopolistic competition. Another study revealed that tourism flows between any pair among the 14 countries of European Union had high quantitative reciprocity rather than univocity (Nowak et al., 2012). The study investigated IIT on strict bilateral flows between two countries of the European Union for the period 2000–2004. It assessed horizontal and vertical IIT in tourism services and concluded that intra-tourism trade between the 14 European countries comprised of trade in services that are differentiated by level of quality. In other words, VIIT was dominant in the European countries. However, evidence showed that horizontal IIT was limited. Earlier studies had considered only horizontal IIT in tourism services and ignored vertical IIT (Lee & Llyod, 2002; Li et al., 2003). Another study separating HIIT and VIIT in tourism services concluded that differences in GDP per capita, income distribution overlap and geographic and cultural proximity are the most important factors for VIIT for European countries (Hanna et al., 2015). The study was based on strict bilateral flows of 23 European countries for the duration of 2000–2008. IIT in tourism services between 25 African countries was observed for the period 2001–2010 (Viljoen et al., 2019). The study focused on bilateral tourism flows between the 25 African countries. Cultural closeness, geographic proximity and the level of development of a destination country were found as the major factors for intra-African tourism. This points toward regional economic integration between the culturally similar, large and geographically closely located African countries. The researchers concluded that intra-African tourism may be for shopping reasons or other reasons rather than leisure as recognized for non-African international tourists. Medium intensity IIT was observed for Russia and its trading partners for the period 2002–2018 (Samarina & Wang, 2020). Prevalence of VIIT for tourism services was observed for Russia. The study concluded that international trade theories and tourism have a correlation. Increasing returns to scale, product differentiation and imperfect competition lead to trade in travel services. The study also concluded that travel services between Russia and Egypt were one-way due to comparative advantage in tourism industry. Evidence showed that geographical proximity and culture cannot be regarded as a major determinant of IIT as Poland and USA had high IIT with Russia compared to Finland and CIS countries. Notably, Finland has 11 border points with Russia and many CIS countries have similar culture. Though there is high IIT in merchandise trade between Russia and CIS countries, the intra-tourism trade was found to be low. Similarly, another study conducted for 20 European countries for the duration 2010–2016 denoted that the traditional approach is not applicable in tourism services (Nowak & Petit, 2020). Strict bilateral flows were considered by the study for three qualities of tourism services – high, middle and low. A summary of the studies is given in Table 15.1.

The study aims to analyze the IIT in tourism services for the BRICS (Brazil, Russia, India, China and South Africa). The acronym BRIC was put forward by O'Neill in 2001. Later, South Africa was included in the group in 2010. This group comprises five major emerging economies who have a potential of high economic growth. The group constitutes 41% of world population with 24% of world GDP and 16% share in world trade (https://brics2021.gov.in/about-brics).

Studies related to BRICS have been on relevance of trade gravity model among BRICS (Jin, 2010), effect of immigration on IIT between Portugal with BRICS as one country group (Faustino & Proenca, 2011), role of tourism in BRICS economies (Pop, 2014), trend in intra-BRICS trade (Chatterjee et al., 2014), role of the BRICS group in international development (Devare, 2015), commodity trade among BRICS in 14 sectors (Raghurampaturani, 2015), trade intensity among BRICS (Singh, 2016), factors affecting trade competitiveness (Kaur, 2018), competition and complementarity in the export products of BRICS (Wang et al., 2018), relationship between tourism and economic growth (Rasool et al., 2021), and the role of international tourism on foreign trade (Garidziari & Meissner, 2022).

Table 15.1. Summary of Studies on Intra-industry Trade in Tourism Services.

Title of the Study	Author(s), Publication Year	Country/Countries Included in Study	Time Period	Major Findings
Intra-industry trade in services	Lee and Llyod (2002)	20 OECD countries.	1992–1996	IIT is high between most countries and remained stable between 1992 and 1996.
Tourism and empirical applications of international trade theory: A multi-country analysis	Webster et al. (2007)	44 countries – developing and advanced	2000–2003	Indonesia, Greece, and Mexico among developing countries; Canada, Netherlands and US among the advanced countries have highest values of IIT.
Intra-industry trade in international tourism services	Hu et al. (2008)	USA and trading partners	1985–2005	The empirical results show application of new trade models, in contrast to the traditional trade theory.
Intra-industry trade in tourism services	Leitao (2011)	Portugal and trading partners	2008–2009	Significant IIT in tourism was observed for Portugal and trading partners with similar conditions
Intra-industry trade and vertical integration in tourism services	Nowak et al. (2012)	14 countries of EU	2000–2004	Tourism flows between EU and 14 countries is based on high quantitative reciprocity. Trade in vertically differentiated products dominates intra-tourism trade in all EU countries.

(Continued)

Table 15.1. (*Continued*)

Title of the Study	Author(s), Publication Year	Country/Countries Included in Study	Time Period	Major Findings
Intra-tourism trade, income distribution and tourism endowment: An econometric investigation	Hanna et al. (2015)	Strict bilateral flows of 23 European countries	2000–2008	VIIT was influenced by differences in GDP per capita, income-distribution overlap and geographic and cultural proximity.
Examining intra-African tourism: A trade theory perspective	Viljoen et al. (2019)	25 African countries	2001–2010	High IIT was observed between countries with cultural and geographic proximity and level of economic development
Russia's intra-industry trade in travel services: Specifics and intensity	Samarina and Wang (2020)	Russia and trading partners	2002–2018	There is a connection between international trade theories and tourism. There is prevalence of VIIT
A reconsideration of tourism specialization in Europe	Nowak and Petit (2020)	20 European countries	2010–2016	Comparative advantages and disadvantages denote serious differences with those obtained by the traditional approach.

Source: Compiled by author.

Studies on intra-industry trade between BRICS countries are for manufactures (Sandrey & Fundira, 2012), agricultural products (Xue-jia, 2013), ICT services (Rajesh, 2018), and manufactured products (Lohani, 2020). An empirical study on IIT in the automobile components industry of Portugal included BRIC as one trade group (Leitao et al., 2010).

2.1 Research Gap

Two major observations are made from literature reviews. Firstly, there are very few studies on measurement of the IIT in services. Specifically, on tourism services empirical evidence is miniscule. Secondly, most studies in tourism services have been conducted for the advanced countries. A handful of studies are for developing and emerging economies.

Studies related to IIT among BRICS are for agricultural products, manufactured goods, and ICT services. There is absence of study on IIT in tourism services between India with BRICS.

2.2 Research Objective

To empirically estimate the intra-industry trade in tourism services between India and other BRICS nations.

3. Research Methodology

Index of Balassa (1966) analyses the IIT between nations with the help of Revealed Comparative Advantage theory. Webster et al. (2007) and Sinclair and Stabler (1997) have also used the Revealed Comparative Advantage theory to measure IIT in European nations.

3.1 Data Source

The study used analytical and descriptive research methodology based on secondary data collected from India Tourism Statistics, Ministry of Tourism, Government of India. Due to lack of export values (receipts) and import values (expenses) of tourism services in India with other nations, the study considers the number of tourist flows. In merchandise trade flows are measured in monetary value, however there is absence of adequate data for bilateral tourism receipts. In fact, foreign tourist arrivals can be regarded as a good predictor for tourism export receipts (Culiuc, 2014). The volume of foreign tourist arrivals is considered to measure the export of tourism services by India to other BRICS nations and the volume of departures of Indians to other BRICS nations have been taken to measure the import of tourism services.

3.2 Empirical Measures of Intra-industry Trade

Grubel and Lloyd (1975) indicator is widely used for estimating intra-industry trade. The indicator was put forward by Balassa (1966) and Finger (1967) in their pioneering works. The Grubel and Lloyd ($GL^k_{i,j}$) indicator estimates the balance trade (i.e., export and import overlaps) between two nations – i and j in total trade of a specified industry k. The index is given in eq. (15.1):

$$GL^k_{i,j} = \frac{\left[\left(X^k_{i,j} + M^k_{i,j}\right) - \left|X^k_{i,j} - M^k_{i,j}\right|\right]}{X^k_{i,j} + M^k_{i,j}} = 1 - \frac{\left|X^k_{i,j} - M^k_{i,j}\right|}{X^k_{i,j} + M^k_{i,j}} \tag{15.1}$$

where $X^k_{i,j}$ and $M^k_{i,j}$ indicates exports of product or service k by i to j and imports of product or service k by i from j in a given year. This approach is called static approach as it measures the time period for a particular year. This method of IIT explains the segment of bilateral balance trade flows between the nations. The range of this indicator lies between 0 and 1. The index value 0 denotes exclusive inter-industry trade, i.e., industry k is either exported or imported by country i to country j in exchange for any other product belonging to different industry. Whereas index value 1 represents absolute intra-industry trade in industry k between the countries ($X^k_{i,j} = M^k_{i,j}$). If the $GL^k_{i,j} > 0.25$, it signifies very less intra-industry trade between nations, if it lies between $0.25 < GL^k_{i,j} > 0.50$, then it infers low level of IIT while if $GL^k_{i,j} > 0.75$, it denotes very high rate of intra-industry trade between the nations.

One of the biggest limitations of Grubel and Lloyd index is that it is a static approach as the index inadequately measures changes in trade of industry k over the periods between the trade partners (Hamilton & Kniest, 1991). On other hand, the GL index does not eliminate the scale effect that is, it does not allow comparison of industries of different size. In 1994, Brülhart gave a solution to this problem by introducing Marginal Intra-Industry Trade (MIIT) or Brülhart index as given in eq. (15.2):

$$\text{MIIT} = 1 - \frac{|\Delta X - \Delta M|}{|\Delta X| + |\Delta M|} \tag{15.2}$$

Brülhart transformed the Grubel and Lloyd index by capturing the changes over a period of time, i.e., the index is a dynamic approach. The Brülhart index also has values 0 and 1. Value 0 denotes marginal trade in the industry is absolute inter-industry trade while value 1 indicates marginal trade in the industry is exclusively intra-industry trade.

4. Results and Discussion

The study used both static and dynamic approaches to measure the intra-industry trade between India and other BRICS nations between 2018, 2019 and 2020. To empirically estimate the IIT the study employs both Grubel and Lloyd (1975) indicator and Brülhart (2008) index.

Table 15.2. India's Intra-industry Trade of Tourism Flows With Other
BRICS Nations – Static Approach.

Country	2018	2019	2020
Brazil	0.77	0.80	0.84
Russian Fed	0.49	0.53	0.20
China	0.57	0.56	0.68
South Africa	0.77	0.75	0.72

Source: Author's own estimation based on India Tourism Statistics, 2021, Ministry of Tourism, GoI data.

4.1 Intra-industry Trade Between India and BRICS: Grubel and Lloyd Index

Table 15.2 reflects India's intra-industry trade with other BRICS nations. The GL index clearly shows that in 2018, India had a very high level of intra-tourism trade with Brazil (0.77) and South Africa (0.77) while with China and Russian Federation, India had moderate level of intra-tourism trade. During 2019 India's intra-tourism trade increased with the other BRICS nations except China. It was very high with Brazil (0.80) followed by South Africa (0.75). In 2020, during the time of Covid pandemic, surprisingly India's intra-tourism trade further increased with Brazil (0.84) and China (0.68) and reduced marginally with South Africa (0.72). However, it declined phenomenally with Russia (0.20). It has been noticed that the tourism inflows (Foreign Tourists Arrivals) and outflows (Indian Departures) have drastically decreased due to the pandemic and consequent lockdown and closure of international flights. However, the inflows from Russia to India were still higher but Indian departures to Russia declined and therefore, IIT reduced with Russian Federation.

4.2 Intra-industry Trade Between India and BRICS: Brülhart Index or MIIT

To measure the change in IIT over the period of time, the study used Brülhart Index or Marginal Intra-Industry Trade index for the same period between 2018 and 2019; 2019 and 2020 and; 2018 and 2020. Results are shown in Table 15.3 where dX^k_1 and dM^k_1 denotes change in exports and imports of an industry k during 2018 and 2019; dX^k_2 and dM^k_2 infers change in exports and imports of an industry k during 2019 and 2020 and; dX^k_3 and dM^k_3 implies change in exports and imports of an industry k during 2018 and 2020 respectively.

The Brülhart index reveals that the tourism service trade flows of India with Brazil (1.0), Russian Federation (1.0), and South Africa (1.0) for the period 2018–2019 denote absolute intra-tourism trade, i.e., the balance of trade in industry k is equivalent to total trade in industry k. However, in the two consecutive periods – 2019–2020 and 2018–2020, the intra-industry trade with Brazil, Russia, and South Africa was very low. Interestingly, with China it was

Table 15.3. India's Intra-industry Trade of Tourism Flows With Other BRICS Nations: Dynamic Approach.

Year Country	2018–2019 $(\lvert dX^k_1 - dM^k_1\rvert)/$ $(\lvert dX^k_1\rvert + \lvert dM^k_1\rvert)$	2019–2020 $(\lvert dX^k_2 - dM^k_2\rvert)/$ $(\lvert dX^k_2\rvert + \lvert dM^k_2\rvert)$	2018–2020 $(\lvert dX^k_3 - dM^k_3\rvert)/$ $(\lvert dX^k_3\rvert + \lvert dM^k_3\rvert)$
Brazil	1.00	0.22	0.26
Russian Fed	1.00	0.30	0.36
China	0.47	0.48	0.48
South Africa	1.00	0.24	0.21

Source: Author's own estimation based on India Tourism Statistics, 2021, Ministry of Tourism, GoI data.

moderate during 2018–2019 (0.47), 2019–2020 (0.48), and 2018–2020 (0.48). The IIT with China was stable despite the global pandemic of 2020.

Brülhart index has been used to explain the problems of structural adjustment in the labor market, but the purview of this study is to gauge the changes in tourism flows internationally. Few studies made a comparison between GL index and Brülhart index (Leitao, 2011; Webster et al., 2007). Likewise, the present study also made a comparison between the two indices. The result reveals a different picture which is similar to the results of Leitao (2011). However, in both the indices China consistently improved its IIT with India.

5. Conclusion

The aim of the study is to examine the intra-industry trade between India and other emerging nations in tourism service flows. Intra-industry trade helps the country to identify the areas to innovate or improve the quality of the products/ services. It also gives the country an opportunity to gain from the economies of scale and product differentiation. The present study used both Grubel and Lloyd (GL) indicator (static approach) and, Brülhart index (dynamic approach) to analyze the intra-tourism trade between India and other BRICS nations. The GL index reveals that the intra-tourism trade between India and Brazil, and India with South Africa were very high while with China and Russia it was moderate during 2018–2020.

To measure the dynamic IIT, the study used Marginal Intra Industry Trade index developed by Brülhart. Empirical evidence denotes that MIIT of India with Brazil, Russia, and South Africa was absolute during 2018–2019 but it decreased drastically during 2019–2020 and 2018–2020. Conversely, MIIT with China remained almost same during the periods.

However, both the indices reflect high intra-tourism trade with Brazil and South Africa during 2018–2019. The result varies for China and Russia over the periods. The empirical evidence indicates that geographical proximity is not a significant factor for economic integration since IIT with Brazil and South Africa is higher compared to China. In future research, the study can be conducted to identify the determinants of IIT in tourism services with reference to India.

6. Limitations

The present study is mainly focused on measuring the intra-tourism trade between India and other BRICS nations using both static and dynamic approach. Horizontal and vertical IIT could not be measured due to non-availability of data on foreign tourism receipts and expenses between India and BRICS countries. In future, the study will be extended to find the determinants of IIT in tourism services.

References

Agarwal, M., & Betai, N. (2021). *Intra-industry trade in manufactured goods: A case of India*. Working papers 21/348. National Institute of Public Finance and Policy.

Balassa, B. (1966). Tariff reductions and trade in manufactures among industrial countries. *The American Economic Review, 56*(3).

Blaskova, M., & Skultety, F. (2015). US intra-industry trade in air transport services: Measurement and results. *Transport Problems, 10*(2).

Brülhart, M. (2008). *An account of global intra-industry trade (IIT), 1962-2006*. Research paper series "Globalisation, Productivity and Technology". University of Nottingham.

Chatterjee, B., Jena, P. C., & Singh, S. (2014). *Intra-BRICS and its implications for India, emerging markets*. Discussion Paper. CUTS International.

Culiuc, A. (2014). *Determinants of international tourism*. Working paper/14/82. IMF.

Devare, S. (2015). *India and BRICS*. SSRN. https://ssrn.com/abstract=2675252

Faustino, H. C., & Leitao, N. C. (2007). Intra-industry trade: A static and dynamic panel data analysis. *International Advances in Economic Research, 13*(3).

Faustino, H., & Proenca, N. (2011). *Effects of immigration on intra-industry trade: A logit analysis*. WP19/2011/DE/SOCUS/CEMAPARE. School of Economics and Management, University of Lisbon.

Finger, J. M. (1967). *Trade overlap and the theory of international specialisation: A statistical study of the Hecksher Ohlin and Linder theories as alternative hypotheses*. Ph.D. Thesis. University of North Carolina.

Garidziari, R., & Meissner, R. (2022). The role of international tourism on foreign trade in the BRICS nations. *Cogent Social Sciences, 8*, 1.

Grubel, H. G., & Lloyd, P. J. (1975). *IIT-The theory and measurement of international trade in differentiated products*. Macmillan Press.

Hamilton, C., & Kniest, P. (1991). Trade liberalization, structural adjustment and intra-industry trade. *Weltwirtschaftliches Archive, 127*(2).

Hanna, J., Levi, L., & Petit, S. (2015). Intra-tourism trade, income distribution and tourism endowment: An econometric investigation. *Applied Economics, 47*(21).

Heckscher, E. (1919). The effect of foreign trade on the distribution of income. *Ekonomisk Tidskrift, 21*, 497–512.

Helpman, E., & Krugman, P. J. (1985). *Market structure and foreign trade.* MIT Press.

Hongbo, T. (2012). Research on Sino-Australian intra-industry trade in services and its influencing factors: Based on the grey relevant analysis. *Science of Science and Management of S. & T.* https://api.semanticscholar.org/CorpusID:156771614

Hu, Y., Han, L., & Li, D. (2008). Intra-industry trade in international tourism services. In *Fourth international conference on wireless communications, networking and mobile computing*, Dalian, China, pp. 1–4. https://doi.org/10.1109/WiCom. 2008.2070. https://ieeexplore.ieee.org/document/4680259

Jin, W. (2010). Research on influence factors of intra-industry trade in BRICs. *Journal of Nanchang Institute of Technology.* https://api.semanticscholar.org/CorpusID: 156929078

Kaur, A. (2018). Factors affecting trade competitiveness of BRICS countries. *Indian Journal of Economics and Development, 6*(8).

Keirkowski, H. (Ed.). (1989). *Intra-industry trade in transportation services, intra-industry trade.* Palgrave Macmillan.

Krugman, P. R. (1979). Increasing returns, monopolistic competition and international trade. *Journal of International Economics, 9*(4).

Krugman, P. R. (1981). Intra-industry specialization and the gains from trade. *Journal of Political Economy, 89*(5).

Lee, H. H., & Llyod, P. J. (2002). *"Intra-industry trade in services" in frontiers of research in intra-industry trade.* Palgrave Macmillan Ltd.

Leitao, N. C. (2011). Intra-industry trade in tourism services. *Theoretical and Applied Economics, XVIII*(6(559)).

Leitao, N. C. (2012). *The determinants of intra-industry trade in the tourism services.* ESGTS, Polytechnic Institute of Santarém and CEFAGE-University of Évora, Portugal. https://mpra.ub.uni-muenchen.de/37444/1/Determinants_of_Intra-Industry_Trade_in_the_tourism_services.pdf

Leitao, N. C., Faustino, H. C., & Yoshida, Y. (2010). Fragmentation, vertical intra-industry trade and automobile components. *Economics Bulletin, 30*(2).

Li, D., Moshirian, F., & Sim, A. B. (2003). The determinants of intra-industry trade in insurance services. *The Journal of Risk and Insurance, 70*(2), 269–287.

Lohani, K. K. (2020, Winter). Static and dynamic analysis of intra-industry trade of BRICS countries. *Theoretical and Applied Economics, XXVII*(4).

Montout, S., Mucchielli, J.-L., & Zignago, S. (2002). Regionalization and intra-industry trade an analysis of automobile industry trade in NAFTA. *Region et developpmenet, 16.*

Moshirian, F., Li, D., & Sim, A. (2005). Intra-industry trade in financial Services. *Journal of International Money and Finance, 24*(7).

Nonejad M., & Haghjoo, M. (2012). Measuring goods quality in Iran's intra-industry trade with G-8 member states. *Journal of Economics and Behavioral Studies, 4*(6).

Nowak, J. J., & Petit, S. (2020). A reconsideration of tourism specialisation in Europe. *Tourism Economics, 27*(8), 1833–1838. https://www.researchgate.net/publication/342959926_A_reconsideration_of_tourism_specialization_in_Europe

Nowak, J. J., Petit, S., & Sahli, M. (2012). Intra-industry trade and vertical integration in tourism services. *Tourism Economics, 18*(6).

Ohlin, B. (1933). Inter-regional and international trade. In *Harvard economic studies* (Vol. XXXIX). Harvard University Press.

Pop, I. (2014). The role of tourism in the economies of BRICS countries. *Knowledge Horizons, 6*(2).

Qing-bo, H. (2013). Research on Sino-Australian intra-industry trade in services and influencing factors: Based on trade gravity model. *Prices Monthly*. https://api.semanticscholar.org/CorpusID:167514961

Raghurampaturani, R. (2015). Revealed comparative advantage and competitiveness: A study on BRICS. *Arabian Journal of Business and Management Review, 5*(5), 1–7. https://doi.org/10.4172/2223-5833.1000152. https://www.researchgate.net/publication/288737267_Revealed_Comparative_Advantage_A_Study_on_BRICS

Rajesh, P. (2018). Intra-industry trade in ICT services in BRIC countries (2005–2017). *International Journal of Financial Management and Economics, 1*(1).

Rasool, H., Maqbool, S., & Tarique, M. (2021). The relationship between tourism and economic growth among BRICS countries: A panel cointegration analysis. *Future Business Journal, 7*(1), 1.

Razvan, S. M., & Camelia, S. (2015). Analysis of the intra-industry trade for the motor vehicle parts and accessories from Romania. *Procedia Economics and Finance, 22*.

Ricardo, D. (1817). *The principles of political economy and taxation.* John Murray.

Samarina, A. S., & Wang, S. (2020). Russia's intra-industry trade in travel services: Specifics and intensity. https://elibrary.ru/item.asp?id=44491663

Sandrey, R., & Fundira, T. (2012). *Intra-industry trade: An examination of South Africa and the BRICS.* The Trade Law Centre NPC (tralac) Working Paper no. S12WP02/2012. https://www.tralac.org/publications/article/4216-intra-industry-trade-an-examination-of-south-africa-and-the-brics.html

Sharma, K. (2002). The pattern and determinants of intra-industry trade in Australian manufacturing. *The Australian Economic Review, 33*(3).

Sichei, M., Harmse, C., & Kanfer, F. (2005). Determinants of South Africa-US intra-industry trade in services. *South African Journal of Economics, 75*(3).

Sinclair, M. T., & Stabler, M. (1997). *The economics of tourism.* Routledge.

Singh, K. (2016). Intra-BRICS trade intensity: An analytical study. *IOSR Journal of Humanities and Social Sciences, 21*(6), 8.

Smith, A. (1776). *An inquiry into the nature and causes of the wealth of nations.* W. Strahan and T. Cadell.

Tang, L. (1999). *Intra-industry trade in services: A case study of international telephone industry, Mimeo.* Drexel University.

Tang, L. (2003). The determinants of international telephone traffic imbalances. *Information Economics and Policy, 15*.

Turkcan, K. (2009). *Vertical intra-industry trade: An empirical examination of Austria's auto-part industry.* FIW working paper series No. 30. Research Centre International Economics, Vienna. https://www.researchgate.net/publication/241769297_Vertical_Intra-Industry_Trade_An_Empirical_Examination_of_the_Austria's_Auto-Parts_Industry

Viljoen, A. H., Saayman, A., & Saayman, M. (2019). Examining intra-African tourism: A trade theory perspective. *South African Journal of Economic and Management Sciences, 22*(1).

Wang, P., Zhao, Y., & Chu, L. (2018). Analysis of competition and complementarity in the BRICS export products. *Advances in Economics, Business and Management Research (AEBMR), 60*.

Webster, A., Fletcher, J., Hardwick, P., & Morakabati, Y. (2007). Tourism and empirical applications of international trade theory: A multi-country analysis. *Tourism Economics, 13*(4).

Webster, A., & Hardwick, P. (2005). International trade in financial services. *Service Industries Journal, 25*(6).

Wei, G. (2013). An analysis of influence factors of service intra-industry trade between China and Japan. *Commercial Research.* https://api.semanticscholar.org/CorpusID:156895660

Xue-jia, L. (2013). Intra-industry trade of agricultural products between China and other BRICS and its influencing factors. *Economics, Agricultural and Food Sciences.* https://api.semanticscholar.org/CorpusID:156945526

Zhao-yi, W. (2012). The empirical study on intra-industry trade in services between Chinese Mainland and Hong Kong. *Journal of Hunan University of Commerce.* https://api.semanticscholar.org/CorpusID:167243596

Chapter 16

Temporal Trends and Determinants of Household Cooking Fuel Choices in India: A Comprehensive Analysis

Namrata Barik and Puja Padhi

Indian Institute of Technology Bombay, India

Abstract

This study examines the temporal trends and determinants of household cooking fuel choices in India. Access to affordable, reliable, clean cooking fuels is crucial for improving household health and mitigating environmental issues. However, a significant portion of the population in developing countries, including India, still relies on traditional solid biomass fuels, leading to adverse health impacts. Using data from India Human Development Survey conducted in 2005 and 2012, this research analyzes changes in fuel choices. It explores the influence of socio-demographic characteristics, education, and accessibility on these choices over time. The findings reveal a gradual transition toward mixed fuel usage but a limited reduction in the use of dirty fuels, indicating the challenges in achieving cleaner cooking practices. Education is a crucial driver of fuel choices, highlighting the need for targeted educational campaigns. Age and household size also play significant roles, with older household heads and larger households exhibiting different fuel preferences. The availability and cost of firewood and kerosene influence fuel choices. The study also suggests developing educational campaigns, improving the availability and affordability of clean cooking fuels, and tailored strategies for larger households. These findings provide guidance for policymakers in promoting the adoption of cleaner cooking fuels and improving household air quality and public health in India.

Keywords: Cooking fuel choices; clean cooking fuels; traditional fuels; mixed fuel usage; transition; households; affordability

Modeling Economic Growth in Contemporary India, 295–320
Copyright © 2024 Namrata Barik and Puja Padhi
Published under exclusive licence by Emerald Publishing Limited
doi:10.1108/978-1-80382-751-320241016

1. Introduction

Ensuring access to affordable, reliable, and clean sources of cooking fuel is essential for improving household health, mitigating environmental pollution, and promoting sustainable development goals (IEA, 2017). The Sustainable Development Goal 7 (SDG 7) seeks to "ensure access to affordable, reliable, sustainable and modern energy for all." The international energy agency (IEA) estimated that around 2.5 billion people depended on traditional solid biomass in 2016; at the current rate of progress, 2.3 billion people will not have clean cooking solutions by 2030 (IEA, 2017). It implies that achieving universal access to the affordable and clean energy (SDG 7) is out of reach (Daniel, 2020). The reliance on traditional solid fuels for cooking in developing countries harms the environment and human health. However, about 40%, particularly in Asia and sub-Saharan Africa, relies on traditional solid biomass fuels such as firewood and charcoal for cooking (IEA et al., 2019). These fuels cause household air pollution, responsible for an estimated 3.8 million premature deaths in 2016 (WHO, 2018).

The households cooking fuel choice also impacts living conditions in rural and urban areas, especially for women and children. The *"energy-poor,"* especially women and marginal communities, suffer the health costs of inefficient combustion of solid fuels in imperfectly ventilated buildings. Various socio-economic factors such as availability or easy access, fuel price, education, awareness, culture or lifestyle influence the cooking fuel choice of households. According to the World Health Organization (WHO), "Clean fuels are fuels with emissions that result in a CO exposure level of less than 7 mg/m^3 and a PM 2.5 level of less than 10 μg/m^3 over a prolonged period" (Price et al., 2021; WHO, 2014). Considering these measures, the clean energy fuels are gas and electricity, ethanol, and biogas. Improving access to modern (clean) energy in can contribute immensely to welfare by decreasing the burden of fuel collection and cooking, saving their time for participation in education and income-generating activities (Heltberg, 2005). Availability and accessibility of these clean cooking fuels are essential to reduce health impact and improve women's productivity.

The economic growth of low- and middle-income countries approaching industrialization goes hand in hand with improved access energy. But the reality is self-collected biomass remains the primary cooking fuel in rural areas, and urban households are more likely to incur fuel expenditures in developing countries. Hence, it is essential to analyze the changes in domestic cooking fuel preferences over an extended period and gain insights into the factors that hinder the widespread adoption of cleaner fuels over Solid Biomass Fuel (SBF) in developing nations. The choice of household cooking fuels in India is crucial in determining the health, environmental, and socio-economic outcomes for millions nationwide. As India undergoes rapid socio-economic transformation, it is essential to comprehensively examine the temporal trends in cooking fuel preferences and understand the various determinants that influence these choices over time.

2. Literature Review

Certain factors deprive households of opting for clean cooking fuel. Further, they bear the economic consequences on education, health, and livelihood. The household fuel transition from dirty to modern fuels is gaining more research attention in developing countries. Though there are numerous studies on household fuel transition studies that examine the driving factors of transition are limited. Heltberg (2004) studied household fuel use and switching behavior in eight diverse developing countries and found that fuel switching is quite advanced in the urban areas of the surveyed countries, except Ghana. However, modern fuels play a relatively modest role in rural areas and are often confined to the top income brackets. Viswanathan and Kavi Kumar's (2005) study shows a wide disparity in expenditure share of "clean" and "dirty" fuels in total cooking fuel consumption between rural and urban households across states using household-level data from National Sample Surveys (NSS) from 1983 to 2000. Urban households have higher chances of switching to clean energy, whereas poor rural households continue with dirty fuel choices due to low education and income levels (Rahut et al., 2020). With rural–urban disparities, various studies reveal that affordability plays a significant role in fuel choices (Liao et al., 2021; Pandey & Chaubal, 2011; Rahut et al., 2017). Pandey and Chaubal (2011), in their study, have analyzed the 61st round of the National Sample Survey (NSS) and found that women between 10 and 50 years of Age with Education and regular salary have a positive and significant impact on the probability of using clean cooking fuel against those who belong to below poverty line, scheduled caste categories with big family size and low landholding. However, socio-demographic and cultural factors affect households' fuel choices. Liao et al. (2021) examined household energy transitions in Low- & Middle-Income Countries (L&MIC) and found that higher levels of household education, incomes, asset holdings, and the presence of credit and subsidy programs are associated with clean energy adoption with variation in energy transition pathways across L&MIC. The study by Rahut et al. (2020) analyses different types of energy used for cooking among urban households in Pakistan. It shows that families with higher education and income mainly use clean energy. Rahut et al. (2014), in their study, attempt to identify and analyze the factors that are likely to influence household decisions of choosing a particular energy source shows that a household's choice of cleaner fuels depends on income, Age, Education, and gender of head of the family along with access to electricity. The range of literature on the gender aspect of households cooking fuel upholds that energy access also has severe gender implications, including women's time and their health. The female-headed households are more likely to choose cleaner fuels. Above all, a clean and cost-effective energy source within the proximity is essential in adopting clean energy (Rahut et al., 2014).

3. Scope and Significance of the Study

For several reasons, understanding how determinants have influenced household cooking fuel choices over time is essential. Firstly, it provides insights into the effectiveness of past interventions and policies promoting clean cooking fuels. By analyzing temporal trends, we can assess whether previous initiatives have led to significant changes in fuel preferences and identify gaps or areas for improvement. This knowledge is crucial for refining existing strategies and designing targeted interventions to drive a more sustainable transition from traditional to modern cooking fuels. Secondly, studying temporal trends in determinants and fuel choices helps us understand the dynamics and patterns of household behavior. By examining changes in socio-economic characteristics, education levels, income, accessibility, and other factors over time, we can identify how these variables have influenced fuel preferences. This understanding allows us to develop a more nuanced understanding of the underlying drivers and barriers to adopting cleaner cooking fuels. Thirdly, analyzing temporal trends provides valuable insights for future planning and policymaking. Policymakers can prioritize interventions and allocate resources more effectively by identifying the factors that have significantly impacted fuel choices over time. It enables them to anticipate and respond to emerging trends and adapt strategies accordingly. Furthermore, studying the temporal evolution of determinants and fuel choices helps us assess the long-term sustainability of clean cooking fuel adoption. By tracking changes over time, we can evaluate whether transitions to cleaner fuels are durable or whether households revert to traditional options. This knowledge is essential for ensuring clean energy initiatives' long-term success and impact.

4. Objectives of the Study

This study aims to comprehensively examine the temporal trends in household cooking fuel choices in India and investigate the intricate interplay between various determinants and these choices over time. By analyzing a balanced panel dataset comprising two waves of data, this research seeks to understand the evolving patterns and dynamics of fuel preferences within Indian households.

- The primary objective is to unravel the temporal trends in cooking fuel choices, shedding light on how these choices have evolved over the study period. By employing statistical techniques and data visualization methods, this study will provide a detailed analysis of the changes in fuel preferences, including shifts in the usage of traditional fuels and the adoption of cleaner and more sustainable cooking fuels.
- The other objective is to explore the influence of various determinants on cooking fuel choices over time. Socio-demographic characteristics, human capital, assets/wealth, and accessibility, such as income levels, education, household composition, and urbanization, are expected to play crucial roles in shaping fuel preferences. By examining the relationship between these determinants and cooking fuel choices across different time points, this study assesses these factors changing influence and relative significance over the years. Understanding the impact of determinants on fuel choices over time is essential to develop effective strategies and interventions. By identifying the key drivers of

changes in fuel preferences, this study can inform the design and implementation of targeted policies to promote the adoption of cleaner cooking fuels.

5. Data

We use longitudinal data from two waves of large-scale India Human Development Survey (IHDS) collected in 2004–2005 and 2011–2012 (hereafter, 2005 and 2012, respectively). The IHDS data are nationally representative and organized jointly by the National Council of Applied Economic Research at Delhi and the University of Maryland (Desai & Vanneman, 2005, 2015). The surveys were conducted through two 1-hour interviews with the whole household or the head of the household. The total number of households surveyed in IHDS I (2005) is 41,544 households comprising 26,734 rural and 14,820 urban households, whereas IHDS II (2012) surveyed 42,152 households comprising 27,579 rural and 14,573 urban. In IHDS I, the rural sample was drawn using stratified random sampling. It contained 13,900 rural households interviewed in the 1993–1994 HDPI Survey and 27,654 new households. The urban sample was a stratified sample of towns and cities within states or groups of states selected by probability proportional to population (PPP).

Out of 593 districts in India in 2001, 384 were included in IHDS I, and the sample is spread across 1,503 villages and 971 urban blocks; on the other hand, IHDS II reinterviewed 85% of original households of IHDS-1, split households residing within the village, and an additional sample of 2,134 households. In IHDS II, households are spread across 33 states and union territories, excluding the Andaman Isles and Lakshadweep, 384 districts, 1,420 villages, and 1,042 urban blocks. IHDS-II covered 85% of the original households, with those households not surveyed the second time either having been unreachable, having moved, or having been struck by a natural disaster (Desai & Vanneman, 2015). To control for the effect of changes in the built environment and constitution of the household due to a move or split, we included only instances where the original household was re-contacted. Thus 6,911 households from the IHDS-I that could not be re-contacted were excluded, as well as the 1,721 households which had split into multiple different households. Out of these 42,153 households, we use only those surveyed in both rounds, i.e., 40,018 households. Thus, final data consist of a balanced panel of 40,013 households. For all Indian rural samples, 28,222 households for 2004–2005 and 27,303 for 2011–2012 are used. All Indian urban sample of 11,791 households for 2004–2005 and 12,710 households for 2011–2012 is used.

The IHDS dataset is a comprehensive survey that covers various topics, including fuel usage, household income from diverse sources, consumption patterns, employment status, and indicators of gender dynamics. It encompasses questions related to both agricultural and non-agricultural self-employment, economic activities of households, the number of contributing members, as well as information on caste, religion, and other socio-economic and demographic characteristics of both households and individuals. The interviews included administering an income/employment questionnaire (typically by the male head of the household) and a household energy/gender/health questionnaire (responded to by an ever-married woman).

Unlike the NSS survey that asks for the primary cooking fuel, IHDS contains a detailed energy module where respondents were asked detailed questions about their use of all energy sources. Khandker et al. (2012) and Ahmad and De Oliveira (2015) pointed out that the energy-related questions in the IHDS are more comprehensive than those in comparable studies, including the Living Standards Measurement Studies coordinated by the World Bank and the NSS Surveys of Consumer Expenditure. The IHDS dataset is disaggregated by housing type and various demographic features such as gender, religion, caste, occupation, and Education (Desai & Vanneman, 2015; Desai et al., 2010).

Additionally, the IHDS includes some information on time spent carrying out certain energy-related practices in the household, including time spent watching television, time spent collecting firewood, and hours of stove usage. All weightings used were the "SWeights" specified for the households in the IHDS-I, and values for relatively unchanging variables (e.g., Caste and Religion) were taken from the IHDS II. The advantage of panel data is that it relaxes the assumption multiple observations within a choice are independent (Alem et al., 2016).

5.1 Variable Description

The primary focus of our study is to examine fuel choices, which include a combination of dirty, clean, and mixed fuels. Our dataset encompasses six different fuel options for cooking: firewood, dung, crop residuals, coal/charcoal, kerosene, and LPG. The IHDS questionnaire specifically lists each fuel type and asks respondents whether their household utilizes that particular fuel for cooking purposes. Notably, the questionnaire does not include electricity as a fuel option. However, based on the 2011 Census data, it is worth mentioning that only a very small percentage of households in India (0.10%) reported electricity as their primary cooking fuel, with even lower percentages in rural (0.07%) and urban (0.15%) areas. Following the literature, we treat firewood, dung, crop residuals, kerosene, and coal/charcoal as dirty fuels. In contrast, LPG is treated as a clean fuel, and a combination of dirty and clean fuels is considered mixed fuel. So our outcome variable, fuel choice, comprises three types of fuel use (Table 16.1).

6. Determinants of Household Cooking Fuel Choice

Various scholars have classified different determinants under four broad categories.

- Socio-Demographic Characteristics
- Human Capital
- Assets/Wealth
- Accessibility

Table 16.1. Variable Description.

Variables	Description	Expected Impact on LPG Adoption
Fuel Choices		
Only clean fuel	= 1 for households using only LPG as cooking fuel	
Mixed fuel	= 2 for households using both clean fuel and dirty fuel as cooking fuel	
Only dirty fuel	= 3 for households using firewood, animal dung, agricultural crop, straw/ shrub/grass, coal/lignite, or charcoal as cooking fuel	
Household Characteristics		
Head's years of education	It is measured in the years of schooling of the household head. It takes values 0, 1, 2, 3, 4, and 5 for no formal schooling, up to 5th, 10th, and 12th standard, graduate, and above, respectively.	Positive
Household size	Number of household members	Positive/Negative
Income	Household's income from all source	Positive/Negative
Household chulha types	Dummy = 1 for households using improved chulha for cooking and 0 if traditional chulha	Positive
Age of the household head	Age of the household head in years.	Negative
Gender	Dummy = 1 for females and 0 for male	Positive
Locality	Dummy = 0 if the household belongs to rural and 1 if the household belongs to urban.	Positive
Fuel Prices		
Log price of firewood	Household's expenditure for the use of firewood (rupees)	Negative
Log price of kerosene	Household's expenditure for the use of kerosene (rupees)	Negative
Log price of LPG	Household's expenditure for the use of LPG (rupees)	Positive

While the energy ladder focuses on the relationship between wealth and fuel, most of the literature additionally examines the impact of other household demographics, Human Capital, Wealth/Assets, and Accessibility. This section discusses the influence of the abovementioned factors on fuel transition over the period.

Socio-Demographic characteristics are the composition of Age of the household head, Gender of the head, Number of adult females, Number of adult males, Number of children, Number of old >65 years, Scheduled Caste/Tribes (SC/ST), Other Backward Class (OBC), Religion, Household size, Fuel prices like firewood price, coal price, dung price, kerosene price, lifestyle. Human capital consists of the education of the household head, the education of adults, the education of adult males, the education of adult females, education of the oldest member. Remoteness and access to the market also influence the household decision to choose cooking fuel-fuelwood versus gas. Contribution of the Accessibility and availability of fuels is necessary to explain household fuel use.

Demographic Characteristics are the composition of the Age of the household head, Gender of the head, Number of adult females, Number of adult males, Number of children, Number of old >65 years, Scheduled Caste/Tribes (SC/ST), Other Backward Class (OBC), Religion, Household size, Fuel prices like firewood price, coal price, dung price, kerosene price, lifestyle.

Access to clean fuels varies globally, and significant differences, specifically between rural and urban populations, were reported by WHO (2013). Figure 16.1 indicates a significant increase in mixed fuel use in both rural and urban India over the studied period. In rural areas, there has been a growth of 7% in mixed fuel use, while in urban areas, the growth is even higher at 9%. This trend suggests that while households in India are transitioning from using a single cooking fuel to utilizing multiple fuel sources for their cooking needs, the reduction in the use of dirty fuels has been relatively small. The percentage of households using dirty fuels has decreased from 78% to 69%, indicating a reduction of only 9%.

Conversely, there has been a slight increase in the adoption of clean fuels, rising from 3% to 5%. These findings underscore the intricate nature of fuel

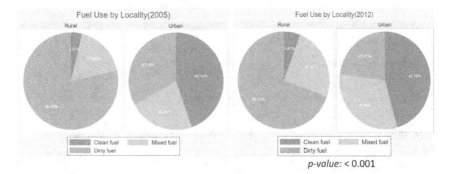

Fig. 16.1.   Fuel Use by Locality. *Source*: Author's calculation.

preferences for cooking, particularly the significant disparities observed between urban and rural areas. In developing countries, rural households, including those in India, heavily rely on solid biomass fuels (SBFs) such as firewood, cow dung cakes, crop residues, and twigs for cooking and heating purposes. The World Health Organization (WHO) estimates that over 90% of rural households in developing countries depend on SBFs (Kituyi, 2004; Masera et al., 2000; Rehfuess & World Health Organization, 2006; Sidhu et al., 2017). Specifically, in India, the rural domestic sector utilizes around 1.2–2.1 kg of biomass per capita per day (Smith, 2017).

6.1 Fuel Use by Educational Level of the Household Head

There is a clear correlation between rural and urban households' education levels and fuel consumption patterns in 2005 and 2012. In rural areas, as education levels increase, the percentage of dirty fuel consumption decreases, reaching its highest point (95% in 2005 and 91% in 2012) in households with no education. Similarly, the percentage of clean fuel consumption increases up to the bachelor's level. A similar trend is observed in urban areas, with higher education levels associated with lower dirty fuel consumption and higher clean fuel consumption. The highest percentage of clean fuel consumption (70% in 2005 and 72% in 2012) is observed among households with a bachelor's education. This analysis emphasizes the role of education in promoting clean fuel adoption and reducing reliance on dirty fuels.

It suggests that increasing education levels can contribute to a shift toward cleaner cooking fuels in both rural and urban. The results confirm previous studies. Baiyegunhi and Hassan (2014) and Gupta and Köhlin (2006) observe that higher education level promotes households to move away from firewood dependence in the direction of using kerosene and LPG in India and Nigeria. In Ethiopia, Gebreegziabher et al. (2012) found that as the education level increases, households are less likely to choose wood and more likely to prefer electricity. Baland et al. (2013) find that education and fuelwood collection have an association in Nepal. Along with time and opportunity costs, taste and education are dominant determinants of fuel switching (Fig. 16.2).

The analysis shows that as the age of the household head increases in rural households (Fig. 16.3), there is a decrease in the percentage of dirty fuel consumption and an increase in the percentage of mixed and clean fuel consumption. The lowest percentage of dirty fuel users is observed for heads above 80 (59.02% in 2005, 69.06% in 2012). The percentage of mixed fuel users is lowest for heads below 15 in both years. The percentage of clean fuel users increases with the age of the head in rural households, with the lowest percentage observed for heads below 15 in 2005 and heads 15 to 30 in 2012. A similar trend is observed in urban households. Overall, the analysis indicates a correlation between the age of the household head and fuel consumption patterns, with older heads more likely to use clean fuels and less likely to use dirty fuels.

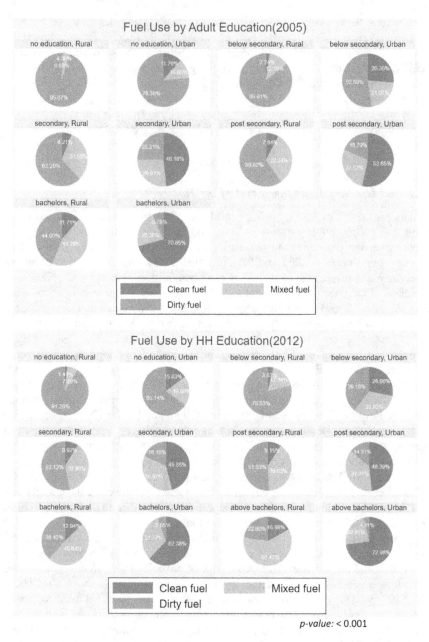

Fig. 16.2.   Fuel Use and Education. *Source*: Authors' Calculation.

Fuel use by households based on Age (2005)

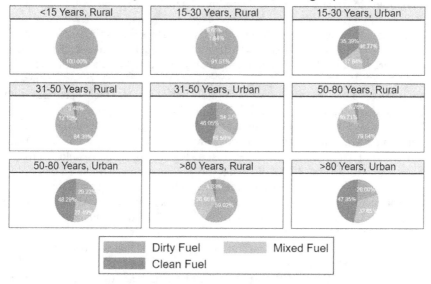

Fuel use by households based on Age (2012)

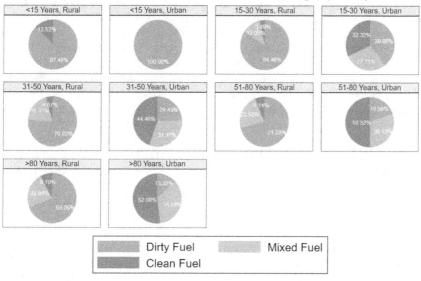

p-value: < 0.001

Fig. 16.3.   Fuel Use Based on the Age of the Household Head.
Source: Authors' Calculation.

Baiyegunhi and Hassan (2014) detect that household heads age induces rural households to deviate toward fuelwood in Nigeria. The reason could be that the older the household head is, the more likely he/she has built her taste around available and affordable fuelwood rather than necessarily efficient fuels. Such desires for traditional fuels support the notion that older people tend to perpetuate more traditional fuel-related habits than young people. Other authors Muller and Yan (2018) find that age and modern fuels preference has a positive association because the use of firewood initially increases but then decreases with household consumption. Firewood seems to be a normal good at low-income levels but an inferior good at higher-income levels (there is an inverse-U relationship between income and wood consumption). Gupta and Köhlin (2006) and Farsi et al. (2007) contribute evidence showing that older household heads are more likely to opt for LNG (light natural gas) to wood in Indian households. These results suggest a life cycle effect whereby young people facing liquidity constraints resort to cheaper fuels while older people can afford cleaner fuels more easily. In addition, Abebaw (2007), An et al. (2002), and Israel (2002) claim that age does not affect fuel use.

The graph shows the fuel consumption patterns of household heads in 2005 and 2012. In 2005, more male households in rural areas used dirty fuel (78%) than their female counterparts (77%) (Fig. 16.4). In urban areas, the usage of dirty fuel was relatively lower, with 32% of male household heads and 38% of female household heads using dirty fuel. By 2012, there was a slight decrease in the usage of dirty fuel across all categories. In rural areas, 69% of male and female households used dirty fuel, indicating a more equitable distribution. In urban areas, the usage of dirty fuel decreased further, with 22% of male household heads and 27% of female household heads relying on it. The adoption of clean fuel showed a modest increase over time. In 2005, only a small percentage of male and female households used clean fuel in rural and urban areas. However, by 2012, there was a slight improvement, with 5% of male and 6% of female household heads in rural areas using clean fuel. In urban areas, clean fuel usage was higher, with 46% of male and 42% of female household heads opting for cleaner alternatives. The comparative analysis reveals some trends in 2005 and 2012. More male household heads in rural areas used dirty fuel than their female counterparts.

In urban areas, there is a smaller disparity between the percentage of male and female household heads using dirty fuel. Gender is another significant factor to consider. Research suggests that female-headed households tend to prefer modern fuels over traditional fuels (Farsi et al., 2007; Rahut et al., 2014; Rao & Reddy, 2007). This preference can be attributed to the fact that women are often responsible for household cooking and are directly affected by the air pollution resulting from the combustion of dirty fuels. Link et al. (2012) demonstrate that many female members in Nepal advocate for the use of fuelwood, as they are typically the primary gatherers of fuelwood. However, a study conducted by Nepal et al. (2011) found that households with children under the age of six tend to reduce their reliance on wood, possibly due to the increased time spent on childcare, which reduces the time available for wood collection. This finding contrasts with the study by Heltberg (2005).

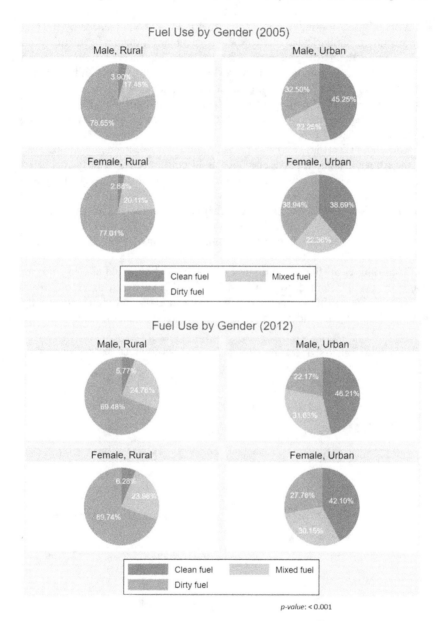

Fig. 16.4. Fuel Use by Household Head. *Source*: Authors' Calculation.

Women's decision-making regarding fuel use may be influenced by the higher opportunity costs they face due to their engagement in income-generating activities, leading them to opt for time-saving fuels. However, Gupta and Köhlin (2006) find that the presence of non-working women does not significantly affect fuel choice in India. These findings indicate that gender's role in explaining fuel use is influenced by a combination of factors, including individual preferences, considerations of time opportunity costs and the bargaining power of women within households.

Household size (Fig. 16.5) also plays a significant role in energy choices. Based on the above graphs, the average household consumption of dirty fuel in rural areas was 5.95 in 2005, which decreased to 4.76 in 2012. In urban areas, the average household size consuming dirty fuel was 5.45 in 2005 and slightly decreased to 4.85 in 2012. For mixed fuel consumption, the average household size in rural areas was 6.14 in 2005 and decreased to 4.95 in 2012. In urban areas, the average household size consuming mixed fuel was 5.89 in 2005 and slightly decreased to 5.06 in 2012.

Regarding clean fuel consumption, the average household size in rural areas was 5.09 in 2005 and decreased to 4.17 in 2012. In urban areas, the average household size consuming clean fuel was 5.03 in 2005 and increased slightly to 4.49 in 2012. These findings suggest that, on average, households with higher

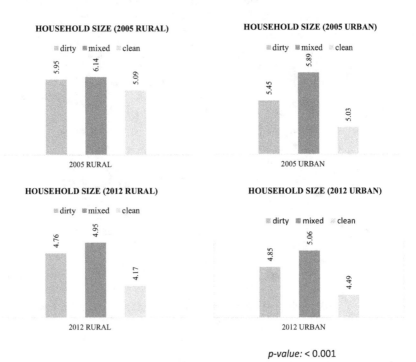

Fig. 16.5.   Fuel Use Based on Household Size. *Source*: Authors' Calculation.

numbers of individuals tend to consume more dirty and mixed fuels. In contrast, households with smaller sizes have a higher tendency to use clean fuels. Multiple studies, including those conducted by Israel (2002) and Abebaw (2007), examine the relationship between per capita energy consumption and household size. Findings from studies conducted by Ouedraogo (2006), Özcan et al. (2013), Pandey and Chaubal (2011), Rao and Reddy (2007), and Reddy (1995) suggest that larger households tend to prefer using dirty fuels, primarily due to affordability constraints. In contrast, Baiyegunhi and Hassan (2014), Guta (2012), and Chen et al. (2006) indicate that household size has an insignificant impact on the transition to cleaner fuels. Heltberg (2004) discovers that larger households are more likely to engage in fuel stacking, using multiple fuel sources simultaneously. Therefore, further research is needed to investigate the nature and specific mechanisms underlying the effects of household composition on fuel choice.

6.1.1 Fuel Use Based on Firewood Prices

In 2005, the percentage of dirty fuel users was highest (85.68%) for free firewood in rural areas and lowest (34.96%) for firewood priced at Rs. 1,001–8,000 (Fig. 16.6). In 2012, the highest percentage (77.28%) was for firewood priced at Rs.

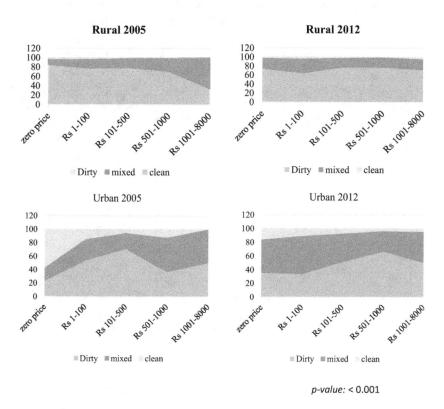

p-value: < 0.001

Fig. 16.6.   Fuel Use by Fuel Prices. *Source*: Authors' Calculation.

501–1,000, while the lowest (63.90%) was Rs. 1–100. In urban areas, the highest percentage of dirty fuel users was in 2005 (71.05%) for firewood priced at Rs. 501–1,000 and in 2012 (66.69%) for the same price range. The lowest percentage was in 2005 (23.26%) for free firewood and in 2012 (33.81%) for firewood priced at Rs. 1–100. For mixed fuel usage, the highest percentage in 2005 was (65.04%) for firewood priced at Rs. 1,001–8,000, and in 2012 (32.49%) for firewood priced at Rs. 1–100. The lowest percentages were in 2005 (11.11%) for free firewood and in 2012 (21.13%) for firewood priced at Rs. 101–500. In terms of clean fuel usage, the highest percentages were in 2005 (3.21%) for free firewood in rural areas and in 2012 (4.36%) for firewood priced at Rs. 1,001–8,000. The lowest percentages were in 2005 (0.71%) for firewood priced at Rs. 501–1,000 and in 2012 (3.50%) for the same price range in urban areas. These findings highlight the influence of firewood availability and price on fuel usage patterns. Access to free or lower-priced firewood contributes to higher usage of dirty and mixed fuels, while higher-priced firewood encourages the adoption of cleaner fuels.

6.1.2 Fuel Use Based on Kerosene Prices

In 2005, the highest percentage of dirty fuel users (86.21%) was observed for kerosene priced at Rs. 1–100, while the lowest percentage was for kerosene priced at Rs. 1,001–3,800 in rural areas (Fig. 16.7). In 2012, the highest percentage

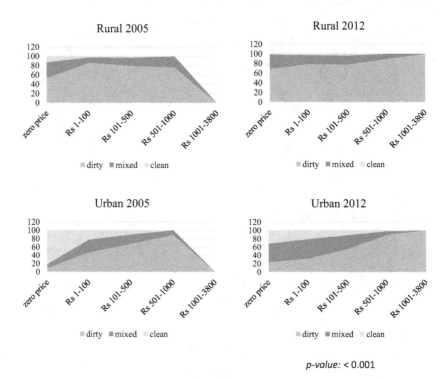

Fig. 16.7.   Kerosene Prices. *Source*: Authors' Calculation.

(100%) was for kerosene priced at Rs. 1,001–3,800, and the lowest percentage (69.23%) was for free kerosene. For urban areas in 2005, the highest percentage of dirty fuel users (89.79%) was for kerosene priced at Rs. 501–1,000, and the lowest percentage was for kerosene priced at Rs. 1,001–3,800. In 2012, the highest percentage (100%) was for kerosene priced at Rs. 1,001–3,800, and the lowest percentage (23.69%) was for free kerosene. Regarding mixed fuel usage, the highest percentage in 2005 was (33.57%) for free kerosene in rural areas, and in 2012 (29%) for free kerosene. For urban areas in 2005, the highest percentage (29.53%) was for kerosene priced at Rs. 1–100, and in 2012 (46.59%) for the same price range. Regarding clean fuel usage, in 2005, the highest percentage (13.01%) was for free kerosene in rural areas, and the lowest percentage was for kerosene priced at Rs. 501–1,000 and Rs. 1,001–3,800. In 2012, the highest percentage (3.71%) was for kerosene priced at Rs. 101–500, and the lowest was for kerosene priced at Rs. 501–1,000 and Rs. 1,001–3,800. These findings highlight the influence of kerosene prices on fuel usage patterns. Lower-priced or free kerosene encourages higher usage of dirty and mixed fuels, while higher-priced kerosene promotes the adoption of cleaner fuels.

6.1.3 Fuel Use Based on LPG Prices

In 2005, the highest percentage of dirty fuel users (99.96%) was for free LPG, while the lowest percentage was for LPG priced at Rs. 501–1,000 and Rs. 1,001–3,000 in rural areas. In 2012, the highest percentage (4.53%) was for LPG priced at Rs. 1–100, and the lowest was for both free LPG and LPG priced at Rs. 1,001–3,000 (Fig. 16.8). For urban areas in 2005, the highest percentage of dirty fuel users (99.4%) was for free LPG, and the lowest percentage was for LPG priced at Rs. 501–1,000 and Rs. 1,001–3,000. In 2012, the highest percentage (0.57%) was for LPG priced at Rs. 1–100, and the lowest was for both free LPG and LPG priced at Rs. 1,001–3,000. Regarding mixed fuel usage, in 2005, the highest percentage (88.27%) was for LPG priced at Rs. 1–100 in rural areas, and the lowest percentage was for LPG priced at Rs. 1,001–3,000. In 2012, the highest percentage (100%) was for free LPG, and the lowest percentage (34.66%) was for LPG priced at Rs. 1,001–3,000. For urban areas in 2005, the highest percentage of mixed fuel users (71.12%) was for LPG priced at Rs. 1–100, and the lowest percentage was for LPG priced at Rs. 1,001–3,000. In 2012, the highest percentage was for free LPG, and the lowest (19.56%) was for LPG priced at Rs. 1,001–3,000. In terms of clean fuel usage, in 2005, the highest percentage (30.60%) was for LPG priced at Rs. 501–1,000 in rural areas, and the lowest percentage was for LPG priced at Rs. 1,001–3,000. In 2012, the highest percentage (65.34%) was for LPG priced at Rs. 1,001–3,000, and the lowest was for free LPG. For urban areas in 2005, the highest percentage of clean fuel users (88.89%) was for LPG priced at Rs. 501–1,000, and the lowest percentage was for LPG priced at Rs. 1,000–3,000. In 2012, the highest percentage (80.44%) was for LPG priced at Rs. 1,001–3,000, and the lowest was for free LPG. These findings emphasize the impact of LPG prices on fuel usage patterns. Lower-priced or free LPG

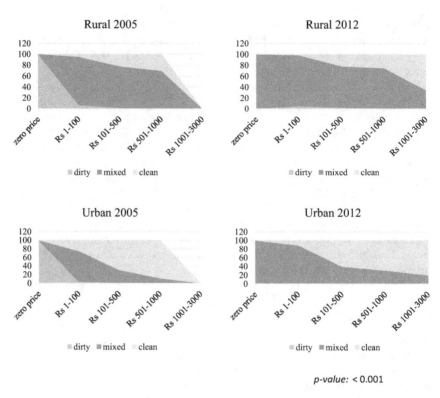

Fig. 16.8.   LPG Prices. *Source*: Authors' Calculation.

encourages higher usage of dirty and mixed fuels, while higher-priced LPG promotes the adoption of cleaner fuels.

Numerous studies have extensively explored the relationship between fuel
prices and household fuel consumption. However, the majority of these investigations primarily focus on analyzing market prices for different types of fuels,
including firewood, coal, charcoal, kerosene, LPG, and electricity. For example,
Jingchao and Kotani (2012) conducted research in Beijing, China, while Farsi
et al. (2007) conducted a study in India. Both studies found that an increase in
LPG prices resulted in a significant decrease in the likelihood of choosing LPG
and a subsequent reduction in LPG consumption. Furthermore, several authors
have observed a negative correlation between firewood prices and firewood
consumption. Lay et al. (2013) studied this relationship in Kenya, whereas Farsi
et al. (2007) conducted a similar analysis in India. Both studies concluded that
higher firewood prices were associated with a decreased preference for firewood as
a fuel source.

Similarly, researchers Muller and Yan (2018) investigated the influence of food
prices on fuel choices. Their study focused on Chinese rural households and
demonstrated that higher consumption of purchased food led to a preference for

cheaper but more environmentally harmful fuels. Conversely, an increase in the price of self-produced food prompted a transition toward cleaner fuel alternatives. These findings suggest that precise estimates of price effects, especially in rural areas, may be approximations in the most accurate econometric models.

6.2 Fuel Use Based on Household Chulha Types

In rural areas, the percentage of traditional chulha users decreased by 1.5% from 2005 (89.26%) to 2012 (87.76%). In urban areas, there was a slight reduction of 0.82% in traditional chulha users from 2005 (72.86%) to 2012 (72.40%). In 2005, the percentage of mixed fuel users was 10.16% for households with traditional chulha and 36.64% for households with improved chulha in rural areas. In 2012 these percentages increased to 11.90% and 45.84%, respectively. Similarly, in urban areas, the percentage of mixed fuel users was 19.6% for households with traditional chulha and 31.85% for households with improved chulha in 2005, and these percentages remained the same in 2012. Regarding clean fuel usage, in 2005, the percentage was 0.58% for households with traditional chulha and 10.03% for households with improved chulha in rural areas. In 2012, these percentages changed to 0.34% and 20.20%, respectively. In urban areas, the percentage of clean fuel users was 7.52% for households with traditional chulha and 36.48% for households with improved chulha in 2005, and these percentages remained the same in 2012. These findings indicate a gradual shift from traditional chulha usage in rural and urban areas. There is an increasing adoption of improved chulha and a slight increase in the usage of mixed fuels. The use of clean fuels has also shown an upward trend, particularly among households with improved chulha (Fig. 16.9).

6.3 Fuel Use Based on Accessibility

Remoteness and access to the market also influence the household decision to choose cooking fuel-fuelwood versus gas. Contribution of the Accessibility and availability of fuels is necessary to explain household fuel use. In rural areas, the average time spent collecting dirty fuel increased from 7.43 minutes in 2005 to 53.87 minutes in 2012. Similarly, in urban areas, the average collection time for dirty fuel was 14.91 minutes in 2005 and decreased slightly to 50.63 minutes in 2012. For collecting mixed fuel, the average time increased in rural and urban areas from 2005 to 2012: from 14.71 to 53.78 minutes in rural areas and from 18.07 to 37.74 minutes in urban areas. Collecting clean fuel took an average of 15.19 minutes in rural areas in 2005, which decreased to 49.4 minutes in 2012. In urban areas, the average collection time for clean fuel was 19.14 minutes in 2005 and increased to 56.8 minutes in 2012. These figures illustrate the changes in the average time spent collecting different fuel types in rural and urban areas over the years. In the literature, the proximity to fuelwood sources is measured as an indicator of the availability of traditional fuels, considering factors such as distance (An et al., 2002; Heltberg, 2005; Kaul & Liu, 1992), households' perceptions

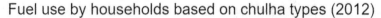

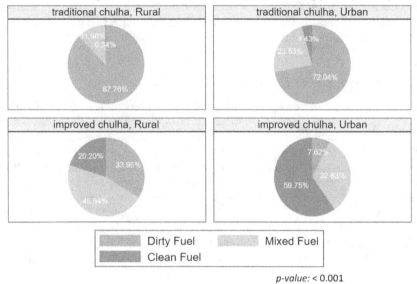

Fig. 16.9. Fuel Use Based on Household Chulha Types. *Source*:
Authors' Calculation.

of geographic location (Peng et al., 2010), and fuelwood availability (Hosier &
Dowd, 1987). Conversely, the accessibility of modern fuels is assessed based on
households' perceptions of community access to electricity (Heltberg, 2004; Lay
et al., 2013), availability of LPG (Gupta & Köhlin, 2006), prevalence of solar
home systems (Lay et al., 2013), and adoption of renewable energy technologies
(Jingchao & Kotani, 2012). Numerous studies highlight that households located
far from fuelwood sources tend to transition toward alternative fuels due to the
higher opportunity costs associated with collection time. Improved access to
modern energy, particularly electricity, is often attributed to driving fuel transition. Heltberg (2004) finds a positive connection between community-level elec-
trification and the usage of LPG in Brazil and India. Lay et al. (2013) observe that
enhanced access to electric power leads Kenyan households to shift from wood
and kerosene to electricity.

Numerous studies indicate income as the primary driver behind the uptake of
modern fuels (Fig. 16.10). In 2005 and 2012, there was a decrease in the percentage of dirty fuel users across different income groups, ranging from low-
income (93.11%) to high-income (58.33%) households. This trend was also
observed in urban areas, where the consumption of dirty fuels followed a similar
pattern based on household income groups. Conversely, the percentage of mixed
fuel users increased from low-income (5.54%) to high-income (33.33%)

Rural

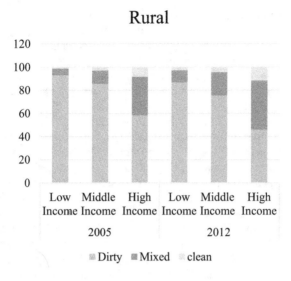

Urban

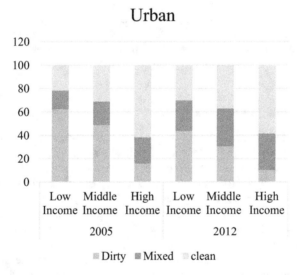

Fig. 16.10.   Fuel Use Based on Income. *Source*: Authors' Calculation.

households in 2005 and 2012. Mixed fuel consumption in urban households exhibited a similar trend across different income groups.

Similarly, the percentage of clean fuel users showed an upward trend from low-income (1.35%) to high-income (8.34%) households in 2005 and 2012. The consumption of clean fuels in urban households mirrored this pattern across various income groups. These findings highlight the changes in fuel consumption patterns and the influence of income levels on fuel choices in rural and urban areas over the specified period. Most authors indicate income as a measure of household earnings, even though household expenditure is sometimes used as a proxy for income because expenditure data are often more reliable and reflect long-term income. Numerous studies indicate income as the primary driver behind the uptake of modern fuels. As their income rises, Hosier and Dowd (1987) find that Zimbabwean urban households tend to move away from wood toward kerosene and electricity. Ouedraogo (2006) finds in Burkina Faso that a higher income prompts urban households to prefer natural gas over kerosene. Baiyegunhi and Hassan (2014) observe that the transition from fuelwood to kerosene, natural gas, and electricity occurs along with rising income in rural Nigeria.

Household expenditure has been utilized as an indicator of income to examine similar trends. Gupta and Köhlin (2006) find supporting evidence for an energy transition in urban India, where households shift from fuelwood and kerosene to LPG (light petroleum gas), primarily driven by higher expenditure levels. These findings align with the concept of the energy ladder, which emphasizes the role of income growth in the transition from reliance on traditional, inferior fuels to the normalization of modern fuels. However, it is important to note that the existing empirical evidence increasingly challenges the notion of a straightforward income-dependent pattern. Heltberg (2004, 2005) observes in various countries that as income increases, households tend to incorporate modern fuels into their energy mix as partial substitutes rather than completely replacing traditional fuels.

7. Results and Discussion

The results of this study shed light on the evolving patterns of household cooking fuel choices in India and offer essential insights for policy and intervention strategies. The increasing prevalence of mixed fuel usage suggests a gradual transition from single to multiple fuel sources, reflecting households' diverse energy needs and preferences. However, the limited reduction in dirty fuel consumption raises concerns about the overall progress in achieving cleaner cooking practices. Despite a modest rise, the low adoption rate of clean fuels underscores the need for targeted efforts to promote their usage. The findings highlight the pivotal role of education in driving fuel choices, emphasizing the importance of educational campaigns to raise awareness about the benefits of clean fuels and their accessibility. The influence of age on fuel preferences indicates that older household heads may serve as catalysts for clean fuel adoption, potentially due to their awareness of health hazards associated with traditional fuels. Household size emerges as a critical determinant, with larger households demonstrating higher reliance on dirtier and mixed fuels, suggesting the need for tailored strategies to address the energy needs of these households.

Moreover, the availability and cost of firewood and kerosene play a significant role in shaping fuel choices, underscoring the importance of improving the accessibility and affordability of clean cooking alternatives. These findings contribute to the ongoing discourse on clean energy adoption. They can inform policymakers in designing effective interventions to promote cleaner fuels, reduce reliance on dirty fuels, and improve household air quality and public health in India.

8. Conclusion and Policy Implications

This study provides valuable insights into the factors influencing household cooking fuel choices in India. The findings suggest a gradual shift toward mixed fuel usage, indicating households' diverse energy needs and preferences. However, the limited reduction in the use of dirty fuels and the low adoption rate of clean fuels raise concerns about the overall progress in achieving cleaner cooking practices. The policy implications of this study are crucial for promoting the adoption of clean cooking fuels in India. Firstly, targeted educational campaigns should be developed to raise awareness about clean fuels' benefits and accessibility. These campaigns should mainly focus on older household heads, who are more inclined toward clean fuel adoption due to their awareness of associated health hazards.

Additionally, efforts should be made to improve the availability and affordability of clean cooking alternatives, such as LPG and biogas, to encourage household adoption. Furthermore, policies should consider the specific energy needs of larger households and develop tailored strategies to address their requirements. This could involve promoting efficient cooking stoves or providing subsidies for clean cooking fuels. Lastly, initiatives should be undertaken to improve the supply chain for firewood and kerosene, ensuring their availability at reasonable prices to discourage their continued use as cooking fuels. Overall, the findings of this study provide valuable guidance for policymakers to design effective interventions that promote the use of cleaner fuels, reduce reliance on dirty fuels, and ultimately improve household air quality and public health in India.

References

Abebaw, D. (2007). Household determinants of fuelwood choice in urban Ethiopia: A case study of Jimma Town. *The Journal of Developing Areas*, 117–126.

Ahmad, S., & De Oliveira, J. A. P. (2015). Fuel switching in slum and non-slum households in urban India. *Journal of Cleaner Production, 94*, 130–136.

Alem, Y., Beyene, A. D., Köhlin, G., & Mekonnen, A. (2016). Modeling household cooking fuel choice: A panel multinomial logit approach. *Energy Economics, 59*, 129–137.

An, L., Lupi, F., Liu, J., Linderman, M. A., & Huang, J. (2002). Modeling the choice to switch from fuelwood to electricity: Implications for giant panda habitat conservation. *Ecological Economics, 42*(3), 445–457.

Baiyegunhi, L. J. S., & Hassan, M. B. (2014). Rural household fuel energy transition: Evidence from Giwa LGA Kaduna State, Nigeria. *Energy for Sustainable Development, 20*, 30-35002E.

Baland, J.-M., Libois, F., & Mookherjee, D. (2013, March). *Firewood collections and economic growth in Rural Nepal 1995-2010: Evidence from a household panel.* CEPR Discussion Paper No. DP9394. https://ssrn.com/abstract=2235492

Chen, L., Heerink, N., & van den Berg, M. (2006). Energy consumption in rural China: A household model for three villages in Jiangxi Province. *Ecological Economics, 58*(2), 407–420.

Daniel, A. M. (2020). Household fuel choice and use: A multiple discrete-continuous framework. SSRN 3562270.

Desai, S. B., Dubey, A., Joshi, B. L., Sen, M., Shariff, A., & Vanneman, R. (2010). *Human development in India.* Oxford University.

Desai, S., & Vanneman, R. (2005). *National council of applied economic research.* India Human Development Survey (IHDS).

Desai, S., & Vanneman, R. (2015). *India Human Development Survey-II (IHDS-II), 2011-12* (Vol. 31). Inter-university Consortium for Political and Social Research.

Farsi, M., Filippini, M., & Pachauri, S. (2007). Fuel choices in urban Indian households. *Environment and Development Economics, 12*(6), 757–774.

Gebreegziabher, Z., Mekonnen, A., Kassie, M., & Köhlin, G. (2012). Urban energy transition and technology adoption: The case of Tigrai, Northern Ethiopia. *Energy Economics, 34*(2), 410–418.

Gupta, G., & Köhlin, G. (2006). Preferences for domestic fuel: Analysis with socio-economic factors and rankings in Kolkata, India. *Ecological Economics, 57*(1), 107–121.

Guta, D. D. (2012). Application of an almost ideal demand system (AIDS) to Ethiopian rural residential energy use: Panel data evidence. *Energy Policy, 50,* 528–539.

Heltberg, R. (2004). Fuel switching: Evidence from eight developing countries. *Energy Economics, 26*(5), 869–887.

Heltberg, R. (2005). Factors determining household fuel choice in Guatemala. *Environment and Development Economics, 10*(3), 337–361.

Hosier, R. H., & Dowd, J. (1987). Household fuel choice in Zimbabwe: An empirical test of the energy ladder hypothesis. *Resources and Energy, 9*(4), 347–361.

IEA. (2017). *Energy access outlook: From poverty to prosperity, World Energy Outlook-2017 special report.* https://webstore.iea.org/weo-2017-special-report-energy-access-outlook. Accessed on September 30, 2019.

IEA, IRENA, UNSD, WB, & WHO. (2019). *Tracking SDG 7: The energy progress report 2019, Washington, DC.* https://trackingsdg7.esmap.org/data/files/download-documents/tracking_sdg7_2019_highlights.pdf. Accessed on September 30, 2019.

Israel, D. (2002). Fuel choice in developing countries: Evidence from Bolivia. *Economic Development and Cultural Change, 50*(4), 865–890.

Jingchao, Z., & Kotani, K. (2012). The determinants of household energy demand in rural Beijing: Can environmentally friendly technologies be effective? *Energy Economics, 34*(2), 381–388.

Kaul, S., & Liu, Q. (1992). Rural household energy use in China. *Energy, 17*(4), 405–411.

Khandker, S. R., Barnes, D. F., & Samad, H. A. (2012). Are the energy poor also income poor? Evidence from India. *Energy Policy, 47,* 1–12.

Kituyi, E. (2004). Towards sustainable production and use of charcoal in Kenya: Exploring the potential in life cycle management approach. *Journal of Cleaner Production, 12*(8–10), 1047–1057.

Lay, J., Ondraczek, J., & Stoever, J. (2013). Renewables in the energy transition: Evidence on Kenya's solar home systems and lighting fuel choice. *Energy Economics, 40*, 350–359.

Liao, J., Kirby, M. A., Pillarisetti, A., Piedrahita, R., Balakrishnan, K., Sambandam, S., Mukhopadhyay, K., Ye, W., Rosa, G., Majorin, F., Dusabimana, E., Ndagijimana, F., McCracken, J. P., Mollinedo, E., de Leon, O., Díaz-Artiga, A., Thompson, L. M., Kearns, K. A., Naeher, L., … Young, B. N. (2021). LPG stove and fuel intervention among pregnant women reduce fine particle air pollution exposures in three countries: pilot results from the HAPIN trial. *Environmental Pollution, 291*, 118198.

Link, C. F., Axinn, W. G., & Ghimire, D. J. (2012). Household energy consumption: Community context and the fuelwood transition. *Social Science Research, 41*(3), 598–611.

Masera, O. R., Saatkamp, B. D., & Kammen, D. M. (2000). From linear fuel switching to multiple cooking strategies: A critique and alternative to the energy ladder model. *World Development, 28*(12), 2083–2103.

Muller, C., & Yan, H. (2018). *Household fuel use in rural China.*

Nepal, M., Nepal, A., & Grimsrud, K. (2011). Unbelievable but improved cookstoves are not helpful in reducing firewood demand in Nepal. *Environment and Development Economics, 16*(1), 1–23.

Ouedraogo, B. (2006). Household energy preferences for cooking in urban Ouagadougou, Burkina Faso. *Energy Policy, 34*(18), 3787–3795.

Özcan, K. M., Gülay, E., & Üçdoğruk, Ş. (2013). Economic and demographic determinants of household energy use in Turkey. *Energy Policy, 60*, 550–557.

Pandey, V. L., & Chaubal, A. (2011). Comprehending household cooking energy choice in rural India. *Biomass and Bioenergy, 35*(11), 4724–4731.

Peng, W., Hisham, Z., & Pan, J. (2010). Household level fuel switching in rural Hubei. *Energy for Sustainable Development, 14*(3), 238–244.

Price, M., Barnard-Tallier, M., & Troncoso, K. (2021). Stacked: In their favour? The complexities of fuel stacking and cooking transitions in Cambodia, Myanmar, and Zambia. *Energies, 14*(15), 4457.

Rahut, D. B., Ali, A., Mottaleb, K. A., & Aryal, J. P. (2020). Understanding households' choice of cooking fuels: Evidence from urban households in Pakistan. *Asian Development Review, 37*(1), 185–212.

Rahut, D. B., Mottaleb, K. A., & Ali, A. (2017). Household energy consumption and its determinants in Timor-Leste. *Asian Development Review, 34*(1), 167–197.

Rahut, D. B., Das, S., De Groote, H., & Behera, B. (2014). Determinants of household energy use in Bhutan. *Energy, 69*, 661–672.

Rao, M. N., & Reddy, B. S. (2007). Variations in energy use by Indian households: An analysis of micro-level data. *Energy, 32*(2), 143–153.

Reddy, B. S. (1995). A multi-logit model for fuel shifts in the domestic sector. *Energy, 20*(9), 929–936.

Rehfuess, E., & World Health Organization. (2006). *Fuel for life: Household energy and health.* World Health Organization.

Sidhu, M. K., Ravindra, K., Mor, S., & John, S. (2017). Household air pollution from various types of rural kitchens and its exposure assessment. *Science of the Total Environment, 586*, 419–429.

Smith, K. R. (2017). Why both gas and biomass are needed today to address the solid fuel cooking problem in India: A challenge to the biomass stove community. *Energy for Sustainable Development, 100*(38), 102–103.

Viswanathan, B., & Kumar, K. K. (2005). Cooking fuel use patterns in India: 1983–2000. *Energy Policy, 33*(8), 1021–1036.

WHO (World Health Organization). (2018). *Household air pollution and health.*

World Health Organization. (2013). *Global action plan for the prevention and control of noncommunicable diseases 2013-2020.* World Health Organization.

World Health Organization. (2014). *WHO guidelines for indoor air quality: Household fuel combustion.* World Health Organization.